CLARENDO.

CLARENDON LAW SERIES

LAW IN MODERN SOCIETY

D. J. GALLIGAN

Professor of Socio-Legal Studies and Director of the Centre for
Socio-Legal Studies, University of Oxford

OXFORD
UNIVERSITY PRESS

OXFORD

UNIVERSITY PRESS

Great Clarendon Street, Oxford OX2 6DP

Oxford University Press is a department of the University of Oxford.
It furthers the University's objective of excellence in research, scholarship,
and education by publishing worldwide in

Oxford New York

Auckland Cape Town Dar es Salaam Hong Kong Karachi
Kuala Lumpur Madrid Melbourne Mexico City Nairobi
New Delhi Shanghai Taipei Toronto

With offices in

Argentina Austria Brazil Chile Czech Republic France Greece
Guatemala Hungary Italy Japan Poland Portugal Singapore
South Korea Switzerland Thailand Turkey Ukraine Vietnam

Oxford is a registered trade mark of Oxford University Press
in the UK and in certain other countries

Published in the United States
by Oxford University Press Inc., New York

British Library Cataloguing in Publication Data

Data available

Library of Congress Cataloging in Publication Data

Data available

Typeset in Ehrhardt
by RefineCatch Limited, Bungay, Suffolk
Printed in Great Britain
by Biddles Ltd., King's Lynn

ISBN 978–0–19–926978–5   0–19–926978–5 (pbk)
ISBN 978–0–19–929183–0   0–19–929183–7 (hbk)

1 3 5 7 9 10 8 6 4 2

Contents

Contents

Contents   ix

Preface

This is the second time a book on law in society has been written for the Clarendon Series. Professor Geoffrey Sawer of the Australian National University, a distinguished constitutional law scholar, wrote the first. It was one of the early Clarendons, having been published in 1965. In the intervening years, the study of law in society has grown from barely existing beyond the classics to the vibrant discipline it is today. The difference between his approach and mine is probably due as much to the transformed nature of the discipline as to personal inclinations. While my predecessor chose an approach that is historical and comparative, I have settled on one that is more in the analytical tradition, which draws on the extensive range of empirical research now available, and benefits from the many approaches and theories in circulation. This has made my task easier in some ways and harder in others. Being able to benefit from the wide-ranging work of other scholars and researchers is the easy part, how to choose from among it and develop a distinctive approach, the hard part.

The object of the Clarendon Series is to provide a critical introduction to a discrete range of legal studies. The recognition of law in society as a discrete subject is proper and timely. It should no longer be regarded as a branch of law or political science, anthropology or sociology, or any other discipline. Each, with its literature and methods, is useful to law in society but none defines or determines the subject. That is not to say law in society is fully-grown or mature, but it has progressed enough to be able to speak of its own subject of study, its own methods, and its own literature. In the spirit of the Clarendon Series, I endeavour here to state and defend an approach to law in society that draws on what has gone before, both in terms of the classics and contemporary writings, yet which is not intended as a survey. H. L. A. Hart, whose *The Concept of Law* features prominently here, was famously economical with citations and footnotes, as had been his predecessors from Hobbes and Hume to the Mills. Here I have tried to steer a middle course between that magisterial tradition and the footnote approach of contemporary writing. I have also followed what I take to be a Clarendon tradition of supplying additional notes at the end of each chapter.

The approach taken here must to some degree be the product of my own education. The enlightened tradition of Australian Universities ensures that those aspiring to be lawyers must also study something else, which for me included political science. Sociology proper had to wait until Oxford where Mrs Jean Floud, who continues to participate in the life of Nuffield College, introduced me to the subject by setting an essay on Durkheim's *The Elementary Forms of the Religious Life*. The Easter holidays of 1972 were ruined but foundations were laid. Mr Kenneth Tite and Mr Patrick Gardiner, both my tutors at Magdalen, guided my interest in politics and philosophy, while the weekly seminars conducted by Ronald Dworkin, Joseph Raz, and John Finnis, together with occasional opportunities to hear H. L. A. Hart, opened up issues and questions about law that, in one way or another, have been my guide ever since. In more recent years, I have learnt immeasurably from my colleagues at the Centre for Socio-Legal Studies, the Oxford Law Faculty, and Wolfson College. The chance to engage in central and east Europe in the early days of the post-communist era, gave me another perspective on the nature and place of law in society, evidence of which will be seen at various points in this book.

From among colleagues and friends, I would like to mark a long association as friend and colleague with the late Peter Birks, who as editor of the Clarendon Series asked me to write this book but did not live to see it. Other friends and colleagues whom I would like specially to thank are Doreen McBarnet, Marina Kurkchiyan, William Twining, and David Wood. From a different quarter, I have learnt much from my long friendship with Mr John Adams and Mr Paul Dodyk, both world-wise attorneys and scholars in waiting. I thank Oxford University Press and its officers for publishing this book and for continuing to maintain the highest standards. Ailsa Thom the Administrator at the Centre for Socio-Legal Studies has given much support and Paul Honey her assistant and Research Support Officer has been of enormous help in producing the final manuscript, and I offer my warmest thanks to both. The graduate students of Oxford constitute a plentiful source of talent and I have benefited from the help of several of them. I wish to record my thanks in particular to Anna Manasca, Chikako Endo, Yossi Nehushtan, Vidya Kumar, and Rhonda Powell for their invaluable assistance.

To those who have been my teachers, some named above and others, this book is dedicated.

Oxford
March 2006

Table of Statutes

Introduction

The icon of modern legal orders ought to be Jeremy Bentham, the jurist and law reformer, who regarded law as a mighty instrument for achieving whatever goals a society wants to achieve. It is often said that law is necessary for the basic social tasks of protecting one from the other and providing the rules for elementary forms of social life in matters of contract, property, and family relations. Law strengthens and makes more secure social relations existing naturally and spontaneously. In contemporary societies it goes much further by changing and redirecting social relations. It is used for the pursuit of positive social ends and goals by regulating a range of activities from employment practices to financial services to human rights. If Bentham is the icon of the age, regulatory law is its creed. Regulation is driven by different motives, some based on efficiency and practicality, others on values such as fairness, non-discrimination, and a sound environment, while in some societies the commitment to human rights is emerging as a force at all levels of law-making. The clamour of factions and the power of special interests can also be the motivation. Just as the modern state regulates extensively, it also provides extensively and uses the law to do so, offering a range of services, including welfare in its various forms, and in the process enacting more rules and creating more organizations and processes. As the state expands its power and the range of its activities, its officials, agencies, and organizations also have to be regulated and restrained to ensure that they operate within the boundaries and according to the expectations of the people. For that purpose, constitutional and administrative law have grown in size and importance.

Law made by states does not exhaust its empire. At the international level it has an expanding part to play in relations between states. It is also moving beyond those relations to embrace individual persons and groups, usually to set standards protecting them against their own sovereign authorities, or to punish them for crimes committed within their own jurisdictions. One form of international law is that of the European Union which has become for its members a major source of both regulation and provision, running parallel to the law of each member state yet having supremacy over it. The European Union is unique, although the tendency towards the creation of regional authorities is increasing. Legal orders need not be based on territory alone but may be particular to peoples, as it was in periods of Roman Law and early medieval law, and continues to be in some societies. They may also be centred on subject-matter as in the case of contemporary orders, such as that of the World Trade Organization. A plurality of legal orders, generally running in parallel but sometimes in competition, enters into and regulates our lives and our actions in countless ways. Legal pluralism is also at work within states where it is not unusual to find distinct legal orders, some relating to specific groups, others based on religion, existing more or less independently of the state system, and whose authority is sometimes accepted by the state, sometimes not.

Law's pervasiveness at the international, national, and sub-national levels guarantees it a significant presence in contemporary societies. The object of this book is to examine that presence, to give an account of it as a social formation that affects the behaviour of citizens and officials, of organizations both public and private, and of nation states. In doing so, I have drawn on the extensive literature that already exists and have used the ideas of H. L. A. Hart and Max Weber, Emile Durkheim and Niklas Luhmann, together with numerous others from Giambattista Vico to my contemporaries. My approach is to provide an account of law in society which is guided by two ideas that are easy to state and hard to apply: that law is a social formation with its own character and features, while at the same time it interacts with and is affected by other social formations. The two cannot be kept entirely separate, but it is nevertheless important to expose and examine law as a distinct social phenomenon as well as study its interaction with others. Some time is taken to explain and justify the adoption of these two ideas and to provide a framework for their analysis. Once the focus of the enquiry is settled, a method of approach is proposed consisting of four principles, what I shall call methodological principles, each of which is useful in guiding the enquiry and revealing features of modern legal orders, some of which are easily neglected.

Within the contours of this general approach, various features of law and its intersection with other aspects of society will be considered. These include such issues as the nature of social rules and the idea of law as a system of rules. Other issues are whether law has particular functions and how legal orders run in parallel The analysis extends to questions of implementation and compliance, and what happens when laws are used to change society. Within this familiar territory, other less familiar matters are interwoven. One is the use of legal theory in examining law in society and in particular the relevance of H. L. A. Hart's *The Concept of Law*.

Another is the narrowing of the enquiry from law generally, wherever and in whatever form it occurs, to those legal orders that have developed in some societies, mainly western and broadly liberal ones. The reason for narrowing the enquiry is that the legal orders of such societies have a distinctive character and form that can be identified and analysed both descriptively and normatively. The benefit of narrowing is to achieve greater depth in probing its character and form. A third feature of my approach is the proposal that, instead of searching in vain for law's functions, a more profitable enquiry would be into how different types of laws contribute to the realization of different social goods. The result is not only a better understanding of law's social role but also an insight into the connection between law and different sets of social relations. Mention of social relations brings us to a final feature of the enquiry, the idea that much is gained by viewing law as an expression of social relations; much is also gained by examining the connections and tensions between the positive laws of modern societies and the spontaneous relations they often try to direct or change.

I

Setting the Bounds of Law–and–society

I.I TAKING LAW SERIOUSLY

Anyone entering into the study of law in society faces the dilemma of either not taking law seriously enough or taking it too seriously. If the view prevails that there is nothing distinctive about it and that its place and importance are marginal to society, law is not taken seriously enough. If, on the other hand, it is thought that law is simply a system of rules that exerts authority over society while being insulated from it, then its character is miss-described and its importance exaggerated. The direction of this study is to do justice to the ideas implicit in the two approaches: that law is both a fairly distinctive social phenomenon and yet closely intertwined with other aspects of society; that law exerts authority over society, and yet in doing so is restrained and influenced by society; that law is in some sense an independent social formation while at the same time being interdependent with other social formations. A study of law in society must draw out these apparently competing qualities. On the one hand it must reveal the qualities particular to law, and on the other hand unravel its entanglement with society. If it is asked why this matters, why we should take the trouble of trying to make sense of a rather complex and untidy situation, then the answer must be that law seeks to direct and guide behaviour and, where necessary, uses force to do so. If to that, which alone should be reason enough, is added the way by which it seeks to direct, guide, and coerce behaviour, the mighty organization of officials enlisted for the purpose, and the heavy cost in resources, then the need to know about it is compelling and the effort worthwhile.

One way of beginning the study and bringing to light issues for further analysis is to consider various ways in which the study of law in society might fail to take law seriously.[1] The step into society in the first place is taken to escape the confines of legal analysis and the certainties of legal

---

[1] Two expressions that occur throughout this book are *law in society* and *law-and-society*; their relationship is this: the object of study is law in society, while law-and-society suggests the process of study.

professionals by considering law as a social formation and the way in which it interacts with other social formations. From there it is a short step to abandoning any sense of law as distinctive, and to re-conceive it at best as one set of rules among many, at worst as of slight social relevance. Since law-and-society research is performed mainly by jurists who want to broaden their understanding of law and who are sometimes disaffected with its doctrinal study, over-reaction in favour of other social concepts is neither unusual nor unexpected, especially when prompted by mistaken claims that legal concepts, being the imaginings of lawyers, are socially worthless. For social scientists, whose textbooks barely mention law, its relegation could be deliberate conversion into more meaningful social categories; it could also be fear of the unknown.

If this is an exaggeration, it is not a gross one and it is done to emphasize the fact that, in order to understand law in its social context, we must regard it as distinct and study its character. The most notable and culpable failure is to assume that law is a mask for something else, for some more basic social categories which are discovered by stripping away the mask. If such ideas have had their heyday, only slightly less culpable is the notion that law, being superficial or super-structural, has no social significance, and can be collapsed, deconstructed, or reduced to something else: power or economics, gender or race, political hegemony, ideologies, or whatever. We may accept that law serves different ends, some good, others bad, without conceding that the legal dimension, the way law directs and structures the actions, through its concepts, rules, and processes, is of no social significance.

A different failure to take law seriously appears when it is assumed that, however plain the law may be, it can always be avoided, modified, or nullified. This tendency appears in different guises and is most blatant in relation to implementation and enforcement, where officials, whether policemen or social welfare officers, parole boards or lobster-fishing inspectors – even judges – are presented as having a subjective discretion to do what they like, no matter what the law says. And in grasping how that discretion is used, we are urged to look beyond the law and to search out the 'real' social factors. A final example is the tendency to present law as if it had one single meaning, as if all laws were the same, as if it were a fixed and simple entity. How often in social science do we come across references to 'the law', when to the lawyer 'the law' means little. The lawyer wants to know what sort of laws are in issue, whether they are laws governing private transactions or relations between officials and citizens; whether they are power-conferring or duty-imposing; what exactly they require or allow; whether there are procedures for applying them, remedies to invoke, and agencies to enforce them. The design or architecture of law, the elements of which are highly variable, is only just gaining recognition as socially relevant.

Law is taken seriously for the purposes of understanding its role in society by examining the concept itself, and then seeing how it interacts with other aspects of society. There are two reasons for thinking this is important: one is that law is itself a distinct social formation with its own character and features; the other is that in the course of its interaction with other parts of society, law neither collapses into them nor becomes part of them. It retains a social character and distinctiveness not only at the level of theory but in practical social situations, which is to say it is itself a set of social categories with meaning and significance for those involved in legal activities. Its distinctiveness is often expressed in terms of its autonomy, although that term has been misunderstood and misused, and perhaps out of caution should be abandoned. The price would be high, however, because autonomy captures a real but elusive quality that is central to law. Perhaps distinctiveness conveys a similar idea, but regardless of the term chosen, the idea is the simple one that law (as shorthand for sets and systems of laws) has an existence, features, and social significance, and in that sense is a social formation different from other formations. This is not to say it is entirely distinct or separate, since it plainly interacts with other parts of society at many points and in many ways, and in that interaction is often compromised, modified, overridden, or ignored, so that the abnormal or pathological case of law can be mistaken for the normal. The claim here is simple and unremarkable: it is that law is a social formation having characteristic features which affect and influence the attitudes and actions of officials and citizens, and which are not reducible without loss into other categories. It follows that the study of law in society has two main parts, the first to understand law, the second to understand its interaction with other social actions.[2]

For these reasons I begin this study with analytical jurisprudence and in particular H. L. A. Hart's *The Concept of Law*. If we are to approach law-and-society with a sound understanding of law, then analytical jurisprudence (or legal theory – the terms are used interchangeably) is a good

---

[2] The distinction between officials and non-officials recurs throughout this book. For simplification purposes, I shall refer to them as officials and citizens, even though the use of the term 'citizens' to refer to non-officials is not exact.

place to start, since the question 'what is law' and 'what are the features of a legal system' have been its preoccupation. Among approaches to analytical jurisprudence, Hart's has several attractions. First, as analytical jurisprudence, which means advancing legal theory by a general description of municipal legal systems, his account is illuminating, has acquired the status of a classic, and on the whole has stood up to critics. The second reason is that, since Hart claims his legal theory is deliberately grounded in social reality, it should be particularly useful for law-and-society. Whether a theory of law could be other than grounded in social reality raises questions (to which I return shortly), yet plainly some are more abstract and speculative than others, so Hart's point is presumably that his account is on the less abstract side and matches what happens in practice more closely than other theories. There is a third reason: Hart goes further by positively laying claim to an interest in the social context of law, which shows itself in two ways. The more fundamental is that his description of law is based on and reflects faithfully the social experience of law. Added to this is the further claim, more in the nature of a throwaway line than a mature thesis, to being *descriptive sociology*, suggesting that his theory of law could be read also as a sociological account of law.[3] These claims need to be examined more closely but, taken as a whole, they are good reasons for using *The Concept of Law* as a way of beginning the study of law in society.

I.2 FROM ANALYTICAL JURISPRUDENCE TO LAW–AND–SOCIETY

Jurisprudence, Hart explains, is concerned to clarify the general framework of legal thought, as opposed to the criticism of law or legal policy. Enquiry into the way we use language reveals the concepts that constitute a legal system; the notion of a rule, being obliged and having an obligation, and the internal as opposed to the external point of view, are examples that: 'help to clarify the framework of legal thought'.[4] In doing so, he sets out to identify and describe the general features of law and legal systems. Rather than define law, his method is 'to advance legal theory by providing an improved analysis of the distinctive features of a municipal legal system . . .', and in the process to provide a better understanding of law, morality, and coercion.[5]

---

[3] It might be thought that these amount to the same thing, since a social account of law is also descriptive sociology, but perhaps there are differences.

[4] H. L. A. Hart, op. cit. Preface.   [5] *Ibid*, p. 17.

In placing the emphasis on a municipal legal system and despite the book's title, Hart gives lesser importance to the *concept* of law. Reference is made to it from time to time, but the main object is the concept of a municipal legal system, by which he means a reasonably developed system of state law. The two aims are not identical so that between them some tension is unavoidable. An enquiry into the *concept of law* is wider and potentially more abstract than the description of a municipal legal system. The former would embrace law not only as it occurs in various contexts, such as customary law or natural law, canon law or informal law; it would also extend to the concept in an abstract sense that is not necessarily tied to practical situations. By imagining a society of angels or saints having law, we could possibly learn something about the *concept* of law, even though it has no relation to reality.[6] On the other hand, the description of a municipal legal system, while still couched in general and abstract terms, is more closely tied to social reality. Finally, whether a description of a municipal legal system is the same as the concept is left open.

Hart's approach limits the enquiry by moving to the margins legal orders that do not qualify as municipal legal systems. What constitutes a municipal legal system can be understood in different ways, but customary systems or other, relatively undeveloped, immature, or traditional legal orders, are pre-legal because they lack some of the qualities of a municipal legal order. Without defining a mature and developed legal order, Hart settles on two essential conditions: a system of primary and secondary legal rules, and sets of officials and institutions to make, interpret, and enforce them.[7] Among the legal systems meeting the two conditions, there is great diversity, ranging from those that barely qualify, through those with a recognizable legal order but little more, to those found in advanced western systems, where the legal order goes beyond the minimum conditions to include additional features. The diversity of legal systems creates another point of tension, partly because a description that includes them all is bound to be general and abstract,[8] and partly because the differences between those barely managing Hart's two hurdles and well-developed legal orders are qualitative and perhaps greater than the similarities. It is not my purpose in this book to propose criteria for classifying legal orders, but rather to identify and describe a narrower notion of a modern legal system, building on the elements of Hart's account.

[6] See J. Raz, *The Authority of Law* (Oxford, 1979).
[7] *The Concept of Law* p. 91 (2nd edn).
[8] See further Joseph Raz, *The Authority of Law*, p. 104.

On the very first page of the *Concept of Law*, Hart writes that, while the book is designed mainly for the student of jurisprudence, it should also be useful to those with other interests, including sociology. The idea recurs in the next paragraph where he writes that the book may also be regarded as an essay in *descriptive sociology*. Beyond that, Hart makes no further mention of the idea, so we are left to deduce what he meant and how one account of law could be read in two different ways.[9] At first sight, legal theory and law-and-society do not have a lot in common; the aim of legal theory is to formulate a general and abstract concept (or description) of law and legal systems, while law-and-society is directed at showing how law interacts with its social environment and how it affects the way people behave. So, legal theory is concerned with the formation of concepts and general descriptions, law-and-society with the unruly world of social practice.

When we look more closely, the two approaches have more to offer each other than at first appears. The posing of two questions shows the relationship between them: how is legal theory formed and, once formed, how can it be used in understanding law in society? As to the first, I begin with a rather bold claim and then modify it. The bold claim is that legal theory, at least Hart's kind, is comprised of a description of legal systems, the description consisting of a number of general features as he knew and experienced them. The general features are expressed in concepts such as social rules, primary and secondary rules, and the internal point of view. The basis of Hart's critique of both Austin and Kelsen is their failure to reflect the reality of legal experience. Kelsen's *pure* theory of law is famously abstract, being concerned with the logical nature of legal norms and the relations among them; nevertheless, the conclusions he reaches and the concepts he proposes must be faithful to the real world of law. In Kelsen's own words: 'its exclusive purpose is to know and describe the object', which is of course law.[10] A theory of a social activity may have more to it than description, but to the extent it purports to be descriptive, it should be an accurate reflection of the activity. A description of law that was wildly inaccurate when tested against the social reality of law would be a poor basis for theory. One arrives at a descriptive theory of law by considering the practical, daily workings of municipal legal systems, and

---

[9] It has been suggested that Hart had second thoughts about this claim; see N. Lacey, *A Life of H. L. A. Hart: The Nightmare and the Noble Dream* (Oxford, 2004).

[10] H. Kelsen, *The Pure Theory of Law* (Free Press, 1938) p. 1. At the same time Kelsen distinguishes sharply between what he is doing and sociological jurisprudence.

singling out the common and essential features. Generalizations are then
formulated on the basis of which concepts can be formed, which may be
refined by further analysis and reflection. Both the generalizations and
the concepts expressing them must be coherent and defensible according
to reason, while at the same time accurately reflecting practical reality. A
concept is not necessarily testable according to social experience, but if it
forms part of a description of social experience and does not accurately
reflect social experience, its utility would be in question.

Now the qualification: put simply, theorization about law is more complex than this. Legal theory, in common with any branch of philosophy,
has its own aims and methods, consisting in the elucidation of the basic
concepts that 'enable us to describe and think about what we observe'.[11]
That elucidation is inspired by reason and imagination, and goes
beyond generalization from practical experience. Theoretical speculation
is likely to be prompted initially by experience and understanding of the
world, but then potentially going beyond into the realm of pure reason.
Philosophical concepts are not necessarily formed in order to describe the
world, although I would maintain that those which are must portray the
world accurately. At the same time, philosophy has its own aims and
methods, which are not primarily concerned with the formation of concepts that are testable by empirical research. Two simple examples illustrate the point. By imagining that society of angels or saints, we might
reach a clearer understanding of the concept of law, even though we have
no experience of angelic or saintly communities and no way of testing
it in practice.[12] The second comes from Max Weber, who was not a
philosopher, but whose notion of *ideal types* serves nicely as a general
theoretical concept prompted by experience, but not a description of
actual social formations. Philosophical elucidation is a different intellectual activity from other forms of social explanation, so that its use in
social explanation may be problematical.[13] Emile Durkheim turned to
sociology, and became one of its founders, precisely because philosophy
was not concerned with empirical evaluation. At the same time, without
suggesting that theoretical analysis should be doing something it is not, it
is surely legitimate for those seeking social explanation to borrow like
bower birds from whatever sources are available, to use whatever concepts
prove useful in understanding practical experience. One might take the

[11] T. Nagel, 'The Central Questions' *London Review of Books*, February 2004.
[12] For this thought experiment, see: J. Raz, *Practical Reason and Norms* (Hutchinson, 1975).
[13] See further: A. Ryan, *The Philosophy of the Social Sciences* (Macmillan, 1970), p. 167.

further step and suggest that if theoretical ideas, whether expressed as concepts or descriptions, do not reflect accurately the practical realities to which they refer or purport to describe, and whether they do or not is sometimes testable by empirical evidence, then there must be a strong case for modifying the concepts or descriptions. These matters are beyond our purposes and need not be pursued further, it being enough to conclude that the precise relationship between philosophical analysis and social reality is still a matter of contention.[14]

Turning now to the second question posed above of how theoretical analysis can be used in law-and-society, the answer is plain: theoretical concepts can be the basis for classifying and making sense of social data. A simple example is the concept of a rule: imagine the difficulty of understanding a range of social activity if we did not have in our minds the concept of a rule, a point Hart makes tellingly in his account. Legal theory provides a refined analysis of what a rule is, of different kinds of rules, what it means to follow rules, how rules are reasons for acting, and so on. Equally useful is the analysis of other concepts like coercion, legal institutions, adjudication, and the distinction between legal systems and other rule-governed orders.

The utility of such concepts for law-and-society is limited in two main ways. Since legal theory is primarily concerned with the elucidation of general concepts and categories, it does not enter into the day-to-day experience of law to consider how those concepts and categories are dealt with there. Legal theory cannot say what happens in practice, when officials or others actually confront rules, for example, while for law-and-society that is its main concern. Nor can legal theory say anything about what happens when legal rules confront other, perhaps competing, aspects of society. By considering these issues, a law-and-society approach identifies patterns of behaviour on which to base further generalizations about legal phenomena and their interaction with other aspects of society. Similarly, since the concepts and categories of legal theory have to be general enough to cover all types of legal systems, they may miss and/or have nothing to say about legal phenomena that are more local and variable, more particular to certain kinds of legal orders. Hart deals with this to some extent by limiting his account to municipal legal systems, which he sometimes refers to as 'modern legal systems'. My

---

[14] For further helpful discussion, see: P. Baert, *Philosophy of the Social Sciences* (Polity, 2005). Some philosophers themselves question the foundations of the philosophical method, suggesting that the search for deep social realities through philosophical reasoning is misguided; see: R. Rorty, *Philosophy and the Mirror of Nature* (Blackwell, 1980).

suggestion is that by narrowing further the enquiry to certain kinds of modern legal systems, their specific features can be identified and better understood.

Legal theories themselves vary in their usefulness to law-and-society, some being more abstract and general than others. The more abstract the theory, the less explanatory power it has with respect to the variety of legal experience, as some legal theories, such as Kelsen's pure theory, show. In concentrating on the logical qualities of legal norms and their relationships, Kelsen distinguishes that objective from other methods of analysis, such as the social.[15] Despite the distinction and his own disclaimer, there is no reason in principle why his account of norms could not be put to use in a law-and-society approach, although its very abstraction means its use would be limited. Hart's approach is importantly different: it is proposed as expressing the social reality of law. We shall return to Hart in a moment, but it should be noted here that his claim is true only up to a point. His account takes a limited view of what counts as the social reality of law and is still mainly concerned with the formulation and refinement of general concepts.

The conclusion we may draw is that legal theory, in providing concepts, categories, and ideas, is a good starting point for an analysis of law in society; at the same time, it is only a starting point, which must be supplemented by considering how law works when it encounters social situations in all their variety. Before developing this idea further, there remains a minor puzzle: how can legal theory be a generalization from social practices and then be used to classify social data and explain its significance. If theory is based on social experiences, how can it help to understand those same experiences? The answer is plain: the student of law-and-society, faced with a mass of social data about how law is working in practice, takes advantage of the concepts developed in legal theory, which represent the accumulated practical experience on which the theory is based. The process is reflexive, for it may be that the particular case shows up something new that has not been accounted for in the general theory, or that aspects of the theory are based on mistakes or misunderstandings. Adjustments are then made to the theory to ensure that it continues to reflect social reality, while adding new concepts where necessary.

---

[15] H. Kelsen, *The Pure Theory of Law* (Free Press, 1938), p. 1.

1.3 HART ON SOCIAL EXPLANATION

Having seen in a general way that legal theory can be of use to law-and-society, let us return to Hart's description of a municipal legal system and his suggestion that it could be regarded as descriptive sociology. This will enable further development of the relationship and at the same time be the basis for assessing its utility for law-and-society. The first point is that Hart's theory is different from others 'such as those of Austin and Kelsen' since it is explicitly grounded in social reality, which means that his concepts, and the distinctions between them, are derived from and should be tested against the practical experience of law. His condemnation of other theories and the presentation of his own is supported by frequent references to that practical experience. As for condemnation, Austin errs because: 'the model of orders backed by threats obscures more of law than it reveals'[16] and is not able: 'to account for some of the salient features of a modern municipal legal system'.[17] In support of his own theory, Hart enlists the analysis of language because it leads: 'to different types of social situations or relationships' and to 'the realities we use words to talk about'.[18] The three concepts fundamental to the whole enterprise – law, coercion, and morality – are considered to be 'types of social phenomena'.[19] Without multiplying the examples, we see how committed Hart is to his theory being grounded in the social reality of law. From that a second point follows: the very same distinctions brought to light by legal theory, and the concepts and categories underlying them, have a social basis in the sense that they form part of the structure of society and affect the way people behave.

In other words, the elucidation of law's qualities and its general concepts adds to our understanding of society by showing how they feature in people's lives, how they use and rely on them, while by their neglect important aspects of social life would be overlooked. Again, the notion of a rule serves as an example: considering how much legal activity is based on rules, it is easy to see the usefulness of an analysis that explains their nature. The same could be said of other concepts and distinctions, such as, the difference between types of rules, the notion of the rule of recognition, what it means to have an obligation, the nature and place of coercion, and above all the introduction of secondary rules, with respect to which Hart says: 'For the introduction into society of rules enabling

---

[16] *The Concept of Law*, p. 48.   [17] *Ibid*, p. 97.   [18] *Ibid*, p. 17.   [19] *Ibid*, p. 17.

legislators to change and add to the rules of duty, and for judges to determine when the rule of duty have been broken, is a step forward as important to society as the invention of the wheel'.[20] It is hardly contentious that these and other concepts, many of which owe their refinement to Hart, provide a sound basis for beginning a study of law in society.

It might be objected that those engaged in law-and-society are perfectly able to devise their own general concepts, and to do so on the basis of empirical research, rather than borrow from a discipline that, for all its good intentions, is still a step away from social reality. It is true that researchers in law-and-society could come up with their own general concepts as some have; but many have not, and the resulting conceptual frailty of law-and-society is all too apparent and one reason why it is still in its early stages. Anyhow, why not benefit from the long tradition of legal theory and exploit its findings to advance law-and-society! Any social explanation has to begin with some concepts, no matter how tentative, and theoretical analysis is the obvious place to look. Finally, it could be thought that the concepts of most use to law-and-society are those developed from empirical research, from the ground up, as those engaged in research like to say. But it should by now be plain that the two are not mutually exclusive: the concepts supplied by legal theory are a way of beginning the enquiry, a way of developing an initial understanding of what to look for and the questions to ask. Empirical evidence could lead to the rejection or reformulation of the theoretical concept, for although legal theorists do not present their theories as hypotheses in the way familiar to social scientists, that is normally what they are. That is not the main reason for using theoretical analysis, nor is it always profitable; the main reason is to get started on a firm footing.

Many years after writing *The Concept of Law,* Hart modified his earlier claim that it could be read as descriptive sociology suggesting instead that it provides 'the tools for descriptive sociology'.[21] If by this he meant that his account provides the elements of law as a social formation on which a fuller account could be built, then he was surely right. The need for a fuller account and what it should contain is brought to light by reminding ourselves of the issues for law in society, and then asking how Hart's account has to be developed to deal with them. The two issues are: the social character of law and its interaction with other aspects of society.

---

[20] *Ibid*, pp. 41–2.
[21] 'Hart Interviewed: H. L. A. Hart in Conversation with David Sugarman' (2005) 32 *Journal of Law and Society* 267, p. 291.

Hart's primary concern is with the first part, the nature of law, and only tangentially with interaction. Considering his aim was to provide an analysis of the distinctive features of a municipal legal system, we should not expect a full account of law in society. At the same time, once an analysis of law avowedly grounded in social reality is embarked on, there is no clear point at which to stop, since the very concept of law as a social formation leads into its relationship with other social formations. This is especially so when the account is grounded on the actions of officials, for it is there that the interaction takes place. Once we examine those actions, it is plain that acceptance of law, for instance, while capable of precise description analytically, is entwined in practice with other social factors from which it cannot be readily separated and which affect the very idea. A law-and-society approach needs to go beyond the analytical concept of acceptance and consider how officials behave in practice. That examination shows, as we see later, that the actual practice of both officials and citizens in accepting the rule of recognition and specific laws is a more complex process than the analytical concept suggests.

1.4 BEYOND HART

Here, then, is the crux of the distinction between Hart's analytical approach and that of law-and-society. The first identifies the features or properties of a concept, legal rules being the main example, whose main feature is its acceptance by someone as a standard guiding behaviour. This is what we understand by a rule. Law-and-society begins with that idea and then goes on to see how rules work in practice. This has two aspects: one is to see how rules are actually regarded and used by officials and citizens, the other to determine how legal rules interact with other social formations. The analytical concept is an initial guide to understanding social actions, but it has to be added to, even to some degree re-assessed, in observing how rules work in practice.

On the basis of the distinction, a general law-and-society approach can be formulated, containing two elements: one is to examine law as a social formation, the other its interaction with other social formations. Both are essential and a corrective to the idea that law-and-society is concerned only with the second, the interaction aspect, as if law itself were a fixed and straightforward phenomenon. On the contrary, law itself is a social phenomenon whose character is formed by social factors. That is why a study of law in society should begin by examining the notion of law itself; only after understanding how law is constituted in a social setting should we move on to its interaction with other aspects of the setting. Again, however, the line between the two elements is not as plain as this suggests for the two are connected; the social formation of law is intertwined with, could even be considered an aspect of, its interaction with other social formations.

In order to develop this approach to law in society, Hart's account has to be both added to and modified in several ways: *first*, some of his concepts need further consideration; *secondly*, other concepts and ideas need to be added; and *thirdly*, the interaction of law with other aspects of society has to be considered. As to the *first*, Hart begins with the concepts of law, coercion, and morality, with a view to showing that coercion has a lesser and different role from that normally ascribed to it, and that morality is related to law but separate from it. The separation of law and coercion is hailed as a major breakthrough in clarifying the concept of law, although from a law-and-society stance coercion plainly has a major place in modern legal orders, and its place has to be reassessed. Hart's interest is elsewhere; having marginalized coercion, he sets out to elucidate law's main features, and encourages the conclusion that his most original contribution is the image of law as a union of social rules of a particular kind, with officials to make, interpret, and apply them. If we were to summarize his account in two words, they would be *rules* and *officials*, both of which are also fundamental to, but insufficient for, a law-and-society approach.

The more developed of the two is the nature of rules, which includes the concept of a social rule, law as social rules, the nature of obligation under rules, what it means to accept rules, the difference between primary and secondary rules, and the rule of recognition. These ideas will be examined here with a view to understanding the nature of social rules and the idea of acceptance; they also show the link between rules and the social context in which they occur, a matter vital to the understanding of law. We shall then proceed to consider the relations between legal rules and social norms, using the latter term to cover rules and standards that intersect with law, whether to complement it or compete with it. Out of this emerges the idea of social spheres as sets of distinct conventions and understandings, the claim being that citizens and officials typically view legal rules from the perspective of sets of social spheres.

Having officials with authority to make, interpret, and apply law is the mark of a legal system as opposed to a pre-legal order in which they are lacking. A legal system, stripped to it bare essentials, consists of general obedience to law by the people and *acceptance by officials* as common public standards of behaviour of the 'rules of recognition specifying the criterion of legal validity and its rules of change and adjudication . . .'.[22] From a law-and-society approach, the place of officials is fundamental and Hart's account of them a good place to begin. It also needs to be developed further to take account of the way officials group together in organizations, which they envelop in institutional conventions and understandings. In modern legal orders, officials have special relations with citizens, and they must also be studied. A noticeable aspect of Hart's account is that, while officials are placed at the centre, citizens are relegated to the margins. The idea of citizens needing only to obey, while officials accept, may be justified in a very general way in relation to legal systems generally, but hardly matches the character of modern legal orders and needs to be reconsidered.

Rules and officials are, then, the two central planks of Hart's account, the examination of which must occupy a large part of a study of law in society. Here is the basis for the *second* line of development: other issues that are not so prominent in Hart beg for attention in law-and-society. One is the prominence of state law: legal theory takes the law of modern states to be the central case of law and by-and-large ignores other rule-based orders claiming legal status. Law-and-society is more receptive, and entertains the idea that contemporary societies may have several legal orders running in parallel. These claims are considered, as are questions about the functions of law, which some would add as a third main plank of *The Concept of Law*. Such a view is, in my opinion, mistaken for although Hart has much to say about law's functions it is not central to his analysis. Nevertheless, the claim of law having specific functions persists and, if true, would have significance for both its nature and its importance. It must then be investigated, in the course of which the emphasis will shift from the functions of law to its social value. Another idea mentioned earlier, which follows from Hart's account of rules and officials, is the distinctiveness of modern legal systems. Narrowing the focus of study to one type of legal order, a type whose practical expression is found in modern western societies, enables a more complete description and encourages discussion of features that are normally neglected, an example being the relations between citizens and officials. The idea that modern western legal systems have distinctive features appears at many points throughout this book, one specific aspect of which is the

[22] *The Concept of Law*, 2nd edn, p. 116.

relationship between developed legal systems and the social conditions supporting it.

The *third* set of issues in establishing a law-and-society approach concerns the interaction of law and other social aspects. On this, Hart and legal theory generally is largely silent, while for the social explanation of law it is a necessary dimension. Interaction of law and other social aspects is, of course, not a neatly separate matter but permeates the social analysis of law at many points and in many ways. It also raises issues that are usually considered under the headings of implementation and compliance, meaning the processes by which groups of officials implement sets of laws and others, usually citizens but also other officials, are expected to comply. Apart from raising general and theoretical issues for law in society, an added attraction is that implementation and compliance have been the subject of extensive empirical research. To sum up, my intention in this book is to use Hart's analysis and the concepts he has formulated as the starting point from which to examine these issues. The result should be a fuller but still naturally incomplete account of the main issues for understanding law in modern society.

1.5 FROM LAW-AND-SOCIETY BACK TO ANALYTICAL JURISPRUDENCE

The utility of legal theory for law-and-society should now be plain, but what about the converse: can law-and-society contribute to legal theory? How can the daily tribulations of lobster-fishing inspectors off British Columbia, the intricate relationships between New York's diamond traders, and the informal rules of Californian ranchers, being so local and particular, possibly be of use to legal theory? One aspect of this issue was touched on earlier with the suggestion that practical experience could provide grounds for modifying or even discounting theoretical concepts and claims. Theoretical concepts and claims of the kind advanced in legal theory, on one view, are in the nature of hypotheses about the social world and, as such, can be tested by evidence. The concept of acceptance of rules as described by Hart, I shall argue, needs to be modified in the light of how acceptance really works. Similarly, the claim that coercion is at the margins of a modern legal system is easily tested. Not all concepts or claims are susceptible to being tested by practical experience for reasons we have seen; whether they are or not depends on how abstract they are and to what extent they are formed from practical experience.

Another aspect of the use to legal theory of empirical evidence gained by studying legal phenomena is whether it can be generalized. The study of cockfights in Bali, religious rites among the Zonde, or the resolution of disputes by Shasta County ranchers, reveals a lot about each of those social worlds; but it is local and particular, and arguably has no wider implications or interest. The celebration of the particular, has good credentials, with some forms of social enquiry limiting themselves in this way, usually from convenience, sometimes from principle. It could be argued, however, that the most detailed and particular study has potential for generalization, for extrapolating from the details one or more hypotheses that could then be tested in other contexts. That is not to say that generalization is the main purpose of social enquiry, but it is a legitimate purpose. The same applies to law-and-society as one type of social enquiry; although empirical studies are often content to investigate a matter simply in order to gain understanding of it, there is both potential and a natural inclination to extract something more.

If, in the course of law-and-society research, matters are revealed that are sufficiently general across legal systems, then legal theory may find them relevant to its own purposes. There is no reason, in principle, against research in law-and-society being informative as to the nature of law, despite its main purpose being to advance the understanding of law in society. It could bring to light matters of interest to legal theory in the form of a novel generalization or hypothesis about law, so that legal theory should be modified to take account of it. Alternatively, on the basis of law-and-society research, current concepts and ideas could be confirmed or questioned. For, as noted before, the concepts and ideas of legal theory are founded on generalizations about the world, even if they are not expressed in that way; and being generalizations about the world they are dependent on accurately reflecting what happens in the world. [23]It might be said that law-and-society has not yet made much progress in developing generalizations about its subject matter, but that is a different issue and more a reflection of a callow discipline than anything deeper. [24]

---

[23] I refer here to Clifford Geertz's famous study: 'Deep Play: Notes on the Balinese Cockfight' in *The Interpretation of Cultures* (New York, 1973). Professor Geertz would not, I think, agree with my claim.

[24] Among recent efforts towards generalization in law and society is Brian Tamanaha's *General Theory of Law and Society* (Oxford, 2003).

1.6 ELEMENTS OF A MODERN LEGAL ORDER

Hart built his description of a municipal legal system around rules and officials. My intention is to narrow the analysis by restricting it to certain kinds of legal systems, and then to deepen it by identifying features that are characteristic of them. Putting aside pathological cases emerging from revolution, war or other crisis, and confining our enquiry to those that are reasonably settled and stable, the legal systems of developed western countries have several features that make them reasonably distinct. These include the extensive use of law to achieve social goals, a developed administration to make, apply, and enforce the law, specific ideas guiding and restraining the use of law and official behaviour, and a high level of acceptance of law. These are very general, but taken together they constitute a very particular type of legal order, which at the risk of confusion I shall designate as a *modern legal order*. Modern legal orders can be seen in reasonably well-developed forms in the societies of western Europe, north America, parts of the British Commonwealth, and occasionally elsewhere. They are the legacy of historical factors particular to those regions and the product of ideas about how societies should be governed and the role of law. Both the particular legal orders and the ideas on which they are based have formed slowly with many set-backs. As legal orders, they run counter to the natural social forces at work, and as a result are fragile and vulnerable to collapse in the face of such forces. Other legal orders in Europe, such as that of Russia or Ukraine, qualify as legal systems in Hart's sense and have elements of the above features; but because they lack other vital elements they are not modern legal orders in this sense. Societies based on totalitarian domination such as the People's Republic of China are also legal systems but could not meet the criteria of a modern legal order, even if other aspects of their traditional law were compatible. Other societies may approximate a modern legal order but fall short in significant ways; they may be under-developed as legal orders, or, although well-developed, lack some of the features described above.

There are two main reasons for introducing this idea of modern legal orders. One is descriptive: within the societies mentioned the elements of a modern legal order can be identified. They are not always fully formed, and practices naturally lapse from the general notion; nevertheless, a reasonably distinct set of practices and attitudes are present which form a coherent conception of a particular kind of legal order. The other reason is normative. Modern legal orders are based on ideas and values that ought to win support and protection. The idea that law is relatively distinct from politics, that legislatures are limited in the use of their legislative authority, that officials hold power on trust and should answer for their use of it, and that law should be used as an instrument for both stability and achieving positive social goals, all warrant our support. They do so because they help in achieving social goods whose value is best appreciated by experiencing societies that lack them, whether they are the countries of East Europe as they recover from Communist rule, the numerous states crippled by corruption and bad government, or those subjected to one form of dictatorship or another.

Having identified the general character of a modern legal order, its more specific features are as follows.

Firstly, law is primarily enacted law made by legislative bodies in their exercise of will rather than emerging from custom, tradition, or common law, with the important result that law is not necessarily grounded in existing social practices. The dominance of enacted law enables the use of law for achieving positive social goals; it also poses the threat of law being in conflict with other social practices.

Secondly, modern legal systems have developed specialized organizations and institutions of officials with authority to make, apply, and enforce the law. Official organizations have specialized knowledge and training, are highly organized, and have the capacity to implement the law. Government organizations are normally separated from each other on a broadly functional basis, although the resulting configuration may take various forms.

Thirdly, coercion is central to a modern legal order and exerts great influence on its nature and working, including enabling officials to enforce the law.

Fourthly, state law has, or claims to have, final authority over other systems of rules within its jurisdiction and does not generally tolerate the existence of competing legal orders. The idea of law claiming final authority over other rule-based orders has its origins in the most elementary idea of law, and still has a role in strengthening the claims of modern states to legitimate authority.

Fifthly, while social relations among citizens are primarily guided by spontaneous social practices, law brings added value in facilitating and protecting those relations, which it has the power to change and often does so by pursuing positive social goals. This regulatory aspect and its frequent use is a significant feature of a modern legal order.

Sixthly, officials have extensive powers, but in exercising them are constrained by their social relations with citizens as expressed in sets of standards, this being one of the most important marks of a modern legal order.

Finally, several of these elements combine to create a distinctive normative structure, which is based on ideas of the rule of law and of which it represents a contemporary version. To that should be added a distinctive role for government institutions, which are generally responsive to those ideas and in whose practices they are expressed. These various features combine to form a sense of a modern legal order, an idea that is developed throughout this book.

NOTES

Not taking law seriously

That the social significance of law is not always noticed or drawn out is an interpretation of research and writing in law-and-society rather than an explicitly expressed approach. However, some examples of a plainly sceptical approach include the following: K. Hawkins (ed), *The Uses of Discretion* (Oxford, 1994).

For a critique of a tendency not to take law seriously in the study of regulation, see: K. Yeung, *Securing Compliance: A Principled Approach* (Oxford, 2004). Her objective is 'to identify a set of constitutional values that ought to shape, inform, and constrain the techniques and strategies used by regulators when implementing regulatory programmes' (p. 4).

The first example in the text is familiar in those approaches that begin with the premise that law is a mask or cover for something else. Much of its force comes from Marx's expression of law as part of the superstructure of society, while real social relations are economic. Later Marxists realized that, although law ultimately serves the economic structure, within that parameter it has some autonomy. A more recent expression of the superficial character of law can be seen in the *Critical Legal Studies* movement, the European version of which has direct lines back to Marxism. The *American Realist* approach (or approaches) constitutes another line of scepticism about legal rules, which in turn has influenced the American version of Critical Legal Studies.

The second example draws on the extensive empirical research that has been conducted into the implementation of law by officials. This includes decision-making by government officials, such as social welfare officers, prosecutors, and regulators; indeed the studies of regulation practically constitute a discipline in themselves. Although these studies have taught us much about the implementation of law, and while any generalization across such a big field must be made with caution, there is nevertheless a certain reluctance to engage with the law itself, to see exactly what it says, and how it influences the actions of officials.

On the tendency of social science to re-describe law in terms of other concepts and categories

R. Cotterrell, 'Law in Social Theory and Social Theory in the Study of Law' in A. Sarat (ed) *The Blackwell Companion to Law and Society* (Oxford, 2004).

On the nature of theories of law

There are, of course, different types of legal theory that divide into descriptive and normative. Analytical jurisprudence is one type of descriptive theory. For recent debate concerning the nature of legal theory, see: J. Coleman, 'Incorporationism, Conventionality, and the Practical Difference,' in J. Coleman (ed) *Hart's Postscript* (Oxford, 2001) and R. Dworkin *Justice in Robes* (Harvard, 2006).

The nature of Hart's theory

One of the issues concerning Hart is whether he was seeking to identify the *concept of law* as the title of his book suggest, or whether he was mainly concerned to *describe the elements of a municipal legal system*. My conclusion is that he was primarily concerned with the second of these and that his account is more suited to it than to the first. There are passages in the text supporting both.

As to his purpose being to describe a modern legal system: his critique of Austin is stated to be his 'incapacity to account for some of the salient features of a modern municipal legal system' (page 97).

It is suggested in the text that the *concept* of law involves a wider enquiry than the description of a municipal legal system. It is also suggested that the *concept* is not tied to actual social experience. This touches on a deeper issue of how concepts are formed; to what extent they are abstractions from actual experience, and so open to empirical investigation, and to what extent they are the product of imagination. We need not enter into this issue here beyond noting the philosophical controversy that lies behind it (see further: A. Ryan, *The Philosophy of the Social*

Sciences (Macmillan, 1970) pp. 167–8; L. Whitehead, 'Comparative Politics: Democratization Studies' in R. E. Goodin and H-D. Klingemann (eds) *A New Handbook of Political Science* (Oxford, 1996) p. 366; P. Baert, *Philosophy of the Social Sciences* (Polity, 2005)).

Language as an entry to social reality

For further discussion of this approach in relation to social psychology, but of relevance to law-and-society, see: R. Harré and P. Secord, *The Explanation of Social Behaviour* (Oxford, 1972). I refer to this work in *Chapter 6*.

In relation to the importance of language as a route to psychology, they write: 'Since accounts are given in ordinary language the starting point for developing a conceptual system for their analysis must be the analysis of the conceptual system of ordinary language.' (page 126).

And later: 'It is partly because the system of rules and meanings under which social life is lived can be grasped by studying the reports and commentaries of social actors.' (page 108).

Legal theory as descriptive sociology

The passage from Hart is worth quoting in full:

'Notwithstanding its concern with analysis the book may also be regarded as an essay in descriptive sociology; for the suggestion that inquiries into the meanings of words merely throw light on words is false. Many important meanings which are not immediately obvious, between types of social situations or relationships may best be brought to light by an examination of the standard uses of the relevant expressions and by the way in which these depend on a social context, itself often left unstated. In this field of study it is particularly true that we may use, as Professor J. L. Austin said "a sharpened awareness of words to sharpen our perception of the phenomena".' (*Concept of Law* p. vii). Hart later added to this quotation Austin's words '[we] are looking not merely at words – but also at the realities we use words to talk about' (page 14).

Among other references to this point in the *Concept of Law* are the following: 'For its purpose is not to guide a definition of law, in the sense of a rule by reference to which the correctness of the use of the word can be tested; it is to advance legal theory by providing an improved analysis of the distinctive features of a municipal legal system and a better understanding of the resemblances and differences between law, coercion, and morality, *as types of social phenomena*' (emphasis added): (page 17).

Among the extensive literature on *The Concept of Law*, the following are especially useful in its relevance to law-and-society:

L. Green, 'The Concept of Law Revisited' (1996) 94 *Michigan L. R.* 1687
M. Payne, 'Hart's Concept of a Legal System' (1976–77) 18 *William and Mary L. R.* 287.

Analytical jurisprudence should accurately reflect social reality

At many points, Hart refers to the point that the concepts of analytical jurisprudence must accurately reflect legal thought and practice, which forms part of social reality.

For instance, his critique of John Austin is based on precisely that point. He writes of Austin: '. . . the model of orders backed by threats obscures more of law than it reveals; the effort to reduce to this single form the variety of laws ends by imposing upon them a spurious uniformity. Indeed, to look for uniformity here may be a mistake, for a distinguishing, if not the distinguishing, characteristic of law lies in its fusion of different types of rules.' (page 48).

Again in respect of the internal aspect of rules, Hart invokes the need to reflect social reality. In distinguishing habits from rules, he writes: 'The third feature distinguishing social rules from habits is . . . so important and so frequently disregarded or misrepresented in jurisprudence that we shall elaborate it here' (page 55). He goes on to show how the internal aspect of rules is fundamental to everyday social practice so that a theory of law which failed to represent it, would be seriously defective.

Similarly, Hart's claim for the importance of the distinction between primary and secondary rules, and the way they combine, is that '. . . most of the features of law which have proved most perplexing . . . can be rendered clear, if these two types of rules and the interplay between them are understood'. He then adds crucially: 'We accord this union of elements a central place because of their explanatory power in elucidating the concepts that constitute the framework of legal thought.' (page 79).

The relationship between Kelsen's *pure theory* and social reality is not easy to pin down. He states: 'A normative order that regulates human behaviour . . . is a social order. Morals and law are such social orders. On the other hand, logic has as its subject matter a normative order that does not have a social character.' (*The Pure Theory of Law* p. 24). The point seems to be that, while a legal order is a social order, the analysis of its logical, normative character does not involve an enquiry into the social aspects; it is rather a different kind of enquiry, based on logic rather than sociology.

Generalization in law-and-society

For discussion, see: R. Kagan, 'What Socio-Legal Scholars Should Do When There Is Too Much Law To Study' in D. J. Galligan, *Socio-Legal Studies in Context: The Oxford Centre Past and Future* (Oxford, 1994).
Compare: C. Geertz, *Local Knowledge: Further Essays in Interpretive Anthropology* (New York, 1983).

On generalization and concept formation

The literature on generalization and concept formation is extensive. Hart was influenced by P. Winch's *The Idea of Social Science and its Relation to Philosophy* (London, 1st edition 1958, 2nd edition 1990); for an analysis of the issues generally, and of Winch's account in particular, see A. Ryan's *The Philosophy of the Social Sciences* (London, 1970).

Legal theory as theory of society

That law is itself a social system and that legal theory is then also social theory can hardly be disputed. N. Luhmann, who discusses the character of legal and social theory deliberately called his major work on law and society *Law as a Social System* (Oxford, 2004), his point being that the legal system is itself a particular social system: 'Our starting point is that the legal system is a sub-system of the social system,' (p. 72).

2

Approaches to Law in Society

2.1 UNDERSTANDING LAW IN SOCIETY

There are different ways of studying law in society, each with its own aims and methods. An historical approach examines the relations between law and events, showing how law has been used at different times for different purposes, how it connects with interests and classes, with political ends and social movements. Notable studies include the early development of modern law in medieval Europe,[1] the use of criminal law in England in the eighteenth century in protecting property,[2] and the transformation of American law in the eighteenth and nineteenth centuries to cope with the rapid advance of business enterprise.[3] Another approach has its setting in political science where the centre of attention is the role of legal institutions, especially courts, legislators, and administrative bodies.[4] Here, the object is to understand how legal institutions fit within the political system, how they work in practice, and how they relate to other political institutions. Economics provides a third approach where, again, its methods and theories are applied to laws and legal institutions to determine how they fit within the economic order and the consequences.[5] The list could go on to include other disciplinary approaches, especially sociology, psychology, and anthropology, the point being that since law is a part of society it is of interest to all forms of social enquiry. Social enquiry has become divided into specialized disciplines, each with its aims, theoretical framework, and methods. The prospect of a unified social science, a grand

[1] H. Berman, *Law and Revolution: The Formation of the Western Legal Tradition* (Cambridge, Mass., 1983).
[2] E. P. Thompson, *Whigs and Hunters* (London, 1975).
[3] M.Horwitz, *The Transformation of American* Law (Cambridge, Mass., 1978).
[4] A good example of an extensive body of research is M. Shapiro, *The Supreme Court and Administrative Agencies* (New York, 1968).
[5] For an analysis of the law and economics approach: N. Mercuro and S. G. Medema, *Economics and the Law: From Posner to Post-Modernism* (Princeton, 1997).

and all-encompassing framework of enquiry, shows little sign of realization.[6]

The approach I take here, rather than being a strict application of any one of the disciplines mentioned, is located within socio-legal studies or law-and-society (nothing turning on the name), which now has its own disciplinary tradition. The object of study of this tradition is law, the aim being to understand it as part of society, having a distinct social form and intersecting with other social forms. Its methods are eclectic rather than pure, with sociology and social theory its main sources of ideas and approaches, while anthropology and political science are constantly invoked. The law-and-society framework itself has room for a range of approaches usually identified with Durkheim,[7] Weber,[8] and Luhmann, as well as numerous more recent writers. Both Durkheim and Weber, two of the towering figures of modern sociology, wrote extensively on law and are a natural bridge to law-and-society, a study of which could hardly escape being influenced by both. Niklas Luhmann, another sociologist and lawyer, dedicated himself more directly to law in society and poses a serious challenge to conventional approaches.[9] His influence is felt and his claims must be considered. Without falling wholly under the allure of any one of these figures, ample reference is made to each in proposing an approach to guide us through the following chapters.

Social enquiry of any kind requires the answering of three main questions: *first*, what is the subject of study; *secondly*, what are its aims; and *thirdly*, how is the study to be conducted. The study of law in society is no exception so that in answering these questions the main features of my approach will emerge.

2.2 THE SUBJECT OF STUDY IN LAW-AND-SOCIETY

To say that the subject of study is *law in society* may be enough to distinguish it from the jurist's concern with doctrine and the legal

[6] For elements of a unified approach see: R. Cooter 'Law and Unified Social Theory' in D. J. Galligan (Ed), *Socio-Legal Studies in Context: The Oxford Centre Past and Future* (Oxford, 1995), pp 50–67.

[7] The main work of Durkheim drawn on is: E Durkheim, *The Division of Labour in Society* (New York, 1994) and *Rules of Sociological Method* (New York, 1938).

[8] Much of Weber's writing on law in society is contained in: M Weber, *Economy and Society (2 vols)* (Ed) G. Roth and C. Wittick (Berkeley, Cal., 1968).

[9] Luhmann's main work is: N Luhmann, *Law as a Social System* (Oxford, 2003) (translated by K. Ziegart).

philosopher's with general concepts and theories, but hardly conveys a clear idea of what it is itself. In order to make that more precise, three lines of approach are identified and their merits assessed. One focuses on the interaction between law and other social formations, a second on both the character of law and its interaction, while a third rejects the relevance of interaction and concentrates on the social character of law itself. The first is associated with much of the empirical research conducted under the heading of socio-legal studies, the third with Luhmann and his insistence that law is a distinct social formation that should be kept separate from its environment; the second is the approach adopted here.

With regard to the first, the focus is on the interaction between law and other social formations where the law itself is taken as a fairly unproblematic constant, so that the kinds of issues arising are: how do people regard law, what happens when they come into contact with it, how they use it, and what happens when they get embroiled in its processes. A good example is a pioneering study, conducted by my own institution, the Oxford Centre for Socio-Legal Studies in its early years, of what happens to the victims of accidents.[10] The study shows how few victims seek or obtain compensation, and explains why; we learn about such matters as what kinds of injuries people suffer, the different types of compensation, why victims choose one rather than another type, and the character of the legal schemes. The study concludes with recommendations for changes and improvements in policy. Other studies of the interaction between law and society go beyond this to include such matters as why people make complaints[11] and what remedies they expect, whether legal representation before tribunals makes a difference to the outcome,[12] and what happens to children and couples after divorce. Another area of research is the implementation of law by officials, including such issues as how they interpret and exercise their powers, whether they apply the law faithfully or tend to assume discretion to depart from it; what factors influence their decisions; and what kinds of relations are formed with those subject to their powers. The study of decision-making by officials is often broadened to include the nature and workings of administrative and judicial bodies, the objective being to understand how institutional and organizational factors influence their practical operation. The other side of implementation by officials is compliance by private parties or other

---

[10] D. Harris *et al*, *Compensation and Support for Illness and Injury* (Oxford, 1984).
[11] S. Lloyd-Bostock, *Law in Practice* (London, 1988).
[12] H. Genn and Y. Genn, *The Effectiveness of Representation Before Tribunals* (London, 1989).

officials, which gives rise to a set of similar issues as to how they receive and deal with law.[13] The relations between law and informal social norms opens up a different line of research, which raises questions such as the conditions under which informal norms are inadequate in regulating social issues and which ones are strengthened or replaced by law. Alternatively, under what conditions are laws modified by or displaced by informal norms, whether by the police, psychiatrists, or a community of farmers. A final area of enquiry to mention is the effect law has in changing or redirecting behaviour, whether of individual persons, associations, or officials. Among the questions here, the principal one is under what conditions is law effective in bringing about social change. Considering how often law is used with that objective, this is of major contemporary interest.

These are the main areas that have come to typify empirical socio-legal research. Of course there are others and it would be wrong to suggest they all have the same aims, or indeed that the aims for which they are conducted are always clear. Nevertheless, taken as a whole, they represent a general approach to law-and-society whose main subject is law's interaction with its social environment. Early studies were directed at showing the gap between the legal ideal and the reality, between the law providing a system of compensation for the victims of accidents and the fact that so few people benefit from it. Later studies matured into a concern, not so much with the gap between idea and reality, as with the social processes set in train when a set of laws is launched to control such matters as environmental pollution or the safety of workers.[14] Laws for the purpose of this approach normally take the form of legislative schemes directed at achieving certain objectives, but research extends to include judicial decisions, especially those of the higher courts aimed at outlawing such practices as racial segregation in schools,[15] or changing the practices of officials through judicial review.[16] As research has developed and its methods become more refined, knowledge and understanding of the interaction between law and its social environment has become quite

---

[13] These issues are considered in Chapters 7, 15, 16 and 17.

[14] Examples are: G. Richardson, A. Ogus and P. Burrows, *Policing Pollution* (Oxford, 1982); K. Hawkins, *Environment and Enforcement* (Oxford, 1983); B. Hutter, *The Reasonable Arm of Law* (Oxford, 1988).

[15] For a sample of the extensive literature on those issues see G. Rosenberg, *The Hollow Hope* (Chicago, 1991).

[16] For a sample of illuminating studies see S. Halliday, *Judicial Review and Compliance with Administrative Law*, (Hart, 2004) and G. Richardson and M. Sunkin, 'Judicial Review: Question of Impact' *Public Law* 79 (London, 1996).

advanced, although its value to policy-makers has not yet been fully realized.

The suggestion that the main concern of this research has been the interaction of law with other social aspects, rather than the law itself, in no way diminishes its importance; nor should it be taken to mean that it has no significance for an understanding of law. On the contrary, for anyone with an interest in law's social role, the body of socio-legal research provides the empirical basis on which generalization about the nature of law can be based; at the same time, that is not the aim of this approach nor has it been much used for that purpose. Once one embarks on a course of generalization as to the character of law, the frame of reference subtly but significantly changes; law is no longer taken for granted as relatively fixed and unproblematic but becomes itself the object of study. The frame of reference now includes both the law and its interaction with society, which go well together, since the analysis of law as a distinct social formation, while of interest and value in itself, also affects its interaction with other social formations. We should think of law as an edifice not unlike a house which, like a house, takes different forms and shapes; and just as the form or shape of a house affects how it is used, the same goes for law.

The basis of this approach, which guides my present study, is that the subject of law-and-society is both the law and its interaction with society. The study of law as a social formation means identifying its elements and examining how they come together to form a distinct phenomenon as outlined in the first chapter. Using this approach, it means following Hart's idea of law as a system of social rules accepted by officials and others as binding on them, and then developing the idea further. More needs to be known about social rules and especially legal rules, about the attitudes of officials and citizens to legal rules, and what it means to accept them as guides to behaviour. The connections legal rules have with coercion and particular functions need to be considered, as does the idea that legal rules are in some way different from other social rules. From these lines of enquiry, more details of which are given in the previous chapter, a general picture of law emerges as a social formation, or, to continue the analogy with a building, we should have a good idea of the legal edifice. Within that edifice, different architectural designs are possible, depending on the nature of the rules and their objectives, the procedures and remedies, and the way officials are organized. Law as a social formation, therefore, has two levels of analysis, one the general meaning, the other the specific designs within it. Following the analysis of law as a social formation, its interaction with other social formations can be considered. The process of interaction has two aspects: one refers to the way various social elements combine and interact in the very formation of law, the other to the way specific sets of laws, specific designs, encounter the social environment.

One reaction could be that this approach lacks clarity and precision. Law as one social formation merges into others, leaving unclear where law ends and others begin; it is also unclear how law can be distinct and yet be intertwined with other aspects of society. To anyone with an eye for conceptual clarity, this must seem unwelcome confusion, prompting the search for a more precise concept of law, one sharply separable from other social forms. That, roughly, is the third approach to defining the subject of law-and-society; it is associated with Luhmann and is a frontal challenge to the approach here. The opposite reaction would be to question the idea that law really is a distinct social formation, to accept that legal rules are just one set of rules among several and proceed from there. Neither reaction is persuasive enough to depose the approach proposed here. The idea that law can be strictly separated from its social environment has a superficial attraction that dissolves on scrutiny, as we shall see shortly. Moreover, it is hard to see why law's social environment, its interaction with society, should be excluded from the study of law in society. The alternative, the idea of law being one set of rules and practices among several, means forsaking any notion of its distinctiveness; that would be unwarranted neglect of a social formation that is not only distinctive but of considerable importance. It does not have the conceptual purity of analytical accounts such as Kelsen's and possibly even Hart's; but imprecision of definition and the ragged edges of practice should not be mistaken for non-existence.

2.3 THE AIMS OF LAW-AND-SOCIETY

Among social theorists, it is recognized that how one goes about studying any aspect of society depends on both the subject of study and the aims and purposes in conducting it. The idea that only one method is available, and that it should imitate the method of natural science, has long passed. Different methods are now acknowledged, although disagreement prevails as to their respective merits; also acknowledged is that the choice of method is inseparable from the researcher's standpoint. The subject of study here has been identified, what then are my aims in studying it? The answer at the most general level is plain: law is a major force in modern societies; it directs and regulates social relations; it dominates other systems of social control and has a mighty administrative machinery to enforce its dictates. It contributes to the life of communities and individuals, in many ways and, despite a capacity for misuse, it is regarded by most not just as a necessary part of a tolerable society but essential to the realization of valued social goods. That is self-evidently a powerful motive for wanting to know more about it, to understand its character, and how it works. The general aim, then, an aim surely sufficient in itself, is to understand this social phenomenon. It becomes more precisely focused in modern societies whose legal orders have qualities differentiating them from legal orders in general. The better knowledge and understanding of those qualities is of interest and importance in itself, but that is not all: better understanding should help in knowing what sustains them for after all they are worth sustaining. And if I am right in claiming that modern legal orders run counter to the forces of natural social formations, even of normal legal systems, then sustaining them is not easy.

Consideration of the general aim leads to others more specific. Law is of interest because it directs and influences people's actions. How it does so, the conditions under which it is effective, and why it often fails, add a point of focus that again resonates through modern societies, since they depend on a high level of respect for law and compliance with it. Hart confines that level of respect to officials, leaving the citizens to obey; my claim is that the achievements of modern societies depend not only on officials but also on citizens, from whom a high level of acceptance as well as obedience is necessary. At the same time, officials have a central role in making, applying, and enforcing the law. How their role is carried out warrants close study, for again more is expected from them in modern societies than pre-modern, and in doing so creates in them points of deep tension. They have the vast powers that are needed to achieve the goals of modern society, especially in regulating social relations contrary to their natural and spontaneous development. Simultaneously, officials have to be severely constrained in the use of their powers. The inherent tension, in turn, makes modern legal orders fragile and vulnerable to collapse. A specific aspect of the general aim concerns the way citizens and officials view the law and deal with it, not only as individuals but as members of associations and organizations. Whenever two or more people have common interests or pursuits, social relations are created among them. Social relations both encourage and are strengthened by the evolution of conventions and understandings, which in turn guide individuals in their actions. Each of us occupies many such sets of social relations and the social spheres developing around them, and it is from those standpoints that attitudes towards law are shaped and actions guided. These aims are already ambitious and to achieve them to any significant degree is a tall order. There is, nevertheless, one further ambition and that is to find, explain, and defend a general framework that transcends other more particular aims for studying law in society.

2.4 FOUR METHODOLOGICAL PRINCIPLES

Now that the subject of study in law-and-society and its aims have been identified, let us consider how it should be done, what methods should be used. Considering that the subject is both law as a social formation and its interaction with other social formations, a description of the main features of both is an obvious starting point. If law is a distinct social formation then it is reasonable to assume certain features that both identify it and distinguish it from other formations. The idea that we should begin by mapping the social world of law 'as accurately and completely as possible' has plain appeal.[17] Mapping means identifying and describing its prominent features. Hart's description of a municipal legal system is a good example of mapping. The main features are singled out, analyzed, and described, and how they combine is explained. The attractions of mapping as a method of explanation are slightly marred by the concern that social formations may not be quite like natural terrains, their features not so obvious and objective as mountains, rivers, and deserts. The added concern, that drawing-up a real map is not itself a straightforward process but dependent to some extent on the cartographer's aims, leads back to the bridge between aims and methods, and why it is important. The bridge reminds us that explaining social phenomena is not a mechanical process conducted by robots; it depends on the observer having specific aims and then classifying and understanding the social world in accordance with them. Philosophers still debate the extent to which the social researcher is or can be a spectator in describing the essential features of an external reality. Whatever the outcome of the debate, it is surely uncontroversial that we bring to any social enquiry a set of background assumptions and values, and a set of issues for which we seek clarification.

But where to start? Legal systems have many parts, some more central

---

[17] These are Patrick Beart's words, taken from his excellent recent book *The Philosophy of the Social Sciences* (Cambridge , 2005), p. 151.

than others; how then is the enquiry limited from among all the possible parts to those that are both important and manageable? Since our main aim in studying law in society is to understand how law works as a social formation, how it affects people's actions, we have a distinct point of view from which to analyze the data and draw the map. The issue then is: what features of law are relevant to its affecting the behaviour of citizens and officials? Durkheim's method in answering a similar question was to develop the notion of *social facts*. Despite social facts being seriously out of fashion, his method is useful in two ways. First, social facts should be taken as those fairly easily identifiable features of the landscape, the social equivalent of rivers, mountains, and bridges. Secondly, the social facts relevant to our enquiry are those affecting people's actions. Durkheim defines social facts in this way: 'When I fulfill my obligations as brother, husband, or citizen, when I execute my contracts, I perform duties which are defined, externally to myself and my acts, in law and in custom. Even if ... I feel their reality subjectively, such reality is still objective ...'.[18] In other words, social facts 'are external to individuals and exercise coercive power over them'.[19] They are not to be confused with the psychological states of individuals. The general approach serves my purposes well by limiting the mapping of law to those aspects that influence, or are expected to influence, behaviour. For social facts, I substitute the term *social formations* on the grounds that the latter have softer edges, allowing that they are themselves formed from several ingredients and are perhaps less objective than Durkheim proposes. On this approach, the elements of a legal order relevant to social enquiry are those social formations that are characteristically legal and likely to influence the actions of citizens and officials. Included among them must be the matters identified by Hart, such as rules of different kinds, officials, and sanctions. They extend to the social relations at the foundation of law, and they include the foundation and shape of legal orders as a whole, and the sets of laws within them. The method of approach, then, is to map those social formations on the canvas of human actions.

The mapping of a legal order is an important first step in the methods of law-and-society; it is the *first* methodological principle. It is not, however, enough. Social formations are external to individuals and exert influence on them; but they do not tell us how individuals respond. They explain the external part of the legal landscape, but not how people

---

[18] E. Durkheim, *Rules of Sociological Method* English edition, (New York, 1938), p. 1.

[19] P. Beart, op cit., p. 23.

regard social formations and deal with them. The example of a rule again
serves us well. Legal rules are part of the external landscape and place
social pressure on people to comply with them; how they then respond
to the rule opens up another area of social activity. Hart enters into
this social world and develops the idea of an *internal point* of view, of
acceptance of the rule as a binding standard, which is different from
another point of view where the rule is a sign that sanctions may be
imposed. Hart is known to have read Weber and appears to have followed
closely his approach to social explanation. Weber defines social explanation as 'the science concerning itself with the interpretive understanding
of social action and thereby with a causal explanation of its course and
consequences'.[20] By *social action*, Weber meant the (subjective) meaning a
person attaches to his behaviour. Weber considered that social activity
consists of the actions of individual persons who pursue purposes and
have reasons for acting in one way rather than another.[21] If we wish
to understand society, it is to the actions of individuals that we must
look. And then we have the *second* methodological principle where the
importance of this method for law-and-society is plain: since law aims at
influencing actions, how citizens and officials regard legal rules, the
meanings they attribute to them, and how they then deal with them are
vital pieces of the legal landscape. With a major qualification: the point is
not the actions of single individuals or their psychology, but the patterns
that can be detected in the actions of individuals.[22]

The methods for studying law in society, so far, consist of two principles: first identifying and describing features of a legal order that can be
identified as relevant to the actions of citizens and officials, and secondly,
examining the meanings attributed to such features by citizens and officials, and the actions that follow. There is, however, another aspect of
behaviour towards law that points to the need for an additional method of
analysis. Both Hart and Weber have an image of persons, whether citizens
or officials, who face the world as individuals and make reasoned choices
as to their actions. The reality is different, for while individual persons
make choices in deciding and acting, each does so from the standpoint of
social spheres, which consist of conventions and understandings as to

[20] G. Roth and C. Wittick (eds.) *Economy and Society: An outline of interpretive Sociology*
(Berkeley, 1968), p. 4.
[21] It should be noted in passing that Weber's claims about reasons being causes is much
disputed; see further, A. Ryan, op. cit.
[22] For further discussion J. Coleman, *Foundations of Social Theory*, (Cambridge, Mass.,
1994).

how to act in different circumstances. As the account in chapter 6 shows, the various social spheres each of us occupies have a major role in guiding and constraining our actions. They greatly reduce the range of choices and the extent to which our decisions are genuinely based on wide-ranging considerations. Their relevance to law lies in the fact that the way citizens and individuals approach and deal with law is significantly influenced by them. The suggestion is not that decisions are determined in advance; it is the more subtle claim that each of us is socialized to some extent, and often to a substantial extent, into accepting as right, reasonable, and normal certain ways of thinking and acting. Once having internalized such conventions and understandings, we act according to them, making our decisions and judgments within their boundaries and being guided by their substantive content. The result is a *third* methodological principle: law-and-society must move beyond the image of the existential person to the socialized, which means focusing on the character of social spheres and their interaction with law.

These three methodological principles taken together constitute a powerful approach to law in society. It is an approach that concentrates on analyzing and describing legal orders and the way officials and citizens respond to them. Although it might be wise to stop here, there is cause for adding a *fourth* principle of a different character. Hart speaks for many when he insists on a distinction between how the world (here the legal world) is in reality and how we would like it to be ideally. Law is separated from morals on that basis. At the same time, not all who seek to understand law or law in society limit themselves in that way. A different and equally justifiable approach, one adopted by Dworkin,[23] Finnis[24], Rawls[25] and Habermas[26] shares with Hart the aim of understanding law, but adds the further aim of positioning law in a moral context, of wishing to understand how law relates to the wider principles and purposes of human associations. Although often clothed in the language of law's functions, of asking what is law for, the aim, however expressed, is to connect law to both its moral and its pragmatic foundations. In making the distinction between relatively developed legal systems in general and a narrower category designated as modern, I have unavoidably made a selection on grounds not fully articulated but necessarily at some level evaluative, reflecting a point of view, a preference for one set of law's

---

[23] R. M. Dworkin, *Laws Empire* (Cambridge, Mass., 1988).

[24] J. M. Finnis, *Natural Law and Natural Rights* (Oxford, 1980).

[25] J. Rawls, *A Theory of Justice* (Oxford, 1972).

[26] J. Habermas, *Between Facts and Norms*, (Cambridge, Mass., 1996).

qualities over other possible sets. The very process of isolating some features of law as worthy of special attention is itself to make a judgment about the place and purpose of law in contemporary societies. And if to that is added, what must become obvious even if not explicitly stated, that modern legal orders have intrinsic features that are desirable and are conducive to attaining social goods of plain merit, then the scope of the enquiry has broadened. A *fourth* methodological principle should, therefore, be added, its focus being on developing the notion of a modern legal order, extolling its advantages, examining the social conditions sustaining it, and understanding the risks inherent in it. On the basis of these four methodological principles, the present study of law in society proceeds.

2.5 LAW AS A CLOSED SYSTEM

Having outlined the four methodological principles for the study of law in society, we must now deal with the alternative approach proposed by Niklas Luhmann. His claim, simply put, is that the proper objects of law-and-society are, first, the law itself, which is a distinct social system within the larger society, and secondly, the social conditions which make law possible and sustain it. The first idea occupies most of his last major book, *Law as a Social System*, his claim being that law should be understood, not in relation to other aspects of society, but as a distinct social system itself.[27] His view is based on several ideas that need briefly to be explained. One is the need to separate law from its surrounding environment, meaning the society around it. How law interacts with its environment is, according to Luhmann, irrelevant to understanding it as a social system. Law is recognized and defined by its separation and its differences from other social formations, not its interaction with them. Another idea is that the real question for law-and-society is how law as a distinct and separate social sub-system is possible and what its elements are.[28] A final claim is that legal systems are closed or *autopoeitic* systems, which means having their own internal basis for deciding what is law, and for classifying actions as legal or illegal. These 'operations' as they are called, cannot communicate with or be directly influenced by factors external to law. Just as you cannot talk to a ringing telephone and tell it to stop, but must enter into its internal electronic network in order to do so, similarly external society cannot communicate directly with law, so that social matters have to be translated into legal forms before they can enter

---

[27] N. Luhmann, op. cit.   [28] *Ibid*, Chapter 1.

the legal system. Both the telephone and the law have their own systems of internal communications that are closed to external factors. Law's operations consist of a binary code that determines whether a matter is legal or illegal, and does so according to its own internal processes.

Luhmann's approach to law-and-society is complex and difficult but merits close consideration. My purpose here is to single out several issues that arise within his approach, and then show why I am not adopting it in full, although relying from time to time on aspects of it. The first matter to consider is what it would mean to take his approach and what the consequences would be. This has two aspects: one concerns the nature of law, the other the relationship between law and society. Concerning the nature of law, Luhmann contends that accounts such as Hart's have failed to provide a basis for identifying law, and have failed because the distinct-iveness – or *closure* – of law cannot be explained as a system of rules. The reason is that the ultimate rule, the rule of recognition, cannot itself be valid but depends on the attitudes of officials. This means that it is subjective to officials and inherently unstable, as opposed to being object-ively observable and verifiable.[29] Instead of focusing on rules, we are asked to think of law as operations and communications that are internal to the system and objectively observable, the object of which is to determine whether a matter is legal or illegal. The unique feature of a legal system is that it translates all kinds of social considerations into the language of law, which is then used to decide specific issues as legal or illegal. This feature of law is an observable social fact that is not dependent on the subjective attitudes of officials, unlike an analysis based on rules. The crucial point is that features and operations internal to law determine its closure and distinctiveness. So, the first consequence of this approach is the need to reformulate the character of a legal system. What then are the consequences for law-and-society? Since a legal system has been described as separate from other social aspects with no direct communica-tion between the two, it follows that a law-and-society analysis would concern itself solely with the internal workings of the legal system, and hence rely on only the first methodological principle. The social environment around law is said to be irrelevant to law-and-society, so that how society affects law, or what influence law has on society may be worthwhile questions but they are not questions for the sociology of law. The one issue that does reach outside the law itself and raises wider social questions is: what social conditions make a legal system possible

[29] N. Luhmann, *Law as a Social System*, p. 130.

and sustain it? This is quite different from asking how legal rules interact with society.

Having seen what it would mean to take this approach to law and society, we should now consider the second main issue: why it should not be adopted here? Or more precisely to what extent it should be adopted. There are good reasons for not regarding this as a compelling approach to the study of law in society. The main reason relates to the nature of law. There is common cause with Luhmann in the conviction that law itself should be taken seriously, meaning that it should be considered the primary focus of a study in law-and-society; there is also common cause in describing law as a distinct social formation. Where our paths diverge is in describing the nature of the formation; one follows social rules (or structures as Luhmann calls them) along the lines of Hart, the other looks to law's operations. The answer is not to choose between them, but to see how both aspects can be put to use in understanding law. The notion of law as operations distinct from social activities reveals an aspect that ought to be included in any description of it; but it does not follow that other aspects, more familiar aspects such as legal rules, should be excluded, nor should the actions of officials and citizens. The issue at stake goes to the very heart of what we mean by law, my suggestion being that according to common, academic, and professional understanding, as reflected in both action and language, law means not the stripped-down, bare-bones version, but one embracing its totality, one that includes rules and human action in relation to rules, as well as the logical operations. In terms of the methodological principles, Luhmann's approach employs only the first, the description of law as a social formation; his account has no place for the other three.

A third matter for consideration is this: what extra dimension does the autopoeitic character of law add, what new issues does it raise? The essential idea is that law is reduced to a set of operations rather than rules, operations based on a binary code that determines whether something is legal or illegal. Those operations, which typically consist in the action of a court deciding one way or the other, can be studied scientifically, the object being to know more about their properties. However, despite often being told how important it is to analyze these operations, quite what new issues they raise for further study remains obscure. One line of enquiry would be to consider how legal operations are conducted with respect to particular subjects, such as contract or financial regulation, giving rise to such issues as: how are these social issues transformed into legal issues, and what problems do they present for a legal system in doing so? These are plainly matters of interest and importance. The trouble is that a study of law's operations only, with the actions of judges, other officials, and citizens being excluded, is necessarily limited and incomplete, since their actions, the reasons they give, and the way cases are framed in legal terms, are normally and naturally considered to be a part of the enquiry into law in society. Since for Luhmann human actors are not regarded as part of law's operations, that enquiry is out of bounds. How operations are then studied separately from actions remains unclear.

This leads on to a fourth consideration, which is to ask just how important it is to view law as observable operations rather than rules. The answer is that this aspect of law is important, even vital, but does not warrant the dominant, practically exclusive place it is given in understanding law. Its main attraction lies in providing a basis for the autonomy of law. The concept of law-as-operations is what is left after all external social and human factors have been removed, so that what is left is a set of operations producing outcomes that are *legal-illegal*. In a sense this is the very core of law, and ultimately could be its most basic element and its distinguishing feature, since no other social system is coded to decide *legal-illegal*. At the same time, having been removed from all human and social contact, it tells us very little about law as the untidy, unwieldy, and socially-corrupted phenomenon we know it to be. Imagine a person who is taken from his social environment, his clothes and all familiar objects removed, his name and identity erased, and his memory obliterated, so that all is left is a biological form, albeit one that works well in the sense that it is a fine specimen of a biological form. We could conclude that this is really what a human being is, and in some sense we would be right, because it is different from any other biological form. It would be a peculiar conclusion and would be reached at a high price of distortion, considering that we normally see human beings enmeshed in dense social environments; we also might wonder at its point. The biological form is, of course, an essential core without which there could be no person, and its importance should be taken into account; but it is just that: a core around which the usual accompaniments form a dense web, which, taken in the totality of its parts, is what we mean by a human being.

A final reason for not embracing the autopoeitic view of law in its full rigour is the idea that law as a social system is separate from its social environment. Critics of Luhmann often try to disprove the autonomy thesis by showing ways in which the boundary between law and its social environment breaks down. That misses the point, which is that law is autonomous by definition. The point of describing it as an autopoeitic system is to indicate its autonomy from all that is not internal to it, from all external factors. Law's autonomy does not mean it has no relations with other, non-legal social factors. As a way of showing the nature of the relations, Luhmann introduces the notion of *structural coupling*, which means at its most elementary that law is influenced by social factors, but only after they are transformed into a form or code that it can absorb within its own system. High language for expressing the simple point that this is what happens whenever a new piece of legislation is enacted: any social issue, which is bound to have economic, moral, and political aspects, in order to become a legal issue has to be expressed in legal language, using familiar legal concepts and terms, and assuming a legal tradition with its web of doctrines and processes. The dimensional divide between law and its environment is the basis for law's autonomy. But it is an artificial and weak base, because in practice there is no real or significant difficulty in converting economic, moral, and political issues into legal language and doctrine. Luhmann and his followers make the mistake of thinking that the conversion must be difficult to make and so, in order to protect law's separateness, should not be included in the social analysis of law. That premise is very dubious; legal orders are adept and well-experienced at making the conversion, normally without difficulty.

Besides the relationship between law and its environment expressed in structural coupling, other aspects of law's relations with the social environment are relevant to law in society. Law is commonly used in modern societies to influence and change the wider social environment. Resources are directed to that end, extensive human and social capital is expended to make law work, and many of the social goals to which law is put, such as the protection of persons and the environment, the regulation of activities that otherwise would impoverish communities and societies, are considered an essential part of modern legal orders. It is reasonable that we should ask what *special attributes* it has in doing so, and what added value it brings to other social mechanisms. And if its success is limited, it is worth knowing why, the point being not only to understand how law might be more effective, but also to learn its limits and shortcomings as a tool of social change and social ordering. For these reasons it is hard to resist the conclusion that both law and its environment matter, and are the proper objects of a study of law in society; they amount to good reasons for sustaining an approach that seeks to understand law as a social formation *and* its interaction with others.

To conclude that law-as-autopoeisis should not be the foundation stone of studies of law in society is not to deny either its importance or its influence, as will be seen at various points in this book. The tendency of law towards autopoeisis, and the need for a certain level of autopoeisis, if law is to be a distinctive social formation, the creation of its own language and concepts, are all factors of considerable value in grasping the elusive character of law as a social phenomenon. Luhmann explicitly acknowledges several times that the two fundamental questions for law-and-society are the nature of law and the social conditions that sustain it; he has much to say about the first but, curiously, little about the second. The second is considered in chapters 13 and 14, although this is no more than a tentative beginning. The idea that law is in some sense more fundamental than rules is used in chapter 4 in developing an idea of law prior to rules, while Luhmann's account of functions within systems helps in analyzing claims made by others concerning law's functions, although itself proving ultimately to be inadequate. The shadow of auto-poeisis falls heavily over the concept of social spheres and assists in understanding their relatively closed character. Whether Luhmann would have approved of such rampant plundering of bits and pieces of his account is unlikely; the short point is that, even though his rigorous approach is not adopted, the study of law in society can not escape its influence.

NOTES

Approaches to law-and-society

Empirical research within the socio-legal tradition rarely makes reference to or use of legal theory, whose objective is to elucidate the concept of law and provide an understanding of legal systems. This is understandable since the main aim of socio-legal research is the encounter between law and other aspects of society rather than the law itself.

There are, of course, outstanding exceptions, prominent among which are W. Twining and B. Tamanaha. The former's extensive writings over many years bring together legal theory and law-and-society. A recent example is: W. Twining, *Globalization and Legal Theory* (Butterworths, London, 2000). The latter has shown in two recent books how each approach is of use to the other: B. Tamanaha, *Realistic Socio-Legal Theory: Pragmatism and a Social Theory of Law* (Oxford, 1997) and *A General Jurisprudence of Law and Society* (Oxford, 2001).

Other references are often found to the need for research in law-and-society to go beyond the interaction of law and society to include examination of law itself. It is stated that socio-legal research: 'has a significant role in the development of legal theory. . . . It needs to draw on broader legal theory to explain what might constitute the "legal" '.: J. Eekelaar and M. Maclean, *A Reader on Family Law* (Oxford, 1994), pp. 1–2. However, in the collection of readings to which this is an introduction, legal theory is barely mentioned.

Law as social facts

For an explanation of *social facts* see E. Durkheim, *Rules of Sociological Method*.

For critiques of Durkheim's notion of social facts see: R. J. Holton, 'Classical Social Theory' in B. S. Turner (ed) *The Blackwell Companion to Social Theory* (Oxford, 1996);
P. Baert, Op. cit;
R. Cotterrell, *EmileDurkheim: Law in a Moral Domain* (Stanford, 1999).

Law as subjective construction and interpretation

Although Weber spelt out his approach in terms of the subjective meanings of individuals, at times he comes close to recognizing, both explicitly and implicitly, that there could be social formations that were outside and prior to those actions, and which influenced them. Two examples demonstrate the point, both interestingly drawn from the social explanation of legal phenomena.

First, collective entities, such as states, associations, businesses, foundations, and so on, must properly be considered: 'as *solely* the results and modes of organization of the particular acts of individual persons, since they alone can be treated as agents in a course of subjectively understandable action'. (page 13) And yet: '. . . the sociologist cannot . . . afford to ignore these collective concepts . . . . These concepts of collective entities which are found both in common sense and in juristic and in other technical forms of thought, *have a meaning in the minds of individual persons, partly as of something actually existing, partly as something with normative authority. This is true not only of judges and officials, but also of ordinary private individuals as well. Actors thus in part orient their action to them, and in this role such ideas have a powerful, often a decisive, causal influence on the course of action of real individuals'.* (pages 13 and 14, emphasis added). Weber was never one to ignore or down-play the full subtleties of social reality for reasons of theoretical purity, as this example shows, although he goes on finally to defend the social-action-as-subjective-meanings thesis.

The *second* example comes from Weber's account of legitimate order. He begins by stating that social action may be guided by belief in the existence of a legitimate order. We might at once object that the very way of expressing the case suggests there is a *legitimate order to believe in* – but let that pass. Weber cites the case of the civil servant who gets to work on time each morning because 'his action is . . . determined by the validity of an order (viz. the civil service rules)' which he obeys both because disobedience would be disadvantageous to him and because of his sense of duty (page 31). Weber continues: that '. . . the order held by at least part of the actors to define a model or to be binding, naturally increases the probability that action will in fact conform to it, often to a very considerable degree'. (page 31). To concede this much is surely very close to conceding that the order has a social existence, which the individual recognizes and which exerts influence on him. There is still an element of individual judgement in each case whether to obey the order, but that is quite different from the claim that society is nothing other than individual actions.

In *Law as a Social System*, Luhmann writes critically of the Weberian approach to social explanation, suggesting that: 'Sociology of law is usually restricted to a vague notion of social action or behaviour, and makes up for the contents that are specifically legal by assumptions about the ideas and intentions of the actor and the "intended meaning" ' (page 83).

He goes on to say: '. . . someone who is consciously oriented to law must already know what he has in mind. The individual must be able to refer to a social system, law, which is already constituted . . . . Therefore, it is impossible to take psychological systems, consciousness, or even the whole human individual as a part or as an internal component of the legal system' (part 84).

Law as a closed system

Luhmann's views on law in society evolved over many years, culminating in his last major work: *Law as a Social System*. The complex and elusive character of his writings make it difficult to be sure of the correct interpretation; of particular help in this regard have been the papers from a symposium held at Cardozo Law School entitled *Closed Systems and Open Justice: The Legal Sociology of Niklas Luhmann* (1992), reported in 13 *Cardozo Law Review*.

What are the issues for further study that arise from law as autopoeisis?

The question in the text asks: what issues are raised by adopting an autopoeitic approach to law, the suggestion being that the answer is not clear. Luhmann touches on this at many points, for example: 'The question is . . . what kind of operations enable a system to form a self-reproducing network which relies exclusively on self-generated information and is capable of distinguishing internal needs from what it sees as environmental needs' ('Operational Closure and Structural Coupling: The Differentiation of the Legal System' (1992) 13 *Cardozo Law Review* 1419, p. 1420).

On why a rule-based approach to law is inadequate

According to Luhmann, rule-based approaches (such as Hart's) to understanding law and the autonomy of law, are unsatisfactory: 'Acceptable legal reasoning has to restrict itself to legal norms, . . . professionally sound practice, and so on. This is how closure is recognized – or "observed" – in the system (every legal theorist will immediately recognize H. L. A. Hart's secondary rules of recognition). However, this does not quite satisfactorily explain how closure is produced in the first place'. 13 *Cardozo Law Review*, p. 1427.

With respect to Hart, Luhmann also writes with reference to the rule of recognition and that it is neither valid or invalid but is simply accepted as appropriate: 'This has all the advantages and disadvantages of a solution which – leaves open the definition of the unity of a system made up by obligations and habits, by valid rules and invalid rules –. It is this point precisely that is the target of the concept of autopoeisis.' *Law as a Social System*, p. 130.

Additional discussions of autopoeisis of special interest include:
J. Priban and D. Nelken (eds), *Law's New Boundaries: The Consequences of Legal Autopoeisis* (Aldershot, 2001); G. Teubner, *Law As An Autopoeitic System* (Oxford, 1993).

3

Law as Social Rules

3.1 INTRODUCTION

The object of this and succeeding chapters is to consider from the point of view of law in society Hart's description of a municipal legal system as composed of social rules. If we are to understand social rules as standards of behaviour we have to understand the social context in which they occur. We also need to unravel the idea of a rule in order to identify several quite different kinds and their consequences. This is not to discard rules, but to make sense of them, which means understanding how they work as standards of behaviour, while at the same time interacting with their social context. In chapter 4, the focus shifts directly to the social context of rules, the object being to retrace the steps of legal evolution from an advanced legal order based on rules, to a notional 'pre-legal order', in which law is not based on positive rules in the modern sense. By moving backwards from rules, to rulings, to acts, law in its most elemental sense is identified as the expression of the primary relations among the members of society. Signs of this elemental sense of law are seen in close-knit traditional societies, as anthropological studies show, where social relations are based on shared understandings and conventions rather then positive rules. Rules, of course, have a place but it is only in more complex and diverse societies that they become the main expressions of social relations and, therefore, of law. The early common law also illustrates these ideas. From these two chapters it is concluded that, although modern law is characteristically composed of rules, the social context, and the social relations expressed within it, are essential to its understanding.

3.2 HART'S APPROACH TO LAW AS SOCIAL RULES

A theory of law that is both analytical and sociological meant several things for Hart. One was to avoid a natural law approach that confused the social reality of law with what we would like it to be. Another was the concern to descend from the abstraction of theories such as Kelsen's, where the connections with reality are uncertain, to a manageable social level. The conviction that municipal legal systems are intrinsically social creations, and should be studied from that point of view, was a third factor. Given these factors, Hart identifies and describes the constant and general features of working legal systems. This means not only the external features and patterns of rules, institutions, and behaviour, but the meaning and significance they have for the participants. By contrast with theorists such as Austin, who begins by stipulating a definition of law and then sets about showing how legal experience fits into and reinforces it, Hart's inquirer comes with a mind open and responsive, building-up a picture of law from the use of language and the experience of practice.

The passage to reality lies in language, in the expressions and distinctions we make in everyday affairs; talk of obligation leads to rules, and rules to the actions and reasons of lawyers, judges, and other officials and, to a lesser extent, laymen as the basis for both the analytical and social understanding of law. Social rules and legal rules, one a sub-set of the other, become the centrepiece of a legal order. In exploiting the notion of rules, Hart distinguishes between an *external* approach which 'limits itself to the observable regularities of behaviour' and an *internal* approach which reproduces 'the way in which rules function as rules in the lives of those who use them'.[1] Austin is associated with the external approach because his account is based on observing those regularities of conduct 'predictions, probabilities, and signs', and has little to say about rules or, more precisely, how they feature in the actions of officials and citizens.[2] Hart explains the internal aspect of rules in one of the most significant passages in the book. Noting that the external observer sees a red traffic light as a sign that people will stop, he writes: '[the observer] will miss out a whole dimension of the social life of those whom he is watching . . . they look upon it as a *signal for* them to stop, and so a reason for stopping in conformity to rules which make stopping when the light is red a standard of behaviour and an obligation. To mention this is to bring into account the way in which the group regards its own behaviour. It is to

---

[1] Op. cit. p. 88.

[2] The common perception that Austin talks only of commands and not of rules, the latter having been introduced by Hart, is wrong; Austin defines law as: 'a rule laid down for the guidance of an intelligent being by an intelligent being having power over him' (*Province of Jurisprudence Determined*, p. 10).

refer to the internal aspect of rules seen from their internal point of view'.[3] Without this perspective on rules, 'a whole dimension of social life' would be missed.

Although not mentioning Weber, Hart might well be following his approach in subscribing to the notion that social action consists in the meanings that people attribute to their actions.[4] When applied to law, this means focusing on the way people use rules, and if we ask why rules should be the focus, the answer is that the astute observer will notice that the language of judges, officials, and others is couched in rules, distinctions, and references that can be explained by reference to rules. Rule-governed behaviour of a certain kind is the central expression of law and, therefore, the subject of legal theory. This does not mean that the way people use and experience rules is *all* there is to law; the critique of Austin is directed at his over-emphasis on certain features – sovereigns, sanctions, and habits of obedience – while neglecting others. It is not that those features lack significance, but that an account concerned only or excessively with them misses the reality of rule-governed behaviour.

The second comment concerns Hart's distinction between the *external* and the *internal*. This is not an easy distinction to unravel, but one aspect is clear: Hart's purpose is to call attention to a type of legal experience – rule-governed behaviour – that Austin left out. His purpose is the social-scientific one of producing a more accurate and complete description of law; it is not to propose that the so-called external occupies a different dimension of knowledge from the so-called internal. The distinction is both misleading and unnecessary. It is misleading because the terminology adopted is well-known in social enquiry where it has a meaning different from Hart's. In social enquiry, *external* means scientific enquiry, the object of which is to describe some social phenomenon by observing it, while *internal* refers to a body of knowledge within a defined system, such as mathematics, computers, or study of the Bible. Each represents a relatively closed environment within which an activity is conducted, the object being to acquire knowledge and understanding within the parameters of the activity. The doctrinal study of law is another example, as the thousands of students from across Europe would have realized when they gathered in Bologna in the twelfth century to study Roman law.[5] Hart's concerns are plainly with the external, scientific study of law, not the internal study of legal doctrine, and in that sense he is an external observer. As external observer,

---

[3] *Ibid.*   [4] Weber's approach is described in *1.3*.   [5] See H. Berman, op. cit.

he is, of course, interested in understanding how those internal to the system, officials and others, understand and deal with rules of law, for that is essential data in the description of a legal system. As for the distinction being unnecessary, there is no reason why a so-called external observer could not come to understand rule-governed behaviour. Anyone adept as a social researcher, whose subject is the social understanding of law, should fairly soon realize that there is more to social life than predictable patterns of behaviour, and that when drivers stop at red lights they may have reasons for doing so besides the fear of a collision or a fine. In order to come to that realization, the device of an internal-external distinction is unnecessary.

3.3 NATURE OF SOCIAL RULES

The prevailing theories at the time Hart wrote were based on law being a set of commands issued by a sovereign and backed by sanctions. One consequence of this approach was that law was tied to the sovereign as a person, an approach that created difficulties in explaining issues, such as what happens when the sovereign changes. By expressing law as rules and severing the link to the person of the sovereign, Hart claims to explain features of law that were otherwise puzzling, features such as continuity over time and capacity for change. Another benefit of introducing rules is to enable a more accurate description to be made of the way people, especially officials, relate to law. Law as commands backed by sanctions suggests that people act in order to avoid unpleasant consequences; the external observer, having noticed patterns of behaviour in the way people react to law, supposedly draws that conclusion. That this would be a misunderstanding becomes clear by substituting rules for commands and an internal approach for the external.

Considering the importance of rules and their internal aspect, we must take time to understand them. For a group to have a rule is to have a standard that its members regard as binding and with which their actions should comply. The *first* element, then, is that rules are standards directing action in one way rather than another: to be punctual for lectures and to drive at thirty miles an hour; to abide by the terms of a contract and to have two witnesses to a will. The point of a rule is that it provides a general standard which is applied in particular cases without having to reassess the merits in each case; predictability and stability result. Rules have to be expressed in language and so an element of interpretation is always necessary; the more scope there is for interpretation, the more scope there is for outside factors entering in, and for the sharpness of the rule and its distinctiveness being blunted.

The *second* element of a rule is that it should be binding, in the sense that those subject to a rule have an obligation to follow it, where failure to do so is to act wrongly. The obligation is expressed, as Hart notes, in words such as 'ought' and 'should' and 'must'. A *third* and closely related element is that to accept a rule as binding is to display a certain attitude towards it, an internal point of view. Following the example of the driver who stops at the red light because there is a rule that he should, Hart explains the idea of the internal aspect of a rule in this way: 'there should be a critical reflective attitude to certain patterns of behaviour as a common standard, and this should display itself in criticism . . . demands for conformity, and in acknowledgement that such criticisms and demands are justified . . .'.[6] He adds that someone who lacked the internal point of view could comply with a rule not because it is considered to be binding, but in order to avoid the sanction of non-compliance.

A *fourth* element is that a rule not only guides actions but is a standard against which actions are judged; it is the basis for explaining and justifying one's own acts, or for judging and criticizing those of others. This idea is expressed by saying that a rule provides reasons for actions, reasons that are sufficient for the purpose in hand. A rule is not necessarily conclusive, since there may be other reasons for overriding it in certain cases; in the absence of such factors it provides a sufficient reason for acting. The *next* element concerns the origin of rules. They derive from a wide range of sources, including a club, a church, or the law; indeed rules of all sorts are all around us and guide a vast range of activities. The claim is that, whatever their context, they share the same properties. *Finally,* the reasons for accepting any set of rules which, varying as they do from one context to another, are analytically distinct from the fact of acceptance and its consequences. People have diverse reasons for accepting a rule, but once accepted, each has an obligation to act according to it. Whether any rule is accepted is a matter of social fact to be ascertained by considering how people act, by observing how they view their actions, and the reasons they give to explain and justify them.

The distinction between primary and secondary rules brings to light another aspect of rules, the idea being that rules confer powers to do things as well as impose duties. The power conferred can be something as simple as entering into a contract or as complex as a statutory scheme

---

[6] H. L. A. Hart, op. cit., p. 56.

empowering officials to regulate the airline industry. The distinction
between duty-imposing rules (primary rules) and power-conferring rules
(secondary rules) adds to Hart's account in two main ways: the order-
backed-by-threats approach of his predecessors had difficulty fitting
secondary rules in at all, and secondary rules have a different social function from primary rules.[7] Their social function, according to Hart, has
several aspects. At a general level, secondary rules are essential elements
of a legal system; they make possible such matters as the enactment of
laws, their application, and their adjudication. At more particular levels,
secondary rules are used by citizens who use the rules to create in Hart's
word: 'structures of rights and duties within the coercive framework of
the law'.[8] A will made according to the law allows you to go to the grave
confident your wishes will be respected, a matter made possible by setting
in train other rules, which create rights and duties in others concerning
the distribution of your assets, with expectations that they will be upheld,
if necessary, by the coercive authority of the state. Secondary rules are
also vital to the conduct of government and administration. Constitutions, as the most fundamental secondary rules in a society, confer powers
on legislatures and other officials to make laws. Those laws may then
create further new rights and duties, as well as delegate powers to
administrative bodies and officials to make further new rules and to
decide on the application of rules, creating in the process additional
rights and duties. Secondary rules conferring powers to do things are
normally joined to primary rules imposing duties on others to comply
with or implement those powers. Without primary rules to support them,
secondary rules would often be of no use. Constitutions for instance,
on closer inspection, are combinations of primary and secondary rules.
The two kinds of rules inter-relate in various ways to form a legal
system to such an extent that Hart considered the union to be the key to
understanding law and legal systems.[9]

   In his analysis of social rules, in showing how they feature in actions
and decisions, and how legal rules are types of social rules, Hart has
brought to light a dimension of plain importance in understanding law in
society. With the addition of the rule of recognition, whose task it is to
unite rules forming a system, the account of law as rules will be complete.
Before moving to that stage, the analysis of rules and the claims made
for them need to be examined from a law-and-society point of view.

----

[7] There has been a lot of debate about the precise character of the two kinds of rules.
[8] Op. cit. p. 27.   [9] Op. cit. p. 113.

The purpose of doing so is worth repeating: Hart's analysis of social rules is the first step, and a fundamental one, in describing the features of a legal system; the next step is to consider those features more closely and then examine their interaction with the social environment.

3.4 CONTEXTUAL CONTINGENCIES OF SOCIAL RULES

Over any claim that social life, including its legal aspects, is structured by rules falls the familiar shadow of scepticism. It takes various forms, the strongest being to question the very idea of rules as social realities, on the basis that the patterns of behaviour all around us are not rule-governed. To reply that we can point to a whole variety of rules, legal rules, rules of clubs, and rules for using the library, is unlikely to change the sceptic's position. They are 'rules' in the sense of prescriptions set out in rule-books, but they have little or no bearing on social life, since actions will always be guided by considerations outside the rules. More moderate versions allow that rules, laid down in an authoritative manner, are amongst the matters to take into account in social actions, but are themselves neither guides to actions nor an accurate basis for understanding them. Being claims about the way rules work in practice, these contentions, at whatever level of scepticism they are pitched, are open to empirical investigation. Hart's frequent reference to rules as the basis for explaining, criticizing, and justifying actions, suggests he believed that such investigations would prove the social relevance of rules, as his own personal experience plainly did.[10]

The sceptical outlook, although unconvincing in its stronger forms, does contain the germ of an idea direct to our concerns. Its claim is that rules are social formations guiding social action, but are not normally complete or adequate guides, since how they work in practice is contingent on their social context. Take a simple example: suppose the university has a rule that a lecture should last for fifty minutes. As a professor of the university, I am bound by the rule and my usual practice is to go for fifty minutes, no more or less. At the same time, I reserve the discretion to start a little later, perhaps to allow late-comers to be seated, or to finish slightly earlier because I covered the material more quickly than expected, or because the audience is distracted, or being my last for the term as a small reward for those who have persevered to the end. In none

---

[10] Neither here nor elsewhere does Hart make reference to empirical research.

Law in Modern Society

of these cases would I feel I had acted wrongly even though a strict reading of the rule would suggest otherwise. I would consider that my actions were justifiable and, if pressed to say why, I would point to such matters as the purposes behind the rule, or that the rule was commonly understand in this way, or that there were other values and interests to be served that require a flexible approach to the rule.

Some aspects of lecturing would clearly be out of step with what is acceptable, and yet they are not covered by the rule. No rule that I know of requires that my lectures be given in English, although that is taken for granted; it used to be thought that one should dress suitably when lecturing, even wear a gown, although understandings have now changed to the point that pretty well anything short of indecency is acceptable. The willingness to explore a subject wherever it leads, and to discuss any matter freely and openly, are implicit in university lecturing, although it would be wrong to use the occasion to advocate a blatantly political line, to incite behaviour contrary to the interests of the university, or to denigrate colleagues. We could go on, and the more we were to, the clearer it would become that the rule is part of and a sign to a social setting comprised of understandings and conventions, interests and values, whose origins and force derive from experience and practice. Each rule has its own little social world of which it is only part, and only by entering that world can we assess a rule's significance and obtain a full understanding of what is required or permitted, condoned or condemned. To settle on the rule, to take it as definitive as to what should or should not be done, without taking account of the factors within the social setting, would lead to an incomplete and inaccurate understanding of the social reality of rules.

Now there are many kinds of rules and the claim may not hold for them all; the rules of some games, such as tennis, appear fairly self-contained, others, such as Scrabble, are eminently flexible and open to argument, as an observer of the game, especially when played by their family members, will soon realize. Once we move away from activities such as tennis, chess, or bridge, to others more inherently contextual – family life, social clubs and associations, the workplace, and the like – rules, even clear and precise ones, become more contextual, more contingent upon surrounding considerations. Legal rules illustrate the point: the common perception that they can always be got around, applied technically, or made to mean the opposite of what they appear to mean, is something of a caricature, but it draws attention to the fact that the surface appearance of rules is often not an accurate sign of what they mean or how they apply. It also touches on the stark reality that different groups interpret the same rules in different ways according to their different points of view and to suit their purposes. Even if we allow that some types of rules are reasonably self-contained, it is hard to dispute the dependence of rules on their social context. And so again we are led to conclude that an account of social action in terms of rules, which fails to account for their contextual character and the contingencies that affect them, is incomplete and may be misleading.

3.5 THREE TYPES OF RULES

The relationship between rules and their contextual contingencies becomes even clearer when different types of rules are identified. The rule about lecturing is one type, let us call it a *clear-line rule*, in the sense that it is clear and specific as to what has to be done: a lecture shall last for fifty minutes, no vehicles in the park, all men to wear a hat. If rules like these are subject to contextual contingencies, then how much more so for other, common types of legal rules. One such type is the rule that requires application of a general standard; let us call them *standard-based rules*, for their significance lies in the action prescribed by the rule being dependent on a general standard that is inherently abstract and open. Constitutions, international covenants, the European Convention on Human Rights, and the Treaties of the European Union supply countless examples, such as due process or free speech, privacy, proportionality, or economic liberty. Reference to the European Union presents another range of rules: notions such as democracy, the rule of law, and respect for human rights, are given legal status in the Treaties and regarded by the Court of Justice as justiciable standards to be interpreted and applied.

The use of rules dependent on standards like these is an invitation to examine their social context, to consider the understandings and conventions of time and place without which they are bare of meaning. Standard-based rules, while perhaps most at home in constitutions and international conventions, are not uncommon in enacted law, meaning statutes, regulations, and the like. The use of standards such as reasonableness, fairness, or good faith, is positively to entrust to officials an element of judgement, merging into discretion, as to what the standard and hence the rule requires. From soft standards that are nevertheless legally binding, it is a short move to 'soft law', in the form of guidelines, opinions, informal codes, and so on, which is a common feature of

modern legal orders, especially that of the European Union.[11] Soft laws
do not have the normative quality of binding rules, but still have some
significance in decision-making, with the differences between them and
clear-line rules often hard to sustain. The common law system, whereby
courts develop legal rules by the accumulation of precedents, was considered by Weber to be a system of substantive rationality rather than one
of formal rules, because its focus was on the practice of courts deciding
cases according to substantive ends and values. Weber may have misunderstood the common law, as some allege, but its ability to be responsive to the social context of cases, to be guided by standards, such as
unreasonableness in administrative law or negligence in tort, in order to
ensure that the law unfolds in step with it, is regarded as its strength. It is
not that standard-based rules are rare or exceptional, since a search of the
constitutions, conventions, statutes, and the common law would probably
show that they are just as common, if not more so, than rules of the kind
'no vehicles in the park' or 'a will shall have two witnesses'.

A third category of rules includes those positively conferring discretion, such as, an official may grant a licence if he considers it reasonable to
do so, a foreigner may be deported if his presence is considered by the
minister to be undesirable, or an employee may be dismissed at a week's
notice. These *discretion-based* rules do not at first look like rules at all;
surely a rule should specify with some particularity what has to be done.
However, they fit within Hart's notion of rules by formulating them
slightly differently: 'it is a rule that a non-citizen may be deported at
the discretion of the minister'. Instead of the power in the minister
(a secondary rule in Hart's sense) being followed by a statement of the
conditions on which he may act (the primary rule aspect), as in the
case of a clear-line rule, here the conditions are left open to be decided at
the minister's discretion. A discretion-based rule not only invites but
positively requires reference to the surrounding social context.

The dependency of rules of all three kinds on their social context has
so far been expressed as a matter of interpretation, but it is more fundamental than that; what at first appears to be a clear rule may come to be
surrounded by additions and qualifications, some of which justify even its
suspension or *non-application* in the particular case. The rule that a lecture
should last fifty minutes may, over time, be regarded as subject to factors
of the kind mentioned above – the state of the audience, the nature of the

---

[11] For an account of soft law in the EU, see L. Senden, *Soft Law in European Community
Law* (Oxford, 2004).

material, the point at which it makes sense to stop, and so on – so that the rule becomes the starting point of deliberation rather than a full expression of it. Here the key point emerges: many rules, especially social or legal rules, are a sign that a certain kind of *deliberative process* has to be gone through, a process of which the rule is a vital but not conclusive part. It requires deliberation as to whether the rule meets the situation, and if it does, what does it mean; it may require consideration of related rules, the weighing of presumptions, and the consideration of factors to take into account. The process requires deliberation as to whether the rule should or should not be applied, whether exceptions should be made to it: should I stop at the red light when no other cars are about, should the dog in Central Park be on a lead, may I finish the lecture after thirty minutes because I have run out of material, shall we allow that dubious word for this game of Scrabble, can an exception be made for this car in the park even though it is clearly a prohibited vehicle. When rules are understood in this way, we can see why, in the case of my lecture, the various modifications, although not precisely in step with the rule, are nevertheless legitimate: the rule neither dictates fully what action should be taken, nor exhausts the range of actions that may properly be taken. The contextual contingencies within which the rule is located answer both, and the action taken is the result of deliberation on the circumstances, the rule, and the contingencies.

Some will see similarities here with the claim made by Ronald Dworkin, who argues in criticism of law as social rules that account must be taken of principles.[12] Principles are more general and abstract considerations than rules, providing a normative environment in which decisions are made; rules, on the contrary, tend to be clearer and more distinctive. The point of Dworkin's argument was to show that, contrary to Hart, law, like social life, is constituted by principles as well as rules.[13] Legal principles, such as act fairly, do not benefit from your own wrong-doing, or treat people equally, are often implicit rather than positively created. Dworkin's purpose in drawing attention to principles was to contest the idea of a rule of recognition by which law could be identified; Hart ultimately accepted that law includes principles as well as rules, but contended that principles also were identified according to the rule of recognition.[14]

---

[12] Ronald Dworkin, *Taking Rights Seriously* (London, 1978).

[13] Hart was sufficiently persuaded to concede that the model of rules had to be modified and it remains a matter of debate among jurists as to how damaging this is for his general theory of law.

[14] H. L. A. Hart, *Postscript to The Concept of Law* (Oxford, 1997, 2nd edn).

While we need not enter that debate, Dworkin's ideas concerning principles fit within my analysis for they plainly form part of the social context of rules.[15] But to stop with principles would be to miss other contextual features, not all of which are properly classed as principles. Principles capture part of the normative environment of rules but not all of it, there being no reason why the great diversity of normative elements – understandings, practices, presumptions, guidelines, factors, and so on – should be herded together as principles. The contextual contingencies, moreover, include cognitive as well as normative elements, cognitive in the sense of ways of thinking about, viewing, and understanding the context. As a seasoned lecturer, I have a sense of the point of lectures, of what is reasonable, and what my colleagues would consider acceptable, even if not all share the same view on all matters. The distinction between normative elements specifying how we should act, and matters of perception and understanding, is not so sharply defined or easily distinguishable when we enter the social context of rules, for how we perceive and understand an issue subtly merges into and is formative of how we should deal with it. In entering into the social practice of lecturing, whose purposes are clear and conventions established, I soon come to know what is expected of a good and reliable lecturer.

3.6 DEFENDING RULES

The most familiar defence of rules is that immortalized by Hart in the notions of *a settled core of meaning* of rules and their *open texture*.[16] Rules rely on language, and although the words used in language normally have a settled core of meaning, there is also an element of open texture requiring interpretation. Hart's defence of the generally settled character of legal rules was originally meant to correct the scepticism of the American Realists, whom he thought overlooked the settled core of meaning and mistook the element of open texture as a sign that 'anything goes'. We need not enquire into American Realism beyond noting Hart's defence, the thrust of which is instructive. After acknowledging that the uncertainties inherent in the general standards of enacted law are similar to those of a system developed from precedents, he goes on to discuss the open texture left to anyone who has to interpret and apply rules. However

---

[15] Nor need we enter the debate over whether there is a distinction between legal and moral principles.

[16] Op. cit., chapter 9.

we phrase it, open texture in applying general rules to particular cases, invites choice and discretion.[17] Neither the formalist's heaven of rules nor the sceptic's rule-less nightmare describe the reality, for every legal system: 'compromises between two social goods: the need for certain rules . . . and the need to leave open for later settlement issues that arise in particular cases.[18] Compromise is necessary because sometimes it is recognized from the start that the activities to be legally controlled are highly variable, as in the case of an industry being required to maintain a safe system of work; it is also necessary where it is impossible to say in advance precisely what activity should be subject to control, of which the standard of due care in negligence is an example. Nevertheless, according to Hart, these are not the central cases of law; for most areas of activity, general rules are formulated in advance or developed through precedent; if they start without a core of settled meaning they soon acquire one. The 'salient fact of social life' is that: 'the life of the law consists to a very large extent in the guidance both of officials and private individuals by determinate rules which, unlike the application of variable standards, do not require a fresh judgment from case to case.'[19]

The object of Hart's defence is to maintain an account of law as rules while recognizing the threat posed by even mild forms of rule-scepticism. If the salient fact of social life is true, then the open texture, and the choice and discretion it brings, lie at the fringe of social life not the core. But notice the subtle stretching of language, the unavoidable feeling that, in defending the salient fact of social life, a cover of orderliness has been drawn over situations where disorder is the natural state. Where the line of compromise falls between settled meaning and open texture is an empirical question that cannot be stated in the abstract and is likely to vary from one situation to another, one society to another. But the problem is more fundamental than one of open texture: it is the more basic one of how to account for social reality, for social reality suggests that there is more to rule-governed contexts than rules. If the extra aspects are regarded as peripheral rather than central, the concept of a rule can be stretched to include it. Alternatively, we could employ Hart's own method of following social reality where it leads and using language as our guide. Sense, then, has to be made of statements that begin: 'this is the rule, but other conventions and understandings must be considered', or 'even though there is no rule, it is clear what must be done, what is expected', for these are clues to the existence of concepts and ideas

[17] *Ibid*, p. 127.   [18] *Ibid*, p. 130.   [19] *Ibid*, p. 134.

that matter to those using them and guide their decisions. No better illustration is needed than the common law,[20] which fits the notion of clear and settled rules only by the largest stretch of the imagination, especially before the relatively late introduction of the doctrine of binding precedent, and even after it. But why stretch the imagination rather than take the common law on its own terms as traditionally a loose collection of ideas, conventions, understandings, and traditions, where the point is less to create clear and settled rules, although some have naturally emerged, than to decide according to the conventions and understandings of society and the legal profession. If the same mistake, of which Austin is said to be guilty, of simplicity at the price of distortion, is to be avoided, then relations between rules and their social context should be examined. That means going beyond the notion of law as rules and bringing to light the conventions and understandings that surround rules.

The key to doing so is a small but significant change to the normal case as Hart presents it. His view of the normal case is one of clear and settled rules, capable of being applied by fitting the rule to the facts of the case, on the basis that the meaning is normally clear and capable of application without reference to anything outside itself, without reference that is to its social context. The amendment I propose is that the social context of a rule, even the clearest rule, is always relevant to its application; it is relevant because the process of deliberation has always to be gone through, not only where meaning is uncertain, but in order to determine whether there are contextual contingencies adding to or qualifying the rule, even to the point of not applying it. The most clear and certain rule may turn out to be unsuitable in the circumstances because it runs counter to the conventions and understandings around it; or its very clarity and certainty may make it unsuitable for the complexity or the needs of the situation. In more unusual cases, informal rules replace formal, as in the case of the Californian ranchers who devised their own.[21] It may be, as Hart contends, that in a well-functioning legal system, most rules are clear enough to be applied by citizens and officials and are, in fact, applied to deal with particular situations; but that, I suggest, is because they have gone through the deliberative process and come to that conclusion. The settled meaning is applied not because it is a settled meaning, but because the decision has been taken that it is the right way to deal

---

[20] Discussed more fully in 4.3.
[21] See R. Ellickson, *Order Without Law* (Cambridge, Mass., 1991).

with the particular case. The basis for judging it to be right is that it is in accordance with the contingencies of the social context.

This conclusion is not that of the realists, who sensed the problem but drew the wrong conclusion; for it is not scepticism of rules that is warranted but understanding how they work. That a modern legal system includes sets of rules is hardly questionable; the contention is that, in order to understand how they guide actions, we have to see them as part of a context composed of norms and understandings, practices and traditions, principles and values; these in turn, as we shall see later, express sets of social relations, which are in turn the foundations of a legal order. This is neither another version of 'anything goes' nor a case of back-door scepticism; on the contrary, the social context of rules is a structured context (although it would be misleading to describe it as a set of rules about rules); what that means and its significance are matters about which more needs to be said. More also needs to be said about the implications for law in society of this critique of social rules. First the case for it should be strengthened.

3.7 STRENGTHENING THE CASE FOR CONTEXTUAL CONTINGENCIES

The thesis I am advancing is not based on an analytical truth about rules, since some rules could conceivably be applied without reference to their social context. The thesis is intended as a description of the way rules work in practice (in accordance with the first methodological principle), just as Hart's salient fact of social life is intended as a description. As descriptions, both generate hypotheses that are open to empirical investigation in relation to different sets of rules. Meanwhile, in the absence of definitive studies, attention should be drawn to other factors that make this account of rules more compelling. Above all, it rings true. There has always been something puzzling about rules, about the idea that you can pick a rule off the shelf to tell you what to do in this case, a different one for the next case. There are rules like that: to land on a square that says 'go to jail, go directly to jail, do not pass go' is a Monopoly player's dread and leaves scant room for deliberation. But most social rules are not like that; most resemble the rules about lecturing, an example that nicely illustrates the thesis. It is also noticeable how rarely in everyday affairs people make explicit reference to rules or to the fact that they are acting on a rule. If social rules are all around us, as often claimed, why do people not refer to them? The answer is not their absence but that we are not normally called upon to explain our everyday actions; the rules tend to be absorbed into the context of norms and understandings, so that we often have a sense of what should be done without articulating a rule. When there is reason to explain or justify, we can probably formulate a rule, although losing in the process some of the subtlety of the deliberative process. Rules are naturally more prominent in official settings, like clubs, the workplace, or government administration, where an official's actions affect others and so have to be explained and justified; recourse to rules is a natural and economical means of satisfying that need. But they are not picked off the shelf or bear on their face instructions as to what to do; they are rather the focus around which takes place a deliberative process of the kind described.

Further support for the thesis can be drawn from different lines of empirical research. One is the tendency for informal rules to grow around formal rules. Formal rules, whether legal or otherwise, are seldom adequate on their own to deal with the 'daily interactions', in Douglass North's phrase, whether among ordinary people or between them and officials.[22] Another line of support comes from the empirical study of areas of rule-governed behaviour; although not directed to this specific issue, studies of decision-making by courts or administrative officials reveal the social context in which they occur, and its influence on how rules are interpreted and applied.[23] They show how officials bring to their task a set of ideas that constitute a point of view, a way of regarding the law which often leads to its modification in order to make it more suitable to the circumstances, sometimes in the exercise of discretion, at other times by assuming a discretion that is not expressly authorized. The idea that judges should create exceptions to the rules, depart from them, or not apply them, in order to take account of the merits of the case is commonly found in widely different legal orders, from the customary to the modern. What counts as the merits may be the judge's subjective view, but in a system that works well, that assessment derives from the informal conventions and understandings shared by judges and lawyers, if not necessarily by the people as a whole.

Another reason for accepting the thesis is that it enables us to make sense of issues that have posed awkward problems. The judicial attitude just described needs to be explained; how is it that judges, or any other

---

[22] See further, D. North, *Institutions, Institutional Change and Economic Performance*, Chapter 5 (Cambridge, 1990).

[23] These issues are examined in Chapters 16 and 17.

officials, have this kind of discretion towards binding legal rules, the reality of which is demonstrated in a recent study of the judges of the House of Lords.[24] According to this study, judges have discretion as to whether they apply a legal rule in any particular case. To say that courts are bound by legal rules and then admit that they always have discretion not to apply them is odd. Similarly, government officials, regulatory agencies, and the like, assume they have leeway in deciding to depart from a rule, modify it, get around it, or decide in opposition to it. A policeman decides to caution when the rule says arrest; the prosecutor adopts a policy of not prosecuting some crimes when his duty is to prosecute all; a housing officer decides to give priority to single mothers who appear to be living virtuous lives, despite its being irrelevant according to the terms of the statute. These practices are taken for granted but rarely explained. They could be regarded as breaches of the rules, as unlawful discretion, as officials arrogating to themselves powers they do not have. By inserting the idea of contextual contingency, they can be understood quite differently. What officials are doing is interpreting, developing, and refining relations between rules and their social context, not playing fast and loose with them. Instead of a world divided between rules on the one hand and what officials do on the other hand, contextual contingency offers a way of absorbing the division into a more coherent whole; it may not resolve all issues, but the idea of coherence in the way officials, from judges to housing officers, behave is more persuasive than one based on a division between theory and reality.

3.8 SOCIAL RULES AND MODERN LEGAL ORDERS

In describing a municipal legal order, Hart positions himself squarely within an approach to social explanation, prominent at the time he wrote, according to which meaningful behaviour occurs within a context of rules.[25] Contemporary philosophers were developing the idea, partly by reference to language and the distinctions made there, and partly by reflecting on the nature of social explanation. In social theory, both Durkheim and Weber had written of the tendency of modern law towards a rule-based system. We do not know how much Hart was influenced by these ideas, although he was familiar with them. To know more about

---

[24] D. Robertson, *Judicial Discretion in the House of Lords* (Oxford, 1998).
[25] Representative of that idea and an influential proponent of it was Peter Winch, op. cit.

their influence would be of interest, but of greater immediate concern for now is that his account should be regarded as an expression of the idea that enacted rules dominate modern legal orders. The prominence of enacted law, according to which officials may enact rules whenever they consider it necessary to deal with an issue, was for Hart a basic feature of a mature legal order, and a sign of its superiority over traditional orders based on custom. Rules and mature legal orders go together because mature legal orders claim the authority positively to pursue social goals, for which rules are a most useful instrument. They are particularly useful because of their detachment from other social formations and their resulting capacity to be applied (or so it is claimed) without recourse, or with minimum recourse, to the social world around them. Against this background, Hart's singling out the determinacy of legal rules as not only a salient feature of social life but also crucial to a mature legal order is understandable.

What, then, are the implications of the preceding discussion for this image of law as social rules? One is the need to modify Hart's salient fact of social life, the claim that the life of the law consists to a very large extent in determinate rules (what I have designated clear-line rules). Whether the claim is true depends on an empirical study of municipal legal systems, which neither he nor anyone else to my knowledge has conducted. Even without such evidence, a cursory perusal of the modern statute book, together with the laws of the European Union, contemporary constitutions, and international conventions, would show how often law is expressed as standard-based or discretionary rules. If to that were added the spread of soft law, which by its nature deals in soft standards, the salient fact of social life is patently implausible. The difficulty Hart had in fitting the common law into his salient fact should have been an early warning sign of the frailty of his thesis. The model of law he appears to have had in mind is enacted law typically in the form of a statute, but even on that basis the evidence is against him, for standard-based rules and open discretions appear to occur in statutes as commonly as clear-line rules. An acceptable reformulation of the salient fact of social life would be to agree that enacted law has a dominant place in modern legal orders, but to add that it consists of combinations of clear-line, standard-based, and discretionary rules. This does not mean that the notion of law as social rules has to be abandoned; provided it is understood that rules come in different forms, the very idea of a social rule is imprecise in that the standards of behaviour social rules dictate can be determinate or indeterminate.

Relations between rules and their social context point to the need for further modification of the notion of social rules. The close ties between rules, even clear-line rules, and their social context have implications for the way they work in practice; recognition of those ties also opens the way for closer scrutiny of their social context and the contingencies within it. As to the first, while legal theory describes legal rules as standards of behaviour, it is only by considering them in their social context that we see *how* they work as standards. Legal theory is concerned with the logical properties of rules while, for law-and-society, the issue is how they work. Legal theory separates the existence of rules from their interpretation and application. Law-and-society is able to absorb the separation, but goes on to say that it must enquire into the whole process: the rules, their interpretation, and their application. That enquiry includes but goes beyond interpretation, a process that inevitably leads to consideration of social context; it extends to the claim that rules are implicated in their social context in fundamental ways. The social context contains or soon develops conventions, practices, and understandings around rules that guide decisions as to their very authority and status, that determines whether and to what extent they need to be creatively interpreted, modified, or marginalized. If clear-line rules are implicated in their social context in this way, then the consequences for those based on general standards and discretion are so much greater. Once the social context of rules is identified, we are naturally curious to know more about it: how does it form, what are its elements, and what does it reveal about law in society. These issues will be considered in the course of the succeeding chapters.

NOTES

Discussion of the concept of law

Among the many commentaries on *The Concept of Law*, the following have been of special use:

J. Raz, *The Authority of Law* (Oxford, 1983) and *Practical Reason and Norms* (Princeton, 1990).

J. Coleman (ed) *Hart's Postscript* (Oxford, 2001).

M. Kramer, *In Defence of Legal Positivism* (Oxford, 1999).

A. Marmor, *Positive Law and Objective Values* (Oxford, 2001).

J. Austin's main writings are: *Province of Jurisprudence Determined* (Cambridge, 1995).

H. Kelsen's main work for present purposes is *The Pure Theory of Law* (Berkeley, 1934).

The differences between Hart's method of approach and that of Austin are not as great as that suggested by Hart. Their common object was to describe law and legal systems, even though they described them differently. Hart explicitly rejects the *stipulative* definition approach, but even that can be exaggerated; Austin gave a definition of law in advance, but then tested it against social reality. Hart did not start with a definition, but selected the concepts that he thought to be basis to law and then set about marshalling evidence for them.

On the character of social rules:

L. Green, 'The Concept of Law Revisited' (1996) 94 *Michigan Law Rev.* 1687.

On the nature and importance of social rules, the following are useful:

P. Winch, *The Idea of a Social Science and its Relation to Philosophy* (London, 1958, 2nd Ed., 1990) Hart makes reference to this book in developing his concept of social rules: see *The Concept of Law* p. 289.

G. Warnock, *The Object of Morality* (London, 1971).

R. Harré and P. F. Secord, *The Explanation of Social Behaviour* (Oxford, 1972).

Internal and external

Considering the similarity between Hart's internal point of view and Weber's account of rule-guided behaviour, it is a puzzle that Hart makes no reference to Weber, here or elsewhere. It is clear that Hart had read Weber: see the account in: N. Lacey, *A Life of H. L. A. Hart: The Nightmare and the Noble Dream* (Oxford, 2004).

Weber's description of rules is contained in: *Economy and Society*, Volume 1, Chapter 1, Section 5. The discussion takes place under the heading *Legitimate Order*. Weber states that 'social action which involves a social relationship, may be guided by the belief in the existence of a legitimate order. The probability that action will actually be so governed will be called the "validity" of the order in question'. (p. 31) He distinguishes customary actions and actions based just on self-interest, which may have a regularity, from a legitimate order. A valid or legitimate order is one in which the maxims guiding behaviour are 'in some appreciable way regarded by the actor as in some way obligatory or exemplary for him'. (p. 31) Weber's point is that an order (legal order) that is considered binding is more stable than other orders, and is more likely to be followed.

In regarding the order as binding, a person has a strong motive or reason for complying with it. This motive or reason is in addition to motives of tradition or pure expediency. But Weber goes on to say that the move from motives of tradition or expediency to the motive provided by belief in the order's legitimacy, is gradual.

Hart comes close to recognizing that the external observer is likely to realize that there is more to law than patterns of behaviour. He writes: 'If, however, the observer really keeps austerely to this extreme external point of view and does not give any account of the manner in which members of the group who accept the rules view their own regular behaviour, his description of their life cannot be in terms of rules at all (page 87)'.

But, we may ask, why would the observer keep to the extreme point of view? The whole idea is somewhat artificial and no more than a device for drawing attention to rule-governed behaviour.

The distinction between following a rule because it is binding and following it in order to avoid sanctions is an important idea in *The Concept of Law*. It is interesting to compare Weber's more sociologically subtle account of a very similar situation. He writes: 'Even in the case of evasion or disobedience, the probability of their being recognized as valid norms may have an effect on action. This may in the first place be true from the point of view of sheer expediency. A thief orients his action to the validity of the criminal law in that he acts surreptitiously. The fact that the order is recognized as valid in his society is made evident by the fact that he cannot violate it openly without punishment'. *Economy and Society* (Volume 1) p. 32.

Rule scepticism

For a recent, representative account of rule-scepticism, see D. Robertson, *Judicial Discretion in the House of Lords*.

Contextual contingencies

The use of *soft law* adds another dimension to the context of rules. *Soft law* means the use of standards that are not legally binding in the way that a rule is legally binding, but which supplement, modify, or interpret legal rules. The point of soft law is to make hard law more flexible, more capable of dealing with complex or fluid situations. It is especially prominent in the European Union and International Law. Soft law takes several forms, including codes of conduct, resolutions, communications, declarations, guidance, and so on. Soft law should be regarded as part of the social context of legal rules, as contingencies within that context. See: M. Cini, 'The Soft Law Approach: Commission Rule-Making in the EU's state aid programme' (2001), 8 *Journal of European Public*

Policy, pp. 192–207; F. Beveridge and S. Nott, 'A Hard Look at Soft Law', in P. Craig and C. Harlow (eds) *Lawmaking in the European Union* (London, 1998).

On the tendency for formal rules to attract informal rules and other considerations, see D. North, *Institutions, Institutional Change, and Economic Performance* which contains a study of informal norms and their relationship to formal norms.

The deliberative process in relation to rules

G. Warnock's *The Object of Morality* has a useful chapter on rules. One passage in particular is relevant to the idea that the application of a rule is subject to deliberation as to whether to apply it, and I would add how to apply it: '. . . as, of course, is very obvious, the applicability in a certain situation of some rule, however "good" the rule may be, is not in general a *conclusive* reason for acting, in that situation, as the rule requires; thus, it is always possible that one might ask, without questioning the rule or its applicability: should I – or why should I – comply with it here and now? The question here is, not whether there is *any* reason to act as the rule requires, but whether there may not be – as there might be – better reason, here and now, for acting otherwise.' (p. 42).

J. Raz distinguishes the *deliberative* stage of a decision from the *executive in Ethics in the Public Domain* (Oxford, 1994). At the deliberative stage, the decision-maker 'considers the merits of alternative courses of action' (p. 206). My suggestion is that notion applies to anyone faced with an authoritative social rule. Deliberation means not only interpreting the rule but also deciding what weight it has and how it fits in with other competing conventions, practices, and understandings.

Realists have naturally defended themselves against Hart's dismissal of their position. As one anonymous defender notes: 'Choosing to study and urging others to study the complex problems of law's leeway areas and its actual societal impact is not to claim that law is a shoreless world of uncertainty'. (H.L.A Hart's 'Concept of Law in the Perspective of American Legal Realism' (1972) 35 *Modern Law Review* 607).

Studies of officials departing from, modifying, or not applying legal rules

I. Loveland, *Housing Homeless People* (Oxford, 1995).

J. Baldwin, N. Whiteley, and R. Young in *Judging Social Security* (Oxford, 1992).

K. A. Shepsle and B. W. Weingast show how the formal legal rules of congressional committees became surrounded by a set of informal rules to deal with specific problems not foreseen in the formal rules in 'The Institutional Foundations of Committee Power' in (1987) 81 *American Political Science Review* 85–104 (discussed in D. North, *Institutions, Institutional Change and Economic Performance*, p. 40). Douglass North discusses the way formal rules become surrounded by informal ones.

The Realists and their defence

For a full and subtle account of the realist's position:

E. Hunter-Taylor, 'H.L.A. Hart's Concept of Law in the Perspective of American Legal Realism' (1972) 35 *Modern Law Review* 35, p. 606.

4

Law Prior to Rules

4.1 FROM RULES TO RULINGS TO ACTS

Relations between legal rules and their social context give rise to questions about the nature of law. Their importance in understanding rules need destroy neither the idea of rules nor the claim that laws are rules; at the same time, some modifications need to be made. For the purposes of legal theory, a state legal order is accurately described as consisting of social rules, provided it is understood that rules take the different forms identified in the previous chapter. The statute book, the Constitution, and international conventions can be consulted to prove the point. The fact that rules depend on social conventions and understandings for their interpretation and application does not dislodge the claim that, in one sense, from one point of view, the law consists of social rules.

From the point of view of law in society the position is different. Since the aim here is to understand the nature of law as a social formation, there is a need to know the elements of which it consists, and in answering that its ties to social context are plainly relevant. Yet even here there is ambiguity. We could retain the view that law consists of rules officially declared and then go on to describe how they are dealt with in practice, how they are interpreted and applied according to contextual contingencies. Law is one thing, its social context another. An alternative view is that legal rules are so intertwined with contextual contingencies, with understandings and conventions, that to consider them as laws in isolation from their social context would be a misunderstanding. On this view, rules are an essential element of law, especially in modern legal orders, but there is more to law than rules; the fuller reality of law consists in rules in their social context. The social context is more than a point of intersection between law and other social elements; it is part of the constitution of law. In reaching that conclusion, we have moved from the notion of law as rules adopted by legal theory to a fuller notion of what constitutes legal reality.

Exploration of that fuller social reality is potentially rewarding. It hints at a different way of viewing law and the experience of law. Imagine we are playing snakes and ladders; having climbed the ladder of rules we then slide down a snake to the social world at the bottom. Supposing we now start with that social world before climbing the ladder back to rules; in other words, supposing we were to explore Hart's 'pre-legal' society. It is often said that law is not only imposed from above but also evolves from below; we now have a chance to see what that means. Being so accustomed to thinking of law as rules, we find it hard to imagine otherwise, and yet the idea of law as rules is a relative newcomer. Giambattista Vico, writing in the eighteenth century, maintains that the earliest people were incapable of grasping universals, and that even early Roman Law consisted in *decrees* of the *duuimvirs*, the officials appointed for that purpose.[1] Decrees were 'injunctions or prohibitions directed at an individual' rather than general rules as we would assume them to be. It was only later 'when intelligible universals had been understood, [that] the essential property of law, its universality, was recognized'.

A similar point emerges from studies of customary societies. Max Gluckman discovered that among the Lozi of Rhodesia the courts or court-like bodies did not judge actions against definite legal rules. The normal test was *reasonable behaviour*, which meant conformity to the role, not the rule, appropriate to a person's social position; customary usages, etiquettes, and conventions helped to indicate what was appropriate. The concept of the reasonable man of Lozi law would be most accurately understood as 'the reasonable and customary occupier of a specific position'.[2] If that seems a world away from our own, we should be reminded that English law, less than a millennium ago, was not expressed in rules as we know them. As J. H. Baker writes 'Decisions settled the matter in hand and were not expected to do more; they were not constrained by the past and did not fix rules for the future. Good decisions are guided by custom and wise counsel as to what is reasonable'.[3]

In order to gain an idea of what law meant in the pre-legal world, we need to retrace legal evolution from *rules* back to *rulings* and from *rulings* back to *legal acts*. Law in its most elemental form is neither a rule nor a ruling, but an act that has legal meaning: applying a seal to a deed, making a marriage vow, agreeing a contract, or settling a will; it could also consist

---

[1] G. Vico, *New Science* (First published 1725) (London, 1999) p. 205.
[2] M. Gluckman, *The Judicial Process Among the Barotse of Northern Rhodesia* (Manchester, 1955), p. 154.
[3] J. H. Baker, *An Introduction to English Legal History* (4th Edition) (London, 2002) p. 1.

in a gathering of people to decide an issue of legal significance. In early societies legal acts often consisted of elaborate rituals and later on were marked by visible signs, so that Gibbon was prompted to write that 'the jurisprudence of the first Romans exhibited the scenes of a pantomime'.[4] Legal acts express the fundamental events and transactions of a society – marriage, transfer of property, exchange of goods and services – but they do more: they express the *relations* between its members, as husband and wife, father and son, owner of property and tenant, contractor and contractee, official and citizen, and as such are deeply social acts. Their recognition as legal derives from their importance in expressing those relations, which in turn constitute the society itself. Nothing is more fundamental to society, more plainly constitutive, than the social relations of its members, for social relations express a society's self-understanding and its continuation over time. Durkheim catches this precisely: social life consists in relations between one and another, or between one and the collective; and if it is to last, social life must take on a definite form and organize itself. Then: 'Law is nothing more than this very organization in its most stable and precise form'.[5]

Social relations are private matters, but also more than private matters: being constitutive of society, they are also matters of common interest and hence of the common good. Law, then, is tied both to the private and the public in a bond that is as real and vital in modern societies as in early societies. Customs and conventions naturally develop around legal acts, giving expression to their regularity and their continuity into the future, but should not be mistaken for the legal act.[6] The point of this analysis is not to provide a definition of law but to catch its spirit in two main ideas: *first*, certain kinds of acts express fundamental social relations among society's members, and, *secondly*, particular attitudes accompanying the acts are attributes that come to be described as legal. We can now see how law, and the attitudes and experiences that are specifically legal, are prior to rules and are expressed without reference to rules. That rules have become indispensable to modern law should not blind us to a sense of law that is real, prior to, and more fundamental than rules.

Disputes occur over legal acts, so ways have to be devised for dealing

---

[4] E. Gibbon, *The History of the Decline and Fall of the Roman Empire* (First published 1776), (London, 1987) Volume V, p. 258.

[5] E. Durkheim, op. cit., p. 25.

[6] In this section, in identifying the specifically legal form in society, I have been much helped by Philip Arlott's book *The Health of Nations: Society and Law Beyond the State* (Cambridge, 2002).

with them. Traditional societies as well as modern ones try to bring the disputing parties together, with resolution by formal process a matter of last resort. When necessary, a *ruling* has to be made not by applying a rule in the sense we would understand, but by determining what social relations reasonably require, for which guidance is taken from all their visible signs and symbols in customs, conventions, and practices. But to imagine that to be analogous to applying rules, the substitution of custom for rules, would be to misunderstand the nature of such visible signs; for while they contain an element of detachment and generality, they are too interwoven with the spirit of the society to allow a sharp differentiation to be made. Rulings make sense not only as conclusions drawn from applying rules to facts, but by a different process, less precise but equally real: what should be done, how someone should behave in this situation, what is reasonable in this society, given its way of organizing itself. The reasonable man of the Lozi is the man who acts according to his role and position. Leopold Pospisil found the Kapauku of New Guinea had a notion, regularly invoked in ruling on disputes, that 'one does not act like that';[7] while Paul Bohannan's study shows that the *jir* or process of the Tiv is likely to conclude with the *ortaregh's* (judge's) stating 'it is plain what must be done'.[8] Whether or not the Lozi, the Kapauku, or the Tiv use legal terms in expressing these ideas, they belong to the same category of acts that, allowing for all the differences between their societies and ours, we regard as legal.

Similar ideas are found in the development of classical Roman Law, with the opinions of the jurists on specific matters, and in judicial decisions of the early common law. In both cases, the judge of the dispute extracts from social relations how the parties should have acted and what was reasonable and supportable in the circumstances. Standards whose terms are more certain and focused are present in elementary form, and in time come to add content to, and even supersede, the idea of reasonableness by making more precise how one should act in different sets of conditions. The language is revealing: reasonableness could be replaced by what is normal, which in earlier usage could have been replaced by *regular*, since reasonable actions are normal and regular actions; *regular* and *rule* both derive from the Latin *regulare*, so making smooth and natural the passage from what is regular to what is by rule. Similar bonds between legal decisions and social relations are familiar in the Islamic

---

[7] L. Pospisil, *Kapauku Papuans and Their Law* (New Haven, Conn., 1971) pp. 97–99.
[8] P. Bohannan, *Justice and Judgment Among the Tiv* (Oxford, 1957) p. 20 ff.

courts. Despite the tendency of commentators from Gibbon to Weber to disparage Kadi justice, by which is meant arbitrary and unprincipled decision-making, closer study depicts a different reality. Laurence Rosen found that in the adjudication of family disputes in village courts in Morocco, judges had extensive discretion. He also found their decisions marked by a high degree of regularity, which: 'lies in the fit between the decisions of the Muslim judge and the cultural concepts and social relations to which they are intrinsically tied'.[9]

As social relations, and hence societies, become more complex, rules are more common and necessary. Small, close-knit societies have a high level of shared understandings, a mechanical solidarity in Durkheim's terms, so that notions of reasonableness and appropriateness are adequate for ruling on disputes and behaviour. Modern societies are marked by more diverse ways of life and more complex social relations, the two being connected, with lower levels of shared understandings the consequence. Again it is hard to improve on Durkheim's account: the division of labour, the forces of diversity and plurality, break the bonds of mechanical solidarity and replace it with a different form, that of organic solidarity. Organic solidarity heralds a different society, a new configuration of relations between people, in which individuals who would otherwise be isolated are linked to one another, and 'instead of developing separately, they concert their efforts'.[10] A new and different social order needs a new and different legal order, an order expressive of those complex social relations.

The direct consequence for law of a new social order is that, in the face of diversity, notions of reasonableness and appropriateness lose or have weakened their capacity to cope, and are replaced by rules. Rules are able to hold the balance among strangers by stating directly the terms on which transactions are conducted; since what is reasonable can no longer be based directly on shared understandings and conventions, it must be conveyed in rules. Rulings now look to rules and are based on applying them; the legal point of view shifts from what is reasonable to what the rules require. Two further consequences are vital to understanding the new legal order. The *first* is that rules can never be more than approximations of the full complexity of social relations. Their fuller and subtler contours, which are understood but impossible to state explicitly and in

[9] L. Rosen, *The Anthropology of Justice: Law as Culture in Islamic Society* (Cambridge, 1989), p. 18. Also quoted in S. Falk Moore, *Law and Anthropology: A Reader* (Oxford, 2005) p. 351.

[10] E. Durkheim, op. cit., p. 21.

advance, remain the context against which rules are interpreted and applied. So, we are back on the ladder from context to rules, and can now see why that context of conventions and understandings remains vital to the social reality of rules. The *second*, equally vital, consequence is that, although rules become the focal point of legal experience, they are only part of it: the reality of law, which in our notional pre-legal society has a wholeness, is split in two, with rules forming only one part.

The other part, the attitudes of the members of society, their understandings of social relations, which we counted above as part of the social reality of law, do not disappear in the new legal order. Their legal status is lost and forgotten, for now positive rules have become the basis of law. Nonetheless, despite being less obvious than in previous societies, and despite being overshadowed by rules, social relations continue to exert their influence by forming the social context of rules. Rules will often be compatible with that context, and, even when they are not, the decision may be taken to follow them to the letter. Equally common, when they are not, when they violate conventions and understandings expressing social relations, their little social world will influence their use, will restrain and modify them, even to the point of marginalization or suspension. Whether in relations among citizens, or between citizen and state, the social world behind the rules keeps a balance and harmony between fundamental social relations and the rules. Social relations are not static and fixed for all times, but respond to and re-form under the influence of legal rules. At times, they are transformed by law, but more typically the relationship is reciprocal and reflexive, with each influencing and being influenced by the other. And so we have now arrived back at the top of the ladder, for we now understand why rules cannot be removed or isolated from their contextual contingencies, from the social world around them. It is in this sense that those contingencies, and the social relations they express, remain part of the social reality of law.

4.2 CASE OF THE COMMON LAW

If the reasonable men of the Lozi, the Kapukau, and the Tiv seem a long way from modern law, they have in common with the common law of England and its transplants elsewhere, as one substantial part of modern law, more than might be supposed. Common lawyers are irritated by suggestions that their system is less than rational or systematic when judged by continental European standards. Many would find no fault with, indeed would relish the thought of, medieval English judges who spoke of the common law as both settled and the product of reason, and in doing so displayed a set of attitudes which, even if nurtured by myth rather than fact, explain much about early legal practice and the evolution of the common law.[11] Among those attitudes was the notion that judges declared the common law rather than made it and that they had a suspicion of enacted law as a potential threat to it. Hart, a former barrister, found the common law settled enough and sufficiently like a system of enacted laws to pose no problem for his salient fact of social life. In his view, despite the obvious differences between a system of enacted law and the common law, the doctrine of precedent, whereby courts are bound by previous rulings (to put it in its simplest form), was enough to transform the common law into rules, which may be applied by both citizens and officials without recourse to a fresh judgement in each new case.

An alternative view is that the common law is 'more like a muddle than a system, and that it would be difficult to conceive of a less systematic body of law'.[12] If it is a muddle, it is a particular kind of muddle in the same way that any system of customary law is a muddle, which is to say that, while there are plainly some settled rules, to single them out as the defining feature of their legal experience would be a distortion. It would be a distortion because the main attribute of a customary legal order is not that it produces a coherent system of rules or even sets of them. It is instead the way *rulings* are arrived at and their relationship to the social context. For the point about customary orders is that judges or judge-like figures make their rulings not primarily by applying settled rules, nor is the formulation of settled rules their main aim. The point, instead, is to make rulings that properly express fundamental social relations, as they are interpreted and reinterpreted from time to time, and what is reasonable behaviour with respect to them. The claims of early judges to be declaring the law rather than making it, far from being a pretence that the common law consisted of a system of settled rules, show a profound insight into the nature of law. For their claim was that the common law, being the legal expression of social relations, was settled in the same way and to the same extent that those relations were settled. Reason was the reason of social relations, and rulings were judgments about what was reasonable in the circumstances. General concepts,

---

[11] J. H. Baker, *An Introduction to English Legal History*, chapter 12.
[12] A. W. B. Simpson, 'The Common Law and Legal Theory' in A. W. B. Simpson (ed) *Oxford Essays in Jurisprudence* (Oxford, 1973) p. 99.

principles, and rules naturally emerged over time as intermediaries between social relations and rulings; nevertheless, in ruling, judges retained the right and duty to determine what was reasonable. Precedents are useful in showing how similar situations have been handled; they also encourage consensus and consistency. Only at a late stage in English law did precedents became binding in future cases, a matter often mistakenly taken to be the defining feature of the common law, when it is a recent, local, and marginal variation thereof. It is easy to see how statutes, being acts of legislative will, could be regarded as a threat to the balance of the common law, although it has been pointed out that, until the modern period, statutes generally were consistent with common law rather than designed to overturn it.

The common law has built into it the capacity to change where social relations change, where the best gauge of that is how people deal with each other in normal and regular circumstances. Law is generated from everyday practices which, in turn, become the basis for rulings. At various points in its history the common law became heavily rule-bound, probably due to the way the courts developed and their organizational character. In this respect the common law differs from customary systems of the kind considered above, which often lack similar organizations. Following periods of excessive rigidity, the common law was brought back into balance by major adjustments, such as that of an equitable jurisdiction growing up in parallel or by the intervention of statute. Where rules became too rigid, or were no longer reasonable expressions of social relations and practices, they were liable to be reformulated or abandoned in favour of a new principle, as shown by the decline of the writ-system in early modern English law in favour of causes of action, and the move in the twentieth century from numerous specific torts with strict rules defining them to a general tort of negligence.

We can now see how the virtue of the common law is said to be its capacity to develop from the bottom up, to deal with the world as it is rather than as we would wish it to be, to respond to social change in a cautious but effective manner. In that sense it is rational and stable, and in the direct line of succession of less-developed customary societies, in which the reality of law is directly and securely tied to experience. At the same time, there are inherent dangers and instabilities. If judicial rulings as the expression of law are to have authority, they must be more than the subjective and potentially arbitrary decrees of judges. The usual remedy of reducing the risks by having general rules is available, and often invoked; but excessive resort to rules would remove the ability of courts to 'let law bubble up' as one senior American judge put it,[13] and that, after all, is the strength of the common law. What, then, are the safe-guards against arbitrariness? The English experience is instructive for the common law has attracted love and hate in roughly equal shares. The first from judges and lawyers who over generations made the common law, who see themselves as continuing an ancient tradition, and who believe it has served society well.[14] And here is both its strength and its weakness. Its strength lies in the common law being the product of judges and lawyers who have historically formed a close-knit profession, in which the conventions and understandings as to its character, and their role in it, are deeply embedded and deeply shared. The organization of bench and bar, the role of the ancient Inns of Court to which judges, barristers, and pupils all belong, and the training process itself, have all ensured historically a high level of consensus and common purpose.[15] This has made the common law possible and protected against excessive arbitrariness on the part of individual judges.

If that has ensured its survival to the present day, it has also led to a long tradition of detestation, which reached its peak in Bentham who, after hearing Blackstone's Oxford lectures, swore to devote his life to its exposure. The root cause of his disdain was the belief that the common law had become the creation of lawyers and judges, over which they exercised a monopoly, whose objective was less to maintain a legal order based on the social good in translating social relations into law, and more in preserving their own privileges. In other words, that the bond between law and social relations had been loosened and corrupted by extraneous concerns.[16] If that were true, then the very point and foundation of the common law, as a classic case of the close bond between law and social relations, would be lost. We need not try to assess the merits of the claim, nor other concerns about the inability of the common law to cope with contemporary societies, nor the alleged isolation of judges and lawyers from the rapid social changes in the post-war period. The point is made for our purposes by seeing the common law as an example, a particularly good example, of how law and the social context of law are inseparable.

---

[13] An expression reported to me by J. W. Adams, a New York lawyer and businessman.
[14] For an example, see P. B. H. Birks, *Unjust Enrichment* (2nd edn, Oxford, 2004).
[15] See: A. W. B. Simpson, *Invitation to Law* (Blackwell, 1988).
[16] For discussion of Bentham's view see: G. Postema, *Bentham and the Common Law Tradition* (Oxford, 1986).

4.3 RULES AND MODERN LEGAL ORDERS

We have moved in this chapter from rules as the focus of law, to the social context of rules, examination of which has led to a sense of law that is prior to and more fundamental than rules. Law, in this sense, is the expression of social relations and the need to preserve them over time. The deeper sense of law is most evident in more traditional societies where positive rules have a minor role, and yet issues similar to those of any society arise as to how people relate to each other, by what bonds they are linked, and how disputes concerning them should be resolved. Law in modern societies has become concentrated in positive rules, enacted in the main by legislators. Yet the same instinct to maintain the basic social relations through law persists; positive rules express one set of social relations, which may not match those emerging more spontaneously in more basic social contexts. Those stated in positive law are likely to prevail, but not without amelioration, modification, or even marginalization by others deeply grounded in social practice. No matter how remote positive legal rules appear to be from fundamental social relations, those relations, reappear in different ways and guises in the actions of judges, officials, and the people, who use the social context of rules as the means for doing so. The significance of the deeper sense of law will be strong in some areas of rules, weak in others.

Now that a way of understanding law in modern societies has been sketched, let us return to the issue raised at the beginning of the chapter: how law is to be understood for the purposes of law-and-society. Legal rules are acknowledged in a modern legal order to be social facts of high significance and, therefore, major influences on behaviour. We should agree with Hart's claim that to miss the way legal rules feature in the actions of officials – and we should add citizens – would be to miss an important aspect of social behaviour. In taking this approach, we implicitly accept the sense in which legal rules are part of the social context. Having made that acknowledgement, and in accordance with the first methodological principle, a law-and-society approach should add that social relations, as expressed in informal conventions and understandings, are also social facts of high relevance to law, such that they are central to a law-and-society approach. Legal rules are also relevant to the internal attitudes of officials and citizens according to the second methodological principle; they are regarded as binding standards to which effect must be given. Similarly for social relations; they are the beacons by which normal social behaviour is conducted and are often more fundamental than legal rules. The intersection of the two is therefore central to law-and-society. To these two levels of analysis should be added the third, the tendency of social relations to be expressed in conventions and understandings that are commonly shared. The result is a complex social setting in which legal rules have a certain distinctiveness, while being at the same time inextricably interwoven with social relations and the social spheres expressing them. The study of that social setting is the basis of the third methodological principle.

To conclude this chapter, a further step may be taken in developing the character of modern legal orders, and in the course of doing so provide another illustration of the interplay between legal rules and social relations. We tend to think of modern law as primarily legislation, with fairly detailed rules governing specific issues, when increasingly legislation is surrounded by the different kinds of rules found in constitutions and international covenants. Generally taking the form of standard-based rules, these two sources of law limit and restrain both the scope and interpretation of legislation. They fit into the structure proposed here in expressing sets of social relations whose importance is considered to justify limiting the powers of legislation. The clearest cases are standards declaring and protecting human rights. It is not hard to see a parallel between those standards and the traditional role of the common law, in maintaining a balance between social relations and law, for in the new order courts – both national and international courts – are required to assess positive law against a new set of standards, which are themselves a restatement of modern social relations. Courts and officials have the opportunity, often readily grasped, of reinterpreting social relations in the light of modern ideas and adjusting positive law in accordance with them. This could be regarded as a renaissance of the common law approach in places where the common law has been largely supplanted by statute, while for those who long ago abandoned it for Roman Law, it could be seen as a second opportunity.

NOTES

LAW PRIOR TO RULES

On law as the expression of social relations

Philip Allott writes in *Health of Nations*: 'There cannot be law without society or society without law. There cannot be good law except in a good society. As a third thing, produced by and producing society's ideas, produced by and producing the everyday exercise of social power, law cannot be separated from the self-constituting of a given society'. (p. 52). The self-constituting of society is expressed most fundamentally in its social relations.

Allot also quotes an illuminating passage from Adam Ferguson's *Essay on History of the Civil Society* concerning *habeus corpus*: 'No wiser form was ever opposed to the abuses of power. But it requires a fabric no less than the whole political constitution of Great Britain, a spirit no less than the refractory and turbulent zeal of this fortunate people, to secure its effects'. (Allot, p. 62, fn. 14).

In seeking to correct what he considered errors and myths about Roman Law, Giambattista Vico insists that the key was to understand that 'Governments must conform to the nature of the people they govern, since they arise from that very nature . . . .' (*The New Science*, p. 411). He continues with reference to the question of why later imperial Roman jurisprudence professed natural equity without the pretence of observing the Law of the Twelve Tables: 'Yet, far from being deceptions such practices were customs arising from human nature. For customs determined states, and states determined precise practices' (p. 412). For *human nature* we should substitute *social relations*.

In his discussion of law in relation to Freud, P. Fitzpatrick notes: 'They [the sons] rely on the relations between themselves, on their 'social fraternal feelings which were the basis of the whole transformation' [quoting Freud] brought about by the paricide. The law comes also from those relations.' (*Modernism and the Grounds of Law* (Cambridge, 2001), p. 33).

On relations between rules, social relations, and social practices

S. Falk Moore remarks in relation to the various ethnographies to which reference is made in the text of the Tiv, the Lozi, and the Kapauku: 'To the extent that all these ethnographies give ample reason to believe that the peoples concerned had very practical arrangements, given their circumstances, and made what seemed to them, very practical decisions, the emphasis on tradition as the sole explanatory factor seems superficial'. (op. cit., p. 100).

Social Relations and legal rules

Examples can be found where legal rules are seriously marginalized by networks of social relations and the practices they induce. A study of small and medium-size businesses in Taiwan shows how social relations lead to business practices that systematically by-pass legal rules and institutions. These businesses found the formal regulated system unavailable to them and so resorted to informal arrangements. It is argued that the arrangements are satisfactory for the effective and profitable conduct of business, and a vital element in the prosperity of the country's economy. See: L. K. Winn, 'Relational Practices and the Marginalization of Law: Informal Financial Practices of Small Businesses in Taiwan' (1994) 28 *Law and Society Review* 193. For comments on the study, see S. Falk Moore, op. cit., pp. 267–8.

R. Ellickson's study of the ranchers of Shasta County shows how close-knit farming communities developed their own informal rules and methods for resolving disputes, even though a set of state laws covered the same matters. Ellickson suggests that adoption of the informal system is explained as maximizing the welfare of the ranchers; an alternative understanding would be that social relations among the ranchers, as they developed through custom and experience, could be more faithfully represented in their own rules than in those of state law. And since there were no particular pressures on the ranchers to comply with state law, the more spontaneous expression of social relations in norms and practices was able to prevail. See: R. Ellickson, *Order Without Law*.

Role of judges

The idea that the underlying social relations influence the decisions of judges and other officials should not be confused with a particular version of *pragmatism*. The pragmatist judge, according to R. Posner, 'regards precedent, statutes, and constitutions both as a source of potentially valuable information about the likely best result in the present case and as signposts that he must be careful not to obliterate or obscure gratuitously because people may be relying upon them'. 'Pragmatic Adjudication' in M. Dickson, *The Revival of Pragmatism* (Durham, NC, 1988) p. 238.

Common Law

J. H. Baker's *An Introduction to Legal History* provides an extended account of the early common law and its development that repays close reading. It contains numerous examples of the close bonds between common law decisions and social relations.

P. Allot, in referring to Hart's account, claims that: 'it misses the sublime essence of common law – the idea that law cannot be stated as a set of existing rules but is a permanent process by which a potentiality of law is turned into am actuality as each case is decided, and as each case produces the potentiality of law for future cases.' (*The Health of Nations*, p. 52).

5

Law as a System of Rules

5.1 THE RULE OF RECOGNITION

From law as social rules we follow Hart in considering law as a *system* of social rules, how social rules unite to form a system of law.[1] The rule of recognition serves that purpose in two ways. First, it links rules together to form a system. It is a master rule or ultimate rule (as Hart often refers to it) specifying the conditions under which new rules of law are created; it is also the basis for testing whether any social rule is a legal rule. It provides the conditions for identifying a legal system as a distinct and separate system of social rules. The rule of recognition could be quite simple, but in practice is likely to be complex, determining which officials have authority to make law, the limits of their authority, and, when disputes arise, who may resolve them. The second task of the rule of recognition is to confer on specific rules their authority as laws. Any law made in accordance with the rule of recognition acquires a binding quality with which officials have an obligation to comply. The binding quality of law derives from acceptance of the rule of recognition and does not depend on additional criteria or justification. As a legal obligation, it is distinct from other kinds of obligation, such as one of a moral or religious nature, its consequence being that legal rules constitute reasons for officials to act in a certain way, and for their actions to be regarded as valid.

The rule of recognition is put forward as a necessary condition of a legal system and vital to its understanding. How does it come about? Hart's explanation again illustrates his desire to tie legal theory to social reality: the rule of recognition is a social fact, its two elements being the convergent behaviour on the part of officials, and an internal attitude which regards that behaviour as obligatory. Whatever rule the officials adopt as a matter of practice is the rule of recognition, which is identified by studying the conventions officials observe, and how they explain and justify their actions in terms of them. The conventions are likely to point

[1] H. L. A. Hart, op. cit., chapter VI.

to a constitution, legislative enactments, customary practice, authoritative declarations, and past judicial decisions.[2] A humdrum case of daily legal life illustrates the point: a judge in an English court makes decisions by applying the statutes of Parliament, the regulations of ministers, and the common law, and increasingly the regulations and directives of European law. In doing so, the judge relies on a set of understandings as to which institutions make law, how they are ranked in the event of conflict, and the duties of a judge with respect to them. The judge normally has no need to articulate these understandings, nor think deeply about them, since they are the basis of adjudication and have been absorbed long ago; they constitute the very activity in which a judge is engaged in joining the bench. As Hart writes: 'For the most part the rule of recognition is not stated, but its existence is *shown* in the way in which particular rules are identified'.[3] If the occasion arises, the judge should be able to give an account that shows how his understandings are based on social rules about legal authority. Non-officials also accept the rule of recognition and rules made under it, but it is not essential for the existence of a legal system that they should, it being enough that the people generally obey. Hart's account does not delve into the reasons for which officials accept the rule of recognition, nor are particular kinds of reasons required for the purposes of legal theory. All that matters is that officials accept, as a matter of fact, a rule of recognition. In case of doubt, its existence and content is pieced together by reference to the actual practice of judges and other officials.

The rule of recognition has attracted a good measure of both admiration and scepticism. It is admired for showing how a description of law has no need to resort to abstract notions, such as Kelsen's basic norm, in order to explain how legal rules form a system of law; social practices and the attitudes accompanying them are enough. Its power and simplicity in showing how social rules are bound together to form a legal system, and how such a system is separate from other sets of social rules, are other reasons for admiration. Scepticism raises its own issues: whether the recognition is a real rule; whether there is one or several; what happens where two or more legal systems are in operation; and how it copes if different officials have different ideas as to what it is. Among these issues and others which continue to engage jurists, two are direct to our concerns: one is what kind of rule it is, the other what it means for officials to accept it.

---

[2] *Ibid*, p. 97.   [3] *Ibid*, p. 98.

5.2 WHAT KIND OF RULE IS THE RULE OF RECOGNITION?

One charge against the rule of recognition is that it is not a rule at all. Critics claim that officials may have good reasons of policy or strategy for acting in accordance with a set of conventions about how law is made and who makes it, but they do not amount to a rule; nor can they explain how conventions create obligations. Conformity of behaviour among officials is not rule-governed behaviour.[4] In his *Postscript*, Hart accepted some of the criticisms of social rules but defended the rule of recognition as a conventional social practice. He states: 'Rules are conventional social practices if the general conformity of a group to them is part of the reasons its individual members have for acceptance'.[5] It follows that the rule of recognition is that set of conventions or practices that judges and other officials actually follow. A convention or practice as a type of rule is to be distinguished from another type of social rule, which consists in members of a group sharing a practice for other reasons, such as moral reasons. The rule of recognition is a conventional rule for Hart because it is that which officials accept as a matter of practice, their reasons being a separate matter.

Once conventional rules are brought to our attention, they seem to be all around. The rules of cricket or chess are of that kind, as are innumerable situations, ranging from social clubs to colleges to professional associations, which are based on convention and which we accept just because they are the rules, because they show how things are done. How often have we heard the expression, uttered in resignation, defence, or enquiry: 'they are the rules!' or 'I am just following the rules!' or 'what is the rule on that?' At stake here is the simple idea that when we enter into various activities or join associations we do so on the basis of the rules by which they are conducted. This is a normal and understandable aspect of social life, for any coming together of people for a common purpose needs organization, and rules are a natural means for doing so. In an effort to strengthen the case for rules as conventions, it has been suggested that conventions have special qualities in that they are often not merely conventions *about* an activity but *constitutive* of it.[6] The rules of chess, for instance, are not just about chess, they 'partly constitute the point or

---

[4] The issue is explained well in A. Marmor, op. cit.

[5] Op. cit., postscript p. 255.

[6] A. Marmor gives a very helpful account in his book *Positive Law and Objective Value*.

value' of chess.[7] Once you decide to play chess, whatever your reasons for doing so, you commit yourself to the conventions that make up the game. In other words, the conventions about chess amount to a set of rules that become binding on you when you enter the game. The idea of rules being *constitutive* of an activity is a familiar one and must be treated with caution, for it is easy to slip into the mistake of thinking that activities, such as tennis, are *just* a set of rules. A moment's reflection shows that there is more to tennis than rules, and indeed that what the rules happen to be is a secondary matter when compared with the point and purpose of the game. With that proviso, it may help in grasping the fairly simple idea put forward above to think of conventions as *part-and-parcel* of what constitutes the activity.

The question is whether that simple idea applies to law. In the first place, it is a common feature of legal systems that officials tend to have conventional rules about what is law and what is not. The trouble is that the conventions are often not comprehensive, covering only part of what is law. The early common law judges had no need to point to a convention about what the law was; they ruled on the basis of what was reasonable according to the customs and social relations of the time, a matter that could not be captured in a meaningful rule of recognition. Some argue that is still the case in modern legal systems: conventions may answer some questions as to what is law and what is not, but for others, officials must seek an answer based on more fundamental under-standings within the society. We are then driven to the conclusion that the rule of recognition is an important feature of a modern legal system for identifying rules as legal rules, but is not complete, for behind it is a deeper world of legal phenomena. I have described the deeper world in terms of social context and contextual contingencies. Bentham describes it in this way: 'a complex network of social institutions, expectations, and regulations'.[8]

This leads on to a second aspect of the rule of recognition: we may be lulled into thinking of rules of recognition as generally being crisp and clear, with statements such as 'laws are made by Parliament, the Constitution states who makes laws, legislation prevails over judicial decisions', confirming that view. Statements like these, however, are likely to conceal a complex social world of contextual contingencies extending, influencing, and modifying the simple rule. Considering the kinds of questions that are asked about rules of recognition, such as in Britain, the

---

[7] *Ibid*, p. 14.   [8] J. Postema, op. cit., p. 256.

relationship between parliament and the courts, or in the United States, the proper role of the Supreme Court, we should expect the contextual contingencies to reach deep into the historical foundations of the society. The deeper the reach, the more scope there is for disagreement among officials, and the less use statements of the rule of recognition will be as a source of guidance.[9] The extent of disagreement in practice, and how far scepticism of the rule of recognition is warranted, are matters on which more empirical investigation is needed. More needs to be known about the social conventions constituting the rule of recognition, how officials regard them, and their workings in practice. Apart from the general and by now obvious point that the rule of recognition, like other social rules, can be fully understood only in its social context, another significant aspect is that different sets of officials are prone to have different views of exactly what it is and how much weight it carries.

5.3 ACCEPTANCE AND THE REASONS FOR ACCEPTANCE

The similarity between law and other rule-based activities is a third aspect of the rule of recognition of interest to law-and-society. If law is a set of social practices constituted by conventional rules in the manner Hart suggests, then acceptance by officials is similar to acceptance of other sets of rules, such as those of a game or a social club. If a society has a legal system, it has a set of conventions as to what the law is, so that anyone engaging in the activity of law accepts those conventions as binding. This means accepting both the conventions as to what counts as law and laws made in accordance with them. Some find this an unsatisfactory foundation for a legal system; they are puzzled as to how simply entering into the practices of law makes the practice binding and capable of creating obligations. Surely for law to create obligations something more is needed, and the usual answer as to what is missing is a moral foundation.[10] Others ask whether the rule is accepted because it is binding, or whether it is acceptance that makes it binding.[11] Despite its importance to his theory, some of Hart's critics consider his account of

---

[9] The skeptical position is put with clarity and force by R. Dworkin in an unpublished paper, *Hart's Posthumous Reply*, which is quoted by A. Marmor, op. cit., p. 5.
[10] See the discussion in J. W. Harris, *Legal Philosophies* (2nd edn, Oxford, 1997) pp. 124–7.
[11] See further J. Coleman, 'Incorporationism, Conventionality, and the Practical Difference' in J. Coleman (ed) *Hart's Postscript*.

the rule of recognition, and what it means to accept it, to be incomplete and wish he had examined it more fully.

The issue of acceptance of the rule of recognition is also central to law-and-society. In the first place, we need to know more about the notion itself; we need to know whether acceptance in a modern legal system has a social dimension not present in other legal orders. Secondly, if acceptance by officials is a general feature of a legal system, what effect this has on their attitude to specific laws. As to the first, a distinction should be made between the *fact* of acceptance and the *reasons* for acceptance. The fact of acceptance means the rules of an activity are adopted for use, while the reasons for acceptance explain and justify their adoption. If you play tennis, by entering into the game you accept its rules as binding on you; when I give my lectures in the university, I abide by the rules as part of the activity of lecturing; becoming a rancher in Shasta County includes accepting the rules about how ranchers deal with each other.

The same applies to law: if you are an official (and also if you are a citizen) you accept a set of legal rules for dealing with certain issues. That means regarding the rules as binding, which in turn means having an internal view of them. The normativity or obligation-creating nature of rules is explained in this way: in entering into the activity, you accept its rules as binding and that applies to tennis, lecturing, or law. This explanation of the normativity of rules is convincing with regard to games and other activities, but is there not something different about law? Both the logic and the sociology are similar: the judge, the policeman, and the welfare officer apply the rules of law as the basis for their daily decisions; being a judge, a policeman, or a welfare officer means being engaged in legal activities and therefore accepting its laws as binding. In none of these cases is the question asked whether the law is binding, since in becoming a judge, a policeman, or a welfare officer that is taken for granted. The newly-recruited police officer in a moment of doubt might ask himself why he ever joined up; once having done so, he is unlikely to ask himself whether the law is binding. A different kind of example comes from membership of the European Community. Once the United Kingdom had joined by signing the Treaty of Rome and enacting the 1972 *European Community Act*, some doubts were raised as to the status of European law within the UK. The doubts were settled within the existing conventions governing the UK and the changes to them brought about by membership of the EC; once the courts declared the status of EC law within the UK, they were accepted without question as binding legal rules.

Support for this approach to the normativity of law is also found in the idea of law as *normatively closed,* an idea associated with Luhmann, by which he means that law is an inherently normative system, working according to certain internal processes or operations, the result of which is a decision of legal or illegal. The rules of law are normative just in the sense that they decide whether an action is legal or illegal; that is the end to which the concept of normativity refers. There is no need to find some external basis for the normativity, since that is law's defining quality, the removal of which means that you are no longer dealing with law.[12] The upshot is clear: if we enter into the legal process, we enter a normative zone in which there is no need to search for a sense of normativity over and above that which comes from entering the zone.

The reason why this account of the acceptance of rules, while hardly contentious in a great range of activities, meets resistance when applied to law has two aspects. One is that law claims an authority backed by force, and the other is because law is often concerned with matters of moral significance. On both counts, it could be said, law needs to be grounded in something more than the manner in which officials happen to converge in their practice of law. However, these concerns, while justified, are rightly addressed in considering the *reasons* for accepting the rule of recognition. It is here at the level of reasons that officials and others decide whether or not to accept the legal practices of the society. At this point, moral and practical issues arise about the law and whether it should or should not be supported. Andrei Marmor puts the point in this way: 'Whether judges, or anyone else, should or should not respect the rule of recognition of a legal system is purely a moral issue that can only be resolved by moral arguments . . . . The existence of a social practice, in itself, does not provide anyone with an obligation to engage in the practice'.[13] 'Moral' here is too strong, unless it is understood in its fullest sense to include the idea that certain social goods are likely to be best secured by a stable and effective system of laws. The securing of those goods may be held to be of moral value, but that is not the point: that they are goods valued by the society is normally reason enough for accepting and entering into the practices of law.

Practices and conventions emerge and grow over the course of a society's history, out of which comes a sense of how to deal with issues of

---

[12] N. Luhmann, op. cit., chapters 2 and 10 in particular.

[13] The general issue is explained with clarity by Andrei Marmor from whose account I have benefited greatly: A. Marmor, op. cit., pp. 1 *ff.*

government and authority, how to govern effectively and yet with restraint, how to ensure that social goods are adequately provided. Among such practices and conventions is the rule of recognition. Nowhere is this historical dimension more deeply engraved on the practice of law than in the United Kingdom where long stability has meant, not only that the conventions and practices are historically grounded, but also that knowledge of them requires delving into historical understandings. At the other extreme, even in the traumatized, new democracies of eastern Europe, fresh beginnings are, on closer scrutiny, deeply intertwined with historical memory and experience.

5.4 REASONS FOR ACCEPTANCE: IS MODERN LAW SPECIAL?

Hart's legal theory is concerned with the fact of acceptance of a legal order not the reasons. The reasons why officials and others enter into and maintain the conventions as to what constitutes law are likely to be diverse, perhaps based on morals, a disinterested commitment to the social goods that result, or pure self-interest. Hume thought that the legal order was secure in the hands of officials because they are paid to preserve it.[14] Hart's need to steer clear of the reasons for (as opposed to the fact of) acceptance is understandable: a general description of a municipal legal system has to cover such a wide a range of legal orders, from the good to the tolerable to the very bad, that it could hardly find common ground among the reasons officials could have for supporting them. In narrowing the enquiry to modern legal systems, we are not so constrained and should ask whether it is enough to note as a social fact that officials accept a rule of recognition without consideration of their reasons. Could it be the case that a modern legal order is characterized by, perhaps is conditional upon, officials having reasons of a particular kind?.

In the first chapter of *Natural Law and Natural Rights*, John Finnis argues that descriptively it may be enough that officials accept a legal order, but if we are to understand the point and purpose of law we must ask from what point of view and for what reasons they accept it. Applying this idea to a modern legal order, we should focus on the social goods that a modern society expects from it; social goods are, in turn, grounded in the social relations characterizing modern society.

[14] D. Hume, *An Essay Concerning Human Understanding* (Ed. L. A. Setby-Bigge) (Oxford, 1888).

One manifestation of social relations is the need for the social goods of security of person and property, and stability in private arrangements and transactions, as displayed in contracts and promises. Since these are the minimum social goods expected of any municipal legal order with settled rules and effective government institutions, they are no basis for separating non-modern orders, such as the former Soviet Union or the People's Republic of China, from modern western legal orders. At a deeper level of social relations, we encounter more exacting expectations as to social goods, in particular, the provision of services and the *regulation* of activities, themselves legitimate, in order to advance and protect other social goods and interests, whether the environment, the workplace, or equal opportunities. A commitment to these goods on the part of officials marks a step forward in the course of which some legal orders that meet the barest conditions of rules and officials would drop away. However, we have not yet reached a point of qualitative distinction between Hart's reasonable mature legal orders and those designated as modern.

That distinction lies in the bond of trust between governors and the governed, and the social good in government and administration being conducted according to the terms of the bond. The difference between a legal order in which officials have whatever powers they choose to give themselves, and to use them however they think fit, is qualitatively different from one in which their powers are limited and for the use of which they must make account to citizens. The difference is that, on the first view, officials hold power for themselves or for interests they serve, while on the second it is held on trust for the people. This is quite distinct from political processes such as the growth of democracy, although a democratic system is more conducive to the bond; instead, it is the specifically legal expression of a set of social relations between citizens and officials that is unique to a few modern legal orders. Its practical expression is to be found in the combination of general principles of constitutional law, and the very specific and often technical doctrines of administrative law. Any doubt as to the significance of this set of social relations in differentiating those that have them from those that do not, would soon be removed by reflection on the difference between social relations between citizens and officials in a communist system compared with a western European model. The realization that officials have only the powers given by law and that they can be held to account for their use, was, for the first generation of law students in the post-communist period, a moment of liberation.

Some would want to express differently this configuration of social relations distinctive of modern legal orders and the social goods they generate. Human rights would be an alternative candidate: they underpin social relations in declaring that each person has certain basic entitlements which must be respected. From this foundation naturally follows the bond between citizens and officials and the restrictions on powers that flow from it. A human rights approach deepens the foundations on which social relations are based, although it is not the only basis for the bond, nor historically a major force. The rule of law is another approach to the same issue, its basis being that the legal system provides a particular form according to which government and administration are exercised. It is enough for now to know that the special relations between citizens and officials are one of the defining features of a modern legal order, and the stance from which the actions of officials are to be understood.

In summing up, two general points should be noted. In the first place, the idea of a modern legal order is starting to take shape. While all recognizably legal orders are directed at providing certain social goods, the distinguishing mark of modern legal orders is the unique combination of the social goods of security and stability, the positive provision of welfare and the restriction of activities through regulation, and finally the containment of official power. The basis of the combination is to be found in the equally distinctive configuration of social relations in modern societies. The second point to note is that the interest in securing these social goods provides officials and others with a set of reasons for accepting the legal order, the corollary being that unless they subscribe to those reasons, modern legal orders will fail. Other factors may, of course, enter into their motives and intentions, but unless there is a shared foundation of disinterested commitment to advancing and protecting the social relations particular to modern societies, the legal order will lose its bearings. These are observations about the social structure of modern societies but, in accordance with the fourth methodological principle, are also normatively compelling. Finally it should be observed, that just as customary societies were vulnerable to changes in their social relations, and were unable to withstand external influences on them, so the social relations of modern societies are vulnerable and difficult to sustain. In this case, it is not the pressure of colonial interference or corrupting influences; instead, the risk is inherent in the very character of the social relations, for they run counter to the forces of natural self-interest and prejudice on the part of both officials and non-officials, and in that way are both artificial and fragile. The idea that government is restrained by its relations to citizens, that every person by dint of being a person has rights, that each must give

to support the other, illustrate the point. This helps to explain why law
has become so prominent in modern societies, at national, regional, and
global levels. It is needed to sustain those artificial and fragile social
relations, and to produce against the odds specific social goods.

5.5 VARIABLE ACCEPTANCE OF RULES

Acceptance of the rule of recognition is presented in legal theory as an
all-or-nothing affair: I either accept the rules about giving lectures or not;
the ranchers accept the community rules about straying cattle or not;
policemen accept the rule of recognition or not. Whether or not Hart
meant to convey acceptance in this way is not clear because of a tendency
to move backwards and forwards between analytical statements and social
reality; and his account should be taken as an analytical statement of the
nature of a rule: a rule is accepted or not. From the law-and-society view,
the idea is implausible, and on this Weber is a surer guide, for Weber
draws a line between the validity of law and compliance with it. He also
notes that *validity*, being itself a belief on the part of the participants in
the legitimacy of a legal order, is a variable. He writes: '. . . for sociological
purposes there does not exist, as there does for the law, a rigid alternative
between the validity and lack of validity of a given order. On the contrary,
there is a gradual transition between the two extremes'[15] You might
accept the rules about lecturing and follow them to the letter, keep contextual contingencies to a minimum, and ignore everything else, short of a
fire alarm. You are more likely to regard the rules as matters to be taken
seriously and generally to be followed, yet see them more as guidelines
than rules, regard them as serving some social good, while recognizing
that other social goods impinge on them, and being willing to give quarter
to conditional contingencies. This pattern is typical of social rules where
acceptance is contingent and often partial. Among the different types of
rules, some encourage more complete and unequivocal acceptance than
others. Quite different from the rules of lecturing are those of the army or
a prison, or those of a sport, where acceptance is likely to be conclusive, in
the first case because argument would be foolhardy, in the second because
you would be out of the game.

The acceptance of social rules is a conditional and variable notion that
can be stronger or weaker, more or less contingent. A rule may be
internalized in the sense that you could not imagine acting otherwise than

---

[15] M. Weber, op. cit., Volume i, p. 32.

in accordance with it, an example of which has been given of a Jewish or Moslem butcher not selling pork, the rule against it being so embedded in the culture of the community that the butcher's breaking it is unthinkable.[16] But most rules are not like that. An Oxford historian, known for his forceful views on many matters including history, is alleged to have said that he held strong opinions lightly. Rules often attract similar attitudes with apparently strict rules being accepted lightly. You might accept a social rule and act on it, leaving open that in some circumstances you would not; or you might accept a rule and act on it, provided there is no better reason for acting otherwise; or a student might accept two sets of rules, say the informal rules that hold among friends and those of the university, knowing they sometimes conflict, but leaving open their resolution. A rule may be accepted as a presumption of how one will act, which can be weaker or stronger, while retaining the option of acting otherwise; we could go further and accept a rule just in the sense that it is a matter to take into account, one factor, probably an important one, among several.[17]

From the contingent acceptance of rules, consequences follow: we now see how groups and individual persons differ in the way they regard the rule of recognition and other legal rules. Instead of all officials having a common attitude to such matters, they are likely to vary; the judge, the policeman, and the welfare officer share a general commitment to the legal system, but in important ways differ. All are concerned with the daily application of the law, but having diverse concerns they approach it from viewpoints tied to those concerns and their professional networks. The most important task for the judge is to uphold the law and to give authoritative guidance, while for the policeman the faithful application of law is only part of a web of other concerns and interests through which the law is filtered; social welfare officers, for their part, regard the law as a tool to be used in relieving poverty or helping those in need, so it is useful to the extent it does that. When these factors are considered, the general commitment to the law appears differently; the settled disposition to uphold the law, another of Hart's terms, is present in each case but variable as to the importance attached to it by officials. Weber approaches the matter slightly differently. He considers acceptance of the legitimacy of the legal order necessary for its coming into existence and continuing;

---

[16] See: A. Etzioni, 'Social Norms: Internalization, Persuasion, and History', 34 (2000) *Law and Society Review* 157.

[17] See: L. Lessig, 'The Regulation of Social Meaning', 62 (1995) *Univ. of Chicago Law Review*, 943; C. Sunstein, 'Social Norms and Social Roles', 96 (1996) *Columbia Law Review*, 903.

at the same time, both citizens and officials may accept its legitimacy in a general way (possibly variable) even if they do not always, in practice, act according to its rules.[18]

The rule of recognition is a metaphor for the acceptance of a system of law as a whole, as a set of social practices and conventions about what counts as law in a society. In societies such as the United Kingdom, and the United States of America and Canada, officials and the people, on the whole, accept the system fairly much without question, although within general acceptance marginal variations occur among groups as to the quality and strength of acceptance. Other western European countries have a broadly similar system of laws, which are generally accepted, although it is said that the Italians, for instance, have a lot of strict laws they take lightly. The history of the European Union presents some challenging issues concerning acceptance, for here a new rule of recognition has been inserted into and made to work in parallel with the national systems of member states. All member states accept, in a general way, the additional legal order, even if experience suggests that at both official and popular levels the quality of acceptance varies across member states. Research conducted in some of the new eastern European democracies shows that, although their legal systems are reasonably well-developed, the levels of acceptance are often low; law is recognized as law but then, in many areas of social activity, more or less ignored.[19] From the mention of these cases, it is evident that the nature and quality of acceptance of the rule of recognition, of the legal system as a whole, is a major variable in the social study of law and plainly warrants further consideration.

5.6 FROM THE RULE OF RECOGNITION TO SPECIFIC LAWS

The rule of recognition confers validity on specific laws made in accordance with it. Statutes enacted by Parliament, regulations promulgated by a minister, and regulations and directives passed by the European Union, all derive their validity from a complex set of rules of recognition. Officials and others regard them as binding because they accept as a whole the system of which these laws are part. We should now make a distinction between acceptance of the rule of recognition, of *the system as a whole*, and acceptance and application of *specific laws*. It is not unusual for a group of

[18] M. Weber, op. cit., p. 312.
[19] M. Kurkchiyan in D. J. Galligan and M. Kurkchiyan (eds), *Law and Informal Practices in Post-Communist Societies* (Oxford, 2003).

officials to accept the system as a whole, but then to have a more contingent and variable approach to specific laws. The police officer belongs to a professional group for whom the upholding of the law is a serious commitment, and yet when it comes to applying the law relating to the arrest, custody, and interrogation of suspects, the imperative of obtaining evidence to secure convictions means that the rules governing these matters are compromised. Not only police officers but also other officials modify, compromise, and sometimes ignore laws in order to attain other ends, or because of the competing strength of professional conventions, or for other reasons. At the same time, all such officials, with just a few exceptions, have a general and unquestioning commitment to the legal system as a whole.[20]

This distinction between acceptance of the system as a whole and attitudes towards specific laws is clearer if we focus on the reasons officials and others have for accepting the legal order. Since they have good reasons for that, a presumption of acceptance of specific laws follows; then, when it comes to implementing specific laws, other reasons come into consideration and may compete with the presumption. Those other reasons will be of different kinds, some based on nothing more than a lack of resources, others attributable to competing values and understandings, others still a concern to advance what are taken to be the purposes of the law, or to prevent their corruption. Studies in law-and-society have long recognized that the degree of official acceptance of, or willingness to depart from, specific laws is a variable in implementation and compliance. Now we can see how this fits within a fuller understanding of the social character of law: the variable character of acceptance, at both general and particular levels, is neither an aberration from how law should be, nor evidence of a gap between law as it is written and law as it is practiced; it is, instead, a central feature of a working legal system. In a modern legal order, it is to be expected that officials and citizens have good and persuasive reasons for accepting both the system as a whole and specific laws; they also have reasons for, at times, giving priority to other concerns.

5.7 CONCLUSION ABOUT LAW AS SOCIAL RULES

The notion of law as sets of social rules combining in a special way is one of the main contributions of *The Concept of Law*. Having considered this

---

[20] In an important piece of research, Simon Halliday found precisely that: S. Halliday, 'The Influence of Judicial Review on Bureaucratic Decision Making', 2000 *Public Law* 110.

notion from a law-and-society stance, we should now draw together the threads of analysis. One of the authors on whom Hart placed store, and whom he cites approvingly, was the philosopher Peter Winch, who made the claim in a book published at the time Hart was writing his, that all meaningful human action is rule-governed.[21] That Hart adopted and shared that view is plain, for his account of law is based squarely on it. However, in a second edition of his book published many years later, Winch retracted vital parts of his original claim; he writes: 'Things became worse . . . where I claimed that "all behaviour which is meaningful (therefore all specifically human behaviour) is *ipso facto* rule-governed." . . . I did, it is true, attempt to qualify this later . . . by distinguishing different kinds of rules, but I do not now think this enough to put things right'.[22] Later, he adds as an approximation of his modified view: 'The kinds of relevance past experience has to current behaviour can be brought out only insofar as that behaviour exemplifies rules or is, in relevant respects, analogous to behaviour which exemplifies rules'.[23] If we were engaged in intellectual history, it would be tempting to say that, had this retraction come earlier, Hart's account of social rules and his salient fact of social life might have been different. He might have acknowledged that rules range from the clear-line to the discretionary, and that even clear-line rules are only part of the social context in which they occur.

Over the course of the last three chapters, several themes have emerged. After following Hart in starting with law as rules, starting at the top of the ladder as it were, we were soon drawn downwards to their foundations, to their social context. Consideration of the social context and the way rules intertwine with its contingent variables requires modification of Hart's claim that rules are generally adequate guides to action, his salient fact of social life. The interplay of rules and context leads on to discovery of a sense of law and legal experience in the expression and maintenance of social relations, a sense readily visible in more traditional societies and the early common law, and prior to and more fundamental than that expressed in rules. In modern legal orders, rules have become the main legal vehicle for expressing social relations, sustaining their foundations, and often changing them. Tensions between those that develop spontaneously over time and those decreed by law are inevitable, while much of the interplay between law and its social context consists of the resolution of those tensions.

---

[21] P. Winch, op. cit.   [22] *Ibid*, Second Edition, p. *xiv*.   [23] *Ibid* p. *xv ii*.

The next set of issues relates to the claim that law is a system of rules held together by a set of conventional rules. Rules of recognition have their own contextual contingencies, which again means reaching down into their social context, comprising here the governmental structure of a society. Rules of recognition, like other social rules, account for part of the social experience of law but are incomplete and cannot account for contextual contingencies within the social context, and in turn the fuller experience of law. Examination of the attitudes of officials towards the rule of recognition shows that the strength of their commitment varies, as does their attitude to specific laws, both due to the influence of the social context. It is as if there were a convention, implicit rather than explicit, allowing officials to have recourse to considerations beyond those stated in the rules. The case for thinking so is strengthened when we consider the reasons officials have for subscribing to the rule of recognition in a modern society. In order to sustain and develop its distinctive social relations, expressed in ideas of security and stability, welfare and regulation and, most of all, controlled government, modern society needs a legal order of a very particular kind. Harmony between the legal order and social relations, as Durkheim envisaged in his concept of *restitutive law*, is hard to create and sustain, but in modern societies is attained to a tolerable degree; that, after all, is one of their main features. Officials have a special role in both creating and sustaining that harmony, their opportunity being the making, interpretation, and application of law. Conventional rules will never be an adequate basis for expressing the relationship between law and its social context. Officials have the opportunity and the duty to maintain harmony between the deeper social relations of a society and law; this means both a commitment to the rules and a willingness to go behind and beyond the rules. It does not signal the end of rules but indicates a better understanding of how they work and their place in society. The importance of rules in social life is not in question, but their presentation as adequate guides to action prospectively, or as an adequate basis for understanding action retrospectively, in law or elsewhere, has to be modified.

NOTES

Hart on the rules of recognition

Hart explains the rule of recognition in this way: 'This is not a necessity, but a luxury, found in advanced social systems whose members come not merely to accept separate rules piecemeal, but are committed to the acceptance in advance of general classes of rule, marked out by general criteria of validity. In the simpler form of society, we must wait and see whether a rule gets accepted as a rule or not; in a system with a basic rule of recognition we can say that before a rule is actually made, that it *will* be valid *if* it conforms to the requirements of the rule of recognition'. *The Concept of Law* (p. 229).

On reasons for acceptance: 'In fact . . . allegiance to the system may be based on many different considerations: calculations of long-term interest; disinterested interest in others; an unreflecting inherited or traditional attitude; or the mere wish to do as others do. There is indeed no reason why those who accept the authority of the system should not examine their conscience and decide that, morally, they ought not to accept it yet for a variety of reasons continue to do so' *The Concept of Law*, pp. 195–199).

On social conventions

The leading analysis of social conventions is:
D. Lewis, *Conventions: A Philosophical Study* (Oxford, 1968).

The idea of constitutive rules

The idea that rules are constitutive of an activity is well-explained in Andrei Marmor: *Positive Law and Objective Values* Chapter 1.

On scepticism of the rule of recognition

R. Dworkin, *Taking Rights Seriously* (London, 1978).
Dworkin has recently written: 'The idea of law as a set of discrete standards, which we might in principle individuate and count, seems to me a scholastic fiction': *Justice in Robes* (forthcoming).
J. Lucas, 'The rule of recognition' in J. Hacker and J. Raz (eds), *Law, Morality, and Society: Essays in Honour of H. L. A. Hart* (Oxford, 1996).

The fact of acceptance and the reasons for acceptance

This distinction also casts fresh light on the *internal point of view* of rules. Once it is realized that the normativity of law derives from its nature as a set of rules, which derives in turn from their being members of a working legal system, then the difference between the official who has the internal view and the person who wants to avoid running into trouble loses much of its force. Both are accepting the normativity of the rules; where they differ is in the reasons they have for accepting it, which affects how they regard the rules. If the internal view means more than accepting the normativity of legal rules, then that must be attributable to reasons outside law. Hart, I suggest, was never entirely clear about the status of the internal view, and tended to merge it with the reasons for acceptance. Weber, recognizing this position, describes it in terms of the *validity* of law, from which derives normativity, and the social reality that people use the rules for different ends: (*Economy and Society*, Volume II, pp. 31–33).

Reasons for acceptance are often expressed in the language of *legitimacy*. According to Weber: 'action may be guided by the belief in the existence of a legitimate order' (*Economy and Society*, p. 31). To believe in a legitimate order is to regard it as binding. 'Such belief naturally increases the probability that action will in fact conform to it, often to a very considerable degree' (p. 31). Three hundred pages later, Weber adds two points. *First*, people comply with legal rules not only because they accept them as legitimate, but also for a variety of other reasons. *Secondly*, it is not necessary for a valid legal act that: 'all those who share a belief in (its validity), actually live in accordance with that belief at all time'. (p. 312).

For further discussion of this point, see : J. Habermas, *Between Facts and Norms* (Boston, Mass., 1996) Sections 2 and 3.

In addition to A. Marmor's book cited above, the following has helpful and important analyses of acceptance of law and its normativity: M. Kramer, *In Defence of Legal Positivism* (Oxford, 1999) Chapter 8.

Internalization of Norms

For discussion of various accounts of internalization see: T. Rostain, 'Educating Homo Economicus' (2000) 34, *Law and Society Review*, 973. Rostain concludes that, to understand how social norms function, it is necessary to understand their social meanings, which must, in turn, derive from the conventions and understandings in a particular social environment.

Conditional acceptance of the rule of recognition

The new eastern European democracies bring out well the idea that law is normative as a matter of its internal character, but then often socially ineffective. These issues are discussed at some length in a set of case-studies, see D. J. Galligan and M. Kurkchiyan (eds) *Law and Informal Practices: The Post-Communist Experience*.

Acceptance of the rule of recognition and acceptance of specific laws

The way officials implement laws has been one of the most focused areas of socio-legal research, much of which illustrates the way specific laws are modified, compromised, or largely ignored by officials, and the reasons for doing so. Among the many examples that could be chosen, the following are important and representative:

G. Richardson and others, *Policing Pollution*; K. Hawkins, *Environment and Enforcement* (Oxford, 1982).

6

Social Spheres

6.1 INTRODUCING SOCIAL SPHERES

Among the various ways in which law interacts with other parts of society, two are of most interest here: one is when officials make, interpret, and apply the law, the other when groups, associations, or individuals conduct their activities subject to the law. In the first case, officials accept and make sense of the law, and then apply it to others, while in the second case, associations and individuals accept the law and apply it to their own activities. Two different images come to mind: one views officials and citizens as individuals discharging duties and exercising powers according to sets of primary and secondary rules, as if this were a largely self-contained task, and as if each were a solitary individual acting for his or her own part. The other image is of officials and citizens dealing with law from a social setting with its own conventions and understandings. The first image is sometimes an accurate representation of what happens but the second is more typical of how people deal with the law.

In order to capture that image and develop it further, the idea of a *social sphere* is introduced. A social sphere may be described as an area of activity in which the participants share understandings and conventions about the activity, and which influence and guide the way they engage in it. 'Social sphere' is not an expression commonly encountered and several more familiar ones could serve just as well. *Institutions* is currently much used; *arenas, practices, traditions,* and *networks of civic engagement* are used from time-to-time, each with its own nuances. Nothing turns on the term, but the idea I want to convey of people acting within an environment structured by conventions and understandings is nicely captured in the notion of a social sphere. Once we recognize the concept, social spheres are all around. The lecturing case is a good example: university lecturers have a common set of understandings and conventions as to the purposes of lecturing and what is acceptable practice. The practice of psychiatry is a powerful case of a denser social sphere, with density expressing the relative power of social spheres in influencing their members.

How, it might be asked, do social spheres fit into the discussion of previous chapters? According to the second methodological principle, the study of law in society focuses on how officials and citizens understand and deal with it. Legal rules have to be interpreted and applied by officials and citizens, while the rule of recognition as a set of practices depends for its effectiveness on being accepted and applied by officials and others. Acceptance is a variable notion, as we have seen, being stronger or weaker depending on the society, and on variations among groups within it; we have also seen how acceptance of the rule of recognition creates a presumption in favour of specific laws. We have discovered the social world in which rules occur and seen how conventions and understandings within it affect the way rules are accepted, understood, and applied. And we have uncovered in social relations the foundations of that social world. In social spheres, we now have a concept that gives structure to that social world and whose study will reveal much about it. That study is guided by the third methodological principle according to which law-and-society needs to go beyond the subjective understandings of individuals and to examine how those understandings are shaped by social formations designated here as social spheres.

6.2 CONCEPT OF A SOCIAL SPHERE

Consider the following case. The *Mental Health Act* of England and Wales, enacted by the Parliament of the United Kingdom in 1983, was designed to give better protection to patients compulsorily detained for treatment. The reforms were the outcome of a campaign aimed at improving the rights of patients by providing measures to protect them against 'unjustified therapy or deprivation of their civil liberty'.[1] Treatment for mental illness is normally voluntary but in some circumstances patients may be compulsorily detained and treated by psychiatrists, who make the decision and who have discretion in doing so. Research conducted into the workings of the new law shows that psychiatrists experience tension between the legal provisions protecting patients' rights and the clinical assessment that treatment is necessary. The result tends to be that clinical assessment prevails over rights. It has been suggested that: 'it is doctors, and corporately the Royal College of Psychiatrists, who have most frequently called for greater restriction of patient freedom and

[1] N. Eastman and J. Peay, *Law Without Enforcement* (Oxford, 1998).

correspondingly greater medical power'.[2] In decisions to compel treatment and when to release patients from treatment, the tension is plain: the doctors are naturally impelled by their training and profession to regard a patient as an object of treatment, with the law as an unwelcome intrusion, an alien force that proceeds according to a different logic and rationale, and which is at odds with the model of treatment. The concern that patients should be dealt with here according to legal rules rather than clinical needs runs counter to the basic premises of medicine in general and psychiatry in particular. It has been concluded that: 'unless the clinical context within which to operate is understood, the legal regulation of psychiatry runs the danger of being either counter-productive or irrelevant'.[3]

The image we are left with is of a professional group conducting an activity within a *social sphere* in which meanings and understandings, conventions and values, practices and procedures about the nature and purpose of the activity, are settled and powerful. Social spheres like this are commonly encountered: professions, such as medicine and law, government agencies, such as the police and welfare officers, businesses, social clubs, and so on; university departments, Oxford colleges, and convents are among countless examples that could be added. When legal rules try to change or modify the behaviour of such groups and associations, they must enter the social sphere and confront the conventions and understandings within it. In some cases the law will be compatible, perhaps reinforcing the conventions and understandings, for instance where existing business practices are given a legal basis. In other cases, the object of the law is to change the conventions and understandings, as in the case of the psychiatrists and mental health patients. Between the two cases, many different shades of compatibility and incompatibility occur.

6.3 FOUNDATIONS OF SOCIAL SPHERES

The idea of social spheres draws on the study of *institutions* which may be taken to be 'the rules of the game in a society or, more formally, . . . the humanely devised constraints that shape human interaction'.[4] Douglass North, from whom this definition is taken, adds that: 'institutions are the

[2] *Ibid*, p. 27.
[3] G. Richardson and O. Thorold, 'Law as a protector of rights' in N. Eastman and J. Peay (eds), op. cit., p. 110.
[4] D. North, *Institutions, Institutional Change, and Economic Performance* p. 3.

framework within which human interaction takes place',[5] the idea being that whenever people come together to carry out some activity, they form rules to govern and guide them. The tendency to do so appears to be deeply embedded in any context of shared activities. Social spheres have more to them than rules, which are an unduly narrow basis for describing the normative environment; values and standards, dispositions and orientations lacking the specificity of rules, also form part of the environment. As the lecturing case shows, cutting short a lecture, or pausing in the middle, or not delivering it in a foreign language, are all explained and justified, not by reference to a rule but to much more imprecise standards and values. A similar idea appears in Philip Selznick's study of the Tennessee Valley Authority where a government agency, created and directed by legal rules, developed its own values and standards for doing its job.[6] This meant 'to infuse with value beyond the technical requirements of the task at hand'. Decisions within and concerning the legal rules 'are structured by socially mediated values and normative frameworks'.[7] In current terms we should probably say that around the rules there developed a set of informal norms, understandings, and dispositions.

The normative context of a social sphere merges into, or perhaps more accurately emerges from, meanings and perceptions, expectations and understandings. This *cognitive* dimension is as fundamental as the normative in shaping the way a participant perceives and understands; it is the basis for developing the activity and distinctive understandings and attitudes about it.[8] W. R. Scott has called it: 'the frame through which meaning is made'.[9] The psychiatrists in our example are trained to think about the practice of their profession in very particular ways; they acquire views as to the character of psychiatry, its ends and purposes, and how a patient fits within them. University professors, police officers, and barristers all have distinctive attitudes and understandings concerning the nature and purpose of their professions. Scott also draws attention to a third aspect of institutions that is less prominent than the other two, namely, its capacity to *regulate* its members. Social spheres have a similar capacity in both setting standards of behaviour and then bringing to bear on their members pressure to comply; a capacity that Foucault might have had in mind in formulating his notion of

---

[5] *Ibid*, p. 4.   [6] P. Selznick, *TVA and the Grass Roots* (Berkeley, 1949).
[7] *Ibid*, pp. 16–17.
[8] The cognitive element is brought-out well in W. R. Scott, *Institutions and Organizations* (London, 1996).
[9] *Ibid*, p. 40.

'governmentality'.[10] The pressures on the ranchers of Shasta County were informal but effective, with deviation from accepted patterns of behaviour resulting in ostracism from a close-knit community;[11] similarly for the New York diamond traders.[12] The psychiatrists, in common with other professional groups, practice against a backdrop of formal as well as informal norms, the former set by law, the latter by custom and usage based around the purpose of psychiatry, its values, and what it means to be a good psychiatrist.

The norms governing an activity derive from different sources. Social activities occurring spontaneously and informally, such as the relations among a group of farmers, are likely to be governed by rules based on agreement, emerging over time and typically unwritten; those of a barristers' chambers are more likely to combine written rules agreed from time to time with informal practices emerging from daily experience. In the case of government institutions, courts, or administrative bodies, the position is different; they owe their existence to a set of legal rules, which are then likely to be encased in a network of informal rules whose purposes are to help in interpreting and applying the legal rules, or perhaps modifying them in accordance with other interests and values.

It is usual to draw a distinction between an *institution* as the rules governing an activity, and an *organization* as the people combining to perform the activity.[13] North describes organizations as 'groups of individuals bound by some common purpose to achieve objectives'.[14] The common purposes could be those of a sporting team, a university department, or a set of barristers' chambers; they could also be those of a government agency or department, a set of courts, or a police force. While the common purpose unites the participants, the institutional rules govern the way the sport is played or the activity conducted. Whether organization is the best term is debatable; it is clumsy and can be misleading, and sometimes *association*, although not perfect, would be preferable. However, the terms are now settled and a change would cause confusion, so let us keep the term *organization* to express the combination of people for a common purpose, and *institution* for the rules by which it is pursued. *Social sphere* often includes both the idea of people combining for a

---

[10] See: A. Hunt and G. Wickham, *Foucault and Law: Towards a Sociology of Law as Governance* (London, 1994).

[11] R. Ellickson, *Order Without Law*.

[12] J. Coleman, 'Social Capital in the Creation of Human Capital' (1998) 94 in *American Journal of Sociology*: Supplement 95.

[13] See for example: W.R. Scott, op. cit. [14] D. North, op. cit.

common purpose and the rules. But it goes further: it envisages an environment of conventions and understandings including but going beyond rules.

The separation of the rules of an activity from the purposes of those engaged in it is often warranted, but not always. It may be true for the farmers of Shasta County whose purposes are to farm and who then devise rules to facilitate their doing so. In other cases, a sharp distinction cannot be drawn between the purposes of the activity for which a group comes together *and* the rules defining the activity.[15] We do not decide to play tennis and then ask what the rules are, since tennis is an activity partly defined by rules. It would be different if our purpose were just to hit a ball backwards and forwards, but as soon as we think in terms of tennis, we are thinking about a rule-defined activity. A similar point applies to institutions created by law, such as regulatory agencies, where the purposes of the officials who staff them are defined by legal rules. Groups associating in this way may have other purposes besides those expressed in the rules of the activity, or adopt them as experience grows, but the role of rules in initiating and defining the purposes of social activities is itself significant.

The relationship between the conventions of an activity and those participating in it is dynamic, in that the performing of the activity may lead to modification of the rules or the creation of new ones. In some cases, conventions made by informal processes or growing out of practices are closely tied to the attitudes and experiences of the participants; in other cases, the conventions are created more formally as rules and are less open to informal modification. If we play tennis, we generally stick to the rules, although two players against one is not unheard of and is still, loosely-speaking, tennis. Legal rules, again, present interesting variations. Where they seek to regulate an activity in which people would engage anyhow, the legal rules may be more-or-less adopted by the participants, or they may be modified, marginalized, or ignored, depending on how compatible or not they are with the activity, and on whether the activity itself is open to change. Where the activity is itself created by legal rules, as in the case of administrative agencies, say, informal rules often emerge in order to interpret the legal rules, or even to modify or marginalize them. This is not to say that legal rules are endlessly malleable, but only that once officials enter into a law-directed activity, a social

---

[15] The force of this point was brought out in Chapter II in relation to the rule of recognition.

process creating informal conventions and understanding begins and potentially affects the formal rules.

6.4 SOCIAL SPHERES AS DISTINCT AND SEPARATE

The image of social spheres so far conveyed is of an activity conducted according to understandings and conventions that are reasonably settled and often powerful. A large part of daily life is lived by each of us, acting in different capacities and for different purposes, within sets of social spheres. We all belong to several and move among them, with overlap between them and with each exerting influence over us. Psychiatrists spend much of their time practicing psychiatry but probably have families; they may belong to a social or sporting club and possibly go to church. Each activity has its social sphere and each leaves its mark on them as they move from one to the other, some more visibly influential than others. Contradictions and tensions often appear in moving from one to the other, with the attitudes and norms of one having to be shed or adjusted on entering another. A coherent plan of life is worth striving for, but in practice it is not unusual to separate one activity from another and to live our lives in fragments.[16] Psychiatrists are probably as liberal-minded, law-abiding, and rights-respecting as anyone else, but when acting in their professional capacity, they are directed by its imperatives and have difficulty coping with those, such as rights-norms, from another sphere. Social spheres help in understanding in extreme cases how a cultivated person degenerates into a torturer or, in a more familiar case, how the same person appears to hold sets of incompatible views.

The notion of *autopoietic* systems developed by Luhmann and others may be invoked to add a dimension to social spheres, and to help in capturing the right emphasis and focus. An autopoietic system has several features. It is an area of activity which 'produces by itself all the distinctions and concepts that it uses'.[17] It 'creates its own territory by its own operations (which are at the same time social operations) . . .'.[18] And finally, such activities are relatively distinct and closed-off from other activities in society; as Luhmann puts it: 'We call those systems

---

[16] For an expression of this idea, see: J. Finnis, *Natural Law and Natural Rights*.
[17] N. Luhmann, *Law as a Social System*, p. 70.   [18] *Ibid*, p. 73.

operatively closed that rely on their own network of operations for the production of their own operations and which, in this sense, reproduce themselves'.[19] An activity such as psychiatry has all three features: it works according to its own concepts of what psychiatry is, and practices it according to those concepts and the conventions enveloping it; it plainly marks-out a territory as being distinctively the practice of psychiatry; and it is closed-off from other activities in the sense that it has its own rules and practices. The rules and practices of psychiatry are self-contained in that they do not rely on, and are unrelated, to the rules and practices of architecture, accounting, or the Church.

An additional feature of an autopoeitic activity as explained by Luhmann, and of importance to the notion of social spheres, is the relationship between an activity and external influences. Luhmann explains the relationship in terms of an activity and its environment, which means simply that activities other than psychiatry, law for instance, can influence what happens within psychiatry, *but only if* they are translated into its language, meanings, conventions, and understandings. The stipulations of law, whose purpose is to restrict psychiatric practice in order to protect patients' rights, cannot automatically become part of the language of psychiatry or enter its social world. Legal norms occupy a different dimension of logic, language, and understanding from that of psychiatry. In order to enter into psychiatry, legal rules have to be translated into its language and enter into its logic, that is to say, have to be expressed in clinical terms. When so translated and expressed, they amount to stipulating that a person who needs treatment should not receive it, or that treatment, once started, should cease before it is completed. The tension between psychiatry as it is practiced and the new imperative is palpable; for once the legal rules are translated into psychiatric terms, taking the form 'stop treatment before the patient is cured', the two are plainly incompatible. It is not, then, surprising that at first the new imperative should be ignored or marginalized, although over time the social pressure for psychiatrists to respect patients' rights may lead them to redefine their own activity, to adjust their ideas about the purposes of treatment, so that it becomes acceptable, *within the activity of psychiatry,* not to treat in some circumstances or to cease treatment in others.

[19] *Ibid*, pp. 80–81.

6.5 DENSITY OF SOCIAL SPHERES

These ideas of autopoeisis help in understanding how social spheres have their own concepts and practices for conducting an activity, how each marks out a distinctive area of activity, which is separate from other activities and fortified against their intrusion. The wider social environment influences each social sphere, but, as in the case of psychiatry, in order to do so it has to be translated into the terms of the social sphere. Not all social spheres are as *dense* as psychiatry, by which I mean that the conventions and understandings defining and directing the activity are not as strong or as closed. The activity of lecturing constitutes a social sphere that is plainly less formed and more open than psychiatry, while psychiatry pales before the rigours of a closed order of nuns. The density of a social sphere is a variable with several consequences. It determines the level of influence exerted on the actions and decisions of individuals; it means that the degree to which one activity is distinct and separate from others varies from one social sphere to another; and finally it means that the difficulty a social sphere has in absorbing external influences is a matter of degree, some being strongly resistant, others relatively open.[20] The significance of these variables becomes especially apparent when considering the influence of law on social spheres.

6.6 SOCIAL SPHERES AND SOCIAL EXPLANATION

The utility of social spheres is in their capacity to explain human behaviour. They show how a social issue is perceived and they guide the way in which it is handled. Much human behaviour occurs within social spheres and is conducted according to their conventions and understandings. Those engaged in an activity accept its conventions as binding and act accordingly; they also use social spheres to explain and justify their actions and as a basis for evaluating the actions of others. Social spheres include rules but are composed of more than rules; they create a mini-world of meanings and expectations, of conventions and practices. To understand social spheres simply as sets of rules would be to miss their fullness and diminish their significance in guiding actions. When I give my lectures, I do not simply adopt a set of rules; instead I enter into an

---

[20] The strength of external influences on a social sphere will also be a major variable.

activity already constituted and structured by a web of conventions and understandings, and the same goes for the psychiatrist, the tennis-player, and the closed-order nun. When conceived in this way, social spheres provide a key for unlocking pockets of social explanation that would otherwise remain hidden, and the means for understanding them.

None of this is to suggest that social spheres give a complete account of behaviour or that they determine the actions of individual persons. Human actions are formed from such a complex of elements and are subject to so many influences that we cannot be sure an explanation, even of our own actions, is ever complete. Some influences are external and obvious, others internal and obscure, and others still buried in the recesses of consciousness. Nor are causal explanations straightforward, since human actions result from decisions by the person to act in one way or another, rather than being the direct effect of external factors. Factors of potential causal effect are mediated through personal choice and judgement. Clearly there are exceptions, and philosophers are locked in debate as to how far causal explanations are appropriate in relation to human actions. For the purposes of the social explanation of human behaviour, the point of focus is the explanation and justification a person is able to offer for his or her actions, leaving it for psychology to explain why those reasons were selected. The argument I am proposing is that social spheres provide both the context in which actions take place and the reasons people give for them; they provide, in other words, the basis for explanation and justification at the level of deliberate action. Social spheres are not a complete basis for explanation and justification; their influence is relative to their density, and even the densest can be over-ridden by competing, external factors. Nevertheless, in the general course of human affairs, much activity takes place within social spheres and is explained and justified in terms of social spheres.

Individual persons have their own attitudes and values apart from social spheres, and are, of course, capable of not following the guidance social spheres offer. The study of decision-making by judges in the House of Lords shows the conventions and understandings according to which they explain and justify their decisions; they include such matters as not interfering in executive government and administration, and maintaining the welfare state.[21] The author of the study does not claim that any particular judge's decision is determined by those conventions or that they wholly explain any decision. The contention is that by studying

---

[21] D. Robertson, *Judicial Discretion in the House of Lords*.

judges' decisions, including the reasons they give in explanation and justification, the influential factors can be identified and they, in turn, derive from the social spheres of high court judges.

The claim that social spheres are a significant influence on people's actions seems, at first sight, counter to the rather different notion that people make rational choices which are guided by their personal preferences and self-interest. The image of individual persons pursuing their own interests runs deeply in certain strands of social explanation and is counter to the claims made on behalf of social spheres. The claim is that the rational person would not necessarily wish to be bound by already established spheres of conventions and understandings. One immediate qualification to this counter-image is that not all actions are taken to further one's own economic interests, since plainly people sometimes act out of altruism, sometimes in order to support one another's interests, or to advance aesthetic or moral goals. To explain all such actions as serving one's own interests would require a very sophisticated explanation.[22] Another qualification is that acting according to the guidance of social spheres is often compatible with the rational pursuit of self-interest; social spheres advance rather than hinder the pursuit of self-interest in various ways, as consideration of why we create them shows. Social spheres also appear to compete with another image of human action familiar in liberal political theory and romantic art as highly individualized, seeking existential meaning and satisfaction wherever the opportunity arises, without recourse to habit or pattern.

6.7 WHY WE CREATE SOCIAL SPHERES

Explanations of why social spheres are created or spontaneously emerge take several forms, ranging from pragmatic concerns and common sense to theories of psychology that eventually give way to neurophysiology. From a pragmatic stance, several advantages are readily identifiable. The first is that social spheres make life easier for us; they simplify and regularize it and make it more predictable; they settle ways of acting in different contexts, so that we need not begin at the beginning each time. It saves time and energy if, whenever I give a lecture, I do not have to agonize over how long it should be, what form it should take, and how it should be presented. The interest of the university provides a second pragmatic reason: the existence of agreed conventions and understandings

---

[22] Douglass North, op. cit., pp. 20 ff.

about lecturing contributes to its smooth running by ensuring consistency across departments, allowing for the booking of lecture rooms on a predictable basis, and possibly saving on the cost and trouble of needing detailed and formal decrees, and administrators to enforce them. These two pragmatic reasons lead to a third: the shared conventions and understandings of a social sphere – psychiatry for instance – assist in developing the activity itself. If the participants are united by a high level of consensus as to the nature of the activity, if the conventions and understandings are clear, they can concentrate on practicing and developing it, instead of being preoccupied with troubling questions about its goals and purposes and how they should be achieved. Where social spheres are less developed, more time is likely to be spent on these matters rather than on the activity itself.

When these common sense factors are applied to society generally, the practical gains are plain: social spheres become efficient in contributing to social cooperation and coordination. Both qualities are most in evidence when the members of a group trust each other, while trust is created by the sharing of conventions and understandings, and the confidence that members will act in step with them.[23] If one adds the impediments of incomplete and imperfect information from which we all suffer in deciding to act, then there is both a need for and comfort in relatively settled patterns of understanding and conventions, even if they are not based on wholly accurate or comprehensive information. The gains in having reasonable levels of security and predictability are of practical value, even if more accurate and reliable information could be acquired by expending more time and energy.[24] In the light of these aspects of social spheres, it may seem hard to justify the claim that they are efficient. *Efficiency* is used here in its true and basic sense, and should not be confused with its use in economics, where it means something quite different. The distinction is important because social spheres are not necessarily economically efficient at all (although in practice they often will be).[25] Their logic is not that of economics, and as a result they are likely to contain aspects which are plainly inefficient economically, because historical leftovers, prejudices, and irrational beliefs may enter into social spheres and form part of

---

[23] For further discussion, see: D. Putman, op. cit., pp. 167 ff.

[24] For discussion of predictability, see: A. MacIntyre, *After Virtue* (London, 1981) pp. 104–5.

[25] For discussion of these issues and especially the economic aspects in relation to institutions, D. North's writings are of very considerable importance; see: D. North, op. cit., Chapter 1.

them.[26] The densest social spheres, and therefore most effective in guiding behaviour, are likely to be those based on deeply shared beliefs, regardless of whether the beliefs are true or justified, and regardless of the worth of the practices they perpetuate. Social spheres contribute in important ways to cooperation and coordination in conducting different social activities, whatever the activities happen to be, whether commendable or despicable. And just as a social order can be based on practices that are good or bad, similarly social spheres tend either way.

6.8 A MORE FUNDAMENTAL ROLE FOR SOCIAL-SPHERES

The practical contribution to social life is plain, but is it all? Something seems to be missing, the idea perhaps that social spheres are somehow more fundamental for both individuals and society. The search for a deeper explanation would lead to issues of cognitive science that are for others to pursue; nevertheless, a few brief remarks are offered attributing to social spheres a more fundamental social role than practical efficiency. It could be expressed in a brief aphorism: lives are lived in social spheres. Just as it is wrong to think that judges are somehow detached from the activity of judging, so that they have to decide whether to accept the conventions of being judges, or that psychiatrists ask themselves as they travel to work whether today they are going to practice the psychiatry for which they have been trained, or that university professors ponder over whether to lecture standing on their heads. Just as it is inaccurate and misleading to think in these ways, it is equally so to think of each of us as *in practice* free, existential beings shifting about in the hope that our lives might then take on more meaning. Some do just that but a more accurate picture is of biological entities which, from the moment of birth, live their lives in a host of social contexts from which they derive meaning, purpose, and direction. According to this image, life outside social contexts – of family, school, friends, professions, and so on – exists biologically but scarcely socially. This is not to say that the bonds of social life cannot be broken, that the iconoclastic life cannot be lived, but it is rare, generally poor, and often unbalanced. Again there is no suggestion of being compelled or determined; whether I become a university professor or a psychiatrist, an expert on Dante or a political philosopher, involves choices, decisions, and a lot of luck. But choice to enter one social sphere

---

[26] See also the discussion in: R. Ellickson, op. cit.

or another is not the point; the point is that our lives are lived in, and take much of their meaning and direction from, whatever social spheres we belong to whether by birth, choice, or fortune.

A more daring step would be to suggest that social spheres are the very basis on which we understand human action, and at least to some degree build a sense of personal identify. Harré and Secord describe human action as being 'generated by the conscious self-monitoring of its performance in accordance with certain sets of rules'.[27] To be a person is to act in accordance with sets of social rules and to monitor one's actions according to them. Harré and Secord do not explain their concept of rules, which anyhow is too narrow for their purpose. If rules are replaced by the concept of social spheres with their webs of conventions and understandings, then the idea of deriving a sense of identity within social spheres is plausible. One may set one's own rules, develop one's own conventions and understandings, but mainly they are settled socially. My actions as a university lecturer are performed according to the conventions and understandings of lecturing, and are the basis on which I perform and judge myself as a lecturer. There is little if anything about lecturing that is not accounted for in the process of acting and evaluating according to the conventions and understandings constituting the activity. If that idea is then extended across the diverse spheres in which we move, most of our daily actions are accounted for within those spheres.

This account displays how human actions are expressed in social spheres; it is, however, so far essentially self-regarding, with the social element missing, by which I mean the relations between people. Harré and Secord only hint at an account of the rules of social relations between human actors without providing one, which is of course our main concern. Robinson Crusoe had rules he set himself, but his actions were not social, at least not until Friday arrived, for social actions consist in *both* human action *and* relations between human actors. How then do human actors relate to each other? They do so through common understandings of the significance of things, and by conventions as to how things should be done. People relate to each other by the same process of action and evaluation that characterize an individual's actions, except here the evaluation is of the other person rather than of oneself. It follows that just as social spheres are the basis for self-action and evaluation, they

---

[27] R. Harré and P. F. Secord, op. cit, p. 93.

also serve as the basis for understanding and evaluating the actions of others. And just as it is hard to find a continuing basis for one's own actions except in the context of social spheres, it is equally difficult to find standards for understanding or testing the actions of others except within social spheres. Social spheres provide the arena for and give structure to the most elementary social relationships between people. If this approach to social understanding has merit, and it clearly needs further development, then the utility of social spheres goes beyond their practical contribution to social life; it extends to clarifying its very foundations as the combination of human action and the relations between human actors.

Social spheres have turned out to be a useful notion in understanding how people act and how they relate to each other. They could be examined in much more depth than is possible here, and their links to similar notions, such as practices, traditions, and institutions established more plainly. It should be understood as part of a long tradition in social philosophy, stretching from the earliest philosophers and social theorists to the contemporary, the aim of which has been how to make sense of human actions in a social setting. But what, it might be asked, is its relevance to the social understanding of law? The answer is that officials and citizens normally encounter law from the perspective of one or other social sphere. The discussion in earlier chapters shows how acceptance of the rule of recognition, and of sets of laws made in conformity with it, is a variable notion that responds to the attitudes of officials and citizens. Social spheres now provide the means for understanding those attitudes, which are largely formed within social spheres.

NOTES

Introducing social spheres

In developing the notion of social spheres, I have benefited substantially from the following:

P. Winch, *The Idea of a Social Science and its Relation to Philosophy* (London, 1958, 1990).

D. North, *Institutions, Institutional Change and Economic Performance*.

R. Putman, *Making Democracy Work* (Princeton, 1993).

Alistair MacIntyre, *After Virtue* (London, 1981).

E. Ostrom, *Governing the Commons: The Evolution of Institutions for Collective Action* (Cambridge, 1990).

The notion of social spheres

The image of the solitary person accepting and applying the law is common to legal theory; it is also Weber's image. It has become associated with *methodological individualism*, which is incompatible with my third methodological principle (see chapter 2.3), the premise of which is that, while individuals are free to act and choose as they wish, in practice their acts are much influenced by their social spheres. That is the claim of Chapter 6.

Social spheres are sometimes examined through the broader notion of *culture*. Fiona Haines defines *culture* as 'a touchstone or well of assumptions which provided the basis for deciding how success for the organizations was to be achieved'. F. Haines, *Corporate Regulation*, (Oxford, 1997). She goes on to show, in an important study of how corporations deal with legal regulation, the significance of 'cultural virtue' that they bring to the regulatory forum (p. 224). The analysis could be expressed equally well in the language of *social spheres*. How a corporation perceives and copes with regulatory demands depends on the character and density of its social sphere (p. 164).

For discussion of legal culture generally, see D. Nelken (ed.) *Comparing Legal Cultures* (Dartmouth, 1997).

On shared social norms and their acceptance, see: E. Ostrom, *Governing the Commons* p. 205–6.

Institutions and organizations

While having benefited greatly from Douglass North's account of institutions, I have suggested some modifications. He writes: 'Conceptually what must be clearly differentiated are the rules from the players. The purpose of the rules is to define the way the game is played. But the objective of the team within that set of rules is to win the game.' (*Institutions, Institutional Change, and Economic Performance*, p. 5). The study of strategies achieving certain purposes within the rules is important; but to link strategies *within the rules* with *common purposes* seems to overlook the point that common purposes are also *defined by the rules*. The ambiguity in *common purposes* can be removed by noting two senses of purposes: one refers to the purposes of the activity as expressed in the rules, the other to purposes in the sense of strategies within the rules. The common purposes for which we play tennis are expressed in the rules of tennis, while the strategies which we adopt to win are something quite different.

The work of W. R. Scott on new institutionalism is of considerable importance in the understanding of institutions and social spheres: W. R. Scott, *Institutions and Organizations* (London, 1995).

Moving across different social spheres

The idea that persons move among social spheres and that their actions, when seen as a whole, do not necessarily form a coherent whole, receives some support from recent work in psychology. R. Harré and P. Secord's *The Explanation of Social Behaviour* (Blackwell, 1972) shows how the social behaviour of a person does not necessarily form a consistent whole. They write:

'. . . in his social behaviour a biological individual may perform in a variety of ways, which taken together, do not form a consistent whole. . . We shall not attempt the impossible task of trying to find an underlying consistency in the social behaviour of a biological individual. Instead we shall begin by supposing that a normal biological individual is capable of manifesting a variety of possible social selves, each of which has some measure of coherence, and may resemble the personas presented on suitable occasions by other biological individuals' (page 92).

Social spheres and social explanation

P. Winch has provided an account of social rules as the foundations of social behaviour and the explanation of behaviour; see: *The Idea of a Social Science and its Relation to Philosophy*. In the second edition, some fundamental qualifications were made to the strength of the original thesis (see Chapter V).

Alan Ryan's *The Philosophy of the Social Sciences* also has an extended discussion of social rules and their importance in understanding human behaviour. On the point that the evaluation of behaviour depends on a context of social rules, he writes: '. . . it is only in the light of rules, and by the standards they provide, that we can intelligibly call behaviour correct or incorrect at all'. (p. 137).

Social spheres sometimes develop quite clear and firm rules, as in the case of the Californian ranchers: R. Ellickson, op. cit.

Density of social spheres

According to D. Putman who develops the idea of 'networks of civic engagement' in explaining the course of democracy in modern Italy: 'The denser such networks in a community, the more likely that its citizens will be able to cooperate for mutual benefit'. (*Making Democracy*

Work, p. 173). Putman also notes that the more dense social networks are, the more control they have over their members.

Social spheres and human action

The Explanation of Human Behaviour, on which I have drawn in this chapter, approaches social explanation in a way similar to Hart. Harré and Secord take the view that language reflects social meanings and distinctions, and rely extensively on the same philosophical tradition as Hart. Of special importance to them is Stuart Hampshire's, *Thought and Action* (London, 1965). They write: ' . . the philosophers we referred to above are recommending a consideration of the kind of explanation of behaviour that is familiar to us as laymen, and that is naturally couched in the subtle and expressive medium of ordinary language' (p. 40).

The force of social spheres in human behaviour can be seen at work in various forms of literature, which often are based on rebellion or rejection, and the consequences that follow. One way of understanding the tradition of tragedy is in terms of social spheres, and the terrible and uncontrollable consequences that follow when fundamental conventions are violated. The very fact that the consequences are terrible and spiral out of control shows how powerful social spheres normally are in directing and containing human actions, and how disordered and unmanageable life is when they are flouted.

Why we create social spheres

Putman discusses at length the importance of civic networks in creating social cooperation. (*Making Democracy Work* pp. 183 ff).

North also examines the advantages of institutions as sets of social rules (*Institutions, Institutional Change and Economic Performance*).

Further ideas in analysing social spheres

Social spheres are linked to, or perhaps another way of describing social capital, by which is meant very loosely trust, norms, and networks. According to D. Putman in his study of civic engagement and democracy in Italy, social capital 'improves the efficiency of society by facilitating coordinated action' (*Making Democracy Work*, p. 167).

Another idea that helps in explaining the continuity and durability of social spheres is path dependency. See A. Stone Sweet, *The Judicial Construction of Europe*.

7

The Reception of Law

7.1 VARIABLES IN THE RECEPTION OF LAW

Several ideas have emerged in the preceding chapters to lay the foundations for the reception of law. Foremost is that of law as a system of rules, which led to the social context of rules and the contingencies within it; from there we moved on to acceptance of law, noting its variability, before introducing the concept of social spheres as shared conventions and understandings in an arena of social activity. The aim of this chapter is to bring these ideas together in considering how groups of officials and citizens deal with the law, how they use it, cope with its demands, or edge it to the sidelines. This process I shall refer to as the *reception of law*.

The reception of law depends on a number of variables. The character of law itself is the first, by which is meant its division into specific categories. So far, law has been left rather vaguely as rules or sets of rules, and the time has now come to make an initial assessment of its categories and the social relations on which they are based. This is intended as an introduction to be added to later on in discussing whether law has distinct functions and the value it brings to society; the point of introducing it to show the connection between the different categories of laws and their reception. That leads to the question of reception by whom, in answer to which a distinction is made between officials and non-officials. Since Hart places the distinction at the centre of his description of a legal system, we need to consider his reasons for doing so and what adjustments need to be made from a law-and-society point of view. This leads us back to the idea that in a modern legal order officials hold positions of trust which gives special significance to the way they deal with law. In placing officials at the centre of a legal system, Hart relegates citizens to the sidelines. They need not accept law as binding standards, it being enough that they obey and that they do so often enough to ensure the efficacy of the system. Apart from the fact that, as Hart makes clear, the language of obedience is suitable in only very particular areas of law, the idea that the people in general should not share in the making and remaking of a legal order, except as subjects whose subservience is needed and gained, if necessary by force, is hard to sustain even from the stance of analytical jurisprudence, let alone law-and-society. The people need to be restored to their position in a modern legal order, and we shall see how this should be done. This brings us back to social spheres, since it is here that the law meets directly the arenas of conventions and understandings from which both officials and citizens view it, and which shapes their reception of it. Social spheres, it is suggested, are vital elements in the reception of law. The chapter concludes with an account of the overall structure within which the reception of law takes place, by introducing in the discussion the ideas of legal architecture and the legal and social environment.

7.2 CATEGORIES OF LAWS

One of the ways of not taking law seriously is to neglect the differences among sets of laws and the purposes for which they are used. It also means neglecting the link between laws and social relations, with specific sets of social relations generating specific kinds of laws. This we must now examine, first by sketching the different sets of social relations, and then isolating the kinds of laws they encourage. An initial classification distinguishes relations between persons from relations between persons and the state. *Relations between persons* cover such matters as family, the entering into contracts and promises, including employment contracts, the holding and transfer of property, and protection of one against harmful actions of another, whether criminal or tortious. *Relations between persons and the state* have three main aspects: the granting of benefits or concessions to citizens, the imposition of burdens on citizens ranging from punishment to taxation to limiting private interests, and restrictions on the exercise of authority by officials. To these should be added *relations between states* as expressed in public international law.

In covering family, contract, property, and wrongs, *private relations* cover the most elementary forms of social life; they are normally marked by consensus among the parties and take place within networks of social norms. Although social norms are capable of dealing with many aspects of private relations, it is usual for communities to build around them a legal structure whose main purpose is to reinforce and make them more secure and stable. It is also usual to provide for the resolution of certain kinds of disputes that arise concerning them, and in respect of some aspects to impose restrictions on them. Legal restrictions are prone to introduce an element of friction, but are justified on the basis that the community as a whole has an interest in the private relations of its members and is entitled to intervene for good cause. Nevertheless, the general thrust of the law of contract, property, and family is in support of arrangements and transactions that are firmly grounded in spontaneous social arrangements.

Regarding *relations between citizens and the state*, the *first* set is illustrated by the benefits modern states confer by the provision of welfare or the granting of concessions. The legal framework sets out the criteria of eligibility and empowers officials to administer them. From concessions which originated as gifts from the state, they tend over time to become rule-based and matters of right. Alternatively, the provision of services may be left to the discretion of officials with various gradations between the two. The *second* set of relations, the imposition by the state of burdens on citizens, divides into several kinds: sanctions that flow from breach of the most fundamental norms of behaviour as expressed in criminal law; burdens deriving from the revenue-raising activities of the state, expressed in laws of taxation; and burdens resulting from the need to conduct private activities in accordance with standards imposed in the interest of or for the protection of others. The differences between the three are significant. Criminal actions are normally condemned by social norms, which are then reinforced by law. The state's need for revenue and the duty of each person to contribute is accepted in principle in modern legal orders, the main point of contention being the proper level of burdens. The legal structure suitable for this purpose states the criteria and gives officials power to determine the level of taxation; it is also likely to confer on officials variable degrees of discretion in fixing burdens and extensive powers of enquiry and investigation into private affairs. The regulation of private activities is different again in that the activities are normally legitimate, the point of regulatory standards being to protect other interests or values, with inevitable tension between the two and a natural tendency to resistance on the part of the regulatees. The legal framework is similar to that already sketched: legal standards are stated and officials are authorized to take measures to implement them, with the threat of sanctions in the background.

The *third* aspect of citizen-state relations is expressed in the idea that, since officials hold power on trust, they must account for it, and in doing so show that standards restricting the way they are exercised have been respected. The standards are expressed traditionally in constitutional and administrative law, which also provides remedies by which private parties are able to initiate proceedings to determine whether the conditions have been met in particular cases. International conventions and regional authorities, such as the European Union, have become another source of standards. Mention should finally be made of the *international legal order* in which three other sets of social relations occur: relationships between states, between international agencies and states, and between citizens and the international order. The importance of all three is increasing in the contemporary world, especially the third, which historically hardly existed at international law. It means that citizens have a direct relationship with the international order from which they derive both benefits and burdens.

The connection between social relations and laws provides a way of viewing the reception of law by officials and citizens. Let us begin with the law of contract: it is mainly directed at making more secure arrangements that exist anyhow. The law does not create contractual relations nor enable people to enter into them; it strengthens that which is already a spontaneous social activity. The consequence is that private parties should not normally have any reason for resisting the law, on the assumption that it is in harmony with existing relations. It need not be, and when it is not, either because it introduces unfamiliar notions or runs contrary to the natural expression of contractual relations, a state of tension is created. The outcome is then hard to predict; the law might be successful in influencing contractual relations, or it might fail and be consigned to the dustbin of laws that are marginalized or ignored. Criminal law is another example: despite the close association between it and the coercive power of the state, criminal law is normally a direct expression of social relations, whereby one does not harm another's person or expropriate his or her property. Criminal law, in its classic form, sustains a close bond with social relations, ensuring its natural reception in society. Problems begin when it over-reaches by imposing prohibitions that have no social foundation. Instead, then, of being a symbol of social solidarity, it is divisive and encourages resistance, which may be contained in the short term by sanctions, but is likely in the long run to prevail.

Since regulation has become so prominent in modern societies, mention of it is warranted. Three sets of relations are involved: (i) regulation restricts private activities on grounds of public interest, which (ii) is an indirect reference to another set of relations between citizens and state, while (iii) at the same time the state is constrained, in the way it implements the regulatory regime, by another aspect of the citizen-state relationship. Consider regulation of the workplace: laws based on the health and safety

of workers impose restrictions on how the workplace is run (state intervention in private relations), the justification being that the state has a duty
to protect workers (state-citizen relations), while in the implementation
of regulatory laws the agency must observe notions of legality, due process, and fairness and reasonableness (state-citizen relations). That such
complex arrangements should result in several points of tension is not
surprising. The running of the workplace is essentially a matter of relations between private parties, but is overridden for some purposes in
order to protect the workers. The likely response of employers to laws
that appear to oppose and inhibit the natural course of private relations
is resistance, while the workers equally naturally may be expected to
urge more exacting protection, resulting in another point of tension, both
between them and the state agency, and between them and the employers.
At the same time, employers insist on strict observance of the protections
that administrative law gives them against the regulatory body, which for
its part may be expected not only to bridle at that prospect, but also to
push at the boundaries of its legal powers in order to achieve its purposes.
The sight of officials apparently playing fast and loose with the laws from
which they take their authority, for the sake of more completely achieving
the purposes behind them, their 'substantive ends' in Weber's terms, is
a familiar one. These examples convey a sense of how the ties between
laws and social relations affect law's reception; they also show how the
points of tension result from the intersection of the two. Tensions are
especially acute in modern societies since they are committed to intervene
extensively in social relations.

7.3 OFFICIALS

Officials have a prominent place in *The Concept of Law* for two reasons.
One is their role in making, interpreting, and applying law; the other is
that officials (rather than the people) must accept the rule of recognition
as binding, and in doing so ensure the effectiveness of a legal order and its
continuing existence. Hart explains that the creation of legal institutions
having the capacity to make new laws, to give authoritative rulings when
disputes arise, and to apply them, signals the passage from a pre-legal to a
legal order. An imaginary pre-legal order would have rules, in the form
of customs imposing obligations, but would lack 'a legislature, courts, or
officials of any kind'.[1] Such arrangements might suit a small, closely-knit

---

[1] H. L. A. Hart, op. cit., p. 89 ff.

community, but could hardly serve a large and diverse society, which needs institutions to deal with uncertainty as to whether a rule is a legal rule, and which have the capacity to change the law; it also needs institutions to overcome the inefficiency that would result unless provision were made for authoritative determinations of the law. Since a pre-legal society plainly has laws, it is the introduction of legal institutions that marks the beginning of a mature legal order.

Legal institutions are described by Hart as sets of secondary rules conferring powers on officials to meet the needs of a developed society. One set confers power to make law, another to decide what the law is, and a third to use the powers conferred by law. Rules conferring powers on officials need to be matched with rules imposing duties stating the terms on which their powers are to be used; they also need to impose duties on others, both citizens and other officials, to recognize the exercise of powers as valid. Legal institutions are constituted, then, by combinations of power-conferring and duty-imposing rules, but the importance of secondary rules – rules conferring powers on officials – as the nub of a developed legal order is left in no doubt in being likened to the invention of the wheel. Legal *institutions*, as sets of rules, are given practical effect through officials forming *organizations*,[2] such as legislatures, executive and administrative bodies, and courts. So, laws constitute the rules of governmental institutions, while officials form organizations to give effect to the rules. To take an example, an administrative agency, which is composed of officials, is created by one set of legal rules, given powers to do certain things by another set, and then guided and constrained in their use by a third set. The three sets of rules are likely to be mixed together in practice, and can be quite complex.

The notion of legal institutions, and the organizations of officials that form around them, is for Hart the second main element of a municipal legal system. Institutions and organizations represent the capacity of a legal system to perform the tasks that he considers fundamental to a developed society: certainty about the law, proper provision for its implementation, and the capacity to change it. They are also fundamental to law-and-society because institutions and organizations are the vehicles through which law is made, interpreted, and applied. How officials come together as legislators, the character of administrative bodies and courts, and the processes of implementation, are all at the heart of legal experience and its intersection with other aspects of society. From a law-and-society

---

[2] The terms *institutions* and *organizations* are explained in Chapter 5.

point of view, several additional matters should be kept in mind in considering institutions and organizations.

One is that organizations of officials, once created, tend to develop their own distinctive identity. For although organizations owe their existence and authority to legal rules, once created, other factors and forces from outside the rules influence the character of the organization. In order to understand the workings of organizations of officials, such as a police force, an environmental protection agency, or a court, it is necessary to consider both the legal rules that create it and confer powers and duties on it, and the effects on the organization of other factors, some flowing from the social environment, others stemming from within the organization. A second feature is the tendency of organizations towards autonomy, to detachment from the legal rules that brought them into existence. Officials within organizations develop a critical attitude to the legal rules, and are inclined to interpret and apply them according to conventions and understandings created within the organizations. And so we are brought back to the realm of social spheres, for the members of a government organization are prone to adopt informal conventions and understandings, partly to make sense of the legal environment and partly to deal with pressures from other factors.

The centrality of institutions and organizations of officials in modern legal orders is also connected to the prominence of enacted law. The move from being the expression of social practices, to being the rules enacted by a legislative body, has consequences for the way legislative, administrative, and judicial bodies perceive their tasks and perform them. Instead of distilling the law from social practices and understanding and, in turn, the social relations on which they rest, as in various other societies including the early common law, legislative bodies respond to a quite different set of factors. Their main duty is now to respond to the political process, regardless of the character of its demands or its impact on social relations. A modern legal order is liberating in that the traditions of the past are no longer the sole guide to the future; legislatures are able to respond to the changing currents of opinion within their societies, or indeed use law to divert them in new directions, not to reflect social relations but create new ones. Liberation has its price; it creates the risk that law, as enacted rules, is divorced from the deeper currents of society, the currents that link it to settled patterns of social relations. The tension between the two, between maintaining settled patterns and creating new ones, reflects itself in the social environment around legal rules.

7.4 BRINGING BACK THE PEOPLE

In his concern to settle on a description wide enough to cover all municipal legal orders, from the good to the bad to the intolerable, Hart had to take account of legal systems sustained by officials with the barest support of the people. As long as officials accept the law as binding and act accordingly, it does not matter for legal theory that the people do not share the internal point of view, do not accept the system as a binding legal order. The society is which this might occur would be 'deplorably sheeplike; the sheep might end up in the slaughter-house. But there is little reason for thinking it could not exist or for denying it the title of a legal system'.[3] However convincing this may be for legal theory, there are several reasons for regarding it, and the distinction made between officials and the people, as unpersuasive for law-and-society. In the first place, it is hard to think of historical examples of a system where citizens merely obeyed and only officials accepted. The more we learn about those qualifying as the most repugnant of recent times, the Germany of Hitler, the Soviet Union of Stalin, or the China of Mao, the clearer it becomes that they had not just the obedience but the positive support of large sections of the population. If examples of regimes that lacked popular support could be found, the chances are their life was short, rendering them a pathological rather than normal case of a legal system.

A second reason is that the analytical distinction itself between the attitudes of officials and those of the people appears on close examination to be problematical. Acceptance is a variable notion as we have seen, allowing in practice a range of attitudes towards the legal system. Some officials and citizens internalize the rule of recognition and countenance no deviation, while acceptance by others is contingent. The citizen who accepts just in the sense that he knows the law to be a set of conventional practices that others will act on, accepts the law in a clear and straightforward sense. Even the person who obeys in order to avoid trouble in some sense accepts, or at least acknowledges, the bindingness of the system. If acceptance means no more than recognition of law's validity, it is a low threshold to meet. If it is taken to mean more than that, then it is still a variable notion whose strength or weakness is gauged by examining the reasons for acceptance. The difficulties of drawing a sharp line between acceptance or obedience are then avoided. The fact that one's

---

[3] H. L. A. Hart, op. cit., p. 117.

reason for following the rules is caution, fear, or moral commitment is a separate matter from the fact of recognition and acceptance. Officials need to have a stronger sense of acceptance than the people, since they must positively sustain the system through their actions; but they also act for a mixture of reasons. It the issue is put in terms of the validity of law rather than the acceptance, it is easier to see that both the officials and the people, even the bad ones among them, normally recognize law's validity; it is only when we enquire into their reasons and motives that the differences between them appear.

There is third and more lethal reason for questioning a sharp distinction between officials and citizens. The language of obedience, as Hart points out, is out of place in relation to much of the law, and especially in relation to transactions between private parties, where the law makes existing relationships more secure. When parties use the law in order to achieve their ends, the language of obedience is inappropriate since the very act of making use of the law constitutes acceptance of it. Even a legal order that verges on the intolerable is likely to provide some facilities for securing transactions and arrangements between private parties, such as binding marriages and contracts. That is normally reason enough for entering into the legal order and relying on it, while to do so constitutes acceptance rather than obedience. In the relations between citizens and officials, those arising from the provision of welfare similarly raise no issue of obedience; the suggestion that the receipt of a benefit, made available by officials according to a set of rules, indicates obedience on the part of the recipient would be stretching language beyond its limits. Receipt need not be a sign of deliberate and positive acceptance of the rules, although the very process of making an application, furnishing information, and generally engaging with officials involves entering into the legal process in such as way as to constitute acceptance.

The criminal law itself is often misrepresented, for even though it is most directly attached to the threat of sanctions, compliance by citizens is often better explained not as obedience in order to avoid sanctions, but as conformity with social norms, to which the law adds confirmation and enforcement. Even a deeply flawed system is likely to reproduce social norms forbidding actions against persons and property, in the form of criminal law. Other offences lacking the support of social norms are often added, for which the fear of punishment is the only reason for obeying, but these are likely to be only part, and often a small part, of the criminal law. That leaves regulation, where the law controls otherwise legitimate activities. At first sight, regulation seems to support a sharp distinction between acceptance and obedience, so that in a society badly governed the people would have no reason to obey standards other than fear of punishment. But when this is considered more closely, it proves not to be such a good example, first, because the language used is normally couched in the softer tones of compliance rather than obedience and, secondly, because regulatory standards are typically open to some degree of negotiation leading to accommodation and compromise, with the threat of sanctions a last and exceptional resort.

The division between officials and people, with the one accepting, the other obeying, as a general feature of a legal system, becomes unsustainable. A distinction that is not straightforward analytically becomes positively untenable when consideration is given to different sets of legal activities and relations for which the language of obedience is inappropriate. And if this is true of a system in which the officials conspire to oppress the people, it is much more so where the two are broadly united in their purposes. This is not to say that officials and citizens are engaged in legal actions to the same intensity, for plainly officials must accept and support the legal order in a positive manner that is not normally expected of citizens. The making of laws, and their interpretation and implementation in authoritative and public forms, is the driving force of a legal order; but in order to succeed, the willing compliance of the people and their broad support is needed. And if pressed to make this more precise, we should go behind the rules of law and again make reference to the social relations that prevail within the society, relations among citizens and between citizens and officials. The social rules constituting law, while at one level the creation of officials, are at a deeper level the expressions of social relations and the attitudes accompanying them. A well-functioning legal order is a sign of harmony between the two, while disruption indicates the opposite; and if the practices of officials become divorced from social relations, the rules of enacted law are then projected into a social void where they will soon wither and become ineffective, or at least have their effects reduced.

7.5 OFFICIALS AND THE PEOPLE: THE TERMS OF DELEGATION

Giambattista Vico argued that the stage a society has reached in its form of government largely influences the character of its law. We can only guess at what he would have made of western societies and their law two centuries and more after he wrote. However, on the basis of his approach we see how the relations between officials and the people reveal essential aspects of modern law. One image that is usually associated with Thomas Hobbes is of the people surrendering their natural powers, without reservation, to the sovereign in return for protection and deliverance from the perils of the state of nature. A different image, associated with the tradition of which John Locke was an early exponent, is of the people delegating some of their natural powers to the state, but with two vital differences: one is that power is held by the state on trust for the people, the other that the people retain certain basic entitlements. Social scientists sometimes put this in terms of principal and agent: in the second case, the state is the agent of the people and answerable to it; while in the first, the opposite is true.

Modern legal orders have so plainly committed themselves to the Lockean image that the relationship of trust between the people and officials must be regarded as one of their defining social qualities. This shows itself in various ways. Legislative officials are elected by the people, hold power on conditions set by the constitution, as interpreted by the courts, and are subject to change at each election. Their powers are also likely to be limited by a range of international conventions and, in many cases, by regional legal orders, of which the European Union is the most notable case. Administrative and judicial officials depend for their powers on legislation, and generally have no powers other than those expressly granted. The powers of administrative officials are also subject to conditions imposed by the Constitution, often by international conventions, regional associations, and principles created over time by the courts. One of the purposes of constitutional and administrative law, buttressed in Europe by European Law and international conventions, is to formulate the terms on which government officials hold powers. The idea that they have no powers other than those conferred by law; that the powers they have must be exercised reasonably, proportionately, and rationally, and in accordance with fair procedures; and that a host of standards, including equal treatment and non-discrimination, privacy and transparency, and the duty to account for their actions through explanation and justification, all are signs that the relations between citizens and officials are based on an elaborate set of conditions guiding and limiting official behaviour. While some conditions may help to maintain the effectiveness of the state itself, they are more directly justified as expressions of relations between citizens and officials.

Several consequences follow for law-and-society. One is that principles express the social relations between citizens and officials in a manner characteristic of modern legal orders, and provide a basis for distinguishing them from others. The notion that legal power is held on certain conditions, expressing social relations between citizens and officials, is often absent. The People's Republic of China, whose legal system has begun to attract interest, is a good example of one in which the idea that officials having legal duties to the people, let alone that they hold power on trust, is largely alien. A World Bank official was recently heard to suggest that, in the language of principal and agent, the order is reversed since Chinese officials are the principal, the people the agents. Another reason for drawing attention to constitutional and administrative law is that they both show in a striking way how closely legal rules and the actions of officials are tied to social relations. It is common to think of them as principles, but they could equally well be put in terms of *standard-bearing rules*. However expressed, they are general and sometimes abstract standards that need to be understood and made specific in the context of actual cases. They show how legal rules reach into the underlying social context for their interpretation and application. That the context is structured by the understandings between officials and citizens is another important social fact. To express the principles of constitutional and administrative law in this way may seem idealistic; after all, officials and the people often differ in their understandings of social relations and their effects for legal rules. That is true of course in the limited sense that there is likely to be disagreement, even serious disagreement, at the more specific levels of action and decision. Legal standards can be clearly stated – 'due process must be observed' – but still need argument and reflection as to what it means in this case; social relations, similarly, can be settled at a deep level but raise complex questions for practical decision-making. It is here that the social environment of legal rules becomes important, and where social spheres have their place; it is also where the attitudes and understandings of the people, as well as the officials, enter into practical decision-making and influence its outcome.

7.6 RECEPTION OF LAW THROUGH SOCIAL SPHERES

The reception of law by both officials and citizens is mediated through the social spheres from which each set of officials or association of citizens views the law. The intersection of law with other aspects of society occurs in general within social spheres, whether of administrators or judges, businessmen or psychiatrists. A distinction should be made between the case where laws have a role in constituting social spheres, as in the case of administrative organisations, and where law intervenes in existing social spheres. The utility of social spheres in explaining how law interacts with other parts of society is then plain: in the first case, one or more social spheres will form around the law, through which it will be interpreted and implemented; in the second case, the reception of law will depend on how it is regarded and handled within social spheres. Where there is competition or incompatibility between the two, it is not simply a matter of the law prevailing over the social sphere, or the social sphere rejecting the law. Instead, the intersection gives rise to a social process that is structured around variables that can now be assembled. These variables help to explain the reception and use of law in society.

One variable is the attitude prevailing within a social sphere towards law as a system; it has two aspects. One is the attitude towards the rule of recognition, which means towards accepting the system as a whole as legitimate and binding. Each social sphere normally involves a set of understandings and conventions about the authority and legitimacy of the legal system. The other aspect relates to a set of standards that form the foundations of the legal order, and which derive, in turn, from the recognition of different sets of social relations within the society. In a stable and well-functioning modern legal system, the level of acceptance of law as a system, and the level of consensus concerning the underlying standards and the social relations on which they rest, is likely to be high among groups both of officials and the people. Variations occur: judges are expected to have a higher commitment to accepting and implementing the legal order than, say, social workers, and we earlier saw why, but it is worth repeating: the social sphere of judges is based on the law, since interpreting, developing, and applying the law to cases that come before them is what judges do. The commitment by judges to those tasks naturally dominates their social sphere, leaving only limited scope for other aims and purposes, and for external influences. For social workers, on the other hand, the law is a vehicle for achieving their wider purposes – the relief of poverty, protection of children, housing the homeless – and, while we would expect to find acceptance of the authority of law, their social sphere is likely also to reflect those other purposes.

Outside the range of governmental bodies, the strength of commitment to law among private and professional associations varies according to other factors. In a well-functioning society, private associations have a general commitment to the law and its values. But in a way similar to social workers, law is not at the centre of their social spheres. The more conscientious and reflective groups, recognizing the social goods that law as a system promotes, are positive in their attitudes and firm in their support, while to others those benefits are vague, perhaps too remote, incapable of inducing anything more than an equally vague sense of commitment. Such attitudes find their expression in social spheres, the one case perhaps leading to strong conventions of acceptance of law, the other generating something weaker. In both cases, law is likely to be regarded as marginal to the more central purposes of practising a profession, making money, or saving souls.

The way a social sphere regards the system of law generally sets the scene for dealing with specific laws. Administrative and governmental bodies, whose main purposes are directly to apply the law, are likely to translate a high level of general acceptance of the system into a high level of regard for specific laws. Meanwhile, the social sphere of a professional body – let us stay with the psychiatrists – while displaying a general commitment to law, is directed more centrally and powerfully by professional conventions and understandings. When competition appears between specific laws and professional concerns, we see why the laws have difficulty in being effective; the explanation lies in the combination of the weaker general commitment to law and the competition between specific laws and strong professional conventions and understandings. To put the matter slightly differently, a general commitment, even a strong one, does not guarantee the acceptance and application of specific laws; it creates a presumption that such laws will be upheld but, like any presumption, is stronger or weaker, and even the strongest is occasionally overridden.

The position could be summed-up in this way: the general commitment to the system influences the way in which laws are viewed, creates a presumption in their favour, but does not necessarily withstand the weight of other factors from within the social sphere. This applies not only in private or professional associations, but also in administrative bodies where it is not unusual to have officials who accept the system without question, but then depart from, modify, or marginalize specific laws. One example is that of inspectors modifying the application of laws protecting the environment, because they hold them to be at odds with such matters as the polluters not being morally blameworthy, or the economic necessities of doing business.[4] Other examples give effect to the views of officials as to which claimants were more deserving;[5] while

---

[4] G. Richardson, *Policing Pollution* op. cit.
[5] I. Loveland, *Housing Homeless People* op. cit.

in another piece of research it was shown that officials simply ignored judicial rulings on matters of general principle, because they could not be accommodated within their social spheres.[6]

7.7 THE ARCHITECTURE OF LAW

A major variable in the way social spheres deal with law is the *architecture* of the law itself. Architecture is concerned with design, with the detailed manner in which laws are expressed, so here again we encounter the need to look inside the structure of a legal order, for to talk of law in a general sense is to conceal a complex and variable social formation. Laws tend to come in sets, so that the architecture of a set refers to such matters as whether they are in the form of clear-line, standard-based, or discretion-based rules; what rights and duties, powers and immunities are specified; what it says about parties, procedures, and remedies; where do the laws originate and what constraints derive from constitutions, bills of rights, and international conventions. And just as the design of buildings allows infinite variation around familiar ideas, the same applies to law. The architecture of law matters because the design of any set of laws affects, or potentially affects, the actions of those required to implement or comply with it.

The full significance of the legal architecture is developed in Chapter 15 but two examples are useful here. In several east European countries, the administrative courts have no remedy for inaction by officials, nothing that is equivalent to the writ of mandamus; the consequences for the behaviour of officials who realize these restrictions on courts are clear to see.[7] In a very different case from the other side of the world, officials charged with regulating lobster-fishing off British Columbia found their efforts regularly frustrated by the insistence by courts that alleged breaches be proved according to the criminal law standard of beyond reasonable doubt. Given the conditions in which the inspectors worked, and the obstacles to obtaining evidence, this meant the regular failure of enforcement procedures.[8]

---

[6] S. Halliday, 'The influence of judicial review on bureaucratic decision making' *2000 Public Law* 110.

[7] See the study of the administrative law systems of numerous eastern European countries as in D. J. Galligan and D. Smilov, *Administrative Law in East European Democracies* (Budapest, 1998).

[8] See J. C. McMullan and D. C. Perrier, 'Lobster Poaching and the Ironies of Law Enforcement' (2002) 36 *Law and Society Review* 679.

That the architecture of law is of fundamental importance to law-and-society seems obvious,[9] but let us be reminded of why it matters. The form and shape of a set of laws is a social formation that enters into the deliberations of officials and private persons, and potentially influences the way they behave. The official charged with implementing laws has to consider what they mean and has to decide what action is necessary, what procedures have to be followed, and what means are available for enforcement. The persons or associations who are expected to comply with laws engage in a similar process of deliberation, and, even if their motive is avoidance rather than compliance, knowledge and understanding of the legal architecture is likely to be an asset in their endeavour. How much legal architecture matters in practical situations, is itself a variable. In social spheres of high commitment to law, the details of design are taken seriously and are at the centre of their social life. The position is very different in, say, a consumer advice centre, for although the whole point of such centres is to advise consumers on their legal rights against retailers, the law may simply be too complicated for the staff to master it.

7.8 LEGAL ENVIRONMENT

The architecture of law is part of a social formation around and with reference to which officials and citizens decide what action has to be taken, what powers are to be exercised, obligations met, and decisions made. Just as the design of a building determines its uses, or at least provides a structure within which uses must be accommodated, so the architecture of law requires certain responses, and influences the form they take. A building, like law, can be a bare structure accommodating a variety of uses, leaving it to the occupants to furnish it to their purposes, or it can be designed with such detail that little is left beyond minor variations of decoration and furnishings. The metaphor applies to law, where questions about different uses are replaced by those about what the law requires and what action has then to be taken. In accordance with the second methodological principle, the way the law is dealt with in the decisions and actions of officials and citizens has to be examined. I shall refer to this as the *legal environment*, the sense of which is gained by

---

[9] There are noble exceptions. Two recent studies that come to mind are F. Haines, *Corporate Regulation: Beyond 'Punish or Persuade'* (Oxford, 1997) and K. Yeung, *Securing Compliance*.

asking what the law requires officials or citizens to do, and what has to be done to give practical effect to these requirements.

Consider the lobster-fishing inspectors: the design of the regulations is complex and detailed, riddled with inconsistencies and contradictions to the point of being unworkable in any literal sense. That is the legal structure the inspectors have to interpret, understand, and apply. What are they to do? Should they ignore some of the rules and apply others, or should they try to reach some accommodation with them all? Or perhaps they should look more to the purposes behind the rules and try to realize them. In the case of psychiatrists, the legal rules protecting patients' rights have to be interpreted to see what they require; having seen that according to any reasonable interpretation they interfere with clinical practice, what is to be done? Can they simply be ignored, allowing time to see what will happen? If enforcement procedures are weak, inaction may work; if patients may bring actions in the courts a new set of issues will be set in train. In other contexts, there may be rules to enforce against others. If so, how is it to be done? If there are discretions to use, what factors are relevant, should guidelines be laid down in advance or allowed to develop with experience? When it comes to compliance or enforcement, how is it to be brought about? If there are different procedures and remedies, which are the most suitable? In short, law constitutes a design aimed at generating actions; in the environment around it, officials and private parties have to decide how to respond.

The idea of a legal environment clustering around sets of laws draws attention to the fact that, while the architecture creates a structure, it has to be interpreted, made sense of, and given practical effect. The legal environment is the setting in which two key notions come together, the first being contextual contingencies, the second social spheres. The first, it will be recalled, means that legal rules have a social context which provides the basis for interpreting them and which means considering how their social spheres should cope with the law.

7.9 LAW CONFRONTING SOCIAL SPHERES

The interaction of law with society, when viewed from the setting of one social sphere or another, may be summarized in this way: *first*, social spheres vary in their conventions and understandings towards laws as a system, which *secondly* influence attitudes towards specific laws, while other factors also enter the scene. *Thirdly*, there is the legal architecture; around which, *fourthly*, a legal environment is created involving decisions as to interpretation and implementation. Yet this is not the full picture. The *final* element consists is confronting the wider social environment. In some cases, this means how to comply oneself, in others how to implement it with respect to others. Having understood the design of a set of laws, having considered as a matter of interpretation what the law requires, officials or private parties now have to give effect to it, and that means considering how their social sphere should cope with the law.

The law may have been interpreted in such a way that this stage is never reached. Examples of this probably occurred in Britain after the recent enactment of the Human Rights Act when government agencies had to consider whether their current practices were compatible with the standards of the European Convention on Human Rights. The likelihood is that some construed both the new legal standards and their present practices in such a way as to conclude that nothing needed to be done. In other cases, even without the benefit of creative construction, the laws are compatible with the social sphere. Imagine an administrative agency whose task is to allocate housing to homeless people in which the practice has grown-up of assessing applicants according to how deserving they are, a matter not provided for in law, and indeed inconsistent with the legal rule that the only relevant test is the applicant's need for housing. A change in the law that allowed consideration of deserts would give effect to existing practices and therefore be easily assimilated. The same compatibility occurs when laws are directed at facilitating or supporting existing activities rather than changing them, as in relation to private transactions where contracts are made more secure, or easier to enter into, or certain business relations are put on a firmer legal footing.

Since law and social spheres are not always compatible in this way, and even creative construction has its limits, many situations remain in which social spheres have to deal with varying degrees of incompatibility with the law. Incompatibility is sometimes deeply rooted, as in the case of psychiatrists confronting laws protecting the rights of mental health patients, at other times superficial, as is often the case with laws dictating procedures, which can usually be assimilated without major disruption of the social sphere. In the face of incompatibility, several approaches are open. The expectation in modern legal orders is that both officials and citizens will change or modify their actions in accordance with the law. That means finding ways of adapting social spheres and the practices they support to assimilate the law's demands. Social spheres and practices vary in the ease or difficulty with which they can be adjusted and modified, some being more dense and entrenched than others. These issues are considered more fully in the final chapters, where several variables are identified. They include not only the density of social spheres, but also the character of the legal architecture and the strength or weakness of the legal environment. Within those parameters, other factors exert their influence; the level of commitment to the law is one, the interests at stake in complying with the law or resisting it another. Where the law strikes at vital interests, resistance should be expected, and may range from stubborn refusal to comply to the exploitation of subtle ways of seeming to comply. Extreme factors, such as the costs of implementation or compliance and the political environment, also effect the actions of officials, citizens, and corporate entities. These matters await fuller treatment later on; the purpose of this chapter has been to bring together the strands of analysis from earlier chapters in providing a framework within which the reception of law takes place.

NOTES

Categories of law

Max Weber begins his extensive sociology of law with an analysis of the different categories of law:

Economy and Society, Chapter VIII. His account is not expressed directly in terms of different social relations, but on the basis of different kinds of legal norms and their functions. Implicit, however, is a pattern of social relations not significantly different from those indicated in the text.

Weber's classification is : public law and private law; criminal law and private law; laws limiting government powers; and substantive law and procedure.

J. H. Baker's historical account of English law traces the growth of the following categories: law of real and personal property; contract and quasi-contract; torts; law of persons; and criminal law; (*An Introduction to English Legal History*, Chapters 13–30).

Relations between citizens and officials

The evolution in modern legal orders is from benefits being concessions or gifts from the ruler, to customary entitlements. Rights in the modern sense are an important issue in the development of modern law. This is also a good example of the shift from law prior to rules to law expressed in positive rules.

Although both crime and tort occur within the relations between private citizens, there are differences in their legal position. Actions seeking remedies for both continue in modern law to be brought by the injured party. Actions for criminal damage are normally brought by state officials, although the private prosecution continues in some jurisdictions. The explanation for the division between crime and tort lies in the claim of the state to have an interest in crime. Crime, in other words, has entered into relations between citizens and officials, despite having its origins in private relations. The resulting neglect of the victim's interest is slowly being remedied in modern legal orders.

In relations between citizens and officials, the notion that the latter hold power on trust has reached a high point in modern societies. Its development has been gradual, as we would expect. The opposite of official power being held on trust is expressed by Weber as: 'the theoretically unrestrained administrative power of the master', (op. cit., p. 645). Weber begins with the notion of *patriarchal power*, by which is meant 'the rule of the households'. In its primitive form, the authority of the household is unlimited. Those subordinated to the patriarch's power have no rights as against him, and norms regulating his behaviour towards them exist only as indirect effects of heterogeneous religious checks on his conduct (*ibid.*) Weber then goes on to explain at length the process whereby state authority becomes subject to rule-based limitations (*ibid*, 652 ff and later chapters XXV and XXVI).

On officials and the nature of organisations

The classic modern account of bureaucratic organizations is Weber's in *Economy and Society* Volume II.

For a range of views that challenge the certainties of Weber's account, see: J. Hassard and M. Parker (eds), *Postmodernism and Organizations* (London, 1993).

Prominence of enacted law

On enacted law, and its prominence in modern legal orders, Phillip Allott, after referring to Austin and Bentham, writes: 'Legislation – intentional law-making – was to become the general paradigm of law. Legislation was reason made law. Law is made by an act of will, not formed by an act of magic'. (*The Health of Nations* (Cambridge, 2002), p. 47).

Gerald Postema traces the growth in the prominence of enacted law in England and shows how, by the seventeenth century 'the conception of the nature of legislative activity had changed': (*Bentham and the Common*

Law Tradition (New York, 1986) pp. 15 ff). He also shows how enacted law was seen by Blackstone and others as a threat to common law.

Bringing back the people

For a critique of Hart's notion that it is enough that people obey, see M. Payne, 'Hart's Concept of a Legal System' in 18 *William & Mary Law Review* 287, at pp. 308–310.

Delegation of powers to officials

Modern constitutionalism is primarily concerned with setting the terms on which officials hold power. A recent illuminating account of constitutionalism directed specifically at the new constitutional orders of central and eastern Europe is: *Limiting Government* by Andras Sajò (Budapest, 2001).

Bentham wrote extensively of the risks of misuse of power by judges and other officials. His remedy, however, was not the checks and balances approach of modern constitutionalism. He considered this approach to be mis-directed, not least because if its irrationality: 'with one hand power is granted to officials and with the other it is withdrawn': quoted by Postema in *Bentham and the Common Law Tradition*, p. 363. Bentham thought publicity the key, or, as Postema puts it, 'the soul of justice'.

8

Law and Coercion

8.1 THE BACKGROUND TO COERCION

Before considering law's role in society, there are two matters following on from the previous chapters that need to be examined. One is the coercive side of law, the other the idea that there are other kinds of law besides state law. The two issues are not unrelated: law's long association with a sovereign state has influenced our view of it, while deflecting attention from other forms of law. Out of the association has grown the idea, prominent in legal and political theory, that law is essentially a coercive order under the control and serving the interests of the sovereign state. The idea found its way into social theories of law, with both Weber and Durkheim subscribing to the view of law as an order of state authority enforced by sanctions. Despite ample evidence from anthropologists that legal orders exist and flourish in societies lacking the concept of the state and its institutions and structures, legal theory has confined itself fairly much to the law and legal systems of modern states. Considering the power of states, the reasons they have developed, and the use they make of law as an instrument to social ends, we could hardly have expected otherwise. Nevertheless, a renewed interest in non-state forms of law has revived old debates about the nature of law and whether in modern, state-dominated societies other kinds of law may exist. These, then, are the next two issues for consideration: the place of coercion in modern legal order, and the idea of legal pluralism and its relevance to modern societies.

The issue in this chapter is the place of coercion in a social account of law. Until *The Concept of Law*, the mainstream of legal theory, of which John Austin's *The Province of Jurisprudence Determined*, first published in 1832, is considered a classic account, defined law as rules, but then went on to define rules as commands issued by a sovereign authority, which people obey because of the threat of sanctions.[1] Hart pointed out

---

[1] J. Austin, *The Province of Jurisprudence Determined* (1832, second edition 1954, London, reprinted, Indianapolis, 1998). The main elements of Austin's account are set out in Lecture I.

several difficulties with the approach, which led to his reformulation of
law as a system of rules. Since then, the place of coercion has been
uncertain. With rules having usurped its lead role as the distinguishing
feature of law, legal theory has relegated coercion to a supporting role,
but one that is ill-defined and to some degree contested. Hart often
makes reference to the coercive environment of law, and regards its
enforcement as one of the social functions to which any society should
attend. It is a 'guarantee that those who would voluntarily obey should
not be sacrificed to those who would not'.[2] Otherwise, he says little
about coercion and sanctions.

The task in this chapter is to examine the place of coercion in modern
legal orders from the point of view of law in society, which means following several lines of enquiry. The first is to look more closely into law's
coercive side in order to understand why it has been depicted traditionally by both legal and social theorists as being central to the nature of
modern legal systems. This leads to the second task, which is to consider
Hart's reasons for reversing that trend by elevating rules to a more central
place and edging coercion to the sidelines. The final task is to consider
whether that relegation has been too severe, and then to develop a law-
and-society approach that rehabilitates coercion by showing its social
significance in relation to specific areas of law.

8.2 THE CLASSIC DEPICTION OF COERCION IN LAW

The coercive character of modern legal systems was long regarded as one
of their defining features. John Austin represents the British tradition,
which he inherited from a line of legal and political theorists culminating
in Bentham, from whom Austin took the main elements of his account.
The subject of jurisprudence was, for Austin, the laws of the state, the
body of rules laid down by political superiors exercising supreme government. Legal rules take the form of commands issued by political
superiors, which create duties in the people, the breach of which leads to
the infliction or threat of infliction of a sanction.[3] Austin is often accused
of peremptorily adopting a definition of law, and while that may be true,
it is closely based on his observation of the character of modern state
systems in which the coercive aspect is prominent. Writing in a different
European tradition, Hans Kelsen is more explicit as to why coercion is a

---

[2] Op. cit., p. 198.   [3] J. Austin, op. cit., Lecture I.

defining feature of modern legal orders.[4] After describing law as a system of norms linked together by a presupposed basic norm, he introduces its coercive character: officials enforce valid legal norms with sanctions. The coercive element sits awkwardly in Kelsen's account. To the main thesis of law as a system of norms, coercion is added in order to distinguish it from other social orders. This is a good but not wholly convincing reason. Kelsen is plain: '. . . if we define law as simply an order or organization, and not as a coercive order (or organization), then we lose the possibility of differentiating law from other social phenomena . . .'.[5] For legal theory, the explanation raises more questions than it answers: first, since coercion is just as much a feature of many other social orders as of law, it is no basis for distinguishing law from them; secondly, it is curious to learn, after an extended analysis of law as a system of norms, which is Kelsen's main contribution to legal theory, that the analysis of norms is equally at home in many other, non-legal contexts, the real difference between them being, not the nature or arrangement of norms, but coercion.

Happily our concerns are with law-and-society not legal theory. From that point of view, Kelsen may be seen as trying to make sense of the obvious fact that in state legal orders coercion plays a prominent part. From Weber, whose own concerns were explicitly with law-and-society, we should expect a fuller account of the place of coercion. Those expectations are only partly fulfilled, but first let us consider what he says. Weber begins with the notion of a *legitimate order* as: 'one that enjoys the prestige of being considered binding'.[6] A legitimate order is also a *valid* order. Legitimacy (or validity) is guaranteed either by subjective beliefs, such as a moral or religious conviction that a particular order should be obeyed, or by the expectation that external consequences will flow from disobedience. Law is a legitimate order externally guaranteed: 'by the probability that physical or psychological coercion will be applied by a staff of people in order to bring about compliance or avenge violation',[7] which is to say that the validity of law, its legitimacy as a binding social order, depends on the expectation of sanctions being imposed in case of disobedience.

This orthodox view of coercion appears to be modified as Weber's treatise proceeds, and is even overtaken by a more complete account of a modern legal order, the main aspects of which are worth noting. The first

[4] H. Kelsen, *Pure Theory of Law* (Berkeley, 1967), p. 33 *ff* and *General Theory of Law and State* (New York, 1961), p. 26.
[5] *General Theory of Law and State*, p. 26.
[6] M. Weber, op. cit., pp. 31, 311 *ff*.   [7] *Ibid*, p. 34.

is the introduction of a distinctively modern kind of legitimate order or authority, *rational legal authority*, and opposing it to other non-modern forms, *traditional* and *charismatic*.[8] In explaining that rational legal authority rests on the 'belief in the legality of enacted rules and the right of those elevated to authority under such rules to issue commands',[9] Weber loosens the connection between legitimacy and the expectation of sanctions, now apparently allowing that beliefs in legitimacy may have a wider basis. The second aspect is the distinction he draws between the *validity* of law, which is a legal concept, and the way in which officials and people *in practice* regard the law, which is the sociological question and which allows the belief in law to be based on social conventions or ethics.

Although the connection between these ideas is neither explained by Weber nor easy to unravel, the point seems to be that validity is a quality of law from a legal point of view, a point of view that also has social significance; at the same time, law is approached from other points of view, which are also socially significant. They are socially significant in showing how both officials and the people deal with law, for which their ethical attitudes and social conventions are relevant. A complete understanding of law in society should accommodate both points of view. There is another, third aspect that enriches Weber's account. He states: 'The purest type of legal authority is that which employs a bureaucratic administrative staff'.[10] His own account of law is very much based around the actions of organizations of officials, including courts, who take for granted the coercive character of law, but in whose attitudes and concerns that fact plays a minor part. The point is that law is founded on the expectations of coercive action being taken, but above that foundation there is room for other concerns, for other attitudes and experiences, the understanding of which is the aim of a social explanation of law. If this construction of Weber's approach is right, the conclusion must be that, while coercion is essential to a legal order, its significance is that of a background factor on which legitimacy and validity are based; beyond that, it has only a limited social significance.

8.3 HART'S REVISION OF THE PLACE OF COERCION

Hart set out to revise the orthodox view of coercion in legal theory. His target was the idea, most closely associated with Austin, that law is a set of

---

[8] *Ibid*, p. 215 *ff*.　　[9] *Ibid*, p. 215.　　[10] *Ibid*, p. 220.

commands issued by a political superior or sovereign, which the people are in the habit of generally obeying, with the threat of sanctions in the event of disobedience. Both Bentham and Austin sought to show that all laws take the form of coercive orders, a matter simple enough in relation to laws imposing duties, such as criminal law or tort law, where the role of coercion is most apparent.[11] It is less obviously so for other matters, such as the laws enabling the formation of contracts or the transfer of property, or laws conferring powers on officials such as judges or policemen. In order to fit the coercive model, laws conferring powers have to be reformulated to show that they are incomplete laws, which, in order to be complete, need to be attached to duty-imposing rules, and thus to coercion and sanctions. So, although laws enabling the formation of contracts or the transfer of property appear to be intelligible as laws, they are really only fragments of laws. It is not just that sanctions may sometimes be used to enforce the terms of a contract or a property transfer; the claim is that because all laws are linked to sovereign orders and sanctions, orders and sanctions are essential to the concept of law. To this general idea, Kelsen added a refinement to the effect that orders requiring the imposition of sanctions are addressed to state officials rather than the parties to transactions.[12]

Hart fastened onto a number of the weaknesses in this approach, some of which concern the idea of a personalized sovereign, others the idea of law as orders. Concerning the second, which is our main interest here, Hart's critique takes three directions.[13] The first is to show that the depiction of law as commands backed by sanctions fails to catch the nature of law; it fails because it misses or cannot adequately express the obvious fact that law is a set of rules. Rules have the characteristics we considered earlier, many of which cannot be explained in terms of orders backed by sanctions; for instance, the idea of laws being binding standards of behaviour, which officials and others accept, cannot be explained in terms of orders or commands. The second line of critique is that the coercive orders approach fails to depict accurately large parts of law: for even if some areas of law, such as criminal law, fit well enough, others do not. It is a feature of any developed legal system, says Hart, that legal rules confer powers on both private persons and officials to do things, in the one case to make arrangements or to enter into transactions, in the other to take measures or to make decisions that are legally binding. The array of

---

[11] J. Austin, op. cit.; J. Bentham, op. cit.   [12] H. Kelsen, op. cit.
[13] H. L. A. Hart, op. cit., Chapters 1–3.

private transactions would not be possible without power-conferring rules, while the structure of government and administration depends on officials having powers to achieve their policy goals. The third line of attack follows on the heels of the second. Legal rules conferring powers have a different social function from the duty-imposing character of orders backed by threats, the function being to enable ends to be achieved and purposes to be fulfilled, which is said to be one of the great contributions of law to social life. Such rules explain legislative, executive, and judicial powers; they also allow private parties: 'to control, to guide, and to plan life out of court'.[14] In singling-out these aspects of law, Hart's intention is neither to deny that sanctions have a place nor that municipal legal systems operate within a coercive framework; at the same time, coercion is not a defining or distinguishing feature of a legal system. While coercion is important in a legal system, power-conferring rules are: 'an additional element introduced by the law into social life over and above that of coercive control'.[15]

8.4 REVISING THE REVISION: A SOCIAL EXPLANATION OF COERCION

Hart's revision of earlier theories of law is celebrated for having prised open the difference between commands and rules, and for highlighting rules conferring powers as opposed to those imposing duties, both of which are among the elements of a social account of law. Nevertheless, what was intended as a corrective should not become a rout, for however we approach law, its coercive character cannot be escaped. It colours the common perception of law and how people talk about it, where ideas such as the following are often encountered. Laws are laws because they are associated with coercion and enforcement; their ties to government bodies make them different from other social rules, even though other social rules may be enforced by the use of force. Laws override other social rules because they have government bodies to enforce them; courts and similar bodies are authoritative because their decisions will be enforced. People rely on the law in conducting their affairs because of the assumption that the law will protect them. The list could go on, but enough has been said to show that, in everyday attitudes, language, and understanding law is associated with coercion, which must then be regarded as a significant feature in an account of law-and-society.

---

[14] *Ibid*, p. 39.   [15] *Ibid*, p. 40.

In unravelling the association between law and coercion, let us begin with the general idea that a modern, municipal legal system is, in a general sense, based on coercion, by which I mean: (i) that laws of whatever kind are generally (but not invariably) linked to enforcement processes of a coercive kind (whether or not the processes are invoked); and (ii) the processes are administered by state authorities authorized to take enforcement action. Without entering into the issue of whether law's coercive character is an essential element of the *concept* of law,[16] we should begin with the fact that, as a matter of observation, coercion is an important feature of a modern legal system, and therefore should have a prominent place in its social explanation.[17] Social explanation has to go beyond merely drawing attention to the generally coercive character of modern legal systems; it must also show how coercion enters into both legal relations and specific areas of law. Criminal law and, to a lesser degree, tort law are often cited as cases of a close association between law and coercion, for here duties are linked directly to the threat of sanctions. Other areas of law, particularly those of private transactions, or those enabling officials to take measures, are considered to be prime examples of laws that are not associated with coercion, and thus prove the case for keeping coercion at the margins. If laws regulating private activities, of which a large part of modern law consists, are mentioned at all, they are liable to be grouped with criminal laws, because they may be enforced by sanctions. These associations are rough-and-ready and rather taken-for-granted; a closer examination from a law-and-society point of view shows how coercion is relevant to each set of social relations and the categories of law that express them.

8.5 SANCTION-IMPOSING LAWS AND THE ROLE OF COERCION

Law often requires that things be done or refrained from, and in doing so runs counter to the interests of those subject to it, or for some other reason lacks widespread support. Here the place of coercion is plain, and has been well expressed by Matthew Kramer, who writes: 'In such circumstances, the only reason for each citizen to comply with the norms is a fear of punishment; the norms in themselves, considered apart from the

---

[16] See further: J. Raz, *Practical Reason and Norms* (London, 1975, Princeton, 1990).

[17] For a recent revision of the issue of coercion in legal theory, see: A. Marmor, *Positive Law and Objective Values* (Oxford, 2001), pp. 42 ff.

sanctions attached to them, do not present people with any reason for compliance'.[18] Laws threatening sanctions occur in three main contexts: criminal law, tort, and regulation. Although it may seem curious, criminal law is not the best example of people obeying the law for fear of sanctions. The core prohibitions of the criminal law, as previously noted, are normally supported by social values and social spheres from which stem powerful motives to comply. The threat of sanctions adds to the pressures. Crimes may be added that lack social foundations, but generally there is a close association between social norms and criminal prohibitions. Coercion is important in reinforcing the seriousness of the standards, which it does by bolstering with the threat of sanctions the social pressures to comply, and then in the event of violation imposing them. Punishment as the imposition of sanctions is necessary to reassure those who restrain themselves that they are not sacrificed to those who do not.

A better illustration of the role of coercion occurs in regulation, where laws are used to restrict or redirect activities that would otherwise be permissible. Its main features were noted in section 8.2: regulatory law consists in setting standards for the conduct of private activities, and then providing mechanisms for their enforcement. It has a wide ambit ranging from business and financial affairs to the environment; it covers matters such as raves, horse races, and the size of apples, together with a host of others, so that the pool of private activities free of regulatory standards is shrinking. More will be said about regulation later, so the main point for present concerns can be briefly stated: regulatory law requires compliance with standards that often (but not always) are contrary to the interests of those required to comply with them, and that often (but again not always) lack deep social or moral foundations. The consequence is that those to whom the standards are addressed have no clear or strong reason to comply (beyond the fact that it is a legal standard), with the further consequence that enforcement or the threat of enforcement by coercion becomes a necessary feature of regulatory regimes.

It may be tempting to question this way of describing regulatory law, since the coercive element is not proclaimed in the manner of criminal law, but is more indirect, more a matter of last resort, with the emphasis being on the standards to be reached rather than the threat of penalties for non-compliance. It is also the case that, even though sanctions are available, they are not often invoked, for one of the lessons of empirical research is that the implementation of regulatory standards is likely to

---

[18] M. Kramer, op. cit., p. 95.

rely on informal processes of accommodation and negotiation, rather than the threat, let alone the use, of sanctions. Sanctions are used so sparingly that to describe these contexts as seriously coercive might be considered a mis-description. It would be equally inept, however, to over-look the role of coercion, a clue to which lies in the idea of *the shadow of the law*. Although now overworked, the idea of the shadow of the law graphically captures the role of coercion in regulation: for the informal processes of negotiation and accommodation, so common in regulation, take place in an environment of understanding and expectations that is influenced by its coercive foundations, by the fact that ultimately the standards set by law can be enforced. That foundation is implicit in dealings between regulatory bodies and the people or firms regulated; it defines the boundaries of the process and influences the attitudes of the participants. The fact that sanctions are only occasionally imposed, usually as a last resort, may detract from, but not remove their importance, and the fact that compliance is often achieved through informal agreement is arguably evidence of the influence of the coercive environment.

The force of the coercive aspect is starkly displayed by imagining a regulatory context without it: the understandings and expectations would be very different; informal agreement would be dependent on persuasion, and the appeal would be to social ends and advantages other than the bare fact that compliance is required and enforceable. In some areas of regula-tion, such ends and advantages could be enough to warrant compliance; the regulated bodies might come to regard the goals of regulation as ones that ought to be supported as a matter of social responsibility, or that in the longer term would advance their own interests, or simply to get the regulator off their backs. The regulatory goals, in other words, over time, could be brought into and internalized in the social spheres of the regula-tees, and influence their own conventions and understandings. Regulation would then become more like self-regulation, where those engaged in an activity formulate their own standards of behaviour and have responsibi-lity for complying with them.[19] The hope in any area of regulation is that the standards will eventually be adopted and internalized in this way, although the process is likely to be slow and always imperfect, so that, at least in the short term, the removal of a coercive environment would result in regulatory failure. To move out of the shadow of the law, to

---

[19] Even self-regulation is not wholly voluntary, either because it takes place within some very general standards set by law or because failure to set suitable standards or to comply with them will lead to standards being imposed by law.

remove the threat of enforcement, would be to transform the social environment around regulatory standards from being essentially coercive to being essentially persuasive. Much as that may be desired, it is not the case.

8.6 PRIVATE ARRANGEMENTS, POWER-CONFERRING RULES, AND COERCION

When approached in this way, many of the puzzles over the role of coercion in law are solved. The analysis that works well for regulatory law can be applied to other areas of law, whether criminal, civil, or administrative. The idea, in each case, is to enter into the context and consider what place coercion has in it: how it shapes the context and influences attitudes and expectations; what its role is in encouraging the adoption of legal standards by those responsible for enforcing them and those subject to them. The significance of coercion can then be seen to vary from one context to another. In criminal law it is patently present, although not quite in the way often supposed; it is not so much a matter of an Austinian sovereign issuing commands under threat of punishment, but rather reinforcing the prohibitions, the core of which are embedded in its social norms. Durkheim drew attention to the importance of sanctions for breach of the criminal law in maintaining social solidarity by reinforcing the shared values of close-knit societies. In more diverse societies, a core of shared values underlying criminal prohibitions is still necessary, but the criminal law is at risk of being used for social ends that are not widely agreed. Given the power of the legislature and the dominance of enacted law, in a modern legal order, criminal law may become an instrument for advancing special interests, with the result that compliance is more dependent on the threat of punishment than shared norms. Even within the criminal law, the role of coercion varies according to the social context in which it occurs and the purposes for which it is used.

This way of approaching coercion applies equally well to the law regarding private arrangements, relationships, and transactions. Hart's account of power-conferring rules was made with these matters in mind – marriages and wills, property transfers and contracts – matters which may loosely be described as private, in that they are arrangements, transactions, or relationships entered into voluntarily by the parties, unilaterally or by agreement. They are made possible, according to Hart, by power-conferring laws, which are different and separate from duty-imposing laws. There is, however, a subtle but important difference

between laws making these arrangements possible and laws in some way
adding to or strengthening those that would be entered into anyhow. The
audacious claim that: 'there could be no buying, selling, gifts, wills, or
marriages if there were no power-conferring rules . . .'[20] is palpably
untenable; people enter into private arrangements, contracts, marriages,
and property purchases as a matter of normal social life and according to
social norms, not because the law empowers them to do so. The role of
the law is not to make these arrangements possible since they exist
anyhow, but, by moving them from the social context to the legal, to
add something of value: possibly to make them easier to enter into and,
once entered into, to give them an added protection. This is sometimes
expressed in terms of co-ordination: the law helps to co-ordinate social
activities which would take place anyhow, the benefits being added
certainty and security. Or, as Bentham put it, the law adds security to the
parties' expectations.[21]

The notion of law as a coordinator contrasts sharply with that of law as
a regulator for, in the first case there is normally no conflict between the
law and private arrangements, while in the second the aim of the law is to
change or control social practices. Coordination means building on social
practices to make them more certain and secure, and in plural societies
to enable them to take place among strangers. This was the point of
Durkheim's concept of organic solidarity: in modern societies, which
are typically diverse as to groups, interests, and values, the law (other
than the criminal part) is *restitutive law*, meaning that it facilitates the
conduct of social life. Arrangements and dealings in such a society are
often among strangers, for which the law provides a common framework,
enabling them to take place under conditions of certainty and security.
For its part, regulation means setting standards that are likely to run
counter to social practices in ways and to degrees that vary.

These differences affect the role of coercion and now we see why: with
respect to private arrangements, coercion appears at first to have no place,
since the laws of contract, property, and trusts are primarily directed at
co-ordinating and facilitating existing social practices. But why would
anyone invoke the law in entering into arrangements of these kinds? If
all the law does is provide an additional set of rules for contracting,
marrying, and dealing with property, when there are already social rules
governing them, what incentive could there be for the extra trouble of

---

[20] H. L. A. Hart, op. cit., p. 32 (2nd edn).
[21] Bentham's ideas are discussed at length in: G. Postema, op. cit., see p. 175 in particular.

following the law? The answer is that the law provides added security; it guarantees that arrangements entered into according to the law will have the protection of the law, which means providing for their enforcement. That incentive is strengthened by the law positively requiring compliance with its forms.

The enforcement of one set of rules depends on there being other rules that impose duties on other parties, meaning both other parties to the arrangements and officials. Hart beguiled us into thinking that power-conferring rules are separate from those imposing duties and, while that is sometimes true, it hides the fact that the two are normally connected, so that the first without the second are futile. Power-conferring rules depend for enforcement on duty-imposing rules, so that a complete statement of the legal arrangements brought into action by the simplest contract must include a set of rules, some giving powers to enter into private arrangements, others imposing duties on other parties and officials to uphold them. Once we realize that laws come in clusters, the place of coercion in private arrangements becomes clear: in asking why people bother to follow the legal forms of contracts or property transfers, rather than some other simpler form, we soon arrive at the conclusion that they do so because legal forms add certainty and security to their arrangements. If we then ask as to their basis, the answer must be confidence in the arrangements being upheld should a dispute or issue arise concerning them, a confidence deriving from the promise implicit in the law that it will be enforced.

The legal connections between the powers of some and the duties of others can be expressed socially as the set of relations that extend from the entering into a private transaction to the actions of officials to enforce it. The need to invoke the procedures of enforcement may be occasional, even rare, in proportion to the volume of arrangements entered into, but that is not the point; the point is that the availability of enforcement, the fact that it is used from time to time, and when used is effective, is enough to create and maintain confidence in the efficacy of legal forms. The benefits of power-conferring laws, the added advantages they confer, the attitudes of confidence they promote, are directly connected to duty-imposing laws, which make enforcement available and which constitute law's coercive foundations. Over time this is forgotten; in an effective legal system, people come to regard the laws as guides to how to do things without ever asking why, taking it for granted that it is in their interest to do so. For, after all, the everyday contract we enter into is a long way away from any notion of legal procedures of enforcement or, to borrow

Norbert Elias' image of a chain, is many links removed from its coercive end.[22] When an issue does arise, however, the possibilities of enforcement soon make their appearance and exert pressure, even if eventually they are not pursued. Perhaps this was Weber's point: in a mature legal order, coercion is its foundation, but that brute fact is so integrated into the very fabric of legal behaviour that it goes unnoticed.

8.7 CONCLUSIONS CONCERNING COERCION

A full account of the place of coercion in a social explanation of law would mean applying a similar analysis to each set of social relations and the laws expressing them. Since these issues appear again in chapter 12 in relation to the social value of law, they need not be considered further here except to note the general direction a complete account should follow. One set of social relations occurs where officials provide services, such as welfare, to citizens, the emphasis being on the powers of officials to confer benefits on citizens; at the same time, the powers must be used subject to various directions and constraints. A citizen aggrieved by the failure of officials to use their powers, or by the way they are used, may invoke duty-imposing rules, which will ultimately be enforced by other officials. From this specific set of relationships between citizens and officials, an appraisal of the general relationship between the two may be made. The granting of benefits is one expression of a social relationship that also covers the imposition of burdens, such as taxation, licensing in its many forms, and penalties. Here officials have powers to do things, while being able to invoke enforcement procedures in the event of non-compliance by citizens. Citizens, for their part, may invoke enforcement procedures aimed at making sure officials use their powers according to the terms on which they are granted, and in compliance with other constraints, such as reasonableness and procedural fairness. The same analysis could be applied to the social relations occuring in other contexts, including international law, the law of the European Union, and the World Trade Organization.

The examination began with the traditional approach of legal theory, according to which coercion is one of the defining features of a legal order. Coercion is so plainly associated with the powers of the state that it somehow had to be fitted into legal theory, even if the fit is not perfect.

[22] N. Elias, *The Civilizing Process* (Oxford, 1994) p. 314.

And yet the objects of legal theory can vary, sometimes aiming at the concept of law, at other times at a description of a municipal or modern legal system. It may be possible to imagine a concept of law in which coercion has no place, but it is more difficult to exclude it from a description of an actual legal system. A law-and-society approach is spared the dilemma since its concerns are with actual legal orders, a concern here narrowed to the notion of a modern legal order. Weber's account is the natural starting point for such an approach, especially one directed specifically at modern legal orders, and yet on this point Weber does not reveal all we should expect. He retains the idea of a legal order being founded on coercion, but without tracing through its consequences for a social understanding of law. Hart offers a fresh approach by exploiting the difficulties earlier theorists had in tying law to coercion. His identification of rules conferring powers to do things is heralded as a breakthrough in analysing the structure of a legal system. It falls short, however, in failing then to show the relationship between rules conferring powers and rules imposing duties. By examining that relationship in different areas of law, I have shown how enforcement and coercion re-enter the legal arena, even parts of it that seem far removed from them. That in turn shows that far from being just a foundation for law, as some suggest, or having no part in certain areas of law, as Hart suggests, from a law-and-society stance, coercion has a subtle, pervasive, and influential role in legal relations.

NOTES

Kelsen's account of law and coercion

The passage from *General Theory of Law and State* is worth noting in full: 'What distinguishes the legal order from all other social orders is the fact that it regulates behaviour by means of a specific technique. If we ignore this specific element of the law, if we do not conceive of the law as a specific social technique, if we define law simply as order or organization, and not as a coercive order (or organization), then we lose the possibility of differentiating law from other social phenomena; then we identify law with society, and the sociology of law with general sociology' (p. 26).

Immediately following this passage, Kelsen considers Eugen Ehrlich's attempt to separate law from coercion. According to Ehrlich, law is the ordering of human behaviour. Kelsen's rejoinder is that this is a definition of society not of law: *(General Theory of Law and State* pp. 26 *ff.)*

Ehrlich's views are stated in *Fundamental Principles of the Sociology of Law* (New York, 1932).

Weber's approach to coercion

Weber develops the notion of *guaranteed law* in *Economy and Society;* he states: 'The term "guaranteed law" shall be understood to mean that there exists a "coercive apparatus": . . . that is, that there are one or more persons whose special task is to hold themselves ready to apply specially provided means of coercion (legal coercion) for the purpose of norm enforcement' (p. 313).

Weber then declares: 'A "legal order" shall rather be said to exist wherever coercive means, of a physical or psychological kind, are available; i.e. wherever they are at the disposal of one or more persons who hold themselves ready to use them for this purpose in the case of certain events; in other words, wherever we find a co-association specifically dedicated to the purpose of "legal coercion" '. (*Economy and Society*, p. 317).

Weber also makes clear that legal orders need not be 'guaranteed by the political authority' (p. 316); provided an order is coercive in this sense, it is legal. This must qualify Weber as an early legal pluralist.

Hart's revision

As the text shows, Hart's view of coercion is significantly different from that of earlier theorists in both the British and the continental European traditions. In both traditions, coercion has been one of the defining features of a legal system. It might be asked, then, how a legal system can be distinguished from other social orders. While Hart is not absolutely explicit on this point, the defining features, or central characteristics, are: (a) a system of rules linked by the rule of recognition, and (b) a set of officials, grouped in organizations, to make, interpret, and implement the rules. Whether this is an adequate basis for distinguishing between law and other social orders, many of which have these two qualities, is questionable. In placing the emphasis on the role of officials, Hart has much in common with Weber, who retains coercion as a defining feature of a legal order, but in the reality of his account it is officials, organized into government bodies, who mark out a modern legal order.

Revising the revision

Weber does occasionally begin to show how the coercive foundation of law penetrates specific areas of law; for instance, he explains that to have a *right* means that the right-holder may invoke the aid of a coercive apparatus 'which is in special readiness for this purpose'. (*Economy and Society* p. 315). He continues, 'This aid consists, at least normally, in the readiness of certain persons to come to his support in the event that they are approached in the proper way, and that it is shown that recourse to such aid is actually guaranteed to him by a "legal norm". Such guaranty is based simply upon the "validity" of the legal proposition, and does not depend upon questions of expediency, discretion, grace, or arbitrary pleasure'. This and other passages suggest a connection between power-conferring laws and the role of coercion; the connection needs to be developed further, as I have set out in my text.

For an attempt to show that Hart's account is closely tied to sanctions: Anon; 'Hart, Austin, and the Concept of the Legal System: The Primacy of Sanctions' (1974–5) 84, *Yale Law Journal* 584, esp. pp. 599–600. It is stated: 'Legal sanctions are typically administered by a centralized official organ which possesses the exclusive authority to punish violations of the law' (p. 600). The author claims that, although Hart did not express the notion of a legal system in this way, it is implicit in his analysis.

In revisiting Hart's revision, my purpose is not to enter into debate as to whether coercion is a necessary element of the *concept* of law; Joseph Raz has shown that it is not. My purpose is instead to take the simple fact that modern legal orders are coercive orders and to show: (a) how coercion enters into different sets of legal relations and actions, and (b) what it brings to each of them. In this regard, legal orders are similar, in many ways, to any social orders, for wherever there are rules there are likely to be coercive means for enforcing them. If a legal order is distinctive, it is in: (a) its systematic provision for enforcement, (b) its being entrusted to a network of government organizations, and (c) in the *security* of the sanctions it imposes.

9

Legal Pluralism: Parallel Legal Orders

9.1 DOMINANCE OF STATE LAW

In modern legal systems, law means the law made and applied by the state through its officials and agencies. Other kinds of law have been influential in the formation of modern law but, having served their historical role, are relegated to subordinate positions. The law of the Roman Catholic Church once ran parallel to secular orders, being in some respects superior to them; it also contributed to the development of ideas and institutions on which modern legal orders are based. Its influence in western societies has long since waned, with Church law surviving in the sense that the Church makes and enforces rules for its members on matters of religion, in the way that any religious or secular association is entitled to, provided they operate within the boundaries set by state law. Roman law was a point of reference in medieval European states even though it was not incorporated into their local legal systems. In numerous non-western societies, religious law continues to operate across territorial boundaries in a manner similar to that of the early and medieval western Church. Customary law remains a worthwhile object of study because of its role in the formation of modern legal orders, and in displaying rather starkly the bond between law and social relations. It continues to have a place in societies that are traditional or in transition to being modern, creating in the process complex relations between customary law and state law. As societies modernize, the role of custom as a source of law reduces until finally it is either subsumed into state law or transformed into social conventions and practices lacking the force of law.

The one form of non-state law in the ascendancy is international law, which is a mixture of the customs and practices among nation states and conventions devised and adopted by them. International law is in the ascendancy in that the international order has become a fecund source of legal standards on a range of matters, among which human rights are prominent. Its practical efficacy depends on nation states agreeing to the covenant, incorporating it into their own legal orders, and then providing suitable implementation. The rise of international law does not signal the end of nation states and national legal orders, as some predict, since its practical efficacy is largely dependent upon states. The recognition of its legitimacy, and the reality of its influence, are features of modern legal orders, which acknowledge its importance, both as a source of universal standards and as a restraint on the legislative licence of nation states. Global Law is not to be confused with international law, which some see as an emerging legal order separate from both national and international law. The precise character of global law remains elusive and its existence uncertain; it is said to arise from practices, particularly in commercial transactions, that generate standards considered by those engaged in them to be binding. It is best regarded a type of informal law and more is said about it in the next chapter on extended legal pluralism.

State law is neither simple nor straight-forward and is open to being perceived in different ways. In one view, its distinctiveness lies in its rules being made and enforced by sets of officials, and by its superiority over competing sets of rules. Sovereign authority resides in the nation-state and, while it is neutral as to the form of government exercising sovereignty, it has tended historically to be associated with imperial or monarchical power. The legacy of that association is one of suspicion of sovereign authority and its laws, which in its modern form is deepened by the claims of sovereign bodies to the right to legislate on any matter they please, to an extent beyond the imagination of the most autocratic medieval monarch, and often regardless of the wishes of the people. The legal apparatus of the state is a mighty instrument for control and regulation which, even in democracies, tends to become divorced from the people and unstoppable in its momentum. Campaigns waged for a smaller state and less law soon founder in the face of real power and the inexhaustible demand for more law rather than less. The state and its legal apparatus have come to be seen by some as intruders on modern sensibilities, an unreconstructed leftover from the past whose demise, although welcome, is unlikely. This image of the state and sovereign authority identifies most readily with a *descending* thesis of government, as Walter Ullmann has called it, according to which power is located in a supreme being who delegates it to human societies through kings and emperors.[1] Power flows from the divine to the secular; kings receive what God gives them while the people depend on kings for what they have. Like the little dogs often depicted under the medieval banqueting table, hoping for scraps

---

[1] W. Ullmann, *A History of Political Thought: the Middle Ages* (Baltimore, 1965) p. 13.

while avoiding the boot, so the people are grateful for whatever flows from the king's benevolence, while ready to cower from his capricious malevolence.

The alternative image begins at the opposite end: here power originates with the people who elect a king or a parliament and determine the powers they are to have, for they have only those powers the people give them and for the use of which they are accountable to the people.[2] This *ascending* thesis of government has competed with its rival and won, becoming in the process an essential feature of modern legal orders. Its history can be traced philosophically through Aristotle, Aquinas, and their successors, while elements of Roman Law, the feudal law of England, and the legal orders of medieval Italian city states like Siena, have all influenced its jurisprudential foundations. There is more to be said historically to show how the ascending thesis has come to characterize modern legal orders, but it is enough for our present purpose to note that the framework of modern law, and the attitudes of officials and the people, makes sense only against this background. Modern constitutionalism is a direct result, as is the basic premise of public law that officials hold power under delegation from the legislature and, in turn, the people.

The ascending thesis also helps to counter the negative image of state law. Instead of being regarded as a powerful apparatus in the hands of autocrats and dictators, it is tied ultimately to the people. What is done by means of state law is done in their name, even if the relationship again summons up the image of a chain with many links in between the people and the state. This distance between citizens and state officials is also characteristic of a modern legal order, and however great the appeal of returning to a closer and more immediate relationship between the two, through such notions as deliberative democracy and communicative action, it is largely an impossible dream.[3] Modern legal orders have a different and more practical response to the social reality of the state: while recognizing the force of Hart's claim that having sets of officials with the capacity to change and execute the law is a major advance on pre-legal societies, modern legal orders also know of the natural tendency for officials, and therefore the law-making and law-application process, towards autonomy and separation from the people. There is no one remedy, no one way to curb that tendency; political strategies can be devised

---

[2] W. Ullmann, op. cit., p. 12.
[3] Compare: J. Habermas, *Between Facts and Norms* (Cambridge, Mass., 1996).

and economic planning can help. Our concern is with the specific and distinctive legal contribution, which lies in public law, in developing a variety of legal doctrines and mechanisms, to ensure restraint and accountability, including standards, such as due process and reasonableness, and processes such as judicial review, the ombudsman, and parliamentary scrutiny. The process is not complete, even in societies which realize that the right response to the modern state is to regulate it not destroy it.

This goes some way towards accounting for the persistence of the modern state and its legal order, how it was able to achieve its dominant position to the point of eliminating rival legal orders, and why it is tolerated, even celebrated. But it is not enough; given its power and the difficulty of controlling it, there has to be more to its continuing dominance over other forms and sources of social control. The answer is found in the capacity of the modern legal order to achieve social goods that could not otherwise be achieved as efficiently and effectively. Hence Hart's claim that rules conferring powers on officials are comparable to the invention of the wheel: modern legal systems are indispensable because they are effective instruments in giving effect to the social relations at the foundation of modern societies. They add security to relations between persons, facilitate the provision of services and welfare, enable the regulation of one set of activities in order to achieve another set of social goods, and control the imposition of punishment. Just how state law contributes to each set of social goods is shown in chapter 12, our present interest being in the principle that modern legal systems are sustained and justified because they not only contribute to the survival of society, but provide the basis for achieving positive ends and goals. This is not to ignore or underestimate the dangers state legal orders pose: they often fall into the wrong hands, and even in the right hands easily get out of control. Bentham held the open publicity of official's actions and constant vigilance by the people to be the remedy; modern societies have learnt the need to add an adequate legal and political order.[4]

9.2 FROM STATE LAW TO LEGAL PLURALISM

Legal pluralism is, to some extent, a reaction to state law; but not wholly since it has two other sources. One is the recognition that, historically, other kinds of law ran parallel to state law; the other is the quite different

---

[4] Discussed in: G. Postema, op. cit., Chapter XII.

tradition of the anthropology of law. The different kinds of law include customary law, Church law, global law as a recent contender, and informal law as a term for what has some of the features of law without quite being law. Legal pluralism is a broad term to express the idea that a society often has a number of legal orders, of which state law is just one – an important one but not the only one. Where there is a multitude of legal orders, they should be studied in order to understand their place in society and their relationship with state law; their study could also increase our understanding of law by revealing aspects that are not present in state law.

Legal theorists make reference to law other than state law in order to elucidate the *concept* of law. Hart uses the contrast between a pre-legal customary society and a municipal legal system to highlight the particular character of the latter. He separated state law from natural law and gave an account of the difference between state and international law. Far from neglecting these senses of law, he explains how each differs from modern legal systems which, for him, were the central cases of law. In the law-and-society tradition, state law has been the centre of attention, although alternative legal orders have come into their own, the argument being that their study is essential to a full understanding of law in society. State law has never been the centre of attention for anthropologists, who have instead (usually) concentrated on traditional and customary communities, which tend to lack a state apparatus and the institutions and organizations of a modern legal system, but plainly have law. According to S. Falk Moore, the anthropological approach, while including state law, 'also encompasses law-like activities and processes of establishing order in many other social domains, formal and informal, official and unofficial, in our own society and in others'.[5]

Legal pluralism is based on two ideas. One is that two or more legal orders can exist side-by-side within the same society or territory; the other is that legal systems derive from sources other than the state and exist as independent fields of law. Support for both ideas is readily found in the world around us. Anyone living in Europe is reminded daily of national legal systems running parallel with that of the European Union, while for Australians, Canadians, and Pakistanis, among others, the intersection of federal and state legal systems is a natural occurrence. The sharing of legal authority between the state and religious legal orders is not unusual, while countries with a colonial past combine in intricate

---

[5] S. Falk Moore, *Law and Anthropology: A Reader* (Oxford, 2004) p. 1.

ways indigenous legal systems with that of the state. As for the second idea of legal pluralism, the post-colonial experience also shows how orders based on custom and tradition, and without a state, are recognizably legal systems. The scope for potential non-state systems spreads beyond the colonial context, with claims of legal status being made for religious orders, ethnic communities, and an array of other groupings, sometimes founded on cultural factors, at other times on economic or territorial considerations. Each has its own system of rules and methods of enforcement, and yet does not look like and is not regarded as a legal order, unless all reasonably distinct, rule-based orders are considered to be legal.

That would serve no purpose as we shall see shortly; nevertheless, the claims of legal pluralism are important in encouraging reconsideration of several issues. The most obvious is the nature of a legal order and what it is that warrants one system of rules being designated as law and another not; and what are the criteria for doing so? Where legal orders run in parallel, issues arise as to the relations between them. Another issue is why the designation as law or not, as the case may be, matters; what is added by regarding a set of rules as legal rather than merely social? Do legal orders other than state law reveal new aspects of law that are relevant to law in society? And finally, the question arises as to whether too much emphasis has been given to state law, and too many assumptions made about its importance in society, perhaps to the neglect of other more informal systems of rules, whether or not classified as legal. Bentham, who must be held one of nature's legal centralists, considered enacted state law was needed in the England of his day simply because the traditional customary orders could not cope with a large and diverse society.[6] Legal pluralists, it need hardly be said, argue fairly much the opposite.

9.3 PARALLEL AND INTERSECTING LEGAL ORDERS

It would be hard to find a better account of legal pluralism in its classic sense than in colonial South America, where three legal systems ran in parallel: not only the law of Spain administered through its colonial governors, and the law of the local population, but also the Church through the Inquisition.[7] Laura Benton depicts the situation in an evocative study

---

[6] See G. Postema, op. cit., Part II.
[7] L. Benton, *Law and Colonial Cultures: Legal Regimes in World History* (Cambridge, 2002).

of parallel legal orders. She explains how overall dominance lay with the Spanish governor and his administration, with the Church having long established its claim over matters beyond the spiritual, while in practice much was left to local laws and institutions. Disputes arose as to which matters fell within which system and where the boundaries among them lay, with intersection and overlap inevitable. Benton shows how, despite suffering restrictions and oppression from the two foreign legal orders, the local population could move among the three, sometimes playing one off against the other, sometimes gaining from one benefits denied by the other. In this and other studies of both the colonial experience and other global encounters among legal orders, Benton portrays parallel legal orders existing and functioning, overlapping, colliding, and reshaping; she explains how they sometimes become absorbed into state law, at other times retaining a plurality where each is distinct but intertwined with others.

The idea of two or more legal orders existing within the same society or territory is neither novel nor problematic. The colonial experience, usually taking the form of a foreign state occupying a territory and imposing its legal system where one or more already existed, is one of the classic cases of legal pluralism. The usual pattern is for a foreign state first to claim jurisdiction for its laws, then to cede some matters to the local order. The range of matters ceded is likely to contract over time, sometimes eventually disappearing altogether as the foreign system gives way to the formation of a new local state; in other cases, the traditional system survives even after a state authority has been created, and gives rise to a complex relationship between the two, a relationship more intricate and subtle than stark ideas of dominance and subservience convey. The pattern developed during colonialism is mirrored in modern cases of pluralism, where within a state system another legal order is recognized as having authority for certain matters. The basis for recognition may be the vestiges of a colonial experience, or common identity of a religious or ethnic kind, or perhaps a distinctive part of the territory.

The legal pluralism of colonialism is by no means the first historical case or the main one. Conquest of one country by another, and the imposition of one set of laws on another, are as old as history, and supply many examples of legal orders existing side-by-side in complex relationships. Quite different historical forms of pluralism are readily found. Relations between secular states and the medieval Church, a Europe-wide organization having jurisdiction over a range of matters, reveal a different version where distinct legal systems run side-by-side, intersect, and overlap. In the latter years of the Roman Empire, law was commonly personal rather than territorial with the result that different orders applied to different peoples within the same territory.[8] Similar parallel legal orders, one secular, the other religious, occur often enough today, sometimes as more-or-less equal partners, at other times with the dominant secular law conceding areas of jurisdiction to the religious, or vice versa. The same pattern of parallel and equal legal orders, in this case formalized, can be seen in federal systems where legal authority is divided among a number of states or provinces and a federal authority. The relationship is not hierarchical but one in which some powers are divided, others shared.

Whether or not any pattern can be detected among parallel legal orders, several formations are familiar: two or more legal orders run side-by-side with well-defined areas of jurisdiction (the Church-state division, a federal system, and the European Union being examples); one is dominant while leaving space for one or more subordinate orders (the classic colonial case and some modern examples); two legal orders compete for control over specific subject-matters or territory (one often being secular, the other religious); or a global order transcends national boundaries and has no direct relationship with them (global business systems being an example). The penultimate case, marked by competition between legal orders, is most common during periods of strife or upheaval, after which a more settled pattern is likely to emerge.

From a legal point of view, parallel orders raise issues about the relationship between them, and again the possible variations are numerous. A complex body of doctrine known as *conflict of laws* determines when one legal order should apply rules and doctrines from another legal order.[9] The division of legal authority among different orders is often provided for in a constitution, as in federal systems, with the courts having authority to settle disputes. Alternatively, parallel orders may have quite different origins but be linked by the constitution, an example being Pakistan, where an amendment to the constitution provides for appeals on certain matters from the highest state court to the religious Sha'ria courts. A variation occurs when a colonial legal system adopts doctrines that incorporate local legal orders, or specify to what extent they will be recognized as having authority. The relationship between parallel orders is not

---

[8] See: P. Stein, *Roman Law in European History*, (Cambridge, New York and Melboune, 1999) p. 30.
[9] See A. Briggs and B. Markepsinis, *Foreign Laws and Foreign Ideas in the English Courts*, (Amsterdam, 1998).

always contained in a precise constitutional document but may rely on political understandings, court rulings, and informal agreements, an image that fits the European Union. The original treaty, the Treaty of Rome, which may loosely be regarded as a constitution, omitted to define fully the relationship between the new European legal order and that of member states, a matter soon remedied by the European Court of Justice in establishing the supremacy of European law. Whatever the formal legal and constitutional arrangements, informal understandings and practices are likely to form around the relationship between parallel orders, often modifying the formal position, or, where no or inadequate formal provision is made, filling the gap informally.

Some of the most complex legal and social issues arise when parallel orders exist without mutual recognition. This often occurs within the bounds of a state system where a community, founded perhaps on ethnic or religious principles, purports to live according to its own laws. Where the state formally recognizes the parallel order as legal, a common enough occurrence in some countries, the position follows the lines described above. It is also often the case that the state does not recognize a parallel order as being a legal system, despite its members holding that it is. The shepherds of Sardinia have their own informal legal order concerning such important matters as the theft of sheep, and avoid the Italian legal system, which for its part does not recognize that of the shepherds.[10] Despite denial of recognition by a state order, an ethnic or religious community may persist in the belief in the authority of its informal order, while nevertheless conducting its affairs within the parameters of state law, and in that way avoiding conflicts between the two. The state, for its part, without making formal concessions, may act in ways indicating an informal acceptance of the authority of the community order. An exemption from wearing a protective helmet when cycling, or allowing headscarves to be worn to school, on one interpretation are no more than signs of respect for other religions; on another they come close to being recognition of another informal legal order. A slight shift in the relationship can lead to conflicts between the two, with the rules of the subordinate order confronting the laws of the state. From a state point of view its law prevails, although the position is likely to be moderated by informal conventions developing over time and structuring the relationship between the two, in ways that allow scope for and tolerance of the rules of

---

[10] See the study by J. L. Ruffini, 'Disputing Over Livestock in Sardinia' in L. Nader and H. F. Todd (eds), *The Disputing Process: Law in Ten Societies* (New York, 1976).

the informal community. It is not necessarily in the interests of the state to exert total legal authority over informal orders, or to take measures to remove or reduce other legal orders, or to curtail their activities. Parallel orders, however designated legally, often preserve a high level of social order among their members, and in that also serve the interests of the state.

9.4 SOCIAL CONSEQUENCES OF PARALLEL LEGAL ORDERS

From a law-and-society point of view, parallel legal orders raise several issues, one of which is implicit in the last remarks: how they intersect, not just in terms of legal or constitutional rules, but informally and in practice. The example of three parallel orders – the state, the Church, and the local – in colonial South America illustrates the complex and intricate points of intersection among them. To extend the study to other parallel legal orders, whether formally provided for or informally created, would be a valuable addition to our understanding of law in society. The notion of social spheres should serve well as a way of focusing on the process of intersecting, or intermingling as Benton describes it, with each legal order constituting a set of social spheres. Viewing the intersection of plural legal orders through this lens, let us consider briefly some of the issues that emerge.

The identity of legal orders, based in Hart's terms on the rule of recognition, raises the question of how one is distinguished from another. Despite there being nothing in the nature of parallel legal systems to question each having its own rules of recognition, the way and extent to which the rules of one take account of, or make provision for the rules of another, requires close examination. The contextual contingencies, a feature common to all social rules, whereby rules are regarded as part of a fuller context of conventions and understandings, are likely to be specially prominent here, showing that the rules of recognition, even of stable state legal orders, are capable of tolerating, recognizing, and even incorporating, the rules and practices of a parallel order. The position is sometimes formalized, with provision being made by state law for the recognition of all or parts of another order; in other cases it is left open to be settled informally by officials and citizens according to the conventions and understandings forming around it. Even where the relationship is formalized, the formalities are bound to be incomplete, leaving room for informal conventions to develop. Where recognition by one of

the other is not reciprocated, relations between the two become complicated. These are just a few of the issues arising within the formal and
informal relationship between parallel legal orders, with the close study
of each a source of so-far-untapped knowledge into the nature of law and
its social foundations.

This brings us to another aspect of parallel legal orders, which illustrates the many points of contact between them, not only at the level of
rules of recognition, but by officials, associations, and individuals in a
myriad of encounters requiring them to interpret, understand, and assess
the relationship, and make sense of it in resolving practical issues.
Whether they are judges engaged in a final ruling, or officials deciding on
the grant of a licence where eligibility involves more than one legal order,
or village elders arbitrating a family dispute, each requires an understanding of both the formal and informal arrangements. Take the last case of
the village officials: the main source of their authority is the local customary legal order, yet the state system also confers certain powers on them,
so that the two run side-by-side without too much concern as to whether
they are consistent, overlapping, or contradictory. Local officials are then
free to move between the two, making the best of both, probably without
too much supervision from either.

Non-official associations, groups, and individual persons also face and
need to make sense of the intersection between two legal orders. They
need to know what is required of them and how to move between the two,
perhaps gaining advantages from one that the other denies. The points of
intersection and the way they are dealt with by both officials and citizens
depend on the social spheres within which they operate, that is, on the
conventions and understandings within which each approaches the task.
Communities develop over time ways of reconciling the intersection of
parallel orders, learning from experience what is acceptable and where
the boundaries lie in practice. It is only when we begin to consider such
practical matters that the depth and range of intermingling of parallel
orders become fully visible. Benton captures the experience of intermingling in the notion of 'a peculiar sub-text of rules about rules',[11] a
notion that resonates beyond the colonial experience to include the many
points of intersection, the many levels of officials deciding on a course of
action, and the diverse groups of people who somehow have to manage.
The only rider is that *rules*, rather than conventions and understandings,
is too sharp a notion to capture the full sense of the intermingling.

[11] L. Benton, op. cit.

Another set of issues for law-and-society arises when we move from issues about the intersection of orders to the character of law itself. Any lingering idea that law can only be state law, or that only state law counts, should be dispelled by even a cursory review of the many examples of parallel orders. The Church had a prominent role in medieval Europe as a distinct legal order long before it assumed the form and authority of a state, it being arguable that its organization as a legal order became the model later adopted by secular authorities.[12] Religious associations which are more loosely formed and lack the organizational structures of the medieval Church, often win recognition as having legal authority over a range of matters, not by delegation from the state, but on the basis of their being distinct, independent legal orders. The colonial experience demonstrates how foreign authorities recognized a variety of indigenous arrangements, some formalized and plainly legal, others more informal and less obviously law. A different kind of potential legal order consists in business and financial transactions that occupy the global sphere without reliance on national systems.[13] And there may be others, whose study should add to our understanding of the nature of law in this wider context.

Whether legal theory will find anything new in the study of plural legal forms of these kinds remains to be seen, while for law-and-society one additional set of issues of obvious interest is this: how does a group or community come to regard its rules as legal, and what effect, if any, does the *legal* dimension have on behaviour. On Hart's account, a set of rules constitutes law if officials have the internal view towards them and regard them as binding. In a customary system, this would mean regarding all rules established by custom as binding, while in more developed orders officials accept a rule of recognition according to which new rules may be made. In some plural orders, the idea of a group of officials is artificial, so that acceptance has to be by the members as a whole. Provided the rules are also generally obeyed, Hart's test of a legal order is satisfied, the result being that an order of rules is a legal order if it is regarded as law by those to whom the rules apply. The trouble with this conclusion is that it provides an unacceptably wide notion of law, for in both language and practice we distinguish between sets of legal rules and sets of social rules that are not legal; it is surely not enough for social rules to become

---

[12] See H. Berman, *Law and Revolution* (Cambridge, Mass., 1983).
[13] For general discussion, see W. Twining, *Globalization and Legal Theory*, (Cambridge, 2000) – General jurisprudence – http://www.ucl.ac.uk/laws/academics/profiles/twining/gen_juris.pdf

law merely by being so regarded. Some additional element is needed, although precisely what is not clear. But being plainly a vital issue for the existence of informal legal orders, we must return to it shortly.

Two final matters for law-and-society arise from the intersection of legal orders. The first is whether the legal dimension of plural orders affects behaviour. This, in turn, has two aspects which are mentioned here rather than developed. One concerns the behaviour of members of the non-state legal order, the other concerns those outside who have dealings with it, particularly the officials of a state system. The second issue takes us back to the intersection with state law where the question is: what is the effect on the actions of state officials where they encounter a parallel legal order? Several possibilities are open. One is where state officials do not regard the parallel order as legal, although even that leaves open questions as to whether it can be considered law for some purposes but not others. Where the parallel order is recognized as legal, the question is how that affects the attitudes of state officials and their treatment of it. It is reasonable to assume that a set of social rules regarded as legal by state officials is treated differently from one that is not; in the social spheres of state officials the difference surely matters. And yet it is far from clear how it matters. Recognition is itself a variable notion; it could be full recognition or only for certain purposes; or it could mean no more than extending to a parallel order greater tolerance than it normally would to a competing set of social rules. Recognition could take the form of limits and restrictions on what the alternative system is permitted to do, leaving it only pockets of autonomy rather than a sense of full authority. As parallel orders become deeply intertwined, it may become difficult not only to isolate the one from the other but also to keep sight of the specifically legal dimension.

NOTES

Nature of Legal Pluralism

Among the many accounts of legal pluralism, the following are particularly useful in their discussion of different aspects:

M. B. Hooker, *Legal Pluralism: An Introduction to Colonial and Neocolonial Laws* (Oxford, 1975).

A. Griffith, 'Legal Pluralism' in R. Banakar and M. Travers (eds), *An Introduction to Law and Social Theory* (Oxford, 2002, Hart).

J. Griffiths, 'What Is Legal Pluralism' (1986) 24 *Journal of Legal Pluralism* 1–55.

S. E. Merry, 'Legal Pluralism' (1988) 22 *Law & Society Review* 869–896.

B. Tamanaha, *Realistic Socio-Legal Theory* (Oxford, 1997).

S. Roberts, 'After Government: On Representing Law Without the State' (2005) 68 *Modern Law Review* 1.

S. Roberts and J. L. Comaroff, *Rules and Processes* (Chicago, 1981).

To the quotation in the text, the following statement from S. Falk Moore should be added: 'An anthropological approach to law inquires into the context of enforceable norms: social, political, economic, and intellectual. This includes, but goes further than, what Western governments and courts define as law'. op. cit., p. 1.

Parallel and intersecting legal orders

L. Benton's *Law and Colonial Cultures: Legal Regimes in World History* shows with clarity the character of parallel and intersecting legal orders.

On the intersection of Roman Law with customary and local legal orders in the Middle Ages and in Medieval Europe, see P. Stein, *Roman Law in European History*.

Global Legal Orders

Much of the recent discussion of parallel legal orders is conducted around the notion of a global legal order. In addition to William Twining's writings, referred to in the text, the following are good examples:

R. Michaels, 'The Re-statement of Non-State Law: The State, Choice of Law and the Challenges from Global Legal Pluralism', *Duke Law School Social Studies Series*, Research Paper no. 81, 2005.

G. Teubner, *Global Law Without a State* (Dartmouth, 1997).

L. M. Friedman, 'Erewhon: The Coming Global Legal Order' (2001) 37 *Stanford Journal of International Law* 347.

On Parallel Legal Orders

R. C. van Caenegen creates a strikingly clear image of legal pluralism in medieval Europe: 'Old Europe had known a legal fragmentation that we can hardly conceive. Europeans had lived under various Germanic tribal laws, attached not to a territory, but to men and women of common descent . . . The innumerable medieval corporations – universities, guilds and crafts – had their own laws and rules, and above it all the Church applied its canons and decretals and the neo-Roman law of the glossators and the commentators'. (*European Law in the Past and the Future* (Cambridge, 2002) p. 23).

In relation to the Trobriand islanders, S. Falk-Moore writes 'Primitive law is not a homogenous, perfectly limited body of rules, based upon one principle developed into a consistent system. . . . The law of these nations consists on the contrary of a number of more or less independent systems, only partly adjusted to one another'. (op. cit., p.77).

The dilemmas facing judges who have to decide cases on the basis of competing legal orders is well-documented in a study of the judicial process in Indonesia, a country of great size and diversity, moving across customary, state, and religious law.

J. R. Bowen describes adjudication in this way: 'Judges in these societies have been finding their interlegal feet amidst a multitude of statutes, court decisions, religious doctrines, and colonial-era treatises on "customary law" '. (J. R. Bowen, 'Consensus and Suspicion: Judicial Reasoning and Social Change in an Indonesian Society 1960–1994' (2000) 34 *Law and Society Review* 97 (quoted in Falk-Moore, op. cit., p. 154)).

Further reference

L Rosen, *The Anthropology of Justice: Law as Culture in Islamic Society* (Cambridge, 1989).

Extended Legal Pluralism: Informal Legal Orders

10.1 EXTENDED LEGAL PLURALISM

If we were to end here we would leave behind a fairly clear picture of the diversity of legal orders, of how they run in parallel, intersect, and compete, together with the suggestion that further study of them from a law-and-society view would be timely. Alas, we cannot end here, for proponents of legal pluralism contend that there are arenas of informal rules which should be recognized as legal orders but are not. Recognition should be extended, it is said, to some of the associations commonly found in a society: economic and business associations, the family, nongovernmental bodies, sporting clubs, and so on; all should be considered as potential legal orders. *Extended legal pluralism*, as I shall call it, refers to those rule-governed spheres which are not regarded as legal orders but perhaps ought to be. The point of such claims is not immediately obvious: why extend the meaning of a legal order in this way and what is to be gained by it? The depth of feeling with which the case is put makes it hard to elicit a clear answer; the best that can be done is to proceed by considering what it is that troubles its proponents and from that isolate the issues.

One troubling notion is *legal centralism*, by which is meant, to quote one of its critics, that: 'law is and should be the law of the state, uniform for all persons, exclusive of all other law, and administered by a single set of state institutions'.[1] If this is meant to be an empirical claim it is plainly untenable for we have just seen several forms of non-state law. A more plausible concern is that excessive interest is taken in state law as a regulatory force in society, the corollary being that other (legal) orders are obscured or neglected, or not given their proper place. A third set of

---

[1] J. Griffiths, 'Legal Pluralism and the Theory of Legislation: With Special Reference to the Regulation of Euthanasia' in *Legal Polycentricity: Consequences of Pluralism in Law,* (ed.) H. Petersen and H. Zahle (Dartmouth, 1998).

concerns takes a different tack: here the emphasis is not on rescuing informal legal orders from neglect or oblivion, but on examining the relationships among them, and particularly between them and state law.[2] It is not enough on this view to draw attention to the existence of informal legal orders; attention should be paid to the ways in which different legal orders interact, intersect, and influence each other.

Before examining these matters, several general comments are warranted. In the first place, it is hardly contentious that a society is made-up of numerous rule-governed orders, some based on formally declared rules, others on informal rules, the range and variety of which are extensive. As a second general observation, these 'multiple forms of social ordering', as Anne Griffith aptly describes them,[3] interact in intricate ways not only with each other but also with state law. The interaction between law and other social formations is indeed one of the two principal objects of a study of law in society; earlier chapters contain an analysis of the interaction and offer a structured approach to it. The scope and density of interactions between parallel legal orders is considered in the preceding chapter, where it is shown how each influences the other: state law influences the understandings and conventions held within other legal orders and, in turn, behaviour; those other legal orders exert their own influence on state officials and their social spheres, in making, interpreting, and implementing law. This framework of interaction provides the setting for detailed studies of specific cases, which are likely to occur within a range, at one end of which the interaction and mutual influence is close and intricate, while at the other end the two are virtually independent of each other. And finally, while social spheres, as a general term to include such formal and informal associations, are powerful influences on the actions of individual persons, state law aims to be the supreme influence. Its influence is of a particular kind, partly because it claims final authority, partly because it has a well-developed set of organizations to implement the rules, and partly because it can resort to coercive enforcement. One reason for the domination of state law, therefore, is that it raises specific issues warranting analysis, whose object is to understand the ways by which it directs and influences behaviour, to what extent it does so, and how it intersects with other influences on behaviour. In setting the record straight on these matters, we see how the general

---

[2] This set of concerns is well-brought out in S. E. Merry, 'Legal Pluralism' (1988) 22 *Law and Society Review* 869–896.

[3] A. Griffith, 'Legal pluralism' in R. Banakar and M. Travers (eds), op. cit., p. 302.

concerns of legal pluralists can be accommodated within the approach to law-and-society set out in this book. It should also be noted that empirical research has long engaged with the interaction between state law and social spheres, even if not always put it in terms of legal pluralism.

10.2 THREE CONCERNS ABOUT LEGAL CENTRALISM

Legal centralism is a stumbling block for pluralists and is held to be a bad thing for several reasons. One is that legal centralism assumes state law to be the only real law, the corollary being that other rule-governed arenas are not law. In light of the examples of non-state law considered earlier, the charge to be plausible would have to be modified to be: the state model so dominates our image of law that legal status is denied to social spheres when it should be acknowledged. This takes us to the core of what counts as law and needs to be examined. A second concern about legal centralism is the assumption that state law is the best way of obtaining social goods, the converse being that informal orders are inferior. Considering the expectations held of state law in modern societies, such a concern is understandable, and further provoked by the familiar sight of law being used without proper consideration being given to other social mechanisms. A final concern is that legal centralism encourages the idea that informal systems of rules are subordinate to state law and operate only within boundaries set by it.[4] Each of these issues will be considered in reverse order.

10.3 RULE–GOVERNED SPHERES SUBORDINATE TO STATE LAW

Since state law claims final authority over all matters within its jurisdiction, it is reasonable to conclude that other rule-governed arenas are subordinate to it. That legal point of view does not meet the pluralist's concern that, whereas legal centralism presents social spheres as subject to it, many in fact emerge, exist, and function independently of it and autonomously. It is not obvious, to whom the concern is addressed although several possible culprits can be found. Legal theorists are one

---

[4] This is one of the main charges made against legal centralism in: J. Griffiths, 'Legal Pluralism and the Theory of Legislation: With Special Reference to the Regulation of Euthanasia:' op. cit.

for they promote the hegemony of state law; state officials are presumably another because they act on the assumption of state law's superiority. Here I take the concern to be with those who conduct law-and-society research, for they allegedly mis-describe social reality, either in over-stating the scope of state law, or in understating the autonomy of other rule-based associations and their independence from state law, or in doing both.

On this interpretation, the critique is narrowed to the claim that at least some social spheres in practice have more independence and auton-omy than legal centralism allows. This, in turn, has two aspects: one is that such associations regulate their own activities, the other is that they do so relatively autonomously of state law. The first is uncontroversial for reasons that became clear earlier: society consists of both purposive and spontaneous activities based around either formal or informal rules, or a combination of the two, which guide behaviour. There is no obstacle to accepting that such rule-based associations and their social spheres have the capacity to regulate areas of social activity. The second part of the claim is that some such associations, such as religious associations, family structures, ethnic communities, voluntary associations, or sporting clubs, are at least candidates to be considered as independent and autonomous, in a way similar to those parallel legal orders considered earlier.

The question, then, is whether such associations or even a selection of them are, as a matter of description, independent and autonomous of state law in a strong sense of both terms. The answer must be a double nega-tive: negative in the legal sense that state law claims jurisdiction over all matters, and negative in the social sense that in modern societies all such associations and organizations are subject to state law, both specific laws regulating them and the general law. The subordination of social spheres to state law is normally recognized by their members and affects their actions. It is impossible to accept that families, professional associations, and sporting clubs, among many others, are in a strong sense autonomous of state law, either legally or socially. State law claims jurisdiction over them, from time-to-time exerts that jurisdiction, and has mechanisms for enforcing it. This is not to say that state law regularly or systematically uses its authority; in fact it leaves many areas of activity remaining more-or-less unregulated by law. The usual situation is that state law regulates some while leaving others to the social conventions that emerge, or are created by those engaged in the activity.

Perhaps independence and autonomy should be taken in a weaker form, with *semi-independence* and *semi-autonomy* being more suitable terms.[5] Insertion of a sense of reality exacts a high price from pluralists, for the strong claim of strong autonomy then becomes the weak and unremarkable one of some or partial autonomy. Some or partial autonomy means several things and is a matter of degree, but is plainly a retreat from the notion that rule-based associations are beyond the jurisdiction of state law. Once it is accepted that state law may, and often does, intervene in social spheres, it follows that autonomy is a variable, conditional on the extent and the consequences of intervention. For to speak of semi-autonomy and semi-independence is to accept a relationship between state law and social spheres in the course of which they interact and intersect in various ways, the close study of which will reveal just how autonomous and independent, or not, an association is at any time.

In judging the degree of independence and autonomy in particular cases, several factors are relevant. *First,* state law normally claims authority over all matters within its jurisdiction, whether or not it in fact exercises its authority. *Secondly,* state law may recognize certain activities as separate legal orders, which means it does not claim authority over them, although as a society becomes more developed and stable, becomes more modern, such recognition is rarer. *Thirdly,* state law may informally cede a degree of autonomy and independence to an arena of rule-governed activity, but it must be contingent, and can be curtailed or removed at a stroke. The authority of state law to reclaim what was ceded is a factor of social significance affecting the relationship between the two spheres. *Fourthly,* when state law does exert its authority over an association or area of activity, the degree of regulation, and hence the restrictions on them, is a major variable in their relationship, the precise contours of which can be ascertained only by close study of the laws. *Fifthly,* when state laws are made restricting the autonomy of associations or other activities, their practical effects vary, depending on how the laws are received by those affected, and on the extent to which they are implemented and enforced by state officials.

Legal pluralism has reason to draw attention to these variables and to the relatively high levels of autonomy and independence of some rule-based associations. It is mistaken, however, in its concepts: it is not independence and autonomy *from* state law in the sense of being outside its control; independence and autonomy occur *within* the jurisdiction of state law and *in* a relationship with it. Within the relationship numerous

[5] See S. F. Moore, op. cit.

issues arise for further consideration, including the effects on rule-based associations of state law's claim to authority over them, the extent to which state law's attempts at regulating such association is successful, and what happens when legal rules of the state run into opposing social spheres. This rather lengthy explanation, while of utility in better understanding the claims of legal pluralism, is a roundabout way of making two fairly simple statements: (a) in the modern state, legal orders tend to claim authority over all activities and associations within their jurisdiction (with occasional exceptions); while (b) at the same time affording substantial freedom to associations to regulate their own activities by their own social rules.

10.4 BALANCE OF STATE LAW AND SOCIAL SPHERES

We are often reminded how awful life would be without law, where law is taken to mean state law. Thomas Hobbes's state of nature with its imagined horrors was a society without law; David Hume declared security of property to be the foundation of society, adding that: 'property is nothing but those goods whose constant possession is established by the laws of society'.[6] Jeremy Bentham kept up the tradition a century later, asserting: 'Property and law are held together and die together',[7] while Hart went further in specifying the kinds of laws needed for survival. Among the four, Bentham must be considered the arch-legal centralist in contending that the task of the state-enacted law is: 'to define anew, to establish and then to sustain, a social and political order and framework for broad scale interaction'.[8] The claims made for the social role of state law are surely extravagant. Much the same can be said for the exuberant claims of legal pluralism, where state law is pushed to the periphery and informal orders take centre stage. *Legal peripheralism*, as R. Ellickson aptly calls it, reduces to negligible levels the significance of state law in ordering society, a position that is no more sustainable than extreme forms of legal centralism.[9] Legal peripheralism finds some perhaps unexpected support in the work of Michel Foucault who, in his search for the seat of power and social regulation, considered state law to be rather marginal. He states: 'one should try to locate power at the extreme point

---

[6] D. Hume, *A Treatise of Human Nature* (Oxford, 1888) p. 491.
[7] Quoted in S. Diamond, 'The rule of law versus the order of custom' (1971) 38 *Social Research* 42.
[8] See the discussion in: G.Postema, op. cit., p. 315.   [9] R. Ellickson, op. cit., chapter 8.

of its exercise, where it is always legal in character.'[10] The issue is surely not one or the other, but rather what kinds of tasks are suitable for informal orders, and which should be the subject of state law. Even that is putting it a little crudely for the two often go together, with the one strengthening the other. They can, of course, also pull in opposite directions.

In seeking a balance between the proper scope of state law and other social orders, a distinction should be drawn between prescriptive claims about how one or the other should be used, and empirical attempts to understand the actual strengths and weaknesses of each in dealing with social situations. The dislike and distrust pluralists have for state law displays itself in prescriptions both as to the limits of state law and the appeal of informal orders. According to the first, state law descends from above rather than ascends from the people, while the administrative and judicial apparatus augments the sense of remoteness, encouraging avoidance and ineffectiveness rather than willing compliance. If to this is added the familiar spectacle of state law's being used for purposes for which it is plainly unsuitable, the concerns of legal pluralists have some justification. Orders of informal norms appear to offer an attractive alternative, growing organically from social practices, lacking a heavy-handed bureaucracy, and responding to people's real needs. The ranchers of Shasta County offer some support for this image. Despite a reasonable set of California state laws setting standards and providing for the resolution of their disputes, the ranchers adopted and administered their own rules and settled disputes informally and apparently successfully.[11]

Studies of post-communist Russia and neighbouring countries show how state law can be ineffective in guiding behaviour. The reasons why include a traditional scepticism among the people about both law and state officials, the use of law by governments to achieve their own ulterior ends and purposes, and the capacity of powerful organizations – the Orthodox Church being a notable case – to resist laws considered contrary to their interests.[12] In moving from the instinctive and prescriptive to the empirical, these studies and others help in identifying the variables that affect

---

[10] M. Foucault, *The History of Sexuality, Vol 1, An Introduction* (New York, 1978), pp. 96–97. The quotation is cited in A. Hunt's and G. Wickham's excellent account of Foucault, op. cit.

[11] R. Ellickson's study of the ranchers is of considerable importance in understanding the relationship between state laws and informal social porders; see: R. Elllickson, op. cit.

[12] D. J. Galligan and M. Kurkchiyan (eds), *Law and Informal Practices in Post-Communist Europe* (London, 2000).

the success or failure of state law and the advantages and disadvantages of informal social norms. That neither of the studies was conducted from a specifically legal pluralist point of view is not that important, since they reinforce the social utility of alternative social orders of conventions and understandings, whether or not legal status is claimed for them. At the same time, legal pluralists should feel some responsibility for grounding in empirical research their prescriptive views about both state law and informal orders.

The case for state law is traditionally founded on the idea that it has certain distinctive functions to serve in maintaining society and achieving social goods. This issue is considered in chapters 11 and 12 where it is argued that we should move beyond claims about law's *functions* and instead identify the advantages and disadvantages different types of laws have in achieving social goods.[13] This is a preliminary analysis and only a first step towards a full understanding of how best to achieve a set of social goals, and when to rely on state law or other rule-based associations. The issue is complicated, and we are a long way from a general theory that would guide the use of each. Our concern for the moment is with legal pluralism and the underlying claim that informal legal orders are more efficient and effective in achieving some social goods than state law. In order to make the claim more credible, legal pluralists need to provide evidence for it, both through empirical research and by formulating general hypotheses. The kinds of questions they need to answer are: under what conditions are informal rule-governed orders likely to arise, and why; how effective are they in achieving social goods, including social order but going beyond it; what variables affect their capacity to do so; and what are the advantages of informal orders over state law.[14] Answers to these questions would help in understanding the role of informal rule-governed orders, but for legal pluralists there is an additional element: they must also show the utility of dividing such orders into those that are *legal* and those that are not.

10.5 THE ELUSIVE LEGAL ELEMENT IN LEGAL PLURALISM

This brings us to the final concern legal pluralists have about the dominance of state law: modern societies contain spheres of rule-governed

---

[13] A preliminary account of different types of laws is given in chapter 8.5 *and* 8.6.

[14] The most sustained attempt to answer some of these questions is Robert Ellickson's *Order Without Law* to which reference is rarely made in the pluralist literature.

activity that are properly-speaking legal orders. The idea that state law is not the only kind of legal order is perfectly sensible and historically authentic, while the idea that all or even most rule-governed spheres are legal orders is just as perfectly unhistorical and untenable. Some legal pluralists nevertheless hold the view that at least some rule-governed spheres should be regarded as legal orders, and that to deny that status is to distort their nature. Any set of social rules, any social sphere, has rules, norms, and conventions that influence behaviour, but they are not generally considered to be law, unless law is defined to mean simply a rule-governed sphere. Extended legal pluralism does not make that claim, and it would do so in vain; at the same time, it has difficulty in defining what it is that makes some informal orders legal orders. Among the questions this prompts, two stand out: one is why it is important to regard rule-governed spheres as law; the other is the criterion for doing so.

Before suggesting answers, one or two preliminary remarks help to set the scene. In common speech we do not normally refer to rule-governed associations as law: the university, financial institution, sporting associ- ation, family, and so on, have rules not laws. Not even the ranchers of Shasta County are likely to refer to their informal code as law.[15] Religious communities, such as those living in British cities, refer to their holy books as law, normally adding the qualification that it is God's law, thus distinguishing it from state law. Such communities often have rules con- cerning secular matters as well, but they are unlikely to be considered law as opposed to conventions or customs. If language reflects reality, then the fact that members of associations, which are supposed to qualify as legal orders, do not consider them to be so is a set-back to the pluralist case. Even in societies where state law is weak and widely disregarded, and informal rule-based systems are strong, as in various former commu- nist countries of eastern Europe, people still make a distinction between law as the law of the state and informal social norms, even though the latter are often more important than law in regulating their lives.[16] So while language itself tells against the stronger claims of legal pluralism, another not uncommon usage may hold a clue to identifying the elusive legal element: although the ranchers, the diamond traders, and ethnic groups do not refer to their rules as law, they might use the term *informal law*, the implication being that it is not law in the full and accepted sense

---

[15] It is worth noting that the study referred to it the previous footnote does not use the concept of legal pluralism; it does not appear in the index, now is it discussed in the text: see R. Ellickson, op. cit.

[16] See: D. J. Galligan and M. Kurkchiyan (eds) op. cit.

but a mirror of law sufficient and to merit the association. To this point we shall return shortly.

Before doing so, we should consider the two questions posed above and remind ourselves of the reasons for wanting to extend the notion of law to a multitude of rule-governed spheres. The claim that state law is given too much prominence and informal orders of rules not enough, even if true, would not itself be a good reason for extending the meaning of law. Nor would it be enough to draw attention to similarities between state law and other rule-based spheres, so that if one were law then the others also should be law. The reasons legal pluralists give for singling out some informal orders as legal are indirect, more a reaction against state law than showing what is to be positively gained. A potential reason could be that the designation of a social order as legal is socially significant; being *legal* adds some quality in the perception of both those subject to the order and state officials. Perhaps colonial officials treated indigenous orders differently, depending on whether they regarded them as legal or not. That might also be the case in a modern society: if officials regard a rule-governed sphere as a legal order, they should be expected to show it more deference than a non-legal one. And if such social orders are properly described as legal, their study should reveal qualities not found in state law, and so increase our social understanding of law.

This must remain, to a large degree, speculative because legal pluralists have not made clear the value of designating a social sphere as a legal order. Assuming that further research would show good social reasons for the designation, what is the elusive legal element? What is it that makes some rule-governed spheres *legal*? Several answers have been given: one describes law, in this case indigenous law, as *concrete patterns of social ordering*;[17] another as *rules evolving spontaneously out of social life*;[18] a third is in terms of *semi-autonomous social fields*.[19] Each of these summons up the idea of a law as a sphere of conventions and understandings; but since many associations of people more-or-less fit that description, it cannot be the basis for distinguishing legal orders from non-legal. Legal pluralists sometimes add a second condition: a social sphere must not only be rule-based but also have officials and institutions to apply the rules. The institutional aspects, so central to Hart's description of a legal system, could then be the basis for eliminating the social spheres lacking them. Its

---

[17] M. Galanter, 'Justice in Many Rooms: Courts, Private Ordering, and Indigenous Law' (1981) 19 *Journal of Legal Pluralism* 1, pp.17–18.

[18] S. F. Moore, op. cit.   [19] *Ibid.*

promise soon peters out because many social spheres, such as sporting clubs or professional associations, are institutionalized, having officials and offices for making, interpreting, and enforcing rules, and yet are plainly not legal orders. A similar fate awaits any attempt to make the capacity to enforce rules the defining feature, for not only is this discredited in legal theory, but many social spheres that we would not wish to designate as legal have that capacity.[20] Each of these factors in isolation fails to capture the legal element, but suppose they are taken together: the combination of a system of rules, an institutional base with officials, and the capacity for enforcement. If these are the key elements of a modern state legal system, then any social formation having them should potentially qualify as a legal order, while those lacking them would not. The criterion, however, is no more successful than the others: a system that is quite plainly legal could lack a developed institutional base, as in the case of some customary systems, or have difficulty enforcing its rules; at the same time, a social sphere could have the combination of elements, as a university and a social club do, and yet not be regarded as a legal order.

10.6 LEGAL PLURALISM, SOCIAL RELATIONS, AND LAW'S AUTHORITY

At this point anyone trying to make sense of extended legal pluralism must be inclined to write it off and close their books. That would be a mistake for in the quest for the *legal* aspect of rule-governed spheres a quite different approach can be taken and something important learnt. Instead of seeking the elusive element in rules, institutions, and coercion, suppose we look to the link between social spheres and *social relations*. In winding back the conceptual as well as the historical clock, we were able earlier to isolate the legal experience that lies behind legal rules (section 4.2). The legal act was shown to be an expression of social relations prior to the formulation of rules. The same process may be the key to extended legal pluralism by drawing attention to the fact that some important social relations are expressed and regulated by social conventions and understanding, independently of state law. These include aspects of relations within the family, concerning property and contractual relations, all of which are essential to social life. The intuition of legal pluralists that various forms of association are the primary means of expressing relations of real significance to society is accurate. Law has its origins in social relations and their

---

[20] Compare: M.Weber, op. cit., p. 317

expression in social conventions; as societies modernize so that state law becomes *the* law, the more important conventions are absorbed into state law. The process of absorption is unlikely to be total; pockets are bound to remain, either because state law has shown no interest in them, or because it allows social orders to run parallel to its own, as in the case of the Californian ranchers. They can also be the sign of resistance or rebellion, as in the case of the Slavic *Zadruga* in relation to imperial Austria.[21] And even in cases of direct conflict, state officials may choose not to enforce state rules, and in doing so tacitly recognize the alternative order.

We now have a defensible basis for extended legal pluralism; we also have another instance of law prior to rules, law originating in social relations, as opposed to law being handed down by state officials. However, despite the appeal of viewing legal pluralism in this way, to conclude that non-state legal orders are all around would be premature, for one vital element is still missing. A characteristic of modern societies is state law's claim to final authority over all other rule-governed arenas. In making the claim, state law is tapping the well of understanding as to the conception of legal authority and its historical basis. According to that understanding, rules are legal rules when they are an expression of that authority, and it is this that separates them from other rules that are authoritative but not finally so. Final authority should not be taken in an absolute sense but as the ultimate standard governing an area of activity. And just as state law claims final authority over all matters within its jurisdiction (or scope of authority), so customary law and Church law claim similar final authority within their areas of jurisdiction. Final authority is distinguished from ordinary authority as the following example shows. Within the social sphere of university lecturers, it is accepted that the combination of university rules and the conventions around them are authoritative standards. Similarly, the ranchers accept that matters such as fencing and straying cattle are governed by binding rules. But in neither case do the standards constitute final authority, for both are subject to state law, even if it does not, in fact, intervene and even if the standards are inconsistent with state law, as in the ranchers' case. That state law is nevertheless present and vigilant is made plain by imagining what would happen if the ranchers were to decide that the penalty for allowing a bull to stray should be the execution of its owner. What is important is that state law claims final authority in a way that other rule-based associations do not; whether or not state law invokes its authority is a separate matter.

---

[21] See: M. Weber, op. cit., p. 316

The claim to final authority does not mean law is exclusive to the state, since parallel legal orders are not uncommon; but parallel legal orders recognized by state law as being outside its jurisdiction are quite different from rule-governed spheres within its jurisdiction. Modern legal systems claim final authority in this way, and for that reason they have difficulty in allowing for the presence of other legal orders within the bounds of their jurisdiction. The analysis does not depend on contending that law always, and in all conditions, claims final authority, it being enough for our purposes that it is true of modern state orders. At the same time, neither language nor experience would be unduly stretched by the suggestion that the social significance of the *legal act* is to state or settle authoritatively and finally, social relations. It is hardly a slide into the pits of essentialism or reductionism to say that, in general, across time and cultures, the specific social significance of law is its claim to authority. That modern states should have appropriated that quality to ensure both their domination and their legitimacy is to be expected. The consequence of the claim of rule-governed spheres to legal authority with respect to some aspect of social relations is that they would be in direct competition with the same claim by state law. There cannot be two different and competing sources of final authority, so any claim by a rule-governed sphere to legal authority must be seen in this light. It is at best a tentative and contingent claim, a true expression of fundamental social relations on the one hand, but an incomplete and imperfect sense of legal authority on the other hand.

The idea of the final authority of law, and its link to social relations, is deepened by reference to two further ideas. One comes from Giambattista Vico who cautions against regarding the forms and institutions of law of one age as being true for another, or for assuming any particular forms to be universal as opposed to local.[22] Each society and each generation create laws and institutions suitable for their purposes, and they modify or abolish those that are not. At the same time, according to Vico, some ideas remain fairly constant in the way people perceive the needs of social co-operation, which in turn concerns the regulation of social relations. Law being at the foundations of social relations is one of those ideas, so that its forms and expressions change, but its place in the minds of the people remains steady. It remains steady not only as a foundation of social co-operation, to which we might add the *authoritative foundation*, but because it is also connected to, and is the profane vehicle for, the delivery

---

[22] G. Vico, *The New Science* (First ed. Naples 1744, current edition: London, 2001).

of justice. Maintaining the balance among persons – the essence of justice – is the task of law. Law looks both ways: to the practical problems of maintaining social relations and to the abstract notion of justice. Final authority is then *just authority*, not in a literal sense for law can be unjust, but in a metaphorical sense that authority aspires to be just authority. In the gathering of people to decide an issue or dispute, whose presence constitutes or more accurately instantiates the law, the link to both authority and justice is then made. For it is the people assembled, whether literally or metaphorically, who have authority to settle matters of social relations, to determine their legality or illegality. The assembly becomes unworkable in more complex societies and is replaced by rules and officials. Some rules of the community express basic social relations, and prevail over others.[23] There is no divide between those rules and law, no extra quality that has to be found to consider them the law; the rules having final authority both socially and linguistically are the law.

To take a large leap from Vico to Luhmann, the latter's claim of law being a set of operations is best understood as a contemporary expression of the idea of law as an authoritative act. Law as operations has been used by Gunther Teubner in an effort to capture the elusive legal element in legal pluralism, where the claim is that global transactions constitute a legal order, which is independent of both nation states and international law.[24] The key to recognizing this order as law is that *transactions* within it are classified according to the binary process of legal–illegal. On its own, this account is lacking, for the legal operation is dependent upon a prior social process that designates the categories of legal–illegal, which in its elemental form was the gathering of the people, whose very gathering constituted the *act* or *operation* and in doing so was the expression of final authority. Since the people assembled cannot be present at every occasion of authoritative ruling, it is expressed through other social means, other processes and officials such as courts and officials, standing in the place of the people assembled. The innate sense of the gathered people being the legal act is replaced by rules. It follows that the operation 'legal–illegal' is not itself the basis for distinguishing a legal order from one that is not; the operation has significance only by being an expression of legal authority, an authority that must be prior to the operation. More precisely, the operation is the conclusion of a social process, whose parts

[23] Op. cit., p. 98
[24] 'Global Bukowina in World Society' in G. Teubner (ed), *Global Law Without a State* (Dartmouth, 1997).

taken together – rules, procedures, officials – constitute legal authority. The question then is: what is the origin of that authority? In answering we could potentially locate authority in a rule-based order that is autonomous and independent of state authority. That could be done, but only if the rule-based order, in this case the global association of persons and entities, has the features necessary to constitute final authority with respect to its members, a matter to be settled by empirical investigation.

Let us draw together the strands of argument. The aim has been to make sense of the idea at the foundation of extended legal pluralism that, in modern societies, there exist rule-governed spheres (other than state law) that ought to be considered law. Proponents of the idea have not succeeded in identifying the elusive legal element, a fact that sceptics have been willingly to point out, before going on to suggest alternatives, none of which satisfactorily meets all the demands. An alternative approach, which tries to isolate and make sense of the central intuition of legal pluralism, and which follows the pattern set in chapter 4, is to consider law prior to rules as the expression of social relations. The similarity between rule-based associations and state law is that both express important social relations. If law in an elemental sense is the expression of social relations, we now see how it is present in social contexts other than state law. However, the temptation to conclude that such contexts are legal orders must be resisted; it must be resisted because the claim to final authority has come to be regarded as a basic feature of law, and it is state law that claims final authority. Since social spheres that could qualify as legal orders come within the jurisdiction of state law, they are subject to it, the consequence being that they cannot claim final authority for themselves and cannot be regarded as legal orders.

So where does this leave extended legal pluralism? The argument here does no harm to the idea of parallel legal orders, nor is state law prevented from consenting to the formation of parallel legal orders within its jurisdiction. What is ruled out is the notion that legal orders spontaneously develop within the jurisdiction of state law and become separate from it. If there is comfort for the ambitions of legal pluralism it is this: rule-governed spheres that express social relations of fundamental significance to a society are likely to intersect with and influence it, perhaps be adopted by state law. Others grow up and exert their influence on behaviour within the boundaries of state law, fairly much untroubled by it; the ranchers, the diamond-traders, and university lecturers are living examples of it. Beyond that, the best that can be offered extended legal pluralism is recognition that some rule-based associations are mirrors of law and as such may lay some claim to be considered orders of *informal law.*

NOTES

EXTENDED LEGAL PLURALISM

Does extended legal pluralism help in a social understanding of law?

Laura Benton cautions against an image of plural legal orders as *stacked*, that is, as a framework in which different levels of law, formal and informal, are stacked 'one atop the other' ('Beyond Legal Pluralism: Towards a New Approach to Law in the Informal Sector' (1994) 3 *Social and Legal Studies* 223, p. 225). Her point is that the boundaries between areas of formal and informal law are: 'difficult, if not impossible, to locate and it is clear that participants themselves operate at times as if the boundaries did not exist' (p. 229). Benton concludes, somewhat equivocally, on the existence of informal legal orders in general, but, in relation to informal economic activities, finds legal pluralism unhelpful.

Benton's perceptive analysis strengthens two matters of importance referred to in the text: one is that social spheres, whether formal or informal, overlap, intersect with, and influence each other. The other is that social spheres vary as to how well they are formed and how distinct they are. Her cautionary words are timely, but we need to go beyond them and acknowledge that social spheres differ enormously as to their *density*, one aspect of which is their capacity to resist influence from outside, and from other social spheres in particular. Some are very dense, others less so; all are influenced by external factors, but the degree of influence depends, in turn, on various factors, including density. We also need to acknowledge that social spheres influence the behaviour of those within them; the extent to which they do so depends on several factors, including their density. So, a healthy dose of scepticism may be in order to restrain the stronger claims of legal pluralism, but it should not be allowed to undermine the existence and utility of informal orders in understanding attitudes to formal law. On this, see the discussion in Chapter 6.

What is extended legal pluralism?

John Griffith has made a major contribution to the case for extended legal pluralism in a series of writings, the most important of which is: 'What is legal pluralism?' (1986) 24 *Journal of Legal Pluralism* 1–55. The trouble with Griffith's claims for legal pluralism is his failure to provide criteria for a legal order; without such criteria, it is impossible to give a descriptive account of the situation in which multiple legal orders are at work. The closest he comes is to propose that law is the ' "self-regulation" of a semi-autonomous social field'; which can be regarded as 'more or less legal according to the degree to which it is differentiated from the rest of the activities in the field and delegated to specialized functionaries' (p. 38).

Sally Engle Merry's 'Legal Pluralism' is often cited as advancing the analysis of legal pluralism, although it is not clear why she puts her discussion in terms of *legal* pluralism. Her analysis is more concerned with the interaction between formal law and informal social orders, and on the way informal orders 'draw on the symbols of the law'. 22 *Law and Society Review* 869–896. Merry's account shows how state law can be regarded as different from and interacting with informal legal orders, without relying on ideas of legal centralism.

Concerning the interaction between different social spheres, this can be studied regardless of whether the spheres are legal orders. Whether or not they are legal orders would be relevant only if their legal quality in some way affected the interaction. I suggest in the text that it could, but that we need more research on the interaction to know. Merry's account does not show that the alleged legal quality affects the interaction.

In later work she states that 'the human rights system represents a new international legal regime'. Does this mean a new legal order? See: S. Engle Merry, 'Colonial and Post-Colonial Law' in *The Blackwell Companion to Law and Society* (Oxford, 2004), p. 580.

Insofar as Merry offers an explanation of what legal pluralism is, she states: 'I think it is essential to see state law as fundamentally different in that it exercises the coercive power of the state and monopolizes the symbolic power associated with state authority'. (p. 879). If coercion is made the basis for distinguishing state law from informal orders, then it fails for the reasons given in the text: many informal orders have coercive powers. Moreover, coercion, as we have seen, is not an adequate basis for characterizing state law: see Chapter 8. Otherwise Merry's definition is circular: the state is distinctive because it exercises state coercive power. Also circular is the claim concerning the state monopolizing the symbolic power of the state.

Classic accounts of extended legal pluralism

For some of the classic accounts of extended legal pluralism, see:

L. Pospisil, *Anthropology of Law: A Comparative Theory* (New York, 1971).

E. Ehrlich, *Fundamental Principles of the Sociology of Law* (Harvard, 1913).

Reza Banakar provides a perceptive and balanced account of the difficulties faced by extended legal pluralism in: R. Banakar, *Merging Law and Sociology* (Berlin, 2003).

Social spheres as subordinate to state law

B. Dupret, M. Berger, and others define legal pluralism as: 'In socio-legal studies, *legal pluralism* means a plurality of social fields, producers of norms which are in partial interaction with each other' (*Legal Pluralism in the Arab World* (The Hague, 1999) p. *xi.*). Except for that unexplained 'partial' so, far so good; they continue: 'It entails depriving the state of its capacity as social actor (as opposite to its multiple constituents), and consequently not considering it merely as the monopolist of legal production, be it directly or indirectly'. How, and in what sense, legal pluralism *deprives the state of its capacity as social actor* is not explained, although this is the key idea in the passage. How do the authors move from *interaction* of social fields to informal fields *depriving* state law of its capacity?

The elusive legal element in legal pluralism

S. Falk Moore develops the idea of a *semi-autonomous* social field; she defines it 'not by its organization (it may be a corporate group, it may not) but by a processual characteristic, the fact that it can generate rules and coerce or induce compliance to them'. (p. 27–8) Griffith commends this for 'locating legal pluralism in social structure' but goes on to point out that it needs to be supplemented by a conception of the legal, which Falk Moore does not provide.

Critiques of extended legal pluralism

A spirited critique of legal pluralism is Brian Tamanaha's 'The Folly of the "Social Scientific" Concept of Legal Pluralism' 20 *Journal of Law and Society* 192 (1993). In pointing out the trouble legal pluralists have had in saying in what sense informal orders are legal, Tamanaha shows that they implicitly try to apply a model based on state law, that is, a model in terms of 'institutionalized identification and enforcement of norms' (p. 206). So, for legal pluralists, law becomes 'concrete patterns of social ordering, delimited by the criterion of institutionalization' (p. 206).

The critique fits the argument of my text, in which I show that rules, institutions, and enforcement are all present in many social spheres that are not legal orders.

However, this is not the end of the argument, and it is not enough to conclude, as Tamanaha does later on in *A General Jurisprudence of Law and Society* (Oxford, 2001), that informal orders are law if the people within them think they are law. My suggestion in the text is that the persistent intuition of legal pluralists that there is something potentially *legal* about some social spheres is well-founded. Once law is located prior to rules as the expression of social relations, it becomes clear that informal spheres may express important social relations, and in that sense are potentially legal. However, in modern societies, their potential is smothered by the claims of state law.

Despite my claim in the text that we must try to locate the elusive *legal* element in legal pluralism, not all take that view. That Max Weber took such a view is plain; he writes ' . . . we categorically deny that "law" exists only where legal coercion is guaranteed by the political authority. For us there is no practical reason for such a terminology.' (*Economy and Society*. p.317). The explanation is that having defined legal orders in terms of coercion, Weber is compelled from a sociological stance to accept any coercive order as legal.

William Twining, a contemporary commentator, reaches an analogous position by arguing that there is no theoretical or practical test for deciding that some rule-bound associations are legal, others not. His reasoning is that, because the concept of law is contestable, and because legal philosophy has no clear boundaries, then an inclusive view of law ought to be adopted. Being inclusive means allowing 'other forms of normative ordering' to be law. The logic of this claim is not wholly convincing; it could also be argued that it is a flight from the responsibility of clarifying and refining the concepts and ideas we study. Moreover, Twining ends his discussion by claiming: 'The central point is that relations between municipal law and other forms of *normative ordering* (however they are labelled) and other interactions (interlegality) deserve the sustained attention of jurists because they are a crucial part of understanding legal phenomena'. General Jurisprudence (Would Congress on Philosophy of Law and Social Philosophy in M. Escamilla and M. Savedra (eds.) *Law and Justice in Global Society* (Seirlle, 2005), p.37 (emphasis added). Despite ambiguities, the point seems to be that jurists should study the *interaction* between municipal law and other forms of social ordering; one can only agree. That is one of the two main objectives of law-and-society; but it has nothing to do either with legal pluralism or with claims that those other normative spheres are somehow legal.

Simon Roberts recently argues against extended legal pluralism by linking law with governing. He writes: 'Law is a concomitant of centralizing processes, processes that at a certain point resulted in the formation of the nation state.' (2005) 68 *Modern L.Rev.* 1, p.13. While his analysis deflates some of the more fanciful claims of legal pluralism, his tying law to the state, a position that would have the concurrence of Hume, Bentham and Hart, is insupportable. It rests on the notion that (a) law is tied to governing (b) that governing is exclusively a state activity. If by *governing* is meant protecting and regulating social relations in a way that is conducive to the realization of certain social goods, then arguably governing is an activity common to any community; (a) would then be true but (b) not, because governing is not restricted to central states. Law and legal relations must therefore be capable of being separate from and prior to state government.

For further discussion:

F. von Bender-Beckmann, 'Comment on Merry' (1988), 22 *Law and Society Review*.

J. Vanderlinden, 'Return to Legal Pluralism: Twenty Years Later' (1989) 24 *Journal of Legal Pluralism* 149.

Global legal pluralism

The global arena has become the site of new research into legal pluralism, notably in the work of G. Teubner. See in particular: G. Teubner (ed) *Global Law Without a State* (Dartmouth, 1997) and his own essay in that collection 'Global Bukowina: Legal Pluralism in World Society' pp. 3–28. See also: F. Snyder, 'Global Economic Networks and Global Legal Pluralism' (Florence, 1999).

Also:

C. Arup, *The New World Trade Organization Agreements: Globalizing Law Through Services and Intellectual Property* (Cambridge, Mass., 2000).

Does Law have Social Functions?

I I . I FROM SOCIAL FUNCTIONS TO SOCIAL VALUE

Common sense and experience show that laws are commonly used as instruments for realizing ends and goals. Constitutions and international covenants, legislation and regulations, judicial rulings and administrative guidelines are all products of deliberate action on the part of peoples and states, of legislators, administrators, and judges, and all may be presumed to have some point and purpose. The law-making process is arduous, often ending in compromise and accommodation rather than the expression of clear intentions and purposes. Nevertheless, the resulting laws are directed at and are the instruments for achieving social goals. Bentham was the arch-instrumentalist and made it sound straightforward: law is an instrument for pursuing whatever social goals are considered desirable within a society. It can be used for good or bad, it can fall into the hands of special interests, or be the engine of cruelty and oppression; it can also be used to advance the good of society. It is sometimes attuned to existing social relations and aims at strengthening them; alternatively its aim may be to change them. The common law is more in touch with social relations but has a diminishing role, even where it once traditionally prevailed, so it is enacted law that should be the main focus of our attention.

The question that must come to the mind of anyone contemplating modern legal orders is: why do we need this mighty edifice of rules and officials, processes and penalties? Social goals are achieved through various means, whether by mutual trust, co-operation, or by offering positive incentives, and it is not obvious when and why laws imposed by state officials are more effective than the others. If co-operation among people and groups is the goal, then there are many ways of encouraging it; if it is best achieved through rules, then social rules emerging naturally within social spheres on the basis of practical experience, seem to be more promising than legal rules coming from the outside and lacking social roots. It is puzzling that, on the one hand, groups and communities have ample means for achieving their ends, while on the other hand the use of law is increasing. Some, among whom legal pluralists must be counted, argue there is too much law and that more reliance should be placed on informal social processes, whether deliberately planned or spontaneously occurring. Even if that were accepted, it would mean only a moderate reduction in law. Others, who need not be dyed-in-the-wool legal centralists, view the modern legal order as a major achievement in the civilizing process, to be celebrated not deprecated.[1] And it is so, not only because it makes more secure and effective arrangements that would exist anyhow, but also, and most importantly, because it enables a society to achieve positive goals that could not otherwise easily be achieved, such as the creation of a better environment, the advancement of human rights, and the provision of services.

The object of this chapter and the next is to examine the value law brings to social life. The discussion concentrates on just two main matters. Questions about the social worth of law are usually posed in terms of its *functions*, the idea being that law performs specific functions in society. Precisely what this means needs to be examined, but if it were true in a general sense that law has a unique role in society, it would be of major significance for its study. Functional accounts are anything but straightforward, and among social scientists tend to be out of favour,[2] but their prominence in discussions of law, both in legal theory and in social explanation, makes them a good place to start in assessing law's social value. So, the enquiry begins with various claims about law's social functions. This leads to the conclusion that generally the language of functions is a synonym for the more everyday notions of point-and-purpose and social effects. There is one exception, one task of law which is overlooked and yet fundamental, the one closest to the precise and technical sense of function as the performance of a necessary task for the existence of the system in which it occurs, which is that of defining, or, as Bentham suggests constituting the legal order. This leads to the second main issue of considering how law contributes to social goods. Here the idea is to consider its role in different situations, facilitating private arrangements, imposing criminal sanctions, regulating private activities, and so on, and then to ask what advantages it brings, what value it adds to other social mechanisms. This I refer to as the *social value* of law.

---

[1] For an original account of the *civilizing process* in the formation of European society, see: N. Elias, op. cit.

[2] For a discussion of functional accounts in social science, see: A. Ryan, op. cit., p. 183 ff.

11.2 FUNCTIONS IN LEGAL THEORY AND SOCIAL EXPLANATION

It has been said that legal theory takes only slight interest in the social functions of law.[3] This does not stop jurists from expressing views on the subject, the following being examples: to control the coercive power of the state; a means of exercising power; to subject human behaviour to the governance of rules; to coordinate social activities; to integrate society; and to settle disputes. An initial difficulty is that at least some, if not all, of these tasks are performed by other social mechanisms. Systems of non-legal rules would qualify with respect to most of them, so they cannot be considered unique to state law. Another difficulty is that legal theorists are still debating whether the functions of law are a necessary element of the concept of law, one view being that a theory of law necessarily includes its functions, which are then the basis for distinguishing law from other social phenomena.[4] Others contest this view, claiming that law's essential features can be identified quite apart from its functions.[5] Hart's work, which contains much about functions, as we see shortly, has been caught up in this debate, but how much his description depends on law having particular functions is not clear.

In the traditions of political and social theory, functions have been central to the understanding of law. M. Kramer, a legal theorist, expresses the point in a way that could be regarded as the culmination of the two traditions: '. . . law has an indispensable role in bringing about the orderliness that is a *sine qua non* of any viable human society'.[6] Early theorists of modern society, of whom Durkheim was the leading figure, wished to discover what held it together, meaning what was the basis for social solidarity in societies marked by diversity and fragmentation. Durkheim found law to be a key element on the grounds that it both expresses and reinforces the social relations of modern society. In a parallel stream of legal and political theory, a similar idea has passed down through Hobbes and Hume to Bentham and Hart that law is necessary for social order, or

---

[3] J. Raz, 'The Functions of Law' in A. W. B. Simpson (ed) *Oxford Essays in Jurisprudence* (Oxford, 1972), p. 278.

[4] R. Dworkin is a leading exponent of this view (*Law's Empire* (London, 1986)). J. Habermas expresses a similar view that law has particular normative functions (*Between Facts and Norms*, Cambridge Mass., 1996).

[5] An example is J. Coleman, 'Incorporationism, Conventionality, and the Practical Difference Thesis' in J. Coleman (ed), *Hart's Postscript* (Oxford, 2001).

[6] M. Kramer, *In Defence of Positivism* (Oxford, 1990), p. 263.

survival as Hart put it, especially in providing security against violence, ensuring the keeping of promises, and protecting property.[7] If social order has an old-fashioned ring, it means simply that a certain pattern of human activity and organization is necessary to achieve those basic social goods.[8]

Coordination has become a familiar concept in expressing the idea that, in order to provide essential social goods, guidance and control through state law is necessary.[9] In considering a modern legal order, we need to go beyond the coordination of existing activities and interests (or, if coordination is taken to be comprehensive, to identify more specific processes within it). The positive pursuit of social goods, such as the removal of discrimination, the protection of human rights, and the creation of a global order should be added. For in order to achieve those goods, the direction, regulation, and restraint of both private and government activities are necessary. The provision of services, especially welfare in its several forms, also needs to be added, as does the need for officials to restrain their use of power and to make provision for maintaining the legal system. However the social goods sought through law are categorized, the idea is that law, with its institutions, officials, and enforcement powers, is essential to their realization. To anyone wary of legal centralism, these claims will invite scepticism; at the same time, the resilience of law over time should leave no doubt as to its importance in society.[10]

Functionalism purports to explain its importance. Since the use of the word *function* is common in our language and since we readily talk about things having functions, a few general remarks may help in setting the scene, before enquiring into law. The first thing to note is that *function* has both technical and common usages. As a technical term, it applies to systems, such as biological or mechanical systems, in which each component has a task to perform in maintaining the whole. As a word of common usage, it is less precise, and is so because it is a corruption of the technical term. Double meanings lead to misunderstandings and this is no exception. Let us begin with common usage: here function has acquired various connotations that can be gathered together loosely as *the*

---

[7] See further on these goods: Hedley Bull, *The Anarchical Society* (London, 1977), chapter 1.

[8] H. Bull, op. cit. Chapter 1.

[9] Coordination is explained in J. Finnis, op. cit., section *X.3*.

[10] On the idea of resilience, see: P. Pettit, *Rules, Reasons, and Norms* (Oxford, 2002), Part II.

object for which something is used. This is made more precise by separating two senses. One refers to the point and purpose of something: a hammer is for hitting in nails, a secretary to type letters, and an aircraft is for flying. Point and purpose are themselves variable because they depend on a context and on whose point and purpose is in issue: in one context and from one point of view, the point and purpose of an aircraft is to fly, a matter taken for granted if the present point and purpose is a bombing raid or to earn profits for the airline company. The main point and purpose is not necessarily the only use to which something may be put: a tennis racket is made for playing tennis but can be used to hit balls for other purposes, to ward off magpies or, at a pinch, serve as a snow-shoe. The dictionary sums-up this idea by defining function as the work something is expected to do, leaving open just what the work is and who has the expectation. So, the first fairly unremarkable lesson is that the function of something is what it is for, according to someone's point and purpose, which in turn depends on the social context in which the issue arises. Functionalism in this sense is common and everyday, and is shorthand for a more complex description of a situation. In order to preserve its common and everyday sense, it is referred to it as *point-and-purpose* functionalism.

Everyday use of function does not end here; point-and-purpose captures much of everyday use but not all. Whereas point-and-purpose is tied to someone's intentions, we often refer to the function of an artefact in the sense of what it is normally used for, meaning what object or effect it normally has. Quite apart from anyone's intentions or purposes, hammers are widely used to drive in nails and tennis rackets to play tennis, which may be translated as: the function of hammers is to drive in nails, of tennis rackets to play tennis. It is then a short step to describing them both as instruments to an end: hammers to achieve the end of driving in nails, tennis rackets to make possible the playing of tennis. The point is even clearer when it is said that law's function is to coordinate social activities: coordination is the end sought, law the means for achieving it. Function, in these cases, refers to the ends to which something is the means, for which the term *social-ends functionalism* will be used (where the ends are of a social kind). The ends can themselves be direct or indirect; we would normally say that the direct object of breaking in a horse is so that it can be ridden, while indirectly it may mean that cattle can be mustered more effectively. There could be disagreement about whether an object or effect is direct or indirect.

A stronger sense of function stems from a variation on the idea that the function of something is what it is used for. Here, the normal objects or effects are considered immanent or essential: the immanent or essential object (function) of a lawn-mower is to mow, a tennis racket to play tennis (or is it to hit balls?), and an aircraft to fly. The tendency to reduce something to its essence, to discover what it *really* is for, is natural enough, but it is a borrowing from, a shadow of, function in its technical sense. To seek essences in social contexts may be harmless, but risks ascribing to an artefact an objectivity that severs its dependence on a social context and its variables. For what is presented as the essence of something, or discovering what it is really for, is itself dependent on a social context in which the something is linked to a goal of that context. This is especially the case when, instead of a lawn-mower, the artefact is law. The essential or immanent quality of a thing is, in fact, that which has been selected as best suited from among the various qualities that best serve the further goal. Claims about the functions of law are often of this kind. When Habermas asserts that law is a means for exercising power or a medium of social integration, he is singling out goals which he considers more important than others, and then claiming that the function of law lies in serving them; by 'function' could be substituted 'job' or 'task'.[11] This use of the concept is referred to here as *essential-qualities* functionalism.

Mention of the essence of things is a step towards, but still a step short of, the full technical sense of functionalism. This sense of functionalism is best illustrated by noting its origins in the biological sciences, the idea being that the performance of certain functions is essential to the life of the organism. Two elements are necessary: a system has certain needs that must be met, or tasks undertaken, in order for it to continue; x has qualities that enable it to serve the needs or perform the tasks, that is, causally to bring about those outcomes. The relationship between ends and means is made stronger by adding a third element: x and only x is capable of doing so. The question is whether this analysis, which makes good sense in relation to the natural sciences, can be transferred to social explanation. Its natural attraction is plain: society is a system with a distinct existence and identity whose maintenance depends on certain social formations. Social formations x survive through thick-and-thin, so that even though some parts of society are in constant change, others show resilience over time.[12] It is unlikely that such resilience is accidental

---

[11] J. Habermas, op. cit.
[12] Philip Pettit inserts this idea of resilience into the understanding of social functions; see: P. Pettit, op. cit., Part II.

or aimless, so an explanation must be sought; from there it is a short step to concluding that *x* performs an essential function in keeping the system going. In relation to law, the same short step leads to the conclusion that law has functions necessary to the survival or wellbeing of society. I shall refer to this as *full* functionalism.

Much more could be said about a concept that has long distracted the attention of social theorists, but we have said enough to turn to law. In *The Concept of Law,* among the many references Hart makes to law's functions, four usages can be identified: (i) the function of social rules is to guide human behaviour; (ii) legal rules serve the two distinct functions of imposing duties and conferring powers, and may be divided accordingly into primary and secondary rules; (iii) legal rules serve a range of substantive functions, such as restraining violence, distributing and protecting property, upholding contracts, allocating power and authority, and punishing offenders; and (iv) legal rules as a system function to assure the survival of a society.

11.3 FUNCTIONS OF RULES

Hart's answer to the question of what rules are for is that they guide behaviour, and they do so by providing standards according to which one's own actions are justified and the actions of others judged. He refers freely to the functions of rules, probably without intending to convey anything more than the common usage of this being what they are for. This approach is marred by two problems. In the first place, Hart draws the function of a rule from its properties, as if to say: that is what a rule is, it guides actions, and so veering towards, if not expressly embracing, the idea of a rule having an essential function. The problem stems from his not distinguishing between the logical or normative properties of rules and their social context. As a matter of their logical properties, rules are guides to behaviour; but that tells us nothing about what they do in a social context, which depends on how they are regarded by officials and the people.[13] The focus then shifts from the logical qualities of rules to the way they are used in practice, which means relinquishing essentialist notions and settling for the uneven extent to which rules actually guide behaviour. A second problem is that even logically rules vary in their behaviour-guiding capacity: clear-line rules give fairly clear guidance, standard-based rules less, while discretionary rules do no more than

---

[13] See further: J. Raz, op. cit.

indicate who has the authority to decide. The most that can safely be said
is that social rules guide behaviour to varying degrees.

Similar problems beset Hart's claim concerning the function of primary and secondary rules as power-conferring and duty-imposing. Here
he makes specific reference to their social functions. After criticizing
the idea that all legal rules can be reduced to the form of primary rules,
he states that this is purchased at a high price, 'that of distorting the
different social functions which different types of legal rule perform'.[14]
As a matter of their logical properties, some rules are power-conferring,
others duty-imposing, but when the move is made to their social context,
whether they confer powers or impose duties depends how they are
used by officials and citizens. The logical qualities of rules are relevant to
that issue but not determinative, since others factors enter into how rules
are used in practice. When viewed in this way, *function* can be replaced
without loss by asking what their point-and-purpose is, and what social
ends and effects they have.

I I . 4   SUBSTANTIVE FUNCTIONS OF LEGAL RULES

This brings us to Hart's third use of function: that legal rules are the
means for achieving substantive social goods, such as discouraging
undesirable behaviour, protecting property, or controlling pollution.
Joseph Raz develops this approach by drawing a distinction between the
direct and indirect functions of laws.[15] Direct functions are those
'achieved by the law being obeyed and applied'.[16] So the direct function
of a rule requiring two witnesses for a will is that wills are made with two
witnesses. Raz then contrasts the direct functions of a set of legal rules
with their indirect, which are described as 'the attitudes, feelings, opinions, and modes of behaviour' that result from the knowing about the
laws 'or from compliance with and application of the laws'.[17] Direct functions appear to be ascertained by examining the terms of a law, but say
nothing about its point-and-purpose or its actual social effects, these
apparently being indirect functions.

Some indirect functions are likely to be intended and foreseen by the
makers of the law, while others are unintended and unforeseen. Those

---

[14] H. L. A. Hart, op. cit., p. 38 (2nd ed.).
[15] J. Raz, 'On the Functions of Law', op. cit.
[16] *Ibid*, p. 289.   [17] *Ibid*, p. 289.

intended are not necessarily realized in practice, while the actual social effects of a law can be quite a surprise. An indirect function of a criminal law could be to strengthen people's attitudes that certain kinds of actions are wrong, although the consequence that they spend less time protecting their own property against theft might be unforeseen. A set of laws making divorce easier could have the indirect effect of encouraging couples to separate, while tougher ones might hold them together.

For the language of direct and indirect functions could be substituted point-and-purpose and social effects; point-and-purpose of the law as seen from someone's viewpoint (legislator, official, or citizen), or as the effects that normally follow from a particular law. Distinguishing direct and indirect purposes or effects is a useful reminder that, in order to take law seriously, the terms in which it is expressed have to be taken seriously. It is also the case that interpretation means entering into the social context of laws and taking account of the contingent factors within them. Some ends and effects are clear from the language of laws, others are attached to the point and purpose of those who make the law, and those who interpret and apply them. Within the interpretive process, there is tension between a more objective approach, which means deriving ends and effects from the language itself, and one that looks more to point and purpose. Direct purposes and effects need to be identified, while recognizing that they are part of a larger scheme of purposes and effects, with mutual influence between them. To isolate one from the other, to consider only the direct ends and effects as specified in the language of the law, is to risk misunderstanding the law, as well as failing to see its place in the wider scheme. Consider wills: the law stipulates a set of rules for making valid wills, which include having two witnesses. The direct ends and effects sought are that wills are made with two witnesses. But, even such a clear rule opens up contingent issues, such as who may be a witness or what constitutes witnessing the will. In answering those issues, interpretation directly enters the social context, so that various levels of purposes and effects are relevant: to ensure the wishes of the testator are carried out, to protect against forgery and deceit, to facilitate the transfer of property, and so on. If faithful adherence to the clear-line rules unavoidably leads to consideration of wider purposes and effects, it can be imagined how intertwined they become when the legal scheme is more complex and the level of faithful adherence lower. This is more striking when we move from the strict language of wills to implementation of a controversial social policy.

The Australian Northern Territory has a large native-Australian population. In the mid-twentieth century, laws were passed providing for individual persons to be made wards of state.[18] The laws provided criteria for identifying those eligible to be made wards and conferred authority on officials to apply them. From perusal of the laws it would be concluded that the direct object was to allow officials to declare certain people wards of state, an arrangement familiar in many legal systems. But to stop there would be to miss both its point-and-purpose and its social effects. The whole point of wardship was to allow state officials to take virtually total control over the ward's life. Even that does not tell us the most important thing: the law was conceived, drafted, and enacted with the intention that it should be applied extensively to aboriginal people as a means for advancing the government's policy of assimilating them into white communities and ways of life. The point-and-purpose of the law and its social effects were to provide state officials with the authority to take aboriginals from their tribal life, by force if necessary, and compel them to live in conditions thought to be conducive to assimilation. The difference between a legal analysis of law and a social explanation is clearly shown in this case: the former looks to the language of the law and goes beyond it only to the extent necessary to interpret it; social explanation also begins with the language of the law but also wants to understand its wider social significance. In the language of functions, a social explanation needs to know both the point-and-purpose of the law and its ends and effects, which means regarding the language of laws as only part, a crucial part but still only part, of the legal environment. A full account of the legal environment means regarding the law as part of a wider web of purposes and effects, where the objects ascertained from language are inseparable, except artificially, from those that lie behind it.

Without knowing the policies sought to be advanced by a set of laws, or the way in which they are implemented, we would miss their social role and significance. A full social account of the wardship laws includes the purposes of the government and its officials, and its actual effects. The example is not unrelated to the idea put forward by Karl Renner that the same laws may have different social purposes and effects in different contexts.[19] Renner wished to know how a set of laws dealing with private

---

[18] This example comes from research conducted by Heather Douglas and presented at a seminar at the Oxford Centre for Socio-Legal Studies on 1 March, 2004. See also H. Douglas, 'Customary Law, Sentencing, and the Limits of the State', 20 (2005), *Canadian Journal of Law and Society* 141.

[19] K. Renner, *The Institutions of Private Property and Their Social Functions* (London, 1949).

property could be used for different economic and social ends. He noticed that the capitalist economy could make effective use of laws and institutions created during an earlier economic order. Otto Kahn-Freund comments, in his introduction to Renner's work, that Renner saw laws as being like bricks: they stay the same but can be assembled in different patterns for different social ends.[20] The relationship between the two is summarized by Kahn-Freund as: 'the functional transformation of the untransformed norm',[21] by which he meant presumably that the same law can have quite different social effects. In a similar vein, my own study of administrative procedure codes in the new democracies of eastern Europe shows that those adopted during the communist period were adapted to the post-communist environment with relatively insubstantial changes.[22] Despite the great changes in the point-and-purpose of the codes, and the transformation of the social context of government administration in relation to citizens, the old codes could be read in a new way in order to serve the new order.

11.5 MAINTAINING THE SOCIAL ORDER

The final reference Hart makes to the functions of law concerns the role of the legal system as a whole in maintaining the social order. Here we encounter a form close to *full functionalism*, the idea being that a society has certain needs that must be met if it is to survive, needs that law provides. By reflecting on human nature and the environment in which social life takes place, Hart identifies factors, such as the vulnerability of each towards others, the need for stability in relationships, the limited resources available to meet demands, and the inevitability that some people will break the rules that others obey.[23] These factors point to the need for rules co-ordinating and regulating activities, while failure to satisfy the need poses a threat to a viable society. There may be other factors we would wish to add, such as the need to resolve disputes or to control the powers of officials, which should also be provided for by legal rules. Hart's approach is pragmatic, common-sensical, and prudential; in the language of functionalism, society has needs, which it is the function

---

[20] O. Kahn-Freund, *The Institutions of Private Property and Their Social Functions*, Introduction, p. 6.

[21] *Ibid*, p. 6.

[22] See my report: D. J. Galligan, *Administrative Procedures and the Supervision of Administration in Hungary, Poland, Bulgaria, Estonia, and Albania* (OECD, Paris, Sigma Paper 17, 1997).

[23] H. L. A. Hart, op. cit., Chapter *IX*.

of legal rules to meet. *The Concept of Law* is ambiguous as to whether these social functions require laws, or whether they could be performed by a combination of laws and informal social rules. The text lends support to the first position, but, since Hart did not discuss the contribution of non-legal rules, some doubt remains as to his view. Whatever it may have been, he gives no reasons for law being the only or even the most important means for achieving the ends needed for social survival. Law has a role, but so do other forms of social co-ordination; so we left them with the question as to what specific and additional value law adds, a matter addressed in the next chapter.

Pragmatic approaches often give way to the stronger view of the function of law in preserving society, the view designated *full-functionalism*. Here it is assumed that society is a special kind of organism, whose elements fit together to make the whole, and where each has a distinct function to perform. Law is one element, indeed it is often portrayed as an essential element, without which the social organism could not function. The origins of this approach, as we noted, are in the biological sciences where complex organisms are composed of constituent parts; society is said by analogy to be a similarly integrated organism. Durkheim gives the classic account: society is compared to the human body, which has essential needs, such as the circulation of blood, the flow of air, and the digestion of food.[24] The function of the organs is to meet these needs, the relationship being one of correspondence, with the function of an organ corresponding to a need. In transferring the approach to modern society, Durkheim aimed to discover what held it together, since being diverse and fragmented, its natural propensity was to fall apart.

The answer, he concludes, lies in two essential social processes, one the division of labour, the other law. The division of labour allows the members of a society to form dense networks of relationships which have the effect of binding them together. At the same time, the relationships are insecure and must be reinforced by law, whose function is to provide a set of rules, processes, and institutions that reflect the social relations people have, and give force and effect to them. The simplest and yet most telling example is a contract, which is said to be the 'supreme legal expression of cooperation'. People enter frequently into contractual relationships, but law is required to make them certain and binding. The same idea can be extended to the many different social relations we have with others, including such matters as property, employment, and the family. Within

---

[24] E. Durkheim, op. cit., Chapter I.

society, states Durkheim, law is analogous to the nervous system,[25] co-ordinating activities in a way necessary to maintain in the one case the body, in the other social solidarity.

Durkheim's account of the functions of law has been influential and repays fuller analysis than is possible here. The general idea that main-taining social stability is a difficult process, that societies will try to find ways of achieving it, and that some, at least, have been reasonably success-ful in doing so, is hardly controversial; nor is the idea that law has a part in the process. The difficulty arises in claiming a necessary connection between social cohesion and law. The first and main difficulty is in show-ing how laws somehow serve a vital need in maintaining societies. They must serve this function by dint of their nature, their essential qualities, independently of the circumstances and engagement of citizens and offi-cials. The invisible hand supposedly guiding markets appears to be at work here also, for the premises of the argument are assumed rather than proved. One premise is based on similarity between society and a living organism, with each being dependent on a set of needs being met by a particular set of processes. The reasoning is circular: from the fact that society has developed a particular type of law, the conclusion is drawn that it must be just the kind of law needed for social cohesion. Each premise and the conclusions drawn from it are open to question.

Is society really like an integrated organism where all its parts are linked in a necessary relationship? Or is it much less organic and more fragmented, consisting of different parts whose interaction varies? Simi-larly, does a society need some particular set of 'system-sustaining reinforcements', as the anthropologist Mary Douglas has put it, or is it sustained by varied, imperfect, and incomplete processes combining in ways not yet fully explained?[26] If these matters can be answered satis-factorily, further explanation is then needed as to how exactly law is functional or meets society's needs in the way required.[27] From the fact that a society has certain elements, such as a division of labour, or religion, or law, it does not follow that they perform a vital function or indeed what causal relationship, if any, exists between them and social survival. Following the demise of the communist system, several Euro-pean countries managed to maintain reasonable levels of social solidarity, although their legal systems were weak and capable of exerting little

[25] *Ibid*, p. 83.
[26] M. Douglas, *Risk and Blame: Essays in Cultural Theory* (London, 1992), p. 137.
[27] For a concise account of functionalism and its difficulties, see: R. Ellickson, op. cit., pp. 149–152.

influence. Social solidarity must have been due to other factors, among which informal social spheres and networks were prominent. But if law has a marginal role in that case, why should we assume it is different in other cases? It is also the case that societies are able to endure practices that gravely undermine security, predictability, and stability, without being destroyed. Closer study of societies that survive such disregard for the basic social goods could identify and explain 'the system-maintaining loops', to borrow again from Mary Douglas; it is also possible that the loops prove to be anything but systematic.

The other main difficulty with functionalist accounts such as Durkheim's relates to the specific role of law in comparison with other social mechanisms, especially informal social norms. Durkheim does not wholly neglect the point, although his treatment is brief: after claiming that any lasting social relations tend to assume a legal form, he considers the objection that some of them are based on custom. After noting that law usually originates in custom, he states: 'There may exist social relationships governed only by that diffuse form of regulation arising from custom. But this is because they lack importance and continuity . . . the law reproduces all those types that are essential, and it is about these that we need to know'.[28] A passage like this, which must be music to the ears of the legal centralist and anaethema to the pluralist, removes at a stroke the possibility of serious social relationships being sustained without the support of law, a view extravagant to the point of being untenable. We should not react by embracing the opposite extreme, but rather accept that both law and informal norms, sustained within social spheres, have a place in social relations and, therefore, in social solidarity. The passage from Durkheim confirms the need to understand better the qualities that law brings to the task.

Before considering that issue directly, brief reference should be made to the empirical evidence, which shows how important social spheres are in forming and cementing social relationships, even to the point of supplanting law. Robert Ellickson's study of life among the ranchers of Shasta County California shows how they created and relied on their own informal rules in place of legal rules.[29] Issues of straying cattle, duties to fence, and the resolution of disputes, were dealt with effectively by social rules, in almost total disregard for the law covering the same matters. It

---

[28] Durkheim, op. cit., p. 26. Between Durkheim and Bentham there is close similarity on this point. See: G. Postema, op. cit., Chapter 5.

[29] Robert Ellickson, op. cit.

may even be the case that some social goods can be attained without rules at all, whether legal or social, as Hedley Bull has shown in the context of international affairs; hence his reference to the 'anarchical society'.[30] Other studies are available to support the same general point that, whatever law's contribution may be, it is unlikely to be that that of full-functionalism, claimed for it by Durkheim.

11.6 DEFINING THE LEGAL ORDER AND LEGAL RELATIONS

There is one sense in which the law has a task or function to perform that is inherent in the nature of a legal order. It consists in defining, or in Bentham's terms *constituting*, the legal order and legal relations within it. This role is more fundamental than guiding behaviour, and takes account of the fact that rules only ever imperfectly guide behaviour and sometimes not at all. One sign of this more fundamental task is the perplexing fact that laws are not generally expressed as guides to behaviour. They are not like the Ten Commandments stating 'thou shalt not' do this or that, but rather tend to describe and define activities as crimes and torts, or specify what powers an official has, or under what conditions a court may review those powers, or what duties an agent has to a principal. Constitutions are perhaps the best example of all; they state the basic elements and doctrines of a legal order, confer powers on officials and organizations, and declare the rights that people have. If the main point of legal rules is to guide behaviour, then this is an indirect and clumsy way of doing so; if guidance is the object, why not follow the divine example and give clear and direct orders?

There is no set pattern in the way laws are stated, but the tendency to describe rather than direct, and the linguistic difference between them, does suggest that, far from being an oddity, a quirk of history and legislative drafting, there is good reason for it. The reason is that prior to any other social role or function of law, the legal order must itself be defined and constituted; in doing so legal relations are also defined and constituted. 'Defined and constituted' means stating what is legal and what is not; it also means settling the terms upon which social relations are conducted. In stating that the official has a wide discretion to deport, and that any decision to deport made pursuant to it is authorized, the law is defining the legal order and settling this aspect of citizen-official

[30] H. Bull, op. cit.

relations. Criminal laws are doing the same when they say that punishments may or shall be inflicted in certain circumstances. The same can be said for constitutions, administrative law, and the law of evidence, to mention just a few. It is no accident that in these areas of law and others, the language is primarily that of description, not direction, and we now see why.

Luhmann's claim that the function of law is to settle expectations should be seen in this light. He claims: 'The function of law is solely to bring about certainty of expectation, especially in anticipation of unavoidable disappointments'.[31] Settling expectations is different from guiding behaviour, and is a more general feature of law. But why should we consider it to be *the* function of law? Settling expectations depends on continuity over time, a quality that is associated with general rules and standards. Yet rules are expelled from Luhmann's legal universe, law instead being operations coding matters as legal or illegal. But it is difficult to see how operations produce certainty of expectations without rules creeping back in. What then creates expectations is unclear. There is another objection to expressing law's functions in terms of expectations: expectations follow from having a defined legal order; they are effects or consequences of something prior, which in this case is the legal order. Settling expectations, in common with guiding behaviour, are effects or consequences of a legal order, not its defining functions. The final reason against Luhmann's approach is of the same kind as that against Hart: not all laws settle expectations, as the case of the official with discretion shows, except in the trivial sense that everyone knows the official has a wide discretion to deport anyone he chooses. If this is what it means to settle expectations, then law's social role is truly slight.

The idea that a significant function or point or effect of laws is to define the legal order is simple but important. Take the analogy of bricks and houses: the most immediate, natural, and obvious way of describing the function of bricks is to build buildings; what the buildings are used for follows on from that and is a different issue; the same applies to legal rules, which are the bricks of the legal order. This approach matches the ordinary meaning of function as the work something is meant to do, for bricks to build houses, for legal rules to build a legal order. It could also be taken a step further: it is the one task or function law necessarily performs, for without it there would be no legal order. The language of functions could be dropped without loss; but, if that is the language of

---

[31] N. Luhmann, op. cit., p. 164.

discourse, its utility is to guide us to the most basic property or quality of legal rules, a property or quality all laws share. Once that is settled, other uses such as guiding behaviour, settling expectations, and achieving substantive social goals can be considered.

This approach, by avoiding the need to force all laws into the form of guides to behaviour or as settling expectations, serves both ordinary usage and common sense. The objection could be made that to express the function of legal rules in this way is trivial or pointless. It is neither. Law is a mighty edifice in society, expressing authoritatively social relations; the first step in its understanding should be to know how the edifice is built, what are its bricks. Bentham considered this the 'primary social task of law' and as Gerald Postema writes: 'The task of law, according to Bentham, is to define anew, to establish, and then to sustain, a social and political order and framework for broad-scale social interaction'.[32] Bentham's view that law's primary task is to define legal relations fits well with the argument of this book. However, his claim is overstated, for enacted law, in which Bentham was a devout believer, does not start with a clean sheet, no matter how much he wished that were the case. On the contrary, enacted law is laid over existing sets of social relations, so that the intersection and competition between the two is a major variable in modern legal orders. That qualification does not detract from the more important point that the first task of law is to define legal relations.

11.7 PURSUIT OF SOCIAL GOODS

Let us turn from attempts to give a functional account of law, especially attempts to show that law is necessary for social survival, and return to Hart and the voice of experience and pragmatism, which suggests that certain practical matters have to be attended to, not only in order to make society viable, but to make life tolerable. Questions about whether law is necessary to sustain society could be true but cannot be tested; those who claim it is accept the case without evidence beyond conventional experience. Let us instead concentrate on questions the answers to which we know or have a better chance of knowing, namely: what social goods are necessary for a tolerable social life, and how to achieve them. Some of the goods traditionally listed were noted above and include: security of person and property, predictability and regularity in social relations, settling disputes, and so on. To this we should add others of more

---

[32] G. Posthema, op. cit., pp. 175 and 315.

contemporary interest: the protection of rights, the provision of social welfare, the protection of the environment, and controlling the powers of officials. Whatever the list, the issues are: what must be done in order to achieve those social goods and what role does law have. It is true that Hart put the matter in terms of society's survival, but it is also true that he was writing within the tradition of British political theory, the tradition of Hume, Locke, Bentham, and the Mills, who were concerned with achieving the goods necessary for a tolerable social life, the assumption being that, if they were protected, society would not only survive but be in good health. The social goods we value are in turn expressed in and reinforced by the social relations of our society.

Once the issue is put in terms of achieving specific social goods, rather than the general and unspecific notion of social order, solidarity, or survival, it is easier to see how law contributes to them, and to assess its strengths and weaknesses in doing so. The language of functionalism can be dropped and replaced by that of plain instrumentalism, for our interest now is in the rules, institutions, and processes that are instrumental to the achievement of social goods. This is still a complex matter on which there is much to learn, but it has a clearer focus and is more manageable than taking social order in the abstract. Rather than asking how important secure contracts are for social order, we ask what is needed to make them secure, or to assume they are significant social goods and then ask what is needed to make them secure, to protect each of us from violence, or to make the right to free speech effective.

NOTES

General approach to functions

Whether functions are part of the concept of law is discussed in J. Coleman, 'Incorporationism, conventionality, and the practical difference thesis' in J.Coleman (ed) *Hart's Postscript* (Oxford, 2001) p. 111.

Coleman's view is likely to be shared by those in the positivist tradition of legal theory: 'One does not need a contestable view of law's functions in order to determine law's essential features' (page 112). See also J.Raz: 'Two Views of the Nature of the Theory of Law' (1998) 4 *Legal Theory* 249.

One of the few attempts by legal theorists to examine systematically the functions of law is: J.Raz, 'The Functions of Law' in B.Simpson (ed) *Oxford Essay in Jurisprudence* (Oxford, Second Series, 1971).

The approach of political theory to law's functions, and the connection to legal centralism, are well-summed up in: R Ellickson, op. cit., Chapter 8.

For discussion of functionalism and legal centralism in post-communist societies, see: D. J Galligan, 'Legal Failure: Law and Social Norms in Post-Communist Europe' in D. J Galligan and M. Kurkchiyan (eds) op. cit. (Oxford, 2003)

Functions of law as a system

Durkheim describes the idea of function in this way; 'Thus to ask what is the function of the division of labour is to investigate the need to which it corresponds.' *The Division of Labour in Society* p. 11.

On the division of labour, the role of the division of labour is not: 'simply to embellish or improve existing societies, but to make possible societies which, without these functions, would not exist. ... It goes beyond the sphere of purely economic interests, for it constitutes the establishment of social and moral order *sui generis*. Individuals are linked to one another who would otherwise be independent; instead of developing separately, they concert their efforts'. (p. 21)

On the function of law: 'The more closely knit the members of a society, the more they maintain various relationships either with one another or with the group collectively . . . the number of these relationships is necessarily proportional to that of the legal rules that determine them. In fact, social life, wherever it becomes lasting, invariably tends to assume a definite form and become organized. Law is nothing more than this very organization in its most stable and precise form, Life in general within a society cannot enlarge in scope without legal activity simultaneously increasing in proportion. Thus we may be sure to find reflected in the law all the essential varieties of social solidarity'. (p 25)

On the difficulties of functionalist accounts

From an extensive literature, the account given by Robert Ellickson in *Order Without Law* is commendably concise, as has been noted in the text.

Also of particular interest is: Mary Douglas, *Risk and Blame* while among the earlier classics are: A.R. Radcliffe-Brown, *Taboo* (Cambrdige, Mass., 1939) and B. Malinowski, *Crime and Custom in Savage Society* (London, 1926).

Philip Pettit offers a fresh approach to functional accounts by suggesting that, instead of trying to make sense of some social activity, such as law, in terms of its performing a specific task in order to meet a specific need, we should seek to explain its resilience. We should try 'to make sense of the fact that in any society some formations are much more capable of withstanding various contingencies than others . . . in particular, to make sense of the resilience of these patterns by reference to their serving an important social function: their having a distinctive effect'. (P. Pettit, *Rules, Reasons and Norms* (Oxford, 2002) p. 170). While the idea of resilience offers a new way of viewing social formations, it is noticeable that by the end of the quote, we are back with the familiar language of functionalism.

Reformulating Functionalism

On reformulating functionalism, it is noticeable that the natural law tradition, as explained by J.Finnis, also emphasizes social co-ordination as a means for achieving the basic goods, rather than social order as a concept and a goal in itself: (J. Finnis, *Natural Law and Natural Rights*).

Defining the legal order and legal relations

While Bentham's account of law as defining and constituting legal relations is of considerable importance, and supports the views expressed in the text, a note of caution should at the same time be entered. Bentham held the task of law to be to 'define anew' the social and political order (Postema, *Bentham and the Common Law Tradition*, p. 315). As Postema explains, law was not the expression of something already existing, but a fresh start. The view I argue for in the text is: (a) that law defines, is constitutive of, legal relations, but (b) they are placed on an existing social framework which includes areas of deeply entrenched social relations. The relationship between existing social relations *and* new social relations created by enacted law is one of the main modulating factors in modern legal orders.

The Social Value of Law

12.1 ASSESSING LAW'S SOCIAL VALUE

The first question that must be asked is how is law's social value assessed? The approach I propose is along the following lines. In modern legal orders, certain social goods are valued to the point of being considered essential, not just to survival but to a good quality of life. Many have nothing to do with law, but some do, among which the following should be included: security of private arrangements and transactions, protection of person and property, the provision of services, restraint on the part of officials, and maintenance of the legal system. Others could be added as sub-sets or independently, an example of the first being the division of protection of persons and property into criminal and tortious acts, and the second example good relations among nation states. The next step is to inquire how law can help in attaining and making secure each social good. This step should be regarded as primarily a description of law's qualities, as part of the mapping of law, in accordance with the first methodological principle. In order to know what actual effects the qualities of law have, we look to the second methodological principle. According to this, officials and citizens receiving law are introduced and empirical investigation is conducted into the way they deal with it. This is the test of how well law performs its tasks. The first step is undertaken in this chapter, although inevitably some reference is made to the second. A feature of the approach is that, by taking account of the role of non-legal formations in attaining social goods, the error of imagining that law is uniquely capable of doing so is avoided. The approach instead includes consideration of how law adds to these other social formations and forces, or, in some cases, competes with and opposes them. The second step of introducing officials and citizens into the process is taken up directly in Chapters 15, 16 and 17.

In proposing this approach to law's social value, I am adopting a view of law as instrumental to social ends; that, after all, is the main reason for having law. To some, however, the true social value of law lies in its being *constitutive* rather than instrumental, and since this idea has gained quite a following, a brief comment should be made. *Constitutive* means viewing law 'as a more pervasive influence in structuring society than as a variable whose occasional impact can be measured'.[1] This is an important aspect of law in society that, as B. Garth and A. Sarat rightly contend, should be taken into account. However, their claim needs to be modified. *Structuring society* appears to mean two related but different things. One is that law organizes the world 'into categories and concepts', the other that it *frames* 'thought and action'. Law, as we saw in the preceding chapter, 'organizes' nothing; law can only state its own categories and concepts, leaving it for citizens and officials to organize the world in accordance with them, or not. The world is organized according to law's categories and concepts only if and when people make decisions and apply them in practice. The expression of law is one thing, how it is received by officials and others a quite separate thing. That, it will be recalled, is the point of the distinction between the first and second methodological principles; it is also the reason for separating the architecture of law from its environment.[2] The idea behind the *constitutive* approach can now be seen. It refers to the way that, quite apart from the use of specific laws to achieve specific social ends, law's categories and concepts infiltrate into people's attitudes and understandings, and in this way affect and influence (or 'frame') their thoughts and actions. And, I would add, the main vehicle through which that process occurs, and the best way of understanding it, is the notion of social spheres. Whether as a direct instrument to social ends or an indirect influence on attitudes and understandings, law is received into social life and social consciousness through the mediation of social spheres. There is no question of having to choose between the approaches; both unlock lines of enquiry in the study of law in society.

12.2 NEED FOR CENTRAL LEGAL AUTHORITY

We are accustomed to the idea that state legal authority brings with it social advantages. A society with a developed legal order is able to achieve social goods more effectively than would be possible in a pre-legal order that lacks central legal authority. Recognition of state law as having final authority is unlikely to be sustained unless it adds to the capacity of other

[1] An example of this approach is: B. Garth and A. Sarat, 'Studying How Law Matters: An Introduction' in Garth and Sarat (eds), *How Does Law Matter?* (Evanston, Ill., 1998).
[2] See Sections 2.4 and chapter 7.

social formations in achieving social goods. What, then, is the distinctive value state law brings to the task? The answer begins with a statement of the case for central legal authority. The kernel of a society is co-operation among its members. Unless we co-operate with each other in a multitude of ways, the barest elements of social order are unattainable. At the same time, it is not always clear that co-operation at any particular time is in my interest or yours; it may be to my advantage to withdraw from a relationship or transaction at the last minute, or it may be to yours. So the question is: what keeps us in, what is the incentive to follow through to the end? This is often expressed as the Prisoner's Dilemma, which is an abstract way of depicting a range of situations in which neither participant knows what the other will do: co-operate or withdraw.[3] Analysts of the prisoner's dilemma are united in thinking that no matter what the other player does it pays each to withdraw before completion, unless there is an additional incentive to cooperate. Robert Axelrod, whose work has become a point of reference, concludes that the necessary incentive is whether the players are likely 'to meet again in the future so that they have a stake in their future interaction'.[4]

Reciprocity and mutual advantage are then the basis of co-operation. Both are served by knowing how others will act in diverse situations and being able to rely on their doing so. Reliance is implicit in some relations, those among friends or within the family; in other cases, relations among strangers being the most usual, social rules become the basis of reliance. They simplify social situations and create certainty in exchanges and interactions.[5] Here we need to broaden Axelrod's account by introducing social spheres: social rules generally occur within social spheres, which are wider than rules and include conventions and understandings from which rules emerge. Social spheres build on social relations and, in providing for the continuity and security of those relations, foster co-operation. Social co-operation normally occurs within social spheres and is guided by the conventions and understandings of which they are composed. If transactions or relations cut across two or more social spheres, another layer is available embracing them both and furnishing the basis for accommodation. Social spheres of different density and scope make possible daily exchanges and interactions where expectations are created and fulfilled. The picture of society is not unlike that of organic solidarity,

---

[3] A recent account is: R. Alexrod, *The Evolution of Cooperation* (1984, New York).
[4] *Ibid* p. 20.
[5] For an explanation of social rules in this regard, see: D. North, op. cit.

which, according to Durkheim, results from the division of labour, and within which each person can pursue his or her own ends, while at the same time reinforcing social order through co-operation, where law plays a major part.

If the twin goals of self-interest and social co-operation are satisfied through spontaneous social spheres, what is the need for central authority? What can it add to a world already highly structured by conventions and understandings? The answer is that co-operation is essential but not enough; there must also be co-ordination. The two might seem so similar as to amount to the same thing, but are importantly different: co-operative activities need to be co-ordinated if common goals are to be achieved. That can happen, as John Finnis explains: 'only if the . . . particular options [pursued by individuals] are subject to some degree of co-ordination', which in turn depends on some person or body whose 'prior concern and responsibility is to care for the overall common good',[6] where the common good means achieving basic social goods. Authority then is both necessary and simply defined: it is necessary in order to move beyond co-operation to co-ordination, and it is exercised by whomever as a matter of fact is able to bring about co-ordination.

Explanations of central authority in these terms are familiar, but incomplete in two respects. In the first place, they project (perhaps unintentionally) an image of society in which individuals pursue their own interests without reference to their doing so in an environment already highly coordinated by social spheres. Individuals sometimes go their own way and flout the constraints of social spheres, which anyhow vary in their density and the guidance they give. Nevertheless, by and large, they provide not just the basis for co-operation but a high level of co-ordination. But that is not always enough to eliminate the need for central authority; social spheres cannot always cope, perhaps because issues are too complex, requiring a special collective effort as in the case of emergencies, or because of conflicts between social spheres, or because social spheres take a direction unacceptable to society at large. The image, then, is of social spheres being effective in co-ordinating daily activities, leaving the state as the ultimate authority to intervene when they fail, rather than its bearing the primary responsibility. This brings us back to the now familiar question as to when state authority should intervene, which is in turn to ask what particular contribution central authority is able to add to those other, more spontaneous processes of coordination.

[6] J. Finnis, op. cit, p. 233.

Another modification to this account of central authority relates to the difference between co-ordination and regulation.[7] The notion of co-ordination is hardly adequate in portraying the role of the modern state in directing society towards positive ends and goals. It does not take account of the world of difference between providing a uniform law of contract and restricting a range of activities in order to promote human rights, the environment, or the interests of shareholders. All such activities are, in a sense, co-ordination, but they are also different, and some are more accurately described as regulation, suggesting not only a more active and positive role on the part of central authority, but also one that meets resistance from informal social formations. Informal social formations have a regulatory capacity, but the form of regulation so common in modern societies imposes external goals on existing social spheres. A bank may come to see that the adoption of anti-discriminatory standards is in its interest, and willingly adjust its practices without legal requirement. Banks and others are not always so conscientious, so it is for central authority to introduce such policies by law, and then take measures for their enforcement. Whether this is an effective way of bringing about change to existing practices raises another set of issues, but regulation is so common that it must be regarded as a central part of state activity.

12.3 LAW'S ORGANIZATIONAL CAPACITY

In order to obtain a clearer sense of how state law contributes to social goods, we need to be reminded of its attributes. Hart's account is now familiar: an imagined pre-legal world of only primary rules lacks certainty; it also lacks regulations for changing the primary rules and for adjudicating disputes about them.[8] The capacity to make clear and certain rules, to change them as conditions require, and to settle disputes authoritatively are, according to Hart, the gifts of a mature legal system, an idea that fits well with Weber's idea of modern societies being based on rational legal authority, a notion encapsulated in clear and certain legal rules administered by a professional bureaucracy.[9] But rules and officials, although essential, are not enough either to distinguish law from other rule-based orders or to explain its capacity in organizing society. Around

---

[7] Preliminary comments are made in Sections 8.5 and 8.6.

[8] H. L. A. Hart, op. cit., pp. 89–96.

[9] Some quibble about the move from a pre-legal to a legal world on the grounds that it is anthropologically inaccurate. This is to miss the point; the contrast is conceptual not anthropological.

those two foundations other elements have to be added: legislative bodies have extensive powers to make laws; they claim authority over other associations and organizations; officials are grouped together to form powerful organizations as government departments and agencies; officials have the power to enforce their decisions. The bare description of legal authority gives an inkling of its capacity but does not capture the full significance of this combination. Consider rules: rules are rules, and legal rules are similar to other rules; but they can be made clear and comprehensive by the organs of government at a level more difficult to achieve in other contexts. The processes for change, application, and adjudication are also capable of attaining precision and authority that are often lacking elsewhere.

These institutional and organizational aspects are crucial: law is made, administered, and judged by sets of officials who are organized, specialized, and divided according to the tasks they perform. These factors allow and encourage a systematic approach that nurtures among officials a sense of detachment and autonomy; it also encourages bureaucratic rationality. Each government organization, with its institutional base of rules, conventions, and understandings, becomes concentrated on performing specific tasks effectively and efficiently, whether making laws, interpreting them, or applying them. At the same time, the organizations and institutions of state, for all their variety, form a fairly cohesive whole, sharing the common enterprise of coordinating society through shared authority. Legal officials are able to view the society as a whole and arrange its affairs in a way not normally available to other centres of authority. They are helped in this by being able not only to make final and binding rulings, but having at their disposal and under their control the resources of the state, and the capacity to enforce the law and their decisions about it. And finally, the law's claim to final authority allows officials to intervene in other social contexts, sometimes to support them, at other times to constrain or direct them.

These qualities taken together convey a sense of the awesome capacity of state legal orders to control and organize society; I refer to it as their *organizational capacity*. Organizational capacity is present not only in good and tolerable legal systems but also in the bad, for as we learn more about law in Hitler's Germany or Stalin's Soviet Union, it becomes plain how much their regimes of terror depended on it. In a modern society, the organizational capacity of the state is itself regulated by law, reflecting the bond of trust between it and the people; in a pre-modern society that bond is absent, and to the extent controls exist they are not legal.

One strength of a state's organizational capacity is the ability to view society as a whole, and to provide for it by sets of general rules, sometimes streamlining existing activities, at other times changing them. By the enactment of authoritative rules, law can bring certainty, clarity, and generality to social situations, a capacity that is especially important when informal practices vary in such matters as, say, the transfer of property or the making of contracts. Its capacity to deal with complex situations of the kind encountered in business and finance is another sign of its utility. The claim to overriding authority, the support of an administrative and judicial structure, and the power to enforce, all add to these strengths and make it a formidable social force, whose utility lies not only in reinforcing existing practices, but in changing them in the pursuit of positive ends and goals. And finally, its tendency to autonomy signals a degree of detachment from society, and insulation from social pressures.

Several weaknesses are equally apparent: the tendency to autonomy means that law is external to the formations guiding everyday activities and often remote from them. Its capacity to systematize and its tendency to autonomy distance it from spontaneous social practices, making it less responsive to them. Law's mode of operation is blunter, less subtle, more rigid, and harder to change than the more fluid conventions and understandings of informal spheres. Its bureaucratic structure is cumbersome and may serve the interests of factions or officials, rather than the common good. Its threat of coercion can be alienating and encourages strategies of avoidance, while resort to coercion is a sign of the failure of law to be adopted into organic practices. And most of all, power in the hands of officials has its own dynamics, whose main features are the tendency to seek more power and resistance to controls. The central dilemma for modern legal orders, as we see time and again in the discussion, is that organizational capacity is necessary to achieve their ends, but poses risks to the social relations they are meant to serve. A more complete analysis might uncover other factors to weigh in the balance, but enough has been said to show that legal authority, despite the power and force at its disposal, has drawbacks which affect its capacity to co-ordinate and regulate. It confirms the obvious but still important point that the utility of law in achieving social goods is likely to vary from one context to another and according to factors that can be stated in advance only in general terms.

Having seen the organizational capacity of state legal orders, we now move to consider its application in specific settings. Two factors guide the analysis: one is the need to achieve social goods, the other the contribution law can make to it. The social goods are divided as follows: security of private arrangements, protection of person and property, attainment of positive goals and values, restraints of officials and maintenance of authority. The aim is to show the contribution of law to these social goods, without using the language of functions and without having to assess its general support for society; instead, general support is judged by its contribution to specific goods.

12.4 SECURING PRIVATE RELATIONS

Law is used to support and make secure arrangements and transactions entered into by individuals, groups, and entities. These include matters from simple contracts to complex financial transactions, from the making of wills to the creation of associations of a corporate, professional, or trade character. They include marriage, trusts, and complex property schemes. Arrangements and transactions of these kinds arise out of and are a natural expression of relations between private parties, including individual persons, groups, and legal entities, which they enter into for their own purposes and generally of their free will. As part of everyday social life, communities devise ways of conducting these activities and protecting them; they develop formal and informal rules for the purpose. It is not as if, as Hart contends, these activities are made possible by law, that law creates rules where none existed before; on the contrary, private arrangements and transactions are entered into and conducted as an integral part of social life according to conventions, understandings, and informal rules. The liberty to engage in such private activities, subject to certain restrictions, is held to be of an essential feature of liberal societies, an expression of fundamental social relations. If the transactions of daily life occur within and are governed by 'dense social network(s)', as Douglas North describes them,[10] networks often created or consolidated within the social spheres of guilds, professions, and business associations, what can law add?

A standard claim is that such networks are effective for small, close-knit, communities, but are of limited use beyond them and are certainly not for complex societies. The evidence is not so clear, with dense social networks being capable of extending beyond the local and familiar to national and international arenas. The practices of merchants, the *lex mercatoria* and its modern equivalent, are examples of rules and networks

---

[10] Douglas North, op. cit, p. 39.

governing international trade, with both evolving from practice and being regarded as binding, largely independently of whether they became part of state law or gain recognition in national courts.[11] The formation of networks of rules and practices governing activities important to the course of daily life and commerce is repeated, locally, nationally, and globally. How effective the networks are in co-ordinating such activities is still moot, although the fact that they persist suggests some degree of success. Since the rules grow out of real-life situations and are based on conventions and understandings, informal networks have advantages that law cannot match. In explaining what law contributes to private arrangements and transactions it is not enough to appeal only to its qualities as a co-ordinating mechanism, as if no other mechanism existed; we must consider instead the instabilities of informal arrangements and how law's organizational capacity helps to overcome them.

Law has the potential to contribute in several ways. One is its role in *facilitating* the intersection of private relations and the conduct of affairs. Much of the need for assistance results from *complexity*: as societies depend on a wide range of exchanges, interactions, and relationships, informal institutions are likely to be stretched beyond their capacity. An increase in social activity opens the way for more complex transactions and disputes, as anyone with experience of the corporate or financial world knows. Multiple parties, the crossing of jurisdictional boundaries, and subject-matter intrinsically complicated, all add to complexity. Formal law, whether deriving from the state or other sources such as the international community, does not eliminate complexity, but it has the capacity to reduce it and provide a structure for its better management.

Another, perhaps more fundamental, issue is *security*. Here state law adds a layer of protection to transactions beyond that available through informal networks. Initially the security of private arrangements is based on family and kinship relations where trust is implicit. When strangers enter the scene, trust has to be found in other relationships, such as those based on common purposes, as found in early European guilds and corporations, vestiges of which survive in modern professional associations. Common purposes generate conventions and understandings, and are reinforced by sanctions. The risk of ostracism, whether from practising as a barrister, doing business in the City of London, or from the farming

---

[11] A recent study of the *lex mercatoria* is R. Applebaum, W. Felstiner, and V. Gessner (eds), *Rules and Networks: The Global Culture of Business Transactions* (Oxford, 2001). The study casts doubt on the independence of such rule-based activities from nation states and courts.

community of Shasta County, is effective in ensuring that the conventions are honoured. However, as societies become more diverse and transactions more complex, the bonds of trust are weakened and often severed; transactions are conducted between parties who are strangers, being neither bound together by consensual ties nor by shared social spheres. Informal rules are more difficult to generate and the parties to transactions have less reason for respecting them. The risks of insecurity in contractual exchanges and property settlements increase, so that other ways must then be found to maintain reasonable security.

The basis of law's utility is now plain. Through its legislative and judicial capacity it lays down rules for the conduct of private transactions; it has the agencies to administer, interpret, and manage the rules and, if necessary, to enforce them. Law adds to the informal transactions and arrangements by constructing around a framework that makes them more secure. By security is meant certainty, stability, and guaranteeing expectations. Take title to land: a community is likely to have ways of proving ownership. Originally it was a matter of common knowledge, later marked by formal symbols, and then by title deeds, which are in time replaced by a central register with the extra security that brings. Similar reasoning applies to contracts, to the modern corporation, to family relations, and many other activities where, in each case, law provides both a framework of rules and the organizational capacity to add certainty to existing arrangements. The law is normally compatible with the intentions and purposes of the parties, and adds to existing customs and practices rather than inventing new ones. It strengthens what occurs spontaneously and gives effect to the parties' purposes, rather than opposing or changing them; its object is to facilitate and make more secure arrangements and transactions that would anyhow take place. Since law adds security, even if marginally, the parties have an incentive to co-operate with and make use of it. The extent to which law is needed depends on an assessment of the adequacy of informal arrangements and the benefits the law can bestow.

In addition to facilitation and security, the law exerts *control* over private arrangements. Control brings with it a change in social relations from those between private parties to those between private parties and officials. They change from officials' supporting private relations to regulating them. The opportunities private activities offer for revenue-raising play a part, but in addition, the state claims a common or public interest in private transactions. A well-functioning private sphere is a legitimate public interest from which flows the law's commitment to its facilitation and security. Another public interest is in ensuring that private transactions are compatible with and respect other social goods and values.[12] This is expressed in the setting of standards restricting the way private activities are conducted. The legal mode changes from facilitation and security to regulation. According to the regulatory mode, contracts must comply with standards of fairness and good conscience, while consumers, purchasers, and investors are given statutory rights to which contracts are subject. Ownership of land is also subject to restrictions based on such considerations as orderly planning and protecting the environment. Two senses of the public interest emerge: some restrictive standards, such as those protecting the environment, are justified by the general public good in having a sound environment; others are for the protection of one or other of the private parties, as in the case of standards relating to the good quality of goods and services. The consequences of the two modes of legal intervention also differ: laws facilitating and securing are likely to be in harmony with informal social practices, while the regulatory mode can be expected to run counter to them. The two modes are not strictly separate from each other, but intersect and intermingle, so that standards that seem at first regulatory and external may be absorbed into the social spheres of private parties, and reflected in their social practices.[13] Regulatory standards may also remain external and foreign, making their adoption unlikely and their implementation problematical.[14]

We now have a structure for understanding legal intervention in private arrangements; it leaves open questions to be answered and issues addressed in relation to specific areas of law. Two additional points merit comment. The general approach does not dictate when law should intervene, or the right balance between law and informal social practices, or how effective legal intervention will be. Legal support for private arrangements, combined with the capacity to enforce them, is said to be 'the critical underpinning of successful modern economies'.[15] More empirical evidence is needed to support this view, which on its face seems compelling. It is not a case of the more law the better; nor does it show in which areas of private activity law should intervene or what form it

---

[12] See further: P. Atiyah, *Introduction to the Law of Contract* (Oxford, 2001, 4th edition).

[13] Intersection and intermingling of regulatory standards and voluntary social practices is an idea developed at length, although expressed in different terms, in: H. Collins, *Regulating Contracts* (Oxford, 1999).

[14] These issues are discussed in Chapters 15, 16, and 17.

[15] See D. North, op. cit., p. 35.

should take. Those matters are decided after taking account not only of the advantages law offers, but also other considerations, in particular, how effective the informal arrangements are; what effects law would have on them (and they are not always good effects), whether the result would be greater effectiveness, and the added costs that might be incurred. The use of law in relation to private arrangements is plainly increasing, sometimes to add to and strengthen them, but at other times for extraneous reasons; since law is a powerful instrument, it is always at risk of being used for factional or ulterior ends.

A second issue for comment is the balance between the two modes of legal intervention, facilitation and security on the one hand, regulation on the other hand. The parties to transactions generally welcome the first, while finding the second problematical. Behind the two modes of legal intervention lie different justifications and ideas about the balance between private and public spheres, between private and public law, and between individual liberty and state control. Modern societies are characterized by both liberal tendencies and the active pursuit of social goals, with tension between them being inevitable. Compromises are necessary but untidy, and prone to lead some to adopt solutions that veer strongly towards one mode or the other. Voices condemning practically any legal intervention in private arrangements may tolerate measures aimed at making them effective, but not regulating them. Rivals at the opposite end of the spectrum argue for a new conceptualization, according to which regulation becomes the dominant mode superseding facilitation and security.[16] The change in social relations entailed in such a move has dramatic consequences: in place of relations between private parties being the dominant mode, with relations between them and officials of secondary importance, the reverse would be the case. The dominant mode would be social relations between private parties and officials, with those between private parties being of secondary concern. We need not adjudicate here the political and ideological merits of such a reversal, except to suggest that modern legal orders, as presently conceived and structured, assume the importance of both sets of social relations and the need for balance and compromise between them, rather than the domination of one by the other.[17]

---

[16] Amongst a growing literature, the best case is made in: H. Collins, op. cit. For critical appraisals, see the essays in: C. Parker, C. Scott, N. Lacey, and J. Braithwaite (eds), *Regulating Law* (Oxford, 2004).

[17] For further comment, see Notes.

12.5 SECURITY OF PERSON AND PROPERTY: THE CRIMINAL LAW

The criminal law, appearing to be at the opposite end of the spectrum in specifying what constitute criminal acts and the punishments for transgression, protects fundamental social goods and the social norms to which they give rise.[18] Integrity of person and property warrant the special protection criminal law and criminal justice provide. Without that integrity other social interactions are inhibited and the settled social relations constituting a society become impossible to form. The criminal law has a dual task: to protect each person from the other and to sustain the foundations of society. Durkheim's account captures well the significance of the second task: the criminal law protects the values of the society, which by the punishment of violations are reinforced and social solidarity strengthened. The task of criminal law is to deter and 'to induce people not to cause harm of serious kinds'.[19] It is also to make possible the formation and continuation of society.

The harm to which criminal law is directed goes beyond the protection of the person and property to include a large number of actions that are not traditionally considered criminal. The harm here is of a lesser order of seriousness and is often based on social goods, such as a clean environment, sound governance of companies, or health and safety of the workforce. In order for laws on these matters to be taken seriously, enforcement is necessary and that usually means making non-compliance an offence. Whether regulatory offences should be regarded as criminal offences is debatable; they are often of strict liability so that the usual standards of culpability need not be proved, and the harm at issue is often best considered as social rather than criminal. But for the law, some would not be regarded as harm at all.[20] Let us put these aside for the moment, for they are more suitably considered under regulation in 12.3, and focus instead on the more traditional sense of criminal law, realizing that it is not an exact term and lacks consensus as to its content.[21]

---

[18] For a valuable introduction, see: A. Ashworth, *The Criminal Process: An Evaluative Study* (Oxford, 1994).

[19] *Ibid*, p. 24.

[20] Regulatory offences make up a large part of the total range of offences and it is estimated that in England and Wales approximately half the total number of offences are of strict liability: *Ibid*, p. 24.

[21] For further discussion, see: H. Gross, *A Theory of Criminal Justice* (New York, 1979), pp. 4–12.

However hard to define precisely, there is a core of harm to persons and property, which is commonly condemned by communities and against which protective action is normally taken. Criminal law is based on this harm and adds an extra layer of protection from it. In this sense, criminal law has more in common with laws facilitating and securing private arrangements than first impressions impart, for both express spontaneous social relations and strengthen the social norms to which those relations give rise. If communities are resourceful in devising informal ways of deterring potential offenders, and punishing actual offenders, as we should expect they are, then what social value is gained by criminal law and process? The usual answer is that criminal law is somehow constitutive of society, so that without it society would collapse or be very different. Criminal law, then, bears a heavy social burden. The answer, however, conflates two ideas, one that the most elementary social life is possible only if certain harms are condemned and prevented, the other that state criminal law is needed to perform those two tasks.[22] The first idea is true and may be justification for the law being used to protect against such harms; but from that it does not follow that law is necessary for the task.[23] Conflation of the two ideas assumes that, without state criminal law, communities would be unable to protect themselves and social relations would be impossible. This is untenable anthropologically and historically; state criminal law may add to the protection informal processes provide in maintaining basic social relations, but that is not an adequate explanation of its social value.

While a complete account of its social value needs a treatise of its own, there are several lines of argument that at least set the scene for further consideration.[24] One is the organizational capacity of modern legal orders; another the tendency towards localization in defining and dealing with crime; the third is the import of legal values. The organizational capacity of the modern legal order, as explained above, enables officials to state the criminal law with acceptable particularity, to detect, investigate, and prosecute suspected offenders, and to take punitive and deterrent action against them. The social impact of actions being declared illegal, and the majesty and solemnity of the criminal process, derive from the

---

[22] Durkheim himself conflated these two matters in failing to consider non-formal legal mechanisms for condemning and deterring crime.

[23] Conflation of the two different ideas is another example of the functionalist fallacy discussed in Chapter 11.

[24] For an account that addresses some of these issues, see: D. Garland, *Punishment and Modern Society* (Oxford, 1990).

organizational capacity of the state. The criminal law's relative effectiveness in deterring the commission of crimes and its connections to justice are due to that capacity. If the legal order lacks that capacity or loses it, society does not necessarily collapse into disorder; since the core of criminal standards is normally embedded in social standards, other informal mechanisms are triggered into action. The disadvantage is that they are unlikely to be as effective over time, or to be applied evenly throughout society.

The tendency of local communities to develop localized norms contravenes the expectation in modern legal orders that the same law applies to everyone. There is no inherent reason why local communities should not define their social relations and the norms protecting them, as is their natural inclination. For a modern legal order, however, more than minor variation cannot be tolerated, for two reasons. One is the claim of authority over other rule-governed activities. The other is the social good of equality before the law, which entails that the law is approximately the same for all. If one questions the value of equality before the law, questions, in other words, why local communities should not be entitled to shape social relations as they wish, then two replies are available. The most simple and straightforward is that equality before the law is highly prized in modern legal orders; it is a defining feature and has entered into social relations. The other is more an empirical claim to which there are many exceptions, but which is likely to be proven generally true: leaving the definition of criminal actions and their enforcement to local forces, being so closely associated with the very survival of the community, encourages distorted attitudes that result in unacceptable harshness of definition, unjustified punishments, and the propensity for discrimination against members or groups. History is replete with examples, and although modern legal orders have not yet escaped from a primordial legacy of excessive punitiveness, progress has been made and, so long as such orders survive, it may be expected to continue.

Equality before the law leads on to consideration of other social goods expressed in notions of due process and a fair trial. That both are imperfectly achieved in practice does not detract from their importance, for in common with equality before the law both could be claimed as among the basic social goods of modern legal orders. It may seem paradoxical that their main practical task is to moderate the organizational capacity of the state, whose importance has just been extolled. A moment's reflection resolves the paradox: organizational capacity imports one set of qualities in sustaining the criminal law, but in doing so runs the risks inherent in officials holding power. Modern legal orders rely on officials' having powers, but at the same time must contain them in order to ensure respect for their equally important relations with citizens, one expression of which is the right to due process and fair treatment at the hands of officials. The dependence of rights on the powers of officials on the one hand, and trust in their capacity for self-restraint on the other hand, compounds the paradox. Here resolution is not so easy, there being no alternative but to record that, while self-restraint by officials is fragile, it is also a pillar of modern legal orders.[25] If the dilemma is how to maintain the balance between power and restraint, the contrast with informal mechanisms for criminal law enforcement is striking: they have neither the capacity nor the commitment to structure such mechanisms in accordance with the social goods of due process and fair treatment. They lack the first because capacity requires organized officials, the second because, according to their social relations, the protection of person and property, being so basic to personal and social survival, is unmediated by competing relations. Without competing relations, notions of due process and fair treatment have no social base.

My purpose is not to propound a full account of the social foundations of criminal law, but to show its social value in modern societies. In ending, there is one loud note of caution to sound. One of the assumptions on which ideas about criminal law are based is the essentially harmonious relationship between social relations and norms on the one hand, and legal definitions of crime on the other hand. On this assumption, criminal law has its origins in social relations, and is then taken over and supported by state law and its agencies. Law takes over both the definition of crime and its enforcement, but does so in a way aimed at maintaining close links with the social relations from which it originates. Without close congruence between the two, the legitimacy of the criminal law and the state's capacity to enforce it would be severely limited. It is probably true to say that the core of the criminal law, its most fundamental prohibitions, retains in modern legal orders reasonably harmonious relations with social standards, which, of course, it helps form. At the same time, a source of tension is the tendency to use the criminal law as an instrument for other social and political ends, whose pursuit, far from being in touch with social standards, is contrary to them and aims to change them. The criminal law takes on a positive regulatory role, rather than one expressing and reinforcing existing social relations

[25] For further discussion of the second paradox, see section 13.2.

and standards. Its social foundations are weakened, it meets resistance, and its effectiveness relies on the threat of sanctions.[26]

12.6 PROVISION OF SERVICES

The provision of services of various kinds is a common feature of modern legal orders, the idea being that the state has responsibilities towards its citizens both collectively and individually. The source of such responsibilities can be explained in different ways according to the kinds of services, and how one views the organization of a society and its governance. Some services, such as education, transport, and policing are necessary for society's survival and well-functioning, others, such as social unemployment benefits, the relief of poverty, and the provision of housing derive from a sense of collective responsibility for those who cannot provide for themselves. Some services are private arrangements between the provider and the recipient, others depend on state officials' acting under legislative authority. The focus here is on the second category, itself diverse in the matters it covers. Since my purpose is to examine the role of law in providing services, concentration on services of a broadly social welfare kind should serve it well. By social welfare is meant the provisions of benefits necessary for a tolerable quality of life to those who need them.

The social relations underlying the provision of benefits are distinctive, different from those so far considered, and open to being framed in different ways. The broad relationship is between citizens and officials; it may be framed as the discretionary conferring of benefits by officials or as the entitlements of recipients. It is characteristic of modern societies that the state takes responsibility for providing a much wider range of benefits than previously. Many now taken for granted were historically not considered the business of the state and left to private associations to be distributed as charity. The landscape of Europe is marked by such charitable institutions as hospitals, schools, and alms-houses, whose origins date back to the medieval period and which were for centuries the main providers of welfare. The history of the great hospital of Santa Maria della Scala of Siena illustrates it well: in addition to serving the medical needs of southern Tuscany, since its early foundation the hospital was an orphanage, an alms-provider, and a refuge for pilgrims, all as a matter of

---

[26] For further discussion see N. Lacey, 'Criminalization as Regulation' in C. Parker *et al*, op. cit.

charity. It remains a hospital but now depends on state-funding, while its other charitable activities have long since passed to the Italian state.

The move from benefits as charity to being the responsibility of the state marks a major change in legal relations between citizens and state officials. A further and more recent change is the idea that benefits are entitlements rather than dependent on official discretion. Despite the tendency to speak loosely of rights to welfare, the position is complex and variable with some benefits having become rights, others remaining discretionary. The law may speak directly of rights, but often leaves it open or ambiguous to be inferred rather than directly declared. Even when rights are declared, their precise content and scope is liable to be subject to elements of discretion on the part of officials in interpretation and application.[27] A more recent and similarly ambiguous shift in the relations between citizens and officials is marked by the growing practice of attaching conditions to the granting of welfare benefits in a manner intended to invoke the language and connotations of a contract.[28]

A neat but imprecise summary of these shifts and changes in legal relations would be: from charity to discretion, from discretion to rights, and from rights to responsibilities. Their history and causes are a matter of interest and importance, but not directly relevant to our present task of identifying the social value of law in providing services. The common ground with other sets of relations we have considered is plain, but there are also differences. The organizational capacity of officials must again be one of the obvious advantages of the state's administering welfare and other benefits. The capacity to create legal structures setting out the basis of distribution, application, and administration of the law, and the arrangements for officials' supervising each other are as important here as elsewhere. The creation of legal structures and the capacity to administer them is vital to, but goes beyond, the effective and efficient distribution of benefits and services; it means in addition the ability to move from relations of charity to legal relations based on rights and duties. That those relations are, in practice, ill-formed and variable does not detract from their importance and the potential for future development. To shift from social relations of charitable concern, relations that bear no legal consequences, to legal relations of rights and duties, is truly significant and rightly judged an indicator of a modern legal order. Its

---

[27] The complexity and uncertainty concerning these matters is well illustrated in: R. Cranston, *Legal Foundations of the Welfare State* (London, 1985).

[28] For discussion of this trend: see A. Paz-Fuchs, *Conditional Welfare: Welfare to Work Programmes in Britain and the United States* (Doctoral thesis, Oxford University, 2006).

natural partner is the related and by now familiar idea that other legal values also enter into relations between citizens and officials. Reasonable certainty in the law itself as opposed to open discretion; fair and suitable procedures for reaching decisions serve both the ends of accuracy, or rectitude as Bentham called it, and other values; and the scope for checking and reviewing decisions – are all ideals attached to law in modern legal orders. In identifying these social advantages, we should not ignore the disadvantages, including the bureaucratic character of government organizations, restricted ability on the part of officials to tailor benefits to the special conditions of each case, and the fact that benefits depend on entering into a legal domain and relations with officials, which may be daunting and discouraging to many for whom charity would at least be easier to collect.

12.7 REGULATORY LAWS

A feature of modern legal orders is the regulation by law of many ordinary activities in which people engage. What looks at first like a diluted version of criminal law is quite different, for where the criminal law, in its core sense, reinforces social standards in condemning harmful actions, those subject to regulation are normally legitimate. Regulation is a variable activity that is not confined to law, but for legal purposes it is usually defined as deliberately attempting to influence or control the activities of others by law.[29] Since this includes just about all law, nothing is gained by calling it regulation. In order to give it utility, its primary sense is taken to be the placing of legal restrictions on activities that are legitimate, the point of regulation being to limit or control them in some way and to some degree, but not to prohibit them.[30] The justification is that regulatory standards are based on goals and values important enough to warrant the restrictions. Manufacturing is a valued activity, both economically and socially, but should not cause undue pollution. Similarly, creating employment is a social good, but it should be performed in such a way that the workers are treated fairly and with care for their safety. Government and administration are themselves subject to regulatory restraints, with considerations of effectiveness and efficiency giving way to due

---

[29] See the discussion in: J. Black, 'Decentring Regulation: Understanding the Role of Regulation and Self-Regulation in a Post-Regulating World' (2001) 54 *Current Legal Problems* 103.

[30] Anthony Ogus' analysis of regulation has been of very considerable help. See A. I. Ogus, *Regulation: Legal Form and Economic Theory* (Oxford, 1994).

process and fair treatment. A hallmark of modern societies, and generally a desirable one, is that law should be used in this way to proclaim and advance values that are held to be important. Importance depends on someone's point of view, and who that someone is constitutes another variable. Regulatory standards have their origins in statutes, constitutions, and international covenants, and how they emerge and become law is an issue that merits more research than is now available. Those that do emerge sometimes command wide consensus, although at other times they are no more than the demands of special interests or passing fashion. The hope in a modern legal order is that regulatory standards are embedded in general values, but even then it is to be expected that interests and sectors subject to regulation will not always be persuaded of their merit or that the costs of compliance are justified. At the sharper end of resistance, the imposition of regulatory standards is held to be an unwarranted restriction on private endeavour, a complaint often heard from some sectors of society.

The very character of regulation shows both the tension inherent in it and why law is needed to create and enforce it. On the one hand, the regulated activities are normally legitimate, while on the other hand, restrictive standards are also based on legitimate social goods. Regulatory law then faces two main difficulties. One is opposition from those who are subject to it; the other is that the regulatory standards, whose legitimacy depends on social support, vary as to the strength of that support. Some standards, such as those imposing safety standards at work, are welcomed by workers and their professional organizations, but invariably seen by employers as unwarranted or excessive. Other standards, of which the recent introduction of the European Convention on Human Rights into English law is a good example, have broad but rather weak social support, with the result that their impact on public and private activities is likely to vary and often be marginal. Sometimes the standards, being the invention of a minister, an agency, or the European Union bureaucracy, lack any firm basis in society. Attitudes to any set of standards are not fixed but are prone to change, as in the case of environmental standards, where studies show the early ambivalence of society towards them. They were novel, they had serious consequences for the economy of businesses, and their moral standing was unclear. Now the standards are more deeply rooted, have become morally compelling, and carry more weight against opposing considerations.

How do these factors relate to the role of law? Regulatory laws are aimed at directing behaviour to comply with new standards; they are the instruments of government for achieving social goods by changing the behaviour of private and public bodies. A second consideration is the reaction of those whose conduct is being regulated. Regulatory standards are sometimes embraced voluntarily, and are most likely to be subject to two conditions: they must be approved of by the regulatees, and be capable of being absorbed into their activities without major change or disruption. Resistance is often to be expected; it may be so weak that compliance, even if begrudging, is not seriously inhibited, or it may be vigorous and resilient. The level of resistance depends on numerous factors, prominent among which is a perception of the standards as incompatible with the aims and methods of the activity, and with the attitudes, conventions, and practices that constitute and support it. Initial resistance may weaken in response to forces and factors other than the law. Social spheres are subject to many different influences, including current ideas and pressures within the wider society. The current concern for human rights is a good example. Organizations of all kinds, both public and private, are influenced by discussion, publicity, and heightened awareness, so that some adjustment to their social spheres and practices should be expected. Other examples could be added: concern for the safety of workers, the need for companies to be more socially responsible, and the growing knowledge of environmental harm – an analysis of each would show how the conventions, understandings, and practices in different contexts have been influenced by streams of social awareness, as well as by law. A third consideration is that the strength of social support for regulatory standards is also a variable affecting the level of resistance from regulatees; the stronger the social support, the greater the pressure on them to accommodate the standards. The strength of support also affects the regulatory body and its members, their attitudes, the mechanisms and strategies they adopt, and the difficulty of securing compliance.

The social value of law under these conditions is now apparent. It is to stipulate standards as to how an activity is to be conducted; to oversee their adoption by those to whom they are addressed; and, in the event of resistance, to take measures to bring about compliance. In setting new standards for society, law is at its most active; it is also here that the gulf between law and social spheres is likely to be most acute. This does not mean the regulatory process is simply a matter of setting standards and taking action to enforce them; on the contrary, although regulatory arenas are coercive, and regulatory bodies may usually invoke sanctions to bring about compliance, such a simplified description would be a mis-description. Between the setting of standards and their enforcement there is a social world consisting of complex relations between regulatory officials and regulatees, where various devices and strategies other than direct coercion are employed, and where compliance effected though discussion, negotiation, and persuasion is probably a more enduring measure of success than enforcement. Nevertheless, the capacity for enforcement sets the tone and determines the environment of the social world of implementation and compliance. The obstacles law faces in changing behaviour and making regulation effective are considered later on.

12.8 RESTRAINING OFFICIALS

Officials in modern legal orders have to maintain a fine balance between two opposing positions. Officials are necessary for the exercise of legal authority, while in its exercise they must sustain a particular configuration of social relations between themselves and the citizens. Undeveloped legal orders lack a secure base for restraining officials through law; with a legal framework that is piecemeal and fragmented, their basis for restraining officials is political rather than legal. Modern legal orders are different, for here trust is the basis of relations between officials and citizens, the terms of which are expressed in constitutional and administrative law. This is where the terms of delegation of authority, the restraining standards, and the lines of accountability are found. Social relations have two main aspects: between officials and the people collectively, and between officials and each person individually, whether as a natural person or through entities such as corporations, partnerships, or other associations.

The social value of law in sustaining relations between officials and citizens consists of two aspects: a structure of laws defining the powers and responsibilities of officials, and the conditions to which they are subject. They include notions such as officials having no authority other than that conferred by law, and the scope of any authority being limited by law. They include standards of fair procedures, such as hearing the case of parties affected by their actions, and a range of other principles aimed at rendering their actions fair, reasonable, and legitimate. The legal expression of relations between officials and citizens is dynamic and developing, as the full implications are realised and new notions become appropriate. Some legal orders have achieved a level of systematic maturity in expressing social relations and enforcing them; others have not yet begun the process, while many are in varying stages of transition. A prominent and difficult aspect of change from communism to liberal democracies in the countries of central and eastern Europe has been the legal restatement of social relations between officials and citizens, and their implementation. Some laws, such as codes of administrative procedure, could simply be read against a new and different set of contextual factors, and re-interpreted without major change; other laws, such as those providing for judicial scrutiny and the transparency of officials' actions, had to be adopted for the first time. The formulation of suitable laws is hard enough, designing suitable organizations and their institutional base, even harder; but the most taxing by far is the change of attitudes needed on the part of officials themselves. This living experiment in social and legal transformation illustrates the natural tendency of government bureaucracies towards autonomy and independence in wielding power; it also shows how difficult and unnatural it is for officials to reformulate their relations with citizens and restrain their actions accordingly.

The key factor in understanding the balance between power and restraint is that officials are responsible for self-restraint. The paradox of officials holding in their hands the power of a sovereign state, and yet being restrained in its use, is resolved by the creation of mechanisms enabling officials to control themselves. The high degree of self-restraint required in developing a tolerable level of social order reaches its peak in the exercise of power by officials. It is sustained over time by its transfer from being a personal matter depending on personal relations, to one that is de-personalized and expressed in legal relations. The means for doing so is a structure of rules, processes, and institutions. Informal social arrangements might have some success through other mechanisms. Under a charismatic leader, officials are expected to implement the leader's wishes and are restrained by that imperative; where custom and tradition prevail, the necessary self-restraint is embedded at the deepest social level, since custom and tradition are a direct expression of social relations, rather than being externally imposed. Two things are different in modern legal orders: one is that relations between officials and citizens are direct rather than mediated through a leader's wishes or the hand of tradition; the other is that officials work within a legal framework whose object is to supply the means for sustaining those relations.

In modern legal orders, the grant of authority to officials is objectified and a measure of autonomy granted to them, removing the elements of caprice in the one case, stultification in the other. The price of objectification and autonomy is restraint. Restraint is then made possible and strengthened by general rules and principles, according to which actions are taken and justified, and by the diffusion of authority among several organizations, each with its own objectives, among administrative bodies and courts, inspectorates and ombudsmen, police and prisons. Implicit in the legal framework is recognition of the special relations between officials and citizens. There is also more: the legal framework marks a particular set of relations among officials. They run parallel to but transcend personal loyalties, hierarchical structures, and group interests; they provide the basis for one set of officials scrutinizing the actions of another without becoming involved in those other sets of relations. Here, then, we have a sketch of the value of law in restraining official actions, the capacity for which is a distinctive feature of a modern legal order. It builds on the notions of both Hart and Weber who saw, but did not adequately expand on, the vital place of officials (in the case of Hart) and bureaucratic organizations (in the case of Weber) in a modern legal order. Law's capacity to create the conditions of official self-restraint could truly be considered the unique gift of modern legal orders; at the same time it is fragile and contingent, always competing with the natural forces of social power and bureaucratic organizations, always at risk of being overpowered by them.

12.9 SUSTAINING LEGAL AUTHORITY

Law's capacity to contribute to social relations and social goods in the several ways shown is itself dependent on sustaining legal authority. That capacity is itself an aspect of law's social value. On Hart's account, legal authority sustains itself through its own rules, which provide for the making of law, its interpretation, and its implementation. Rules make provision for the institutions and organizations necessary for those purposes. One of the reasons Hart describes a modern legal system in terms of rules rather than sovereigns is the ease in explaining their continuity, their institutional basis, and the distribution of powers and duties among institutions. The practical expression of these ideas is again found in constitutional and administrative law, stating the general structure of institutions, powers, and limitations on them, the latter developing those ideas further, and applying them to a secondary level of institutions and organizations.

We should here recall the discussion of the rule of recognition, acceptance by officials of the system of rules as authoritative, and their settled disposition to act in accordance with it. Their attitudes and actions derive from social factors formed within their social spheres and on which they depend for their strength. In one sense, then, the authority of law can be reduced to the attitudes of officials, which are conditional upon informal conventions and understandings. To take such an approach, however, would be to miss the point of law as a system of rules, for we have seen how officials subscribe to the system as a whole; that is, in accepting the rule of recognition, they commit themselves in a general way to all other rules made in accordance with it. The necessary modifications to the effect that officials in practice give variable weight to legal rules, while subscribing to the system as a whole, do not detract from its main point. The point being that a developed legal system contains rules whose purpose is to maintain itself. The application of the rules requires the actions of officials and others, but that process should not be confused with, nor thought of as another way of stating, the fact that law creates its own authority and makes provision for its continuation.

12.10 CONCLUSION

The discussion of the last two chapters can now be brought to a close. Chapter 11 began with an examination of the claim that law has functions to perform, including the preservation of a society and its good order. Several senses of functionalism were identified and the argument made that these were better described in the vernacular language, either of point and purpose or social effects. Whenever the language of functions is used, it can usually be translated into these more manageable notions; provided it is understood, which often it is not, that nothing is gained or lost by its use. The one exception is the familiar claim that law, as a system, has certain functions in sustaining a society. Although this lends itself to stronger or weaker formulations, I have shown good reasons for regarding the stronger as unfounded, on the grounds that they are based on circular reasoning, neglect the role of informal norms in maintaining society, and are unsupported by testable evidence. The notion that law as a system has certain tasks to perform, without which society would not be possible, could eventually be shown to be true, but so far it has not. To be sceptical about the stronger claims of functionalism is not, of course, to doubt the importance of law in society. But how and why it is important is best shown by abandoning claims about the system as a whole, and instead assessing its usefulness in achieving and making secure specific social goods. We have a good idea of the social goods we value in a modern legal order; the question then is: how do law and officials help in achieving them. In order to make such assessments, we must first have an idea of legal authority and the capacity of officials grouped in government organizations. The next step was to consider how the combination of law, legal authority, and the organizational capacity of officials contributes to several examples of social goods. Not all have been included in the assessment; law's role in tort and in international relations has been largely passed over, but the approach developed here could be applied to them and others. The analysis here should be seen as an approach, which could guide further research, rather than a complete project. We have also noticed the tensions and fine balances, the dangers and the fragility of law in modern legal orders, both in a general way and in relation to specific matters.

NOTES

Assessing law's social value

For another formulation by A. Sarat (and W. L. F. Felstiner): '. . . law is inseparable from the interests, goals, and understandings that shape or comprise social life. Law is part of the everyday world, contributing powerfully to the apparently stable, taken-for-granted quality of that world and to the generally shared sense that as things *are*, so *must* they be. . . . Interpretivists believe that law permeates social life and that its influence is not adequately grasped by treating law as a type of external, normative influence on independent, ongoing activities'.: *Divorce Lawyers and Their Clients* (New York, 1995), pp. 10–11.

For further statements of the constitutive or interpretivist approach:

M. McCann, 'Law and Social Movements' in A. Sarat (ed), *The Blackwell Companion to Law and Society* (Oxford, 2004).

J. Bringham, *The Constitution of Interests: Beyond the Politics of Rights* (New York, 1996).

Advocates of law's constitutive role pay attention to positive law infiltrating to influence attitudes and understandings; they might also pay attention to law prior to rules and to the way social relations are themselves expressions of law: see Chapter 4.

On state authority and capacity

Norbert Elias in his classic account, *The Civilizing Process*, writes: 'But when the external threat or possibility of expansion lapsed, the dependence of individuals and groups on a supreme co-ordinating and regulating centre is relatively slight. This function only emerges as a permanent, specialized task of the central organ when society as a whole becomes more and more differentiated, when its cellular structure slowly but incessantly forms near functions, near professional groups and classes'. (p.315) He continues: 'The formation of particularly stable and specialized central organs for large regions is one of the most prominent features of Western history'.

Private arrangements as regulation

For an excellent introduction, not only to tort law but as a description of private law generally, see: T. Weir, *Tort Law* (Oxford, 2002).

Hugh Collins has stimulated debate concerning the balance between private law and regulation in: '*Regulating Contract*' and summarized in 'Regulating Contract Law' in C. Parker, C. Scott, N. Lacey, and J. Braithwaite (eds), *Regulating Law* (Oxford, 2004). The main claim is that contract law should be reconceptualized as a regulatory mechanism. From the reasons given for seeing contract law in this way may be extracted the general idea that the law of contract is a form of governance in that it constitutes 'the basic rules governing most market transactions and, therefore, one of the principal sources of wealth'. (p. 13) As a form of governance, by which appears to be meant form of regulation, the law of contract should be analyzed according to the standards it sets and how effective they are. Although there are many aspects to this idea, only one general comment is recounted here.

The re-characterizing of the law of contract as regulation means a radically different understanding of social relations. Instead of contract being an activity entered into by private parties for their own purposes, it becomes an activity directed at the social goal of efficient markets. But why should we think of contracts in that way? Its drawbacks are plain. First, it ignores the social fact that people enter into contracts as necessities of daily life and for a host of different reasons which, in most cases, have nothing to do with markets or their efficiency. Second, it mistakes the *description* of a social activity – making and keeping promises – with *consequences* that may or may not result from it. Contracts may have effects on market efficiency, but that is a consequence of contracts not a description of them as a social activity. An accurate description has to make sense of the social relations and social practices expressed in contracting. Such a description supports a regulatory mode as opposed to a private arrangement mode only at the price of inaccuracy. Other aspects of the claim that contract is regulation are examined in *Regulating Contract*. See in particular the essays of J. Stapleton, 'Regulating Torts' and P. Cane, 'Administrative Law as Regulation'.

Securing person and property: the criminal law

The conflation of (a) society's need to protect person and property and (b) the need for the criminal law is apparent in the following: 'The criminal law ... establishes rules of conduct whose observance allows us to enjoy life in society, and in addition provides punishment for violation of those rules, for the rule would not be taken seriously enough by enough people to be generally effective ...': H. Gross, *A Theory of Criminal Justice*, p. 10. See further N. Lacey's perceptive introduction to *A Reader on Criminal Justice* (Oxford, 1994) and N. Lacey and C. Wells, *Reconstructing Criminal Law* (London, 'second ed., 1998).

The social value of the criminal law is typically expressed in terms of its contribution to social survival. A. Ashworth writes as follows: '... the chief aim of the criminal law is to contribute to the preservation of society itself' (*Principles of Criminal Law* (Oxford, 1991)). This is achieved by prevention and deterrence (see *The Criminal Process*, p. 23) and by inducing people not to cause harm of serious kinds (*Principles of Criminal Law*, p. 11). While these statements are accurate, my object in the text is to show the specific contribution a system of criminal law and justice makes to those general aims, which are also included in the aims of other social practices and mechanisms, and are not particular to criminal law and criminal justice. My argument is that their contribution differs according to different kinds of societies, and that modern legal orders have distinctive features, which in turn influence the tasks and the social value of criminal law and criminal justice.

The common law expresses criminal law in general standards rather than detailed rules, the justification being that this allows closer correlation between law and social norms and practices. It is arguable that because the criminal law is meant to express those norms and practices, its standards should be general and open, leaving them to be interpreted and applied in ways reflecting their origins. Where juries and lay magistrates are used, this is especially true, for both are a direct link to social norms and practices. See further: A. A. S. Zuckerman, *The Principles of Criminal Evidence* (Oxford, 1989) Chapters I and II. Zuckerman writes: 'In the public debate about the right to trial by jury those arguing against its erosion do not rely on the jury's ability to determine objective truth accurately. Rather, their argument is founded upon the desire to be judged by reference to the current social standards'. (p. 43)

It is one thing to accept that the contextual contingencies of legal standards inevitably vary from one community to another, especially in jury trials, decisions by lay magistrates, and in relation to sentencing, but quite another to leave to each the definition of the standards themselves.

Provision of services

On rights in relation to the provision of services and the balance of rules and discretion, the following accounts are noted:

J. Baldwin, N. Wikeley, and R. Young, *Judging Social Security* (Oxford, 1992) is an excellent empirical study of the adjudication of claims for benefits in England and Wales.

I. Loveland, *Housing Homeless Persons* (Oxford, 1995) is another empirical study of considerable value in examining the exercise of authority by officials in allocating housing.

D. J. Galligan, *Discretionary Powers: A Legal Study of Official Discretion* (Oxford, 1986) contains an analysis of discretion from a broadly legal and contextual point of view.

C. Sampford and D. J. Galligan (eds), *Law, Rights, and the Welfare State* (London, 1986) contains a collection of essays on rights in relation to welfare and examines problems in relation to social and economic rights.

Law as regulation

For a greatly expanded sense of regulatory law, see the collection of essays in S. Piccioto and D. Campbell (eds), *New Directions in Regulatory Theory* (Oxford, 2002). Regulation is defined in the opening essay as: 'the means by which any activity, person, organism or institution is guided to behave in a regular way, or according to rule': S. Picciotto, op. cit. 'Introduction: Reconceptualizing Regulation in the Era of Globalization', p. 1.

Maintaining the legal order

Luhmann's account is of interest and importance in showing how closed systems like law maintain themselves. The self-maintaining operations which he describes could not occur without the role of officials.

See further: J Raz, 'The Functions of Law' in Simpson, *Oxford Essays in Jursiprudence*.

Restraining officials

The centrality of self-restraint on the part of officials is part of the deeper social significance of self-restraint for modern societies; see: N. Elias, *The Civilizing Process*.

Form of Modern Legal Orders

13.1 DISTINCTIVENESS OF MODERN LEGAL ORDERS

Societies express social relations in laws whose forms vary. A glance at legal systems at different points in history shows that some retain a customary basis of general standards of the kind familiar to the Lozi, the Kapauku, and the Tiv, as well as the early common law; others rely on detailed rules enacted by a legislature. In the thirteenth century, the idea that laws should be stated in clear and simple rules, so that those subject to them know what to expect and how to arrange their affairs, inspired the Republic of Siena to print its Constitution in Italian rather than Latin, a notion previously unheard of; and just to be sure it did so in very large letters.[1] A study of the administrative courts of Poland shows how judges cling to the formalist idea that they are simply the mouthpieces of the law, law meaning the formal rules of the civil and administrative codes, and are reluctant to consider the more open standards of the Polish Constitution and European Union law, even though obligated to do so.[2] The debate as to the right balance between detailed rules and open discretion has never been concluded and probably never will, with some law-makers still seeking the elusive goal of a heaven of rules, others taking refuge in broad discretion. The debate may anyhow have been overtaken by the notion that enacted law, and the powers granted by it, are subject to a higher layer of general standards of the very kind the Polish judges cannot steel themselves to apply. The Parliament at Westminster and officials empowered by it, long used to unlimited sovereignty, are coming to terms with the force of standards of the European Convention on Human Rights and the treaties and judicial decisions of the European Union. Legal systems accustomed to a single or dual source of law-making are suddenly faced with rules and standards from multiple sources.

---

[1] An original can be seen in the Archivio di Stato in Siena.
[2] D. J. Galligan and M. Matczak, *Strategies of Judicial Review* (Warsaw, 2005) pp. 1–37.

Different sets of social relations give some guidance as to the normative structure of law, with those relating to property and contract naturally encouraging clear-line rules, while the more positively purposive provision of goods and services, or regulation of activities, seem to fit a more standard-based and discretionary approach. Closer study soon shows so many exceptions in practice that it is hard to sustain anything but the weakest presumption one way or the other. The diversity of the normative structure of law is matched by that of the institutions and organizations responsible for it, with some embedded in a complex arrangement of courts, officials, and lawyers, others lacking all but the most basic distinction between legal organizations and other social formations. Law and legal systems plainly appear in many shapes and forms, offering more or less guidance, being more or less distinct from other social formations, standards, and arrangements.

At the same time, the form or shape of modern legal orders is distinctive and different, not only from traditional societies based on custom, but also from those that, although quite developed, lack the qualities of a fully modern system. On this matter, legal theory and law-and-society diverge; whereas Hart followed the tradition of legal theory in describing the qualities shared by all relatively mature legal systems, those more directly concerned with a social account of law have narrowed the focus to modern legal orders. What matters is not the name (and *modern* is not necessarily the best) but the fact that some legal orders, those designated as modern, have qualities that others lack. According to Durkheim, modern social relations consist in the division of labour and the fragmentation it causes, with modern law expressing those relations. Much of Weber's work was directed at developing the idea of *rational legal authority* as the ideal type of a modern legal order, and the social conditions conducive to it.[3] *Bureaucratic law* is proposed by Roberto Unger as a stage some societies reach with only a few going on to become *legal orders* in their fully developed sense,[4] while according to P. Nonet and P. Selznick *responsive law* is suitable for a genuinely modern society.[5] These accounts and others raise issues about the nature of modern law, the claim being in each case that certain features may be generalized to form a distinct concept of a modern legal order. It is not my present purpose to analyze

---

[3] Weber's account of formal and substantive law is contained in op. cit. volume II.

[4] R. Unger, *Law in Modern Society* (London, 1976).

[5] P. Nonet and P. Selznick, *Law and Society in Transition: Toward Responsive Law* (Berkeley, 1978).

these views systematically, but instead to draw on them in developing a better understanding of the form law takes in modern legal orders.

13.2 SOCIAL RELATIONS IN MODERN LEGAL ORDERS

The configuration of social relations expressed in law leads directly to the foundations of modern legal orders. Social relations are revealed by unravelling laws as shown at various points in this book; it is those sets of social relations that both make modern legal orders distinctive and separate them from others. The configurations in any legal orders are: between citizens as private parties, between citizens and officials nationally (and internationally), among officials nationally (and internationally).[6] What then is distinctive about these sets of social relations in modern legal orders? The main background factor is a high level of regard on the part of both citizens and officials for the authority of law, a factor that at once separates modern orders from other systems where it is lacking. From this background, the special features of social relations emerge. In relations between citizens, freedom to enter into arrangements and transactions is prized; once entered into, their security and stability is expected. Relations between citizens and officials have several aspects, the first and most important being that officials hold authority in accordance with the *ascending* model, meaning that authority originates in the people rather than descends from on high. Secondly, officials are expected to provide the legal framework for security and stability of private arrangements among citizens. Thirdly, officials are empowered actively to direct society in order to achieve social goods, either by their positive provision or by restricting citizens' activities. Fourthly, officials hold power on trust, are obligated to act according to the terms of trust, and are accountable for their actions. Fifthly, the terms of trust include the obligation to maintain the legal order. Regarding the international sphere, we may be brief: state officials have duties created by the international order, while the status of citizens is beginning to gain recognition. A comparison of legal orders according to these criteria shows a qualitative distinction between those that more-or-less measure up and those that fall well short. Measuring up is, of course, a matter of degree and, in that sense, the notion of modern legal orders could be considered an ideal type; at the same time, a

---

[6] The international aspect of relations among officials is well-established, that between citizens and international officials is in its early stages.

comparison of the legal order of the former Soviet Union with that of the United Kingdom shows the qualitative differences.

From this account, two questions follow: what kind of legal order is needed to express and preserve the sets of social relations and the expectations they create? And what social conditions are needed to sustain it. The answer to the first question, which this chapter addresses, lies in examining the legal structure commonly found in modern legal orders, and then considering how it is linked to and protective of social relations. This divides into three separate but related issues: the normative structure, the institutional and organizational arrangements, and the ideas supporting them. The social conditions that sustain this legal structure is the subject of the next chapter.

13.3 NORMATIVE STRUCTURE OF MODERN LEGAL ORDERS

According to Hart's salient fact of social life, a mature legal system normally provides adequate rules for guiding actions and resolving disputes, where the rules are clear and certain enough for the purpose. We have examined the foundations on which legal rules are separated from other social rules to enable this claim to be made: the move from a pre-legal to a legal system marked by the adoption of mechanisms for adjudication, certainty, and changing the law, together with the grouping of officials as legislators, administrators, and courts. As law becomes relatively autonomous, as it separates itself from moral and social norms, it develops its own method of reasoning and encourages the creation of a legal profession as its guardians as well as its practitioners. We have noted the difficulties implicit in this account: the contextual contingencies of rules and the issues they raise; the hidden ambiguities in moving among clear-line, standard-based, and discretionary rules; and the straining of language in viewing all mature legal orders as rule-based. The one feature of modern legal orders that stands out above others is just how varied its normative structure is as between the three kinds of rules, sometimes with clear rules, at other times heavily reliant on general standards, and with lashings of discretion thrown in. Legislators have a choice as to how they structure the law governing a matter, and in choosing are swayed by other considerations besides the need for clear and certain rules. Administrators responsible for implementing the law normally find their powers and duties expressed partly in clear rules, partly as general standards, and partly as discretion, while the position of the judge is not very different. From the citizen's point of view, clear guidance is available in some matters, while others depend on how an official interprets a general standard or uses discretion.

If the ideal is clear-line rules, then far from being a heaven of rules, modern legal orders barely reach limbo. Hart's salient fact of social life is better understood in the shadow of Weber, who was less concerned to describe municipal legal orders than to identify an ideal type of law characteristic of modern societies. For 'ideal type', one could substitute the possibly more familiar notion of a central or focal case, for each expresses a theoretical model informed but not necessarily wholly reproduced by practice. Weber sought to capture the essence of modern law in the notion of legal rational authority as opposed to authority based on charisma or tradition, arguing that systems of domination strive to cultivate a belief in their legitimacy.[7] Rational legal authority gains legitimacy by acceptance of the legality of enacted rules and the right of officials to issue them.[8] Rational legal authority divides into formal and substantive law, each being a form of law competing with the other for prominence. The essence of the distinction is that formality is the expression of law in tightly constructed rules, while substantive law is based on general standards linking law to values. Formalism, according to Weber, enables law 'to operate like a technically rational machine',[9] whereas the law is substantive when it is based directly on 'expediential and ethical goals' to which direct recourse should be made in its application.[10] Formal legal authority reaches its purest form in bureaucratic organizations where the authority of each official is specified by rules. Each form of law is the product of social forces, notable in western societies, producing a level of legal formality not found elsewhere. The revival of interest in Roman Law in medieval Europe, the development of Canon Law and its application across the Continent, the emergence of secular states with their need to govern through centralized bureaucracies, and the growth of free markets are among the factors that explain the formalization of law in western Europe. Weber claims that European societies and their western offspring developed a unique level of legal formality compared with other societies. Progress is not only one way since tendencies towards substantive rationality pull in the opposite direction. Weber notes that, although the Roman Catholic Church made an important contribution to the formalization of law, the tendency within it to match law to moral standards was a power-

---

[7] Explained and discussed in: M. Weber, op. cit, Chapter III.   [8] *Ibid*, p. 215.
[9] Weber, op. cit., Volume II, p. 811.   [10] *Ibid*, p. 810.

ful countervailing force. The concerns within modern law for a *social law* based on notions of justice and human dignity, to which might now be added human rights, pose similar threats to its formality.[11]

Although aspects of Weber's account merit closer scrutiny than is possible here, his main point emerges plainly: the characteristic form of law in modern societies is rational legal authority, within which there is interplay between its formal and its substantive aspects. Here Hart and Weber are united in their concern to show that the distinctiveness of municipal law (for Hart) and modern law (for Weber) lies in its relative formality, its relative detachment from other social forces, and its tendency to comprehensiveness. Both are, in their own ways, endeavouring to formulate the central case of law, the full unfolding of a legal order. As important as both are in this endeavour, their sketchy outline should be made more specific in two ways. One concerns the interplay between rules, standards, and discretion, for here what is implicit in both should be drawn out more fully. Discretionary powers in the hands of officials primarily (and private entities) are such a common feature of modern legal orders that they can neither be accommodated as an exception to the rule of rules, nor adequately provided for in a notion of formal law. Discretionary authority, in the sense more fully explained in 15.6 but briefly expressed as the authority to decide and act in the relative absence of directions as to how to decide and act, is as central to the character of a modern legal order as rules or standards. And it is so, because we know that for officials to provide the social goods which the people expect discretion is necessary. Discretion is a central and positive feature of a modern legal order, not a corruption of or deviation from the ideal legal form.

The other addition stems from the need to move beyond the image of law as a single layer of rules – law as unilayered – to one in which law is multilayered. That means, in a given context, the presence of two or more layers of rules and standards, often deriving from different sources, all of which have some bearing on decisions and actions. Discretion is a simple and striking example: one set of rules (the statute) confers discretion and defines its scope; another set (the common law) places constraints on how the discretion may be used; while a third set consisting of several potential sources (the Constitution, European Union law, the European Convention on Human Rights, or other international covenants) adds another layer of direction and constraint. The multilayering of law is not

---

[11] *Ibid*, p. 886.

unique to modern legal orders, but it has come to have such prominence, and to be the source of such high expectations, that it must be granted the status of a distinctive aspect.

The tension within this normative structure is plain: enacted law and the delegation of authority to officials are necessary to achieve the social goods expected in modern societies; at the same time, extensive legislative power is dangerous and a threat to other legitimate expectations arising from the bond of trust between citizens and officials. The resolution is equally plain: legislative authority and its delegation are made subject to a range of standards deriving from multiple sources, some created by the legislature, others deriving from elsewhere. An accurate image of modern legal orders is not then one of unilayered rules conferring powers and imposing duties, but instead one of rules, standards, and discretion emanating from several sources, with different points and purposes, intersecting and influencing each other in various ways. In order to capture this form of a legal order we must reassemble the components: rules in the sense of clear-line rules still occupy a central place, but instead of being the ideal to seek and from which departure is deemed a failure, we now see that legal contexts are constituted differently. They are now constituted by combinations of clear-line rules, standards, and discretion, conferring powers and imposing duties, some offering direction in deciding and acting, others placing constraints on how decisions are made and what is decided. The first test of legitimacy is whether there is rule-based authority for what is done and whether the right rule has been applied. That is now part of a fuller, more diverse, and rather subtle sense of legitimacy. Instead of the test being whether there is a single rule to justify the decision, the test now is whether the decision has been made in a way that is justifiable according to the prevailing web of rules, standards, and discretions. Where discretion is conferred, its limits are set by rules and its exercise is constrained by standards. Legitimacy is less precise than simply applying a rule; it is more complex and it naturally allows a prominent place to the contextual contingencies. It has the complexity of modern art rather than the clear lines of the classical; it is, however, an accurate portrayal of the normative structure of modern legal orders.[12]

---

[12] For an extended analysis of discretion and the normative legal framework around it, see my earlier book *Discretionary Powers*. A more recent and illuminating account of the modern legal form is M. M. Feeley and E. L. Rubin, *Judicial Policy Making and the Modern State* (Cambridge, 1998).

13.4 MATCHING NORMATIVE STRUCTURE AND SOCIAL RELATIONS

We have two ideas to draw together. One is that modern legal orders express distinctive sets of social relations, the other that the normative structure is complex and diverse, building on, but going beyond, the idea of rules. The question is: how do the two fit together? In relations between citizens as expressed in private arrangements and transactions, where law's value lies in facilitating and making them secure, clear-line rules are likely to be prominent, with some recourse being had to standard-based rules. To the extent that entering into transactions involves officials, registering a company or partnership for instance, elements of discretion are inevitable but moderate. In making transactions secure, where officials have a fuller role in providing and implementing remedies, the concern for predictability and stability would normally best be met by clear and certain rules, subject again to standards and discretion. Where standards and discretion occur, courts and other officials are expected to reduce uncertainties by formulating guidelines and developing precedents. The position is similar but slightly different in relation to criminal law and civil wrongs, where duties are imposed on citizens and officials to respect the person and property of others. Duties that reflect social norms – reasonableness, negligence, provocation, and dishonesty, for instance – are often expressed in standard-based rather than clear-line rules, allowing police and prosecutors, courts and juries, to draw on well-understood notions. Where the duties of criminal law or tort are not based on social norms but artificially created by enactment, a higher level of rules would be expected. At the same time, since the criminal law, in particular, has become a positive instrument of social control in modern societies, creating crimes artificially and without roots in society, the resort to standards and discretion rather than clear rules has advantages.

The normative structure of modern societies is most visible in relations between citizens and officials. Laws distributing social goods have provoked debate as to their appropriate form. Their aim being to achieve social ends, such as the relief of poverty, the rehabilitation of offenders, and the creation of a healthy and well-educated society, a natural inclination towards general standards and generous discretion is predictable. The need to distribute scarce resources strengthens the inclination. Since the goods distributed are among the most essential, a countervailing pressure towards rights and rules is also predictable. The incommensurability of the two, and tension between them, reflects uncertainty in the underlying social relations and the most apt legal expression of them, an uncertainty that modern societies have not resolved. Regulatory laws raise a different set of issues: they require the restriction of otherwise legitimate private activities in order to attain positive social goods. Again, modern societies have not resolved at the level of social relations tensions between the two; the need for a clear and predictable legal structure, as a natural expectation where private activities are at stake, is offset by the purpose of regulation being to achieve social goods, such as safe working conditions, equal opportunities, and the protection of shareholders. The usual outcome is once again a variable legal structure, with shifting combinations of rules, standards, and discretion. One advantage of more open legal structures dominated by standards and discretion is that negotiation and accommodation between officials and private parties is made easier.

These two cases illustrate the character of the legal structure sketched above. Both show its shifting nature as a mixture of clear-line rules, standards, and discretion. In displaying the uncertainties and tensions in underlying social relations, the two cases show why the legal structure has that form, and why, for all its contradictions and unevenness, it is the standard normative form of modern legal orders. We also see how purposive action delegated to officials for the pursuit of social goods needs the relative freedom of discretion rather than the close direction of rules. That freedom, if left unrestrained, would lead down routes in conflict with the social relations between citizens and officials. Their maintenance relies on discretion being guided and restrained by standards deriving from the multiple sources described above.

13.5 SUPPORT OF OFFICIALS

It is a paradox that officials grouped together in a variety of governmental organizations are necessary for the viability of a modern legal order, and yet also pose its greatest threat. The central place of officials in sustaining a legal system is made plain by both Hart and Weber for reasons that have been explained and need not be repeated except in the briefest terms.[13] For Hart, their role is in accepting the rule of recognition and then having authority to make new laws, to give authoritative rulings, and to apply the law. Their importance for Weber was not dissimilar, although

---

[13] The principal sections are: Chapter 5 and Sections *7.3* and *13.7*.

his emphasis fell on the capacity of organizations to implement effectively the policies of government. To these features I have proposed the addition of two more. One is the tendency of organizations of officials to develop an institutional character of conventions and understandings, formed partly from its legal environment and partly from other factors both internal and external. The result is a social formation that tends to detach itself from other formations and to develop a distinctive character, a tendency depicted in the notion of *autopoeisis*. The significance of autopoeisis is that officials act from within an institutional setting and are influenced by it. The other addition is that modern legal orders are made possible only by self-restraint on the part of officials, on their accepting restrictions on the range of their powers and the manner of their use. The basis for restraint is the social relationship between citizens and officials, according to which authority ascends from the citizens, is held on trust, and is to be used according to acceptable standards. The restraints are self-imposed and self-policing, for who is there after all to control the controllers or regulate the regulators?

The paradox is most stark in modern legal orders: on the one hand there is a commitment to the active pursuit of positive social goals, while on the other hand officials must act under restraints which are more than mere irritations, but confront the natural dynamics of government organizations, and are likely to be perceived as interference. The relationship between the two is asymmetrical: bureaucratic organizations are powerful, self-restraint weak. How, then, do officials resist the temptation of converting powers into licence and following the natural sway of bureaucratic organizations? The hope that a question so basic to contemporary societies should have been well considered is disappointed, so that instead of being able to draw on a bank of understanding, I propose three ideas that need to be studied further, but which open up promising lines of enquiry. The *first*, introduced in 7.7, concerns the normative structure: the point being that the creation of rule-based and standard-based contexts, itself provides officials with the basis for acting, justifying their actions, and evaluating those of others. Both actions and evaluations are depersonalized and assume a sense of disinterested detachment, where the issue is whether an action has been taken in accordance with the prevailing rules and standards. A link can be seen between this and the idea introduced in chapter 11 that, in its pristine sense, the function of law is to constitute the legal order, so that anyone entering it has a basis for action and evaluation of action. Law, in short, creates its own criteria as to which actions are legitimate and which are not.

Important as that process is, it is not enough, for we do not yet have a link between officials and the normative structure of modern law. Here we encounter a *second* idea: the link is constituted by officials accepting the normative structure as binding in the way previously discussed. The key to acceptance is not the solitary official trying to form suitable attitudes to the law, a figure whose model would be Dworkin's Herculean judge.[14] The key and an alternative image is that officials belong to organizations whose social spheres of conventions and understandings include commitments to the authority of the law. They derive their perceptions and norms principally from within their organizations in the manner of and subject to the various qualifications described previously. Social spheres provide more than an initial set of understandings and conventions; by being the constituent parts of a continuing social entity, they constantly reinforce attitudes, while being strengthened by the very fact that officials in practice act according to them. Scope for adjustment and change is not eliminated, although organizations tend to build social spheres of high density, so that conventions and understandings adopted and internalized exert strong influence on their members and erect barriers against easy adjustment.

The normative structure of modern legal orders is adopted and internalized within the social spheres of government organizations, influencing officials' attitudes and providing them with a legitimate basis for upholding the legal structure as a matter of course, as if that were the natural order of things. The description has, to some extent, been over-simplified in order to show the force of social spheres and organizations; the strength of officials' commitment to the legal order varies, other factors compete, and organizations differ in the degree of influence they exert over their members. Nevertheless the key to understanding how officials exercise self-restraint, in accepting and acting in line with a fragile legal order, is found within their organizations.

Organizational pluralism is the *third* factor in considering the role of officials in sustaining modern legal orders. The network of officials needed to perform the tasks of modern government is extensive and diverse, covering legislative and administrative bodies, courts and other supervisory authorities, and a range of semi-governmental and non-governmental entities. Once organizations reach a level of general acceptance of the legal order, they become mutually reinforcing in maintaining it. Just as individual officials are supported by their own organizations in

---

[14] A point made by M. M. Feely and E. L. Rubin op. cit. (Cambridge, 1998).

their attitudes, similarly each organization finds support in belonging to a network whose members share a commitment to the legal order. Mutual support is expressed in various ways, in the co-operative relationships among organizations, the overlap of their activities, and their cross-checking and cross-balancing roles. Organizations in a modern legal order participate in a macro-social sphere which provides shared conventions and understandings running parallel to those at a micro-level.

The relations among organizations and the degree of influence exerted by their shared social spheres are matters awaiting fuller examination. Courts, as one set of organizations, have a distinctive and definitive role in both setting standards and providing leadership to other organizations. Their role as judicial bodies is unique in having the final say in interpreting the law, a matter given added importance where law is multi-layered and general standards prominent. Courts are expected to be independent of other organizations, whether public or private, not because adjudication is, simply speaking, the law. The reason is that lack of independence would prevent the courts being even-handed in their treatment of other officials and organizations, the idea being that the faithful upholding of the law by courts reinforces law's authority throughout society. We do not know with any certainty whether this is true, nor whether the courts are influential in reinforcing the commitment of other officials and organizations to law's authority, since empirical evidence is both limited and inconclusive. The post-communist societies of Eastern Europe have struggled to create strong and independent courts, only to discover that administrative agencies and government departments are still anchored in attitudes and practices from the past. Courts may over time have a significant role in changing such attitudes and in encouraging a high level of acceptance of the legal order by officials. The most that can safely be said is that the self-restraint of officials is at least partly dependent on the mutual reinforcement of government organizations, and probably non-government ones as well. It is likely that, within the process of mutual reinforcement, courts have an important place, although that must remain somewhat speculative until more evidence is available.

13.6 SUPPORTING IDEALS: THE RULE OF LAW

We now have an account of the normative structure and how officials support it; the third aspect of modern legal orders is the set of ideas on which it is based. This is loosely described as the *rule of law* which has several meanings, some based on the innate qualities of rules, others linking law to ideas of liberty, democracy, and rights. Rather than adding to the numerous accounts already available, the object here is to identify the set of ideas that are implicit in modern legal orders, implicit in the sense that they guide the actions of officials and citizens, normally by being adopted in their social spheres; also in the sense that in explaining and justifying actions reference would be made to them. These ideas have their origin in the rule of law, which has the following qualities: first, legal contexts are defined by, infused with, and constrained by legal rules and standards; secondly, certain qualities are built into the rules; and thirdly, the rules are applied by officials according to certain conditions.

According to the first quality, legal contexts, especially those involving officials, are characteristically created by rules conferring powers to take certain kinds of actions, while at the same time limiting their nature and range. Rules both confer powers and limit them, the limits being both procedural and substantive. Officials have authority only if the law confers it, and have no authority other than that so conferred. This simple idea is fundamental to a modern legal order and distinguishes it from those in which officials do as they like, as the party decrees, or as special interests demand. In the early days of post-communism, students from central and eastern Europe, who were raised under communism, when studying western legal ideas, found this to be so different from the role of officials to which they were accustomed that it was almost impossible to grasp. Having stated the general principle, we should enter some caveats and project the rule of law on to a modern legal order. *Rules* do not mean Weber's formal rules, nor are they confined to Hart's salient fact of social life; instead rules mean combinations of clear-line, standard-based, and discretionary rules, intersecting, overlapping, and sometimes competing. Rules are not interpreted and applied by mechanical means, or even by simply applying the text as the Polish judges and most other judges from that region believe. Instead, rules and standards have their own social world where contextual contingencies come into play and exert their influence. Legal contexts are *infused* with multiple layers of rules and standards deriving from several sources and exerting varying degrees of influence. For all its complexities, contingencies, and avenues of escape, this idea of legality persists as the foundation of a modern legal order. [15]

Accounts of the rule of law draw a distinction between *rule by law* and *rule of law*, the first connoting nothing more than using rules (or some-

---

[15] For an account on similar lines and from which I have benefited, see M. M. Feeley and E. L. Rubin, op. cit. (Cambridge, 1998) especially Chapter 6.

thing similar to rules), the second requiring that the rules have certain qualities. According to this idea, a sovereign body could use law to rule just in the sense that decrees are issued without regard for notions of generality, autonomy, or equality. Roberto Unger suggests that, at some point in some societies, legislation progresses from being 'public and positive' to being 'general and autonomous'.[16] *Generality* means the use of general categories and concepts that apply to all who come within their terms, the contrast being with laws applying to some but not others, or are *ad hominem*, or deal with only some cases within a wider class. *Autonomy* means that laws are applied according to their terms without reference to other beliefs, rules, or values. *Equality* of treatment is not always recognized as implicit in the rule of law, but a moment's reflection shows that a rule, couched in general terms and faithfully applied, imports the limited sense of equal treatment that all whose circumstances come within the rule will be treated in the same way. It is equality in a limited sense because it says nothing about the content of the law, so that the line between the two is bound to be uncertain and unstable. Equality before the law could be the stimulus for groups to claim that formal equality without substantive equality lacks merit, but we need not pursue the issue here. A related but quite different aspect of equality arises when the question is asked: who is subject to the law? King James I's contention that he could not be subject to the law since it was his law, has long been overtaken by the notion that all are subject to the law, including, with few exceptions, the organs of government.[17]

These ideas are implicit in modern legal orders. The values of generality and equality are taken for granted, with the rider that both are relative notions so that what is general or equal to one may appear to be particular and unequal to another. Both concepts are, to some degree, artificial, since in cases of contention their evaluation depends on the (probably unexpressed) substantive view as to what constitutes generality or equality. Clear-line rules at first seem natural allies of both, indeed are immanent in the very nature of a rule; however, it is not hard to find rules aimed at particular cases. The fact that standard-based rules, such as procedural fairness or proportionality, are open-textured does not prevent their being general or those subject to them being treated equally. The standard of procedural fairness applies generally to all administrative actions,

---

[16] R. M. Unger, op. cit., p. 52.
[17] For a recent retelling of an old story see G. Robertson, *The Tyrannicide Brief* (London, 2005).

even though precisely what is required, and therefore what constitutes equal treatment, varies according to the circumstances. The normal expectation is that, through interpretation and experience, abstract standards will be made more precise by rendering them into rules and guidelines, and, in this way, enhancing both generality and equality. The prevalence of discretion in modern legal orders poses difficulties for ideas of generality, for the point of discretion is to deal with the particular case as seems most fit. However, ideas of generality and equality have deep social roots. Sentencing and parole practices, which traditionally are highly discretionary, fell into disrepute because they violated basic ideas of equal treatment. The over-reaction in favour of almost mechanical rules removed some inequalities, but spawned a host of new ones, an experience shared by the British social security system when it tried to remove discretion by rules. It may be ironical, but discretion properly used facilitates the reaching of a higher level of real equality and generality than rules or standards; the trouble is the risks are high. For that reason, a rough balance of rules, standards, and discretion is common; and it is probably the safest way of achieving a reasonable level of equality and generality while, at the same time, realizing the social goods for which power was given in the first place. Finally, equality in the sense of all being subject to law has special importance in modern legal orders, both as a condition of power being granted to officials, and as a mechanism for holding them accountable for its use.

The application of legal rules according to their terms, often referred to as its *autonomy*, is the final aspect of the ideas implicit in modern legal orders. There are two main ideas: officials decide and act according to the terms of the rules, and in so acting they respect the constraints on their powers. This is the correlative of the first idea that law confers, defines, and limits the authority of officials. That decisions should be made according to the rules and standards of law is as fundamental as its counterpart that officials have only the powers given by the law. To grasp its point in modern legal orders, we have first to expunge the image of formal rules being mechanically applied, and plant in its stead the image of a complex of rules, standards, and discretion depicted earlier. Account then has to be taken of contextual contingencies and the scope they unlock for variable interpretations; account also has to be taken of the fact that legal designs can be incomplete, internally inconsistent, and impossible to apply. A third matter to note here for fuller explanation in chapter 16.2 is this: the extent to which officials have authorized discretion not to apply the law is unresolved, although they often assume the right to do so. Despite this armoury of qualifications, in whose wake the idea of law's autonomy might appear in tatters, the idea remains intact that law is a recognizable social formation that all are obligated to take seriously. Every legal arena is marked by a legal design whose existence is recognized; each creates a legal environment in which citizens and officials have to meet and deal with that design; and each interacts with the fuller social environment around it. Officials know they have to account for their actions by showing that they have entered into this environment and tried to make sense of it. With regard to the second idea – that the application of law is constrained by standards – we can be brief: enough has been said to make plain that even the widest discretion, the most purposive grant of authority, has constraints on its use, some stemming from the original grant of authority, others from those multiple sources displayed earlier. Compliance with these standards is as important to the legitimacy of authority as respect for the terms of the empowering statute, which signifies another gap between legal orders that are modern and those that are not.

13.7 INSTABILITIES

A question Luhmann asks but never answers is: what are the conditions sustaining law as a social system? Without attempting to answer his question, we should consider a slightly different one: what are the social conditions that are conducive to modern legal orders? A preliminary foray into that issue is the subject of the next chapter. A prior matter, and the note on which to end this chapter, is to mark the more visible instabilities in the conception of modern law whose elements have just been described. They revolve around three axes: the risks of enacted law, organizational rebellion, and the collapse of ideals. Since modern legal orders turn on these axes, change or disruption could jeopardize their survival.

Enacted law's empire

As customary law has waned in modern societies, enacted law is in the ascendancy. Enacted law means mainly laws made by the deliberate act of officials, normally in order to achieve specific social goals. The primary form is legislation made by parliament or similar bodies, with administrative regulations and judicial decisions having secondary but still major significance. In modern legal orders, including those of the common law tradition, enacted law is the main source of law, affecting all subject matters from private transactions to governmental regulation. The making of enacted law is sometimes motivated by the concern to render into law existing practices and social norms; at other times it creates law in otherwise empty spheres; while in others still it seeks to modify or redirect social practices and norms. Considering how much enacted law there is and how important it has become, its provenance is worth considering. The simplest explanation for its rise is that law is regarded as an instrument by which governments advance their political goals. At their most crude, laws are no more than the expression of a government's will, which may be the expression of disinterested concern for the common good, but it is just as likely to be capricious, misdirected, or captured by special interests. Since modern societies are normally democratic, legislation may be justified as expressing the will of the people acting through their elected representatives, and pursuing social goals for the common good. Despite the restrictions imposed by constitutions and bills of rights, legislators retain extensive law-making authority. Our interest here is not in the substance of that authority but in the form of laws emanating from it. The reality is that legislative bodies have discretion largely unfettered as to the form of their decrees. Clear-line rules of general application are one form, but legislative decrees are just as likely to be couched in the language of purposes and standards, or left to the discretion of officials. History gives little guidance, since it is only relatively recently that standards, such as the rule of law or due process, have been invoked to define the parameters of law's formal qualities. As constraints they are weak, so that enacted law as the expression of legislative authority is apt to take whatever form the enacting body gives it.

The character of enacted law is the product of its origins which lie in the authority of the head of a household. The head of the household, according to Weber, wields a patrimonial authority over his household that is personal and, subject only to recognized traditions, practically absolute. Family is extended to include kin, retainers, slaves, and employees. Of a fourteenth century Tuscan merchant it is written: 'Servants and children alike were subject, in law, to the *podestas puniendi* of the head of the family; they could be beaten and starved and even sent to prison at his caprice'.[18] The expression of authority is as likely to be in the form of orders addressed to one or other member of the household, as a general rule applying to all. Patrimonial authority is expressed in numerous ways – as rules, orders, ad hoc decisions – according to the needs of the

---

[18] I. Origo, *The Merchant of Prato* (London, 1954) p. 197.

household. Some households become powerful over time and emerge as political authorities, extending beyond kith and kin, but retaining the same form of patrimonial authority. The evolution of kingly authority in England illustrates the point. The authority of both old English and medieval Norman kings was organized around the king's household. Authority was personal and absolute, subject only to accepted traditions and the bounds of loyalty. The three main functions of government, legislative, executive, and judicial, were the personal prerogatives of the king, while all authority held by members of the king's household were held in his name and at his pleasure. As one scholar described it: 'At the court everything centred around the king's person. In him all power resided, though at times he might share it with certain members of his immediate family.'[19] Even as offices became separated from the family and the household, they were still the expression of the king's personal power to rule, the connotation being that he ruled his kingdom as any man ruled his household. His actions, decisions, and orders could be issued as he thought fit and in whatever form he chose. The history of English constitutionalism is, then, the history of steps taken, initially to curb the personal discretion of the king, and later that of Parliament as his successor, while as late as the early twentieth century A. V. Dicey deprecated those very qualities of Parliament's unlimited legislative authority.[20] What has changed little after a millennium is that legislation is the act of an unlimited sovereign, an idea that derives directly and without rupture from that of the king's household. Lacking roots in social practices, it is the opposite of customary law.

The relevance for our current concerns is in showing how enacted law, especially in the hands of sovereign bodies and their delegates, does not conform either theoretically or historically to any ideal, let alone to any natural social inclination that law should be in the form of general rules or that it should encourage autonomy and equality. The natural tendency is in the opposite direction, for sovereigns like heads of households must act in such ways as appear to them to be effective and expedient in achieving their ends. From those concerns might come pressures towards modern ideas of the rule of law; Machiavelli thought that pure expedi-

---

[19] L. M. Larson, *The King's Household in England Before the Norman Conquest* (1904 quoted in C. B. Chrimes, *An Introduction to the Administrative History of Medieval England* (Oxford, 1959).

[20] A. V. Dicey, *The Law of the Constitution* (London, 1961).

ency alone would tempt leaders in that direction.[21] That may be true and it may be enough to ensure the rule of law. At the same time, arguments of expediency are an unstable base for the expression of social relations and the organization of government; and the point remains that the rule of law rubs against the natural grain of government. And if this all seems remote from the modern state, just glance through a volume of contemporary statutes or regulations to see that, where much has changed, much more has stayed the same. The concerns for generality and autonomy are rebuffed by the stronger demands of government to be expedient, to hedge its bets, and to keep future options open. Just as the natural order of running a household is to retain discretion to take whatever action in whatever form the situation needs, it is the same for the modern state. If enacted law is to meet ideals of generality and autonomy, it will be the result not of qualities inherent in government, but of countervailing social forces.

The tensions inherent in enacted law are increased by several other factors to be mentioned in passing. One is that enacted law often lacks roots in social norms and practices, a feature that is most visible when its aim is to change social norms and practices. Another is attributable to the active state, the commitment to ordering and changing society in a host of ways, according to an agenda that acquires its own momentum which, once launched, is hard to stop. Foucault considered the law a much less significant or potent method of governance and discipline than other more informal and insidious forms, among which social spheres are prominent.[22] Nevertheless, law in modern societies is ambitious in its goals and active in their pursuit, so that impatience with legal forms and constraining standards is predictable. Another way of viewing the same matter is in terms of overloading the legal order. Some theorists express this as *juridification*, an evocative term for turning social issues into legal matters.[23] *Over-juridification*, the attempt to convert complex social, economic, and political issues into law, may lead to a breakdown in the ordered structure of the legal system, forcing it to cast off constraints that are only lightly attached. Over-juridification expresses a concern that the normative structure of modern orders lacks the capacity to cope with

---

[21] For an imaginative account of the Machiavellian approach: see S. Holmes, 'Lineages of the rule of law' in J. M. Maravall and A. Przeworski (eds), *Democracy and the Rule* of Law (Cambridge, 2003).

[22] See: A. Hunt and G. Wickham, op. cit.

[23] For instance: N. Luhmann, *Law As a Social System* and G. Teubner, 'Juridification: Concept, Aspect, Limits, Solutions' in *Juridification of Social Spheres* (Berlin, 1995).

complex social issues, and is at risk of being undermined or even destroyed by them.

Without attempting a full analysis of this idea, several aspects should be noted. The first is that the normative structure of modern law is more capable of responding to the social demands made on it than often imagined. Discretion has long been a means for introducing flexibility into law, while resort to purposes and open standards are common features of any legal order. All are ways of enabling the unlimited variability of economic, social, and political life to be transformed into legal forms. The notions of rule-based authority, of multi-layered standards guiding and restraining authority, of organisational pluralism and official self-restraint and cross-checking, together with avenues of complaint and scrutiny from citizens and non-governmental associations, endow modern legal orders with the capacity to respond to the ambitions of enacted law. Alarm over juridification is usually stimulated by an obsolete image of the legal structure, more akin to Hart's salient fact of social life than to the more complex structure described here. The claim that overuse, or use for unsuitable purposes, is having a harmful effect on the form of law is a hypothesis whose confirmation depends on extensive empirical investigation. Empirical investigation requires a statement of the form of law and then an assessment of whether or not specific areas of law fit within it or undermine it.

Until that is done, it is difficult to know how seriously the concerns of over-juridification should be taken. After a cursory review of three areas of law – contract, family, and employment – a certain scepticism is warranted. All three, being areas of private arrangements overlaid by a regulatory structure, display the usual tensions between laws facilitating and making secure arrangements spontaneously entered into, and law regulating them in order to achieve positive social goods. All three also exhibit the expected mix of clear-line rules, open standards, and discretion, the second two being naturally more prominent in the goal-oriented regulatory aspects. Among the three, the tendency is most pronounced in employment law, where ideological goals are closely tied to the legal order, and fluctuate from one generation to another. Collective bargaining is prominent at one point,[24] the promotion of employment and strengthening of relations between management and workers at another,[25] while

---

[24] A. C. L. Davies, *Perspectives on Labour Law* (Cambridge, 2004), p. 3.
[25] H. Collins, 'Regulating the Employment Relation for Competitiveness' 30, (2000) *Industrial Law Journal*, 17.

economic efficiency and rights regulation are said to be currently prominent.[26] Despite the prevalence of goals and standards coloured by ideology and politics, and despite its complexity and more than a hint of instability, there is little evidence of concern among jurists specialized in the subject that the rule-of-law form has been weakened or threatened. Concerns that the form of law is being eroded in modern legal orders should be taken seriously; but just how real the threat is remains uncertain and unproved.

Organizational rebellion

If modern legal orders rely on the self-restraint of officials, rebellion is conceivable. What is there to stop officials, grouped as they are in powerful organizations with the instruments of coercion at their disposal, from defying the bonds of self-restraint, a phenomenon beyond contemplation in stable, modern societies, but in most others the normal state of affairs. Again, the Machiavellian case may be enough: officials are much more likely to have their way and further their interests by clothing themselves in legal weeds than rude power. That may be a factor but there is plainly more to it. Self-restraint is collective and institutionalized, aided and strengthened by organizational pluralism. Lapses here and there can be accommodated, so that even if one set of officials or another confounds the bonds of restraint, the system as a whole should survive and the deviation be remedied.

At the same time, the risks are plain. The bonds of restraint confront the natural tendencies within organizations towards the effective pursuit of goals. Being steeped in ideals rather than in social practices, the restraints are weak and fragile. Their internalization in the social spheres of organizations needs to be so deep-seated that negation is impossible to imagine or to occur, although the difficulty of reaching that point should not be neglected. Organizational pluralism is stronger or weaker in its capacity to restrain the behaviour of officials, and is at risk of being undermined by both major upheavals and gradual opposition. Organizations are composed ultimately of groups of individual persons, and stand or fall by their actions; organizations, nonetheless, have limited resistance to the rebellion of individuals. Rebellion in one part of an organization easily spreads to others and may infect the whole while the rebellion of one organization has a similar effect, so that the accumulation of isolated failures puts the whole system at risk. The pressures at work are easy to

---

[26] S. Deakin and G. Morris, *Labour Law* (London, 2001, 2nd edn.), p. 57

detect, but to determine their likely outcome in practice, we need more empirical knowledge than now available.

Collapse of ideas

As governments of liberal societies rush to enact legislation allowing for exceptional measures to be taken against those suspected of terrorist activities, some see the beginning of the end of the rule of law. That conclusion is unwarranted, but it does show the vulnerability of ideals, and that to trifle with them is to threaten them. Ideals are often discarded as little more than the vehicles for vulgar interests, and although there is some truth in that, ideals also have a capacity to become ingrained in the social spheres and social consciousness of a society. And when to them is added the armour of government and non-government organizations, it is improbable that they will collapse under the weight of a few rash actions of government. Nevertheless, a cautionary tale lies in the craven ease with which ideas, that one day are taken to be constitutive of a society, to express its fundamental social relations, are the next day presented as contingent inconveniences. Ideas, by their very nature, are liable to change as other conditions change. Ideas are capable of achieving some autonomy and independence from material and practical interests, as we have seen. However, they are always vulnerable to collapse, and are most at risk when the practices of governments and officials no longer provide regular affirmation. Ideas of the rule of law, as they are expressed in modern legal orders, survive and develop only with the practical and ideological support of the organizations of government and civil society. If that support were withdrawn or subtly shifted, the ideas would soon wither.

NOTES

On the force of law

The main authority on the form of law is Max Weber who argues that modern western societies have developed a distinctive form of law: *Economy and Society*, Chapter VIII, Part VIII.

A similar idea, although described differently, is central to Durkheim's account of law is a highly differentiated (modern) society: *The Division of Labour in Society*, Chapter III.

A more recent account is R. M. Unger, *Law in Modern Society*, Chapters 2 and 3.

Unger's idea that legal order is disintegrating in modern societies is taken further by Nonet and Selznick in their brief but stimulating book, *Law and Society in Transition: Towards Responsive Law* (New York, 1978).

On the normative structure of modern legal orders

Feeley and Rubin give an extended analysis of the legal framework of judicial policy-making in relation to prisons. The main issue, in their view, is how that process is constrained or limited; they state: 'Principles such as the rule of law are now treated in functional not categorical terms – the operative question is whether the policy-making process is subject to constraint. Our claim is that the process of creating doctrine, when performed properly, is inherently constrained . . . . . the unity of legal doctrine and the rule of law in judicial decision making generate constraints that are inherent, or in-dwelling, in the process of doctrine creation'. (*Judicial Policy-Making and the Modern State*, p. 210).

Legal values in relation to discretion are analysed in D. J. Galligan, *Discretionary Powers*, esp. 2.32.

On the proposal that Responsive Law is the key to developing law in modern society, see P. Nonet and P. Selznick, *Toward Responsive Laws: Law and Society in Transition*. Responsive law is based on the limits of rules and the alternatives of identifying the *purposes* of a grant of official powers.

Purposes are partly objectively determined and partly arrived at by the participation of divers groups and interest. For a critique of this approach: see D. J. Galligan, *Discretionary Powers*, section 2.33.

The rule of law

Definitions of the rule of law are plentiful; among those of particular historical interest are:

Hart, op. cit, Chapter IX.

F. A. Hayek, *The Road to Serfdom* (Chicago, 1944).

F. A. Hayek, *Law, Legislation and Liberty* (3 Volumes, Chicago, 1973–1979).

J. Raz, 'The Rule of Law and its Virtue' in *The Authority of Law*.

L. L. Fuller, *Law and Morality* (New Haven, 1969 second ed.)

J. Habermas, op. cit.

For a recent survey of different versions of the rule of law and their historical origins:

B. Tamanaha, *On the Rule of Law*, (Cambridge, 2004).

On the rule of law in relation to discretionary powers:
D. J. Galligan, op. cit.

On the rule of law in relation to regulations:
K. Yeung, op. cit.

Instabilities in modern legal orders
On weakening the normative structure by over-juridification:

G. Teubner (ed) *Juridification of Social Spheres and Dilemmas of Law in the Welfare State* (New York, 1988).
N. Luhmann, op. cit.

On contract law

H. Collins, *The Law of Contract* (London, 2003 fourth edn.)
G. Treitel, *The Law of Contract* (London, 2003 11th edn.)
D. Campbell, 'Reflexity and Welfarism in Modern Law in Context' 20 (2000) *Oxford Journal of Legal Studies 473*.
S. Smith, *Contract Theory*, (Oxford, 2004).

On family law

J. Herring, *Family Law* (London, 2004, second edn.)
F. Burton, *Family Law* (London, 2000).
J. Eekelaar, 'What is Critical Family Law?' 105 (1989) *Law Quarterly Review* 244.
M. King, 'Future Uncertainty on a Challenge to Law's Programme: The Dilemma of Parental Disputes' 19 (1992) *Journal of Law and Society* 271.

On employment law

S. Deakin and G. Morris, *Labour Law* (London, 2001).
H. Collins, *Employment Law* (Oxford, 2003).
A. C. L. Davies, op. cit.
K. Ewing, 'Democratic Socialism and Labour Law' (1995) 24 *Industrial Law Journal* 103.

14

Social Foundations of Modern Legal Form

14.1 ACCOUNTING FOR THE FORM OF LAW

The last chapter ended with an account of the instabilities of the legal form in modern societies. On the one hand, the legal form has a specific normative structure, the institutionalized support of government and non-government organizations, and a foundation of ideals; on the other hand, the innate tendencies of enacted law, the potential rebellion of organizations, and the collapse of ideals create instability. The trend of modern societies towards fragmentation of social relations and the fracturing of social solidarity augment the instability. The more complex and pluralist a society, the more determined the trend, so that the issue for the founders of modern social explanation was to find the bonds holding it together, the forces countering natural disintegration. As one of the founders, Durkheim considered a legal order composed of rules transcending local and group divisions to be a major unifying factor. We have seen the value law adds to informal social arrangements and need not doubt its salutary effect on a fragmented society. The issue now is how that legal order came about rather than its consequences, and on that Durkheim is silent. If the tendency of modern societies is towards diversity and fragmentation, the question is: what contrary social factors could there be to foster a legal order that fosters common purposes rather than divisions and similarities rather than differences? Followers of Marx, another of the founders of modern social understanding, look below the surface to learn that the legal order, in promising generality and equality, is a clever device for concealing differences and rewarding special interests. Law cannot change the divisions of class and wealth but can hide them, and there is no better way than through a legal order that promises equality of treatment under general rules and a coercive apparatus with which to implement them.

To erect a total explanation on the back of an elementary truth about economic and class divisions inevitably means losing, purging, or ignoring much of social life. The disinterested concern to make sense of events and their social consequences, the willingness to engage the awkward and the unruly, to omit nothing, leads to Weber, the third of the founders of modern social explanation. It is Weber who, having in common with Durkheim a sense of the special character of modern law, asks what brought it about. Weber saw no grand historical scheme, no collapse of one economic and political order into the unfolding of another. What he saw were close ties between the legal order on the one hand and the economic, administrative, and political systems of modern societies on the other hand. He considered the form of modern law to be distinct from other forms of law and unique to a few societies, it being the direct result of social forces at large in western societies. The rise of the sovereign state and its need to rule over diverse groups; the conflicts between the Roman Catholic Church and rising secular states; the growth of commerce and industry, and the creation of the free market with its need for legal certainty; the new interest in Roman Law as an abstract and formal legal order; each of these and others, according to Weber, influenced the form of modern law.

My objective is not to conduct a close study of Weber's ideas on the legal form, but to give an account of the social factors that explain it. This means identifying the social factors that could reasonably be regarded as contributing to the distinct form of modern law. The risks in such an enquiry are plain. Considering the difficulty of marshalling all the factors that contribute to a social formation as complex as law, any attempt is bound to be incomplete. The best that can be done is to isolate those factors whose presence seems likely to contribute to and support the legal form. The most obvious approach to take is the historical, the adducing of evidence from which conclusions as to causal connections are drawn. But an historical account is both complicated and beyond my present concerns, and is anyhow best left to historians. An alternative is to work backwards, so that instead of asking what brought about the legal form historically, the question is: given that this legal form has appeared and is sustained in some societies, what are the social conditions on which it depends? In answering, we are guided by history, but the account is descriptive and inductive, based on making connections among social factors, rather than explaining historically. This is what Foucault meant by a *genealogical* approach, using the past to illuminate the present, in this case to reveal the social foundations of modern law. Instead of searching for origins and evolutionary paths from one stage of development to another, this method concentrates on understanding the present, allowing that it is as likely to be unplanned and unforeseen as the outcome of deliberate action or irresistible social forces.[1] The factors most relevant to this genealogical reconstruction divide into those external to the legal order and those internal to it, the first including private interests, the interests of the state, and the rule of law, while the second refers to the process of evolution within the legal order itself.

14.2 FROM TRUST TO RULES TO LAW

If we know why groups develop social rules to govern their arrangements and transactions, it should be easier to ascertain why they take the further step to legal rules. It has been accepted from Hobbes to Hume to Hart, that rules protecting social goods, particularly security, property, and contract, are necessary for survival. The contrast between situations where rules have a minor place with those where they are prominent helps to explain why. Take, as an example, the family where matters of daily life are conducted largely without rules; expectations and under-standings are based on affection, empathy, and trust, with rules having a minor part. For most matters, they would be simply out of place. Once relationships move outside the family or similar associations, problems arise: the distance between one group and another grows, so that strangers are treating with strangers, trust is weakened, and the risks are greater. How can we rely on the stranger honouring his promises, not repossessing the land he has sold, or taking what he wants by force? Outside the family, the trust that prevails naturally within it has to be created artificially; informal social rules are one way of doing so. Whereas family relations were once the guarantees of security and predictability, rules now take their place. Rules state the conditions of the transaction and the consequences of breach or failure to deliver, and provide pressures for compliance. Informal rules would not work without an initial foundation of trust which, as the rules prove to be reliable in practice, becomes more secure.

Informal social rules are normally adequate in daily life for the conduct of private transactions and arrangements, both in setting the terms and in mounting pressure to ensure compliance, and nothing more is needed. Sometimes, in relation to some matters, a society takes the further step

[1] M. Foucault, *Discipline and Punish: The Birth of the Prison* (London, 1977) and *History of Sexuality* (London, 1981); for explanation of Foucault's idea of *genealogy*, see P. Baert, *Philosophy of the Social Sciences*, (Cambridge, 2005) pp. 163 ff. Weber may have been an harbinger of Foucault for his approach was similar if simpler.

and adds to informal rules a layer of legal rules. The added utility law brings to private arrangements is explained in *12.4*: added security, the capacity to handle complexity, and state control. Legal rules normally build on informal social rules by adding to their capacity to deal with complex transactions and guaranteeing security in their execution. The move from social rules to legal rules is in no way inexorable, nor do all societies make it. The Chinese practice of creating relationships of trust between the partners to business transactions, according to well-understood social conventions, continues in contemporary China. It continues not because of a shortage of legislation, for that now exists in abundance, but because the tradition of basing relationships on trust has served well for a long time. As a result, legal rules are often ignored in favour of informal relations, to the perplexity of foreigners. The Chinese are caught between the two worlds, between traditional practices and pressure from westerners to adopt their rule-based approach. The move towards a formal legal approach is visible and could be explained by insistence from western business on having a system it can understand; it could equally be that in the modern world of global business the formal system has advantages over the informal. The Chinese case leads one to ask: why is it that some societies are able to manage their affairs on a mainly informal basis, with legal rules and state enforcement present but not prominent, while others are impelled to reliance on formal legal rules and state institutions? When does the need for those added facilities and protections become so pressing that a society moves from an informal base to a formal one?

Since the formal approach is most pronounced in western countries of a democratic, liberal, and free-market kind, it is there that we should search for the conditions that have led private interests to seek security in formal legal arrangements. Weber's explanation is that some economic interests prize the predictability and stability of a formal legal order, although he goes on to say that economic interests alone would not be enough to bring it about.[2] What other factors are needed he leaves open. In imagining what they could be, it is perhaps enough to invoke an image of a burgeoning business environment in which the subject matter varies widely, the parties, of whom there may be many, are situated around the globe, and the transactions are complex. From such an image, we get an inkling of the limits of informal rules, and why the extra security of legal rules and the institutions to enforce them, are desirable.

[2] M. Weber, op. cit., Volume II, pp. 813 and 884.

Relations between the parties is a major factor, as we saw, the idea being that informal rules will be adequate where the parties trust each other enough to be able to rely on them. That condition is most likely to be met in small, close-knit groups, such as a farming community or a restricted profession, such as barristers, or business associations in the nature of guilds.[3] As private transactions move beyond these circles, the level of trust in informal rules is likely to diminish, so that the greater security of formal law becomes appealing. Other factors are also relevant, including the difficulty of establishing common, informal norms because of distance, cultural diversity among the parties, or the complexity of the matter. The introduction of law into private transactions does not mean abandoning the informal norms in favour of the formal, but adding a layer of protection to them. As trust is strengthened, the parties are likely to relax the formal rules in favour of more informal conventions and understandings, the outcome being a complex relationship between the formal and the informal.[4] The best source of predictability and stability is not, in general, the law but good private relations; when they fail, as sometimes they do, the law provides incentives for settlement and, on rare occasions, enforces the arrangements.

14.3 PRIVATE INTERESTS AND THE STATE

In understanding the social conditions of the legal form, relations between private interests and the state should not be discounted. In the absence of good relations between the two, an economy is unlikely to prosper, while the effects on law are difficult to gauge. If the common law is the primary source of law, it can generally be relied on to decide cases and create a body of precedents that are responsive to the informal understandings and expectations of private interests. Some consider its capacity to protect private interests, by way of contract and property, to be its glory. In the case of enacted law, the position is more volatile. Arbitrary and unpredictable interference by the state has long been regarded as anathema to stable private arrangements and the enemy of enterprise. General rules, together with judicial supervision of their application, are considered a necessary protection, a barrier to executive

---

[3] See Robert Ellickson's account: op. cit. pp. 249 ff.
[4] See further: S. Macaulay, 'Non-Contractual Relations in Business: A Preliminary Inquiry' (1963), 28 *American Sociological Review* 55.

arbitrariness and a belt of security for private interests.[5] Obsolete traditions and arbitrary practices, as Weber notes, are both incompatible with a modern legal order and impediments to the freedom of the middle class to engage in private enterprise. General rules have the capacity to reduce the privileges of one group in favour of a wider group, a capacity invoked by the middle class in attacking the special privileges of the upper class. The liberal state normally supports private interests, while other kinds of states may be their enemy. Democratic societies should be a guarantee of some protection, for there is no natural division within them between the state and private interests, and it may be expected that private interests will balance each other to prevent domination of some over others. More could be said about these complex relationships than is possible here, but it may fairly be concluded that co-operation between private interests and the state, a mutuality of interests, should go some way towards explaining both the prosperity of western societies and the formation of their legal orders.

It is convenient and sometimes accurate to think of private parties as united in their interests and concerted in their causes; more often they are locked in competition, either to protect their privileges against each other or to win privileges from which they are excluded. The struggle of the plebeians of early Rome for property rights, finally recognized in the agrarian laws of Servius Tullius, could be taken as the first such encounter, often repeated over the course of history.[6] The French historian, Fernand Braudel, suggests that the one problem occurring most frequently in Europe between the fifth century and the present was the struggle over *libertates*, not liberty in the modern sense but privileges, or in modern terms *rights*: 'protecting this or that group of people or interests, which used such protection to exploit others, often without shame'.[7] *Libertates* include such matters as being able to engage in commercial or professional activities, to contract freely outside one's own group, or to own and transfer land or other property. In a society accustomed to supreme liberty in these matters, where the restrictions on free engagement in any activity are few and related to qualifications rather than privilege, it is hard to imagine a society in which many of those same, normal activities were confined to classes, groups, or guilds. How

---

[5] F. A. Hayek made this one of his lifelong themes; see op. cit. (Chicago, 1944); J. Raz also draws attention to this aspect of general rules in: 'The Rule of Law and Its Virtue' in J. Raz, op. cit.

[6] Described by G. Vico, op. cit., p. 68.

[7] F. Braudel *A History of Civilizations* (New York, 1987) pp. 315–6.

instrumental the law has been in the movement from liberty as privilege to liberty in the sense of freedom to engage as one wishes, is yet to be examined. What is clear is that such movement is a significant factor in the formation of modern law.

A word of caution often repeated by Weber and worthy of Foucault should be recorded: between private interests and the emergence of modern legal orders there is no necessary link. Whether the one leads to or even encourages the other depends on such a range of conditions that it is hard to predict when one outcome rather than another will result. The social factors favouring such a link have to be set against others pulling in the opposite direction. One is cost; the cost of engaging in the formal legal processes has to be balanced against the gains in security. Cost may be a disincentive to cultivating a modern legal order, as is shown by the popularity of informal processes, rather than courts, in settling disputes. Another factor, perhaps less obvious, is that a formal legal order may inhibit private activities rather than secure them; the buccaneering spirit of Rhodes in Africa or Clive in India would have found an order of legal rules unhelpful to their cause. In the history of private enterprise, the ear of the prince or the favour of the executive may be worth more than the best made laws.

14.4 RULING OVER DIVERSITY

The modern legal order can be traced, it is said, directly to the organization of the Roman Catholic Church when, in the late twelfth century, it exerted authority over matters that had lapsed into the hands of local secular states or the Holy Roman Emperor but which, it was claimed, were properly Church matters.[8] If the Church's claim to authority, the so-called Gregorian Revolution, were to succeed, it would need an organization that could transform local laws and customs into a set of general and positive laws, applying and capable of being enforced throughout Christendom. The implementation of positive law depended on an administration of Church courts and officials who had the necessary professional skills. The reinvigorated interest, prominent at the time, in classical Roman Law as a system of universal concepts and rules, was not confined to the Italian universities or destined only for adoption in the provinces, but infiltrated the Church and influenced its lawyers and

---

[8] See H. Berman, *Law and Revolution* (Cambridge, Mass., 1983).

judges.[9] If Church law, in both its Canon and Civil forms, were to apply uniformly across Europe, it would have had to achieve some level of generality and universality. The thesis, according to Harold Berman, is that in the Church's assumption of authority, its legal approach to implementing that authority, and a bureaucracy to carry it out, we have the seeds of the modern legal system, whose utility was slowly recognized by secular states. Its elements are simply stated: law is the legislative enactment of a superior authority rather than customary; it strives for generality in its concepts and rules; it has a civil service to apply and implement the law; and professional courts as interpreters and enforcers, which are reasonably separate from the Pope and the administration. Without imagining that from the combination of these elements a modern legal order sprang into life, we see here an immature outline of later developments. Weber also attributed to the Church a decisive role in the formation of state authority and public administration, which he describes as the emergence of a rational mode of legal authority, as distinct from traditional authority based on custom or charisma. Rational authority vacillates between the formal qualities of rules and substantive standards; the new legal order, although no exception, was formal enough to warrant a separation being made between the law on the one hand and non-legal standards on the other hand.

In considering how the character of the modern state contributes to the formal tendencies of the legal order, we begin with legislation as the main source of law. Having seen its tendency towards expediency and particularity rather than generality and autonomy, we should ask what motive rulers and officials could have for making their behaviour predictable, for separating law from politics, and generally for imposing on themselves the discipline of a legal order. Among the possible reasons, two stand out. One is evident from the Church's attempts to impose its law over the great diversity of communities, groups, and interests of medieval Europe. Since one aim was to set standards that all could meet, laws had to reach some level of generality; and since another was to eradicate local variations, a distinction between general legal standards and those of local custom or practice was imperative. Formality was not pursued relentlessly, for the Church's main interest was in correct outcomes rather than formal rules, the general point being that ruling over diversity promotes the generality of laws and their separation from local custom. Since modern western states are in similar positions in

---

[9] See P. Stein, op. cit., Chapters 3 and 4.

needing to legislate for diverse communities, the same discipline of generality and autonomy that promoted the Church's legal order applies to
them. To this it should be added that ruling according to general
standards avoids the need to frame laws for the needs and character of
each group or interest, a time-consuming, costly, and divisive endeavour.

14.5 FROM PRIVILEGE TO EQUALITY

A second matter encouraging the formation of a modern legal order is the
state's interest in having laws that treat its citizens equally, an end towards
which general and autonomous laws contribute. That interest is most
visible when society reaches a balance among groups and interests, a
balance of rough equality, where no one dominates the political process to
such an extent that that others are excluded from consideration. Without
attempting an historical explanation as to why some societies achieve the
balance and many do not, beyond noting in western societies and some
others the decline of dominant groups and the wider sharing of power
and resources, we may exploit its importance. Once special privileges are
surrendered, so that the political process is open to all, with new groups
having access to avenues of influence, the law responds accordingly. From
being an instrument serving the interests of a few, it assumes a more
general form. It becomes a vehicle for recognizing a degree of equality in
meeting the demands of diverse groups and for dealing even-handedly
with them. The special interests of different groups are not ignored;
indeed the modern statute book is swollen with what are in effect special
laws. The difference is that they are presented as general laws to be
administered and adjudicated by professional bodies at a distance from
the political process. By law's being presented in this way the claims of
different groups are met, while the commitment to equality and fairness,
even if in a rather formal sense, helps to ensure political legitimacy. To
this should be added that although some groups are more powerful than
others, they still depend on the cooperation of others, which in turn
strengthens the need for both recognizing their interests and doing so
according to law.[10]

Questions as to the categories of equal treatment and their converse are
matters to be settled in the political process, a matter on which western
societies have made progress. The qualification to contract and own

---

[10] For development of this point, see: S. Holmes, 'Lineages of the Rule of Law' in
J. M. Maravall and A. Przeworski, op. cit.

property is common to all (with minor exceptions); equal pay for equal work is considered right in principle, even if not fully realized in practice; discrimination on such grounds as race, religion, and gender is regarded as wrong. We know that our societies have left behind in principle, although not completely in practice, the idea of special privileges, whether by luck of birth or fortune; we know that the *libertates* which have been at the core of social conflict are no longer contestable but entitlements of all. The connections between those notions, which are fundamental in modern societies, and the form of law are plainly visible: equality of treatment for its part requires laws that are distinct and general, while special laws are identified with unjustifiable privilege and special status for individual persons and particular groups. If such ideas were no more than ideas, aspirations rather than realities, concessions to be wrung from the powerful, their influence would be lesser. But they have, in fact, won the support of powerful interests over a long course of history, whose genealogy begins with the landless plebeians of early Rome and then follows countless paths, including the peasant revolts of medieval Europe, the demands of the rising middle classes of seventeenth-century England, to the modern foundation of labour unions. It embraces the mobilization of popular movements throughout history, culminating in those of feminists and gays, with race and poverty yet to have their day. The influence of such movements on the form of law cannot be calculated in the abstract, but on close study should prove to be decisive. As for the present, they are now so closely associated with the self-image of modern societies, so fundamental to its legal structure, that neglect or reversion, while possible, would be difficult.

For further support of the thesis, we need only to look at societies that have not reached a stage of liberties and rights for all, but which preserve special privileges for some to the exclusion of others, on such grounds as birth, class, gender, party, religion, or tradition. The maintaining of such a system, which is the normal tendency of societies, requires close co-operation between the state and special interests, requires in effect common cause, whether between the Russian Orthodox Church and the Russian state, or the aristocracy of Saudi Arabia and its brutal tools of government, the tribal demands on an undeveloped state, or the powers and privileges of the Chinese Communist Party. The degree of common cause among such groups and interests determines the character of the legal order, which is a powerful support for what is inherently insupportable against the aspirations of the citizens at large. As such an instrument for special interests, the legal order is trapped in special laws, subservient administrators, and compliant courts; it is identified with the state and the privileges the state supports. The legal order cannot achieve separation from the apparatus and designs of the state, it cannot reach a recognizable level of autonomy and distinctiveness, and falls short of that threshold of rules that defines modern law. In a global age where ideas have no boundaries, such systems are harder to sustain and the process of modernization is harder to restrain. But as long as a society clings to an order based on privileges, unless it takes the road to *libertates* for all, a road along which western societies have travelled some distance, its legal order will lack the qualities of a modern system.

14.6 DYNAMICS OF GOVERNMENT ADMINISTRATION

We have so far uncovered two incentives for resisting the tendencies of enacted law to arbitrariness and particularism, while encouraging the formation of a modern legal order: one is the need to rule over diversity, the other the effects of equality. Another has its origins in the nature of administration, the thesis being that a developed system of public administration tends towards rule-based formality. In doing so it takes two directions. One relates to the inner dynamics of administration, by which is meant the tendency of a complex organization to structure itself by rules; the other is a corresponding tendency for administrators to govern through rules.

As to the first of these, complex organizations such as those of government tend to form a pattern with certain features: they are hierarchical, tasks are specified and objectives set, while the efficient and effective completion of tasks and achievement of objectives is the guiding aim. At first, this seems counter-intuitive, for in a small, personalized office, evaluation and judgement according to the merits of the situation is the natural approach, where rules would be seen as a hindrance. In a large organization, such direct contact between means and ends is impossible; evaluations made by numerous staff, each according to personal judgement, would be a route to disorderly practice and inconsistent outcomes. Rules are then the basis for both the orderly conduct of business and the coordinated delivery of outcomes. Rules of organization, rules of procedure, rules for fixing targets and assessing results, become the basis of effective performance. These rules become a system in which its members have vested interests, and as a system they are protected from extraneous influences, developing in the process ways of ensuring their own survival. Organizations of this kind are such paradigms of rule-based actions that Weber drew from them his notion of formal rational authority.

Their internal dynamics influence the way administrative organizations use their authority to govern. Weber suggests that the more a ruler relies on administrative bodies to rule, and delegates to them powers of implementation and enforcement, the more formally rational their method of administering will be.[11] The thesis seems persuasive. As long as the ruler rules as head of the household, rule is personal, arbitrary, and unpredictable, and its implementation left to members of the household. As societies modernize, the division widens between the ruler who decides and administrators who implement, until the point is reached at which the ruler no longer dictates as head of the household, but is transformed into a legislative authority, while administrators, now organized and professional, implement the legislation. Their first duty is to do so effectively and efficiently, and the laws most suited for implementation by administrative bodies cannot be those expressed in personal, moral, or religious concepts, nor those half-formed and badly articulated, nor those that are incomplete, prone to change, or impossible to make sense of. On the contrary, the inner dynamics of administrative bodies as complex organizations, combined with the need to implement laws effectively and efficiently, urge the need for laws bearing the hallmarks of rules that are reasonably formal, distinct, and rational.

Where laws fail to meet those conditions so that administrators are left with excessive discretion, their usual response is to formulate their own rules, simplifying in cases of complexity and rationalizing inconsistency. The tendency to structure discretion through administrative rules and guidelines is documented and the reason for it is plain: discretion does not fit easily within the dynamics of administrative organizations, nor is it conducive to the effective and efficient pursuit of stated goals. Rules are easier and safer: as guides to what has to be done, they can be clear, and if not clear they will be made so by the gloss of administrative rules. In judging effectiveness, to have applied the rules is a surer and better guide than to claim having used discretion wisely, as well as properly. The alternative to rules is neither 'the simple and summary decrees of a Turkish cadhi', as Gibbon claims, nor even 'the first engine of tyranny';[12] but it

---

[11] M. Weber, op. cit., Volume II, p. 809.
[12] E. Gibbon, op. cit., Volume V, p. 303. The need to correct the misleading image of *khadi justice* was noted earlier; see: L. Rosen, *The Anthropology of Justice: Law as Culture in Islamic Society* (New York, 1989).

is not without reason that discretion sits uneasily in the seat of administration. This is not, of course, to argue that administrators necessarily apply the law to the letter, that they never depart from it, or impose their own dispositions. Administrators deal with the law from the standpoint of a highly developed set of social spheres, and from that standpoint they are apt for their own purposes to construe it, add to it, or let parts fade away. The argument here contests none of that; it contends only that the natural domain of administrative bodies is one of rules, without specifying which rules or whose, and that the shortcomings of enacted laws will be remedied by the creative cures of administration. Government bureaucracy exerts influence over the character of legislation, not only by dint of its general power, but also because it is involved in the process of legislation, from the initial drafting to the final proclamation, and in the course of that process is well-placed to ensure a form that fits within its organization and matches its understanding, as well as serving its purposes. And, as Weber pointed out some time ago, those factors are conducive not inexorably but nevertheless significantly to the form of modern law.

14.7 SEEDS OF SELF-RESTRAINT

It is one thing to show that rulers and officials have good reasons for moving from personal rule of the household to a rule-based legal order, quite another to explain the further step of limiting their own actions by law. Law here includes not only positive legislation, but also standards from the multiple sources described in 13.2. The taking of the step to limit their actions by law is essential to modern legal orders, because it is a necessary consequence of the relations of trust between citizens and officials; it is also one of the main differences between modern orders and others. Taking the step involves self-restraint on the part of rulers and officials; self-restraint in regarding their own actions as governed by law, and limiting the use of force in compliance with the law. In isolating the social conditions that would make sense of their subordinating themselves to the legal order, a good place to begin is with a Leveller tract of the sixteenth century called *Vox Plebis*, in which the writer declared it 'a most sure Rule in State policy, That all the Laws that are made in favour of liberty, spring first from the disagreement of the people with their Governors'.[13] With that quotation, Alan Harding concludes his study

---

[13] Quoted by Alan Harding in his illuminating study of the legal foundations of the state. See, A. Harding, *Medieval Law and the Foundations of the Modern State* (Oxford, 2002), p. 340.

of medieval law in England and France, in which he shows how that disagreement, at the centre of law and politics, contains within it the key to the modern state.

The competing images of authority descending from above or ascending from below define the parameters within which disagreement takes place. The constitutional histories of England, France, and other European states could be understood as the unfolding of the bitter disagreement, manifested in tracts, laws, and conflicts over the centuries. Descending theories, concisely put by James I as 'to be grieved with the Law, is to be grieved with the King' (a dangerous position to take), slowly gave way to compromise and qualification, until a point was reached at which the peoples' claim of authority was irresistible. The dream of the Levellers in the seventeenth century that: 'The Commons must listen to the people if they really wished to "make this nation a state free from the oppression of kings and the corruptions of the court" ',[14] in the nineteenth became a reality. The social relations between the people on the one side and rulers and officials on the other, characteristic of modern legal orders, are now established: the sovereign or head of state is a constitutional figure, the parliament is the law-maker and is elected by the people, and officials have their powers defined and limited by law. Nation-states remain intact, but accept membership of an international order from which flows constraints on their actions. These movements took many paths and display themselves in many guises, a striking case of which is the practice of judicial review, sometimes hailed as the twentieth-century apogee of constitutionalism, whereby courts determine whether not only administrative officials, as well as legislative bodies, have acted within their legal powers and restrained their actions in line with multiple standards. The social conditions that made this reality possible here and elsewhere are less plain. If *disagreement* between the people and their rulers over how they are to be governed is the key, what is it that enables the people of one society successfully to lay claim to the ascending vision, while those of another endure the yoke of the descending? How is the 'common cry of curs', whose love Coriolanus prized 'as the dead carcasses of unburied men', transformed into the voice of authority and sovereignty?[15] Since the history of western law and politics is concentrated in this question, and since we do not know the answers, it is enough to offer a few brief remarks. In the first place, even if power in the hands of the

---

[14] *Ibid*, p.339.
[15] W. Shakespeare, *The Tragedy of Coriolanus* (London 1990,), act III, scene 3, line 122.

few is the natural state of society, it is inherently unstable, an instability that provoked Niccolò Machiavelli to instruct the Prince on practical strategies to overcome it.[16] The recent collapse of regimes throughout central and eastern Europe has revealed how fragile those apparently impregnable orders were; and it is surely no coincidence that all were based on rule of the few, with officials accountable to the few rather than to a legal order. Such systems were not without benefits, but the balance of social goods finally is not enough, or not enough of the right kind, for they fail to sustain the support of the people. That leads to a second observation: the support of the people is essential to preserve any form of rule, no matter how strong. In its absence or loss, inherent instability and fragility will be manifest. There are many ways of shoring up weaknesses and some manage well over long periods; however, the weaknesses remain, perhaps dormant, liable to be awakened by events whose occurrence can be as swift as it is unexpected.

14.8 FOUNDATIONS OF THE RULE OF LAW IN MODERN LEGAL ORDERS

The normative structure of modern legal orders is a version of the rule of law whose features are set-out in section 12.5 and worth repeating: first, legal contexts are defined by, infused with, and constrained by rules and standards; secondly, certain qualities are built into the rules and standards, which, thirdly, are applied by officials according to certain conditions. This account of the rule of law has been reached by describing the practices that prevail in modern legal orders and the ideas supporting them. However, we should not imagine, that the rule of law has been a beacon guiding the course of legal history. Any society, no matter how undeveloped and pre-modern, is likely to have a legal order which contains some element of the rule of law even if it is nothing more than that there ought to be rules that are reasonably general and consistent applied. Considering the close interweaving of law and other social norms and values, even that might be unwarranted, based more on reading into history, ideas common to us now, than reality. As recently as a millennium ago, English law could have been described neither as a system nor as distinct from customs, practices, and moral beliefs, let alone one grounded in the rule of law.[17] The formalizing tendencies of Roman Law

---

[16] N. Macchiavelli, *The Prince*.
[17] This is well brought out in J. H. Baker, op. cit.

had more influence on continental jurisdictions and the ideas behind them than it did on the English system and its descendants. The common law and ideas informing the common law were for them the breeding ground of the rule of law. Some find elements of it as early as the agreement between King and barons represented in Magna Carta; common law judges of the seventeenth century had a more developed but still immature notion in mind during their contests with the Sovereign; but none could have imagined the rule of law in its modern form, nor its grip on contemporary societies. As a philosophical idea, as a precept for a good society and good government, the rule of law in some form can be traced back to the earliest writings that survive, but both its current form and its prominence are of recent origin, reflecting the concerns of modern liberal orders and reacting to the events of the twentieth century. As a measuring stick for evaluating societies, for blaming or praising them, for befriending or ostracizing them, the rule of law has been admitted in our age to that almost holy trinity of liberty, democracy, and human rights.

It searching for its social foundations in modern legal orders, we encounter a puzzle: is the rule of law a legacy of western law, an idealization of what has been achieved, or is it a set of ideals that have influenced western law? Common sense and experience over a long period have shown what kind of legal framework is needed to stabilize private transactions, curb governments and officials, and encourage liberty and equality. Some societies have developed such a legal framework, which could be regarded as a state of equilibrium brought about by the interplay of social forces of the kinds considered earlier. On this view, the rule of law, as a set of ideals, has little or no influence on the bringing about of that equilibrium. In legitimating what has been achieved, and in converting what has been achieved in some societies into a goal that ought to be sought by all, the rule of law may have utility, but that is different from attributing influence to it in bringing about social change. A different view is that the rule of law is an expression of natural law ideas, or alternatively a set of moral ideals, rooted in the political and moral basis of western societies, about how government should be conducted, competing interests accommodated, and people treated. On this view, as a set of ideals, the rule of law has exerted a powerful influence over the form of modern law; rather than being a rationalization of what has occurred, it is prior to and instrumental to the occurrence.

14.9 COMPETING EXPLANATIONS

On this idealistic view, which is likely to win the support of lawyers and judges, the ideals of the rule of law have their origins in early philosophical speculation, have developed slowly over the course of western history, and have been formative of the western tradition. The early form of that tradition perhaps emerged in the crucible of Church-state relations, and was extended and refined over time, both as a set of ideals and in the formation of legal orders. Great constitutional moments have been the milestones, liberal instincts the incentive, with each encouraging and strengthening the other, culminating in a match of the ideals of the rule of law and its realization. Such a case would have to be built on showing, not only how ideas about the rule of law have evolved and matured, but also how they affected the actions of legislatures, administrators, and judges. The one does not lead inexorably to the other, and great ideals can have a life of their own while leaving no noticeable mark on social practices. That is surely the exception and it would be remarkable if ideals like the rule of law were found to have no social use. Fortunately, the reconstruction of history is not our task and can be left to others; ours is to consider, in an a-historical way, how the ideas of the rule of law could be a formative influence on the form of modern law.

The notion of a legal tradition is one approach to the task. A tradition grows out of a combination of ideas and practices. From its beginnings, as a way of seeing and approaching an issue, a tradition grows into a framework of conventions and understandings, which guide individuals and organizations in their actions. It is another way of describing sets of social spheres with their roots in history, from which the rule of law has evolved incrementally rather than abruptly, learning from experience, and building foundations on trial and error. The case, then, would be that a legal tradition based on the ideals of the rule of law could develop and guide the actions of those who are engaged in legislation, administration, and adjudication. Its foundations would be even more secure if it were to spread beyond officials, so that groups and associations in the wider society came to regard it as the normal way of doing things, and an instrument to be deployed on their behalf. By regular affirmation from above by officials and from below by civil society, the tradition infiltrates a multitude of other social spheres, and becomes embedded in society's consciousness as well as its actions. To conclude with the impression that a tradition forms its roots out of ideals or goodwill while partly true, would be to omit the importance of self-interest, for nothing is more potent in cementing its place in society than the dependence on it of a group, class, or profession. The legal profession is the natural guardian of the legal tradition, whose zeal in its defence is both genuine and well-rewarded.

It is one thing to imagine a legal tradition with these hallmarks, but another to be persuaded of its efficacy in containing the actions, let alone winning the hearts, of those who most count, the legislators and the administrators. This is the dilemma for accounts based on the power of a legal tradition: given the pressures from other sources, what possible motive could officials have for resisting them, and preferring instead to restrict their actions in accordance with abstract notions of the proper legal form, the autonomy of law, and the special role of lawyers and courts? The combination of altruism and reward is usually enough to gain the support of lawyers and courts, but what is there to win over legislators and administrators? Here the force of the opposing view begins to show, for according to it, they are not won over; their actions instead are driven by other social forces with which the rule of law cannot compete. For no matter how firm their commitment to the rule of law may appear, it is likely to crumble in the face of other forces. Explanation of the rule of law would then have to be located in the need to protect and balance private interests, and as a means for effective and legitimate government. The sceptical view attributes the form of modern legal orders to those other factors rather than the rule of law. They may be expressed in terms of the rule of law, but only because that adds weight in legitimation.

This argument is part of a wider debate about how far ideas, whether in such forms as culture, tradition, religion, civilization, and the like, explain political behaviour.[18] The sceptical view is that, despite the common tendency to assume that ideas influence behaviour, there is no empirical support for it. Weber advanced the claim that the religious basis for the accumulation of wealth explains the 'spirit of capitalism', which, in turn, explains why Protestant countries developed earlier and better than other countries.[19] However, it has been suggested that, when Weber's work is closely scrutinized, the connections are not demonstrated.[20] A strong version of this claim would be that, whenever actions

---

[18] A good example of an extensive literature is: S. Holmes, 'Lineages of the Rule of Law' in J. M. Maravell and A. Przeworski (eds) op. cit.

[19] M. Weber, *The Protestant Ethic and the Spirit of Capitalism* (New York, 1952).

[20] See A. Przeworski, 'Why Do Political Parties Obey Results of Elections?' in Maravell and Przeworski, op. cit., p. 124.

are apparently based on ideals, it will usually be found that the real basis is personal or group interest, in the sense of economic or political or other material advantage.

14.10 SOCIALIZATION OF THE RULE OF LAW

This brings us to one of the oldest and most contested issues of social explanation: to what extent are actions guided by ideas, and to what extent is the real basis, the foundation to which all else can be reduced, self interest or some other material return? The issue, appearing in many different guises, comes down to whether the grid of ideals, principles, and values of a society, has some degree of independence in guiding and explaining actions, or whether they are no more than expressions of, and vehicles for, underlying interests. Without entering into the general controversy, we must here be content with a few remarks concerning the rule of law and competing interests.

Two pieces of legislation, both of which we have encountered before, serve as a starting point; they are The Mental Health Act, 1983 and The Police and Criminal Evidence Act, 1984. The object of the first was to give better protection to those afflicted with mental disorder against compulsorily detention and treatment, while the second proclaimed the rights of suspects and regulated the powers of the police during the investigation of crime. Since neither group has significant power or the support of influential lobbies and indeed face strong opposition, attempts to account for the laws in realistic or materialist terms face plain difficulties. The most obvious and compelling explanation in both cases is that enough civil servants and legislators, supported by elements of public opinion, became convinced that the rights of mental health patients and suspects should be given better protection. An explanation of how that came about is still awaited, but whatever factors were important, the concern for rights, rather than the force of material and practical interests, is likely to be prominent. Dedicated civil servants and campaigning parliamentarians who became committed to the cause may have had interests in sponsoring the legislation, so that the line between acting for ideals or for self-interest is hard to draw. Even allowing for that, it would be hard not to conclude that principles of how people should be treated were significant; and if ideals carry weight here, why not elsewhere?

It helps to distinguish between two different issues: one is whether a person or group has accepted a set of ideals, the other the reasons for doing so.[21] People plainly accept ideals of all sorts and act on them. To explain and justify actions on that basis is (as we saw in the discussion of social rules) such a common course, so taken-for-granted, that its significance may be overlooked. The rule of law, as a set of ideals, may be accepted as a basis for one's actions in just that manner. We talk freely and intelligibly of a society having accepted the rule of law, indeed we say it of modern societies generally. By it, we mean that a society has adopted the rule of law as a set of standards to govern aspects of public life, the expectation being that its officials will then act accordingly. The next step is to notice that acceptance varies in its intensity, from absolute through strong to weak, a significant matter when it has to compete with other concerns. The societies of western Europe, which have modernized and built their rule of law tradition over a long period, are likely to have a strong commitment, while for those of eastern Europe, which adopted the rule of law after recently emerging from communism, it is weak.

Among the ways of testing the degree of commitment of a society to a set of ideals, the level and quality of institutional and organizational support is of special note. In the case of the rule of law, public expressions of support for it in documents, such as international conventions, constitutions, and the treaties of the European Union, are one sign; other signs can be gleaned from the statements of government officials, their daily practices, and their attitudes. However, among these factors and others, perhaps the most important is the position of courts and lawyers, for the very basis of their profession is the notion of law as a distinct social form, the practice of which requires special knowledge and training. To them is entrusted custody of the rule of law, not as a special task or favour, but as the basis of their existence. More than dedication may be needed, but it is surely necessary, for where courts and lawyers neglect the nature of their undertaking, or are unable to achieve it, the chances of the rule of law emerging or surviving are slight. Where they are secure in that undertaking, the daily affirmation of the rule of law through both declarations and practices, as a foundation stone of society, has a significant effect on attitudes and practices that go well beyond those of laws and courts.[22]

There is one final step: the reasons for acceptance, which are reasons of three kinds: strategic, practical, and idealistic. A strategic calculation of

---

[21] We have here another instance of the same distinction made in Chapter 2 in relation to the rule of recognition.

[22] What exactly lawyers and courts mean by 'the rule of law', or how faithfully they apply it, is not the point; what is important is affirmation of the ideal.

how best to achieve certain goals – the cooperation of others, domination over them, holding on to power, legitimacy – will motivate the more Machiavellian to adherence to the rule of law; others might bow to international pressure or wish to qualify for financial aid to which rule-of-law conditions are attached. Practical reasons relate to the advantages of having a settled mode of making, expressing, and applying law, which removes the anxiety and cost of wondering each time how best to achieve one's aims without being confident of the answer. Limited knowledge and information, uncertain outcomes, and the saving of time and energy, all add to the importance of having a settled legal form. For the idealist, the inherent appeal of the rule of law, and its connections with other values, such as liberty, equality, and respect for rights are sufficient reasons in themselves.

From this account of the variables influencing the role of the rule of law in social practices, we may conclude that the realists have a point in their claim that the main reason for officials, especially legislators and administrators, accepting the rule of law is strategic, based on the utility of the rule of law as a means to other ends, such as power, co-operation, and security. Officials conduct their activities in accordance with the rule of law, because that has proven to be an effective way of achieving desired goals. At the same, it is plain that the rule of law has become entrenched as a set of values, independently of other social goals, that influence the form of law. Such influence will be at its peak where there is a developed tradition, which has a high level of support in the social spheres of officials and citizens, and which, above all, has strong institutional and organizational support, especially from courts and lawyers. By the combination of factors, the rule of law is projected as a social force influencing the behaviour of officials, which in turn affirms the tradition, increases its security, and augments its social force.

The test comes when the rule of law has to compete with other interests, as is seen in the following case: in the aftermath of terrorist activities, the British government seeks extra powers in the interests of security. We may assume that the measures are incompatible with the rule of law in various ways (although in reality that might not be so clear), so that between security and the rule of law there is direct competition. Part of the interest of the case is that the government is not trying to use the rule of law as a strategic means for achieving its ends, but instead claims a conflict between the two, the resolution of which must favour security. If the government expected that to be an end of the matter, with an easy victory for security, it was mistaken; counter-claims based on the rule of law, in the press and the courts, the Bar and in the common rooms, have been vigorous and persistent, so that, as I write, no clear victory has emerged for either side. The capacity of the rule of law to stand its ground, to force compromise and reconsideration, reveals tenacity that must be unexpected to the realists. The reasons are plain: British society has a strong, public commitment to the rule of law; in the actions and consciousness of officials and citizens, it has a long and vigorous tradition to reinforce it; and it has lawyers and courts who fully grasp its point, while having the power and prestige to defend it. Or, to put it slightly differently, the conventions and understandings that have formed around the rule of law are deeply implicated in the social structure of the society, to such an extent that they form part of it and determine how we see and deal with issues, a process strengthened by the support of powerful institutions and organizations. This is not to claim that in cases of competition the rule of law will prevail, for plainly it will often be defeated or compromised; but it would be equally mistaken to imagine that it carries no weight. Several variables come into play, so that the one conclusion we may state with confidence is that social behaviour is guided not only by interests but also by ideals. If we are know the interplay between them, we must look closely at those variables. And as regards the form of law in modern societies, the conclusion should be that in its evolution, the rule of law is, under certain circumstances, a significant force in social explanation.

14.11 EVOLUTION FROM WITHIN: LAW AS A SOURCE OF THE LEGAL FORM

Quite apart from the external influences on the form of law in modern societies, the impetus may come from within the law itself. This is not to negate the effects of external forces, but to isolate factors within the law that may have had a part in the genealogical process. Consider the issue in the context of the English legal system. In the passage from a legal order that was based largely on customary law, some parts local, other parts central; where the administration of justice was a task of the King's household; whose judges were members of the King's advisory councils and generally lacked legal training; and where the boundaries between law, morals, and religion were written in the sand – from that beginning how did the same system evolve into the one we now have?[23]

---

[23] In depicting the early English legal system in this way, I have relied heavily on Sir John Baker's masterly account: see J. H. Baker, op. cit.

What had happened that by the early sixteenth century Sir Thomas More could be concerned that the common law had become too rigid, too rule-bound, and needed equity to mitigate its rigours?[24] What justified Lord Coke in the seventeenth century being able to speak credibly to the King of the 'artificial reason of the law', when they were his courts, his judges, and his law? The civil law tradition of continental Europe could be interrogated in the same way in explaining progress from local, customary systems, which were hardly discernable as legal orders, stretching across the old Roman Empire and beyond, to those formal, codified systems of the late eighteenth century? Common to both traditions is a long and gradual passage, driven and shaped as much by accident as purpose, marked by turning points whose accumulation over time created their modern forms. Some of those turning points were decisive, but which ones must be a matter of conjecture. The limiting of arguments in court to distinct legal doctrines is one such point, and possibly a decisive one.[25] The separation of courts from legislative and executive authority could be another, the rise of the legal profession and the appointment of judges with legal training a third. Continental jurists tend to place great store by the appeal of Justinian's restatement of Roman Law for its reconstruction of a full and abstract legal order, although a common lawyer could make no such claim.

Our purpose is not the historical one of showing how these two different systems culminated in similar legal orders, but instead to understand how factors internal to them could stimulate the development of their modern forms. One line of explanation is found within the notion of a tradition, a notion earlier depicted as a subject matter or undertaking around which gathers a set of ideas, institutions, and practices that develops over time. The designation of modern law as it developed in western jurisdictions as a tradition (or traditions) is both fitting and natural.[26] The practices consist in the legal process, which culminates in decisions of legality or illegality; the institutions are primarily those of courts and lawyers; and the ideas, while often inchoate and in flux, combine views about the nature of the legal enterprise, its normative foundations, and the rules that should direct its practical decision-making. A tradition is born out of historical events, and is constantly shaped and reshaped by events; yet at the same time it gains a certain

---

[24] *Ibid* p. 107.
[25] N. Luhmann, op. cit., p. 248.
[26] Harold Berman has done much to explain the western legal tradition and I have drawn extensively on his admirable book, *Law and Revolution*.

distance from events, forms a protective immunity from them, sufficiently to allow an internal structure to be created, to become, in a sense, master of its own house. The result may be over time a distinctive understanding of itself and its role, a refinement of the ideals behind it, the rules for daily use, and the form of its practices. It is not the work of an invisible hand, nor is it the direct outcome of external events or in any sense pre-determined. It is, instead, the product of individuals making decisions in the course of their practice, applying and extending the rules and understandings, and constantly choosing one path when two or more are open and reasonable. External events might preclude some options or insist on others; there may be setbacks and false paths; the tradition may even be dissolved, as has been the fate of many. However, some survive and flourish, and they do so by weaving their way between external demands and exploitation, internal needs and integrity. The description could be given more forcefully in the language of systems and *autopoeisis* and, while some fall comfortably within their strictures, the notion of a tradition varies too much to allow a natural association of the two. Traditions can be more or less closed, more or less immune from external influences, and can vary in the density of their internal workings.

NOTES

On law and social organization in modern societies

Durkheim regarded the legal order as an 'external symbol' of the social organization of a society: *The Division of Labour in Society*, p. 24. Areas of law, such as domestic law, contractual law, commercial law, and administrative and constitutional law, all express a form of social organization based on co-operation, which in turn derives from the division of labour (p. 77). To take an example: the law of contract is 'the supreme legal expression of cooperation' (p. 79). Contract based on reciprocity is 'only possible where co-operation exists and this in turn does not occur without the division of labour'. (p. 79) In short, the law of contract has the purpose of harmonizing functions that are special and different (p. 80).

On genealogy

M. Foucault describes genealogy in this way: 'Genealogy is grey, meticulous, and patiently documentary. It operates on a field of entangled and confused parchments, on documents that have been scratched over and recopied many times. On this basis, it is obviously that Paul Ree was wrong to follow the English tendency in describing the history of morality in terms of a linear development – in reducing its entire history and genesis to an exclusive concern for utility . . . (genealogy) rejects the metahistorical deployment of ideas, significations, and indefinite teleologies. It opposes itself to the search for "origins" '. *Hommage à Jean Hyppolite* (Paris, 1971) p. 145.

For comment and discussion, see A. Sheridan, *Michel Foucault: The Will To Truth* (London, 1980) and A. Hunt and G. Wickham, op. cit.

For further discussion, see P. Beart, *Philosophy of the Social Sciences*

On Chinese law

For recent accounts of Chinese legal developments see:

S. Lubman, *Bird in a Cage: Legal Reform in China After Mao* (Stanford, 1999).

R. Peerenboom, *China's Long March Towards Rule of Law* (Cambridge, 2002).

W. J. Diamant, G. Lubman, and K. J. O'Brien, *Engaging the Law in China* (Stanford, 2005).

Weber's account of western legal orders

Modern law consists of *legal propositions*, that is: 'abstract norms the content of which asserts that a certain factual situation is to have certain legal consequences'. Legal propositions: 'give rise to the rights of individuals to prescribe, or prohibit, or allow, an action vis-à-vis another person'. That is the legal point of view; the sociological is that: 'such legally guaranteed and limited power over the action of others corresponds to the expectation that other persons will engage in, or refrain from, certain conduct or that one way himself engage, or fail to engage, in certain conduct without interference from a third party'. *Economy and Society*, p. 667.

Weber analyses at length the pre-modern existence of special legal communities where law is tied to the members of the community, not as *lex terrae* but as *professio iuris* or personal law. Since conflicts naturally occurred between members of different legal communities, some measure of 'common legal principles' had to be devised. This need increased with the growth in diverse social relations across communities (p. 696).

From libertates to rights

Fernand Braudel writes: 'Imagine that it might be possible to assemble the sum of our knowledge of European history from the fifth century to the present . . . and to record it . . . in an electronic memory. Imagine that the computer was then asked to indicate the one problem which recurred most frequently, in time and space, throughout this lengthy history. Without a doubt, that problem is liberty, or rather liberties'. (*A History of Civilizations*, p. 315). Liberty means not to much individual liberty but 'the liberty of groups'. *Liberties* were: 'the franchises or privileges protecting this or that group of people or interests'. (p. 316)

Liberties, in this sense, depend on special laws granting them to special groups. Groups here were defined not on economic or technical qualities, such as factory owners, farmers, or plumbers, but on status as noblemen, knights, or members of a guild (Weber, *Economy and Society*, pp. 698–9). Weber's approach is consistent with Braudel's analysis. The question then to answer historically is how European societies made the transition from special and particularistic laws to generally applicable norms. Weber's explanation is based principally on: (a) the extension of the market economy, and (b) the bureaucratization of the organizations of legal communities.

Dynamics of governmental administration

Weber formulates the relationship between government administration and the rationalization of modern law in this way:

'The more rational the administrative machinery of the prince's hierarchs becomes, that is, the greater the extent to which administrative "officials" were used in the exercise of power, the greater was the likelihood that the legal procedure would also become "rational" both in form and substance'. (*Economy and Society*, p. 809). Weber did not consider there were deliberate policies on the part of wielders of power, but rather the result of the needs and dynamics of administration.

Self-restraint on the part of officials

That governments and administration are limited by law is generally regarded as a principal feature of the rule of law. For a recent summary of this idea see B.Tamanaha, op. cit., Chapter 9. His discussion identifies several means which help to explain this idea, including the social understanding that government and administration would act within the law and this becomes a routine activity (p. 115–6). Although not intended as a full social explanation, those notions fit well with the discussion in Chapter 13, where it is suggested that institutional plurality is itself a major factor in maintaining official self-restraint.

On the need for support of the people

Sir John Fortescue seems to have had in mind the importance of popular support if even the strongest monarch is to survive and rule. He argued against the claim that is would be good for the King if the commons of England were poor as they were in France. He writes '. . . when any rising has been made in this land by the commons, the poorest then have been the greatest causes and doers therein . . . what would happen if all the commons were poor? Truly, it is likely that this land should be like the realm of Bohemia, where the commons, because of poverty, rose upon the nobles, and made all their goods to be common'. (*On the Laws and Governance of England* (Ed. S.Lockwood, Cambridge, 1997)) (Originally written around 1471).

15

Implementation and the Architecture of Law

15.1 INTRODUCING IMPLEMENTATION

Most compliance with law is voluntary, but individual persons, groups, and entities often need to be prompted or even coerced and, to that end, legal systems have rules and create organizations, processes, and remedies. The process of implementation by which officials try to bring about compliance by others with law is the subject of this chapter and the next; the position of those who are expected to comply is considered in the final chapter. The study of implementation and compliance means applying ideas developed in the course of the preceding chapters in a more specific and focused manner. The way in which officials and citizens perceive the law and deal with it is at the heart of a social account of law, as the first three methodological principles show. Much of the preceding analysis and discussion is directly or indirectly about the process of interaction between law and those applying it or subject to it, while the structure within which it takes place is described in chapter 7. In the following three chapters, we have the opportunity of examining the interaction and reception more closely and, in doing so, to draw on a wealth of informative empirical research.

Different groups of officials implement laws in different ways and according to different legal and social variables. It is the courts upholding the law that come first to mind, not only to lawyers and judges but to the popular imagination. We read about them in the newspapers, while cinema court trials are a distinct genre; in real life some of the stranger events end up before them. Even if they steal the limelight, the courts are only a small part of the vast apparatus of agencies and organizations, departments and officials bearing the day-to-day burden of applying and enforcing the law. In addition to governmental bodies, a host of informal institutions in both the public and private arenas also contribute to implementation, while ordinary people, acting alone or jointly with others, by their initiative have a major part in inducing others to comply.

No attempt is made in this chapter to examine the many types of implementation or the various parties involved in it; that subject awaits another treatise. Here, the object is quite specific: to understand how laws relate to and interact with the social environment of implementation. The approach is the by now familiar one of understanding law as a distinct social formation, and then examining its interaction with other parts of the social environment. Within the structure of interaction, the three layers of analysis earlier isolated are now examined more closely: first is the law itself, the legal architecture, then the social environment created by the law, and finally the fuller social context in which implementation occurs. The analysis is conducted with particular reference to laws that are broadly regulatory in character, meaning officials applying legal standards in order to direct or restrict the activities of others. A similar analysis could be made of enforcement of the criminal law, or of the courts as implementing bodies, rather than administrative officials. Some reference is made to courts, but since a selection of issues is necessary, the emphasis is on administrative officials, partly because they carry the main burden of responsibility for implementation, and partly because they have been the subject of extensive empirical research. The patterns that emerge in relation to them are likely to apply to other organizations, subject to suitable adjustments being made.

Since the terms can be confusing, some clarification is needed. Those who are subject to a law are expected to *comply* with it, meaning to act according to its terms. They often comply on their own initiative but may have to be prompted to do so by someone else. *Implementation* is the process whereby one body takes measures to apply the law to a situation before it, or to bring about compliance by another. A social security officer implements the law by applying it to applicants, while implementation by a regulatory agency usually means applying it to the regulatee, who is expected to take whatever action the law and the regulator require. Implementation is used here to include the many different forms it takes, including formal and informal measures, persuasion as well as coercion. The distinction between implementation and compliance leaves room for ambiguity: the social security officer, in applying the law to a case, both implements it with respect to others and complies with it himself. The ambiguity and any resulting confusion is reduced by confining implementation to the process whose object is compliance whether by oneself or another. *Enforcement* adds another dimension: where implementation is secured by coercion or the threat of it, enforcement is the term often used. In one sense, it is an important element within implementation, meaning procedures directed to the imposition of penalties, while in another sense it means a procedure to punish a party for not complying, rather than to bring about compliance. Even in that sense it is not unrelated to compliance, since part of the point of penalties is to encourage compliance in future. For ease of reference, *implementation* is used here to refer to any measure, including enforcement, taken by a party the object of which is to apply the law, where to do so usually requires action by another party.[1]

15.2 IMPLEMENTATION BY OFFICIALS

The focus here is on officials taking action to bring about compliance with the law by others. Underlying the process are several factors of which it is timely to be reminded. One is that in modern legal systems officials generally accept the authority of law and consider it their duty to implement it. Another factor is that officials are grouped into organizations which are formed by law and are given their authority by law, the aims and purposes of which law defines. Rather than being external to organizations of officials, law is their foundation. It creates organizations, stipulates their purposes and tasks, and provides the rules and standards to guide their actions. Organizations of officials, once created, tend to develop their own social world, tend towards autonomy and autopoeisis. Around organizations and institutions grows a more complete social world, with conventions and understandings, practices and approaches, influenced not only by law but by other social factors as well.[2] From one set of officials to another, the result is variation in the strength of the convention of acceptance of law as a whole. Another result is that organizations of officials approach specific laws from the standpoint of their social spheres, which influences their conduct of the implementation process.

Although the main focus here is on implementation by officials, the role of third parties should not be overlooked. Officials sometimes act on their own initiative, but often depend on a third party filing a suit, registering a complaint, or in some other way triggering them into action. This opens up questions about what action individual persons, groups, or private entities take when the non-implementation of law affects their

---

[1] The emphasis here is on national legal orders; for a study of implementation of international law, see: D. J. Galligan and D. Sandler, 'Implementing Human Rights' in S. Halliday and P. Schmidt (eds), *Rights Brought Home* (Oxford, 2004)

[2] This section builds on earlier chapters, especially 5, 6, and 7.3.

interests. It could be as simple as feeling dissatisfied with denial of a welfare benefit, or as serious as bodily injury suffered through the negligence of another. It could be a prisoner aggrieved that prison officers are not properly applying the rules against discrimination, or a multinational corporation alleging unfair competition on the part of a rival; the possibilities are many. Among those to whom the law offers redress, most take no action, as an early study of the victims of accidents demonstrates: only a tiny fraction of those harmed received compensation or took action towards it.[3] On the other hand, some groups and interests regularly use the courts and other institutions as a natural and unavoidable part of doing business. Large corporations and similar entities fall into that category, with the recent case of a chief executive officer lamenting that the growing legal costs of bringing and defending actions had a serious impact on the company's profits. Other groups of a different kind, ones that have been alienated from the social mainstream, indigenous minorities for instance, may discover that legal processes can be used to further their cause. The Australian aboriginal people is a case in point: after two centuries of practical exclusion from Australian society, they began to use the courts to win recognition of limited rights to land, which had consistently been denied them in the political process. Indigenous groups in other countries have had similar experiences. The ways and extent to which individual persons, groups, and entities use the law, and invoke the aid of legal agencies, raise many issues about implementation and the role of law in society more generally, but I shall not attempt to consider them in this chapter.

Another major variable is the nature of the implementing body, whether a court, administrative agency, regulatory body, or a variety of others. Anything more than a passing reference to them is beyond the scope of this work, although a systematic study of their different approaches and capacities would be of great value. Closely associated with the different types of organizations are the processes and procedures of implementation, which also take various forms. Judicial processes are associated with the courts, although many non-courts exercise functions of a judicial kind. By judicial process is meant interpreting the law and applying it to a set of facts, with the addition in modern legal orders of reasons explaining and justifying the decision. Hart expresses the judicial paradigm as the adjudication of legal rules by a professional, independent judiciary after a hearing conducted according to often

---

[3] D. Harris *et al*, op. cit.

elaborate procedures. The paradigm is only ever imperfectly realized; rules have to be interpreted, standards given content, and gaps filled in, and the law has to be kept in tune with changing conditions and ideas, in the way explained in chapter 3. Once courts are placed in their social context, their practices look less distinctive and the judicial paradigm is brought down to earth. For courts, in common with other sets of officials, are organizations with purposes to pursue and tasks to perform. They work within a structure of legal rules and standards to which they add their own social spheres. The study of judicial culture and practice has made a slow start, especially in Europe compared with the United States, where the study of courts has long attracted research by social scientists as well as lawyers. Despite some major contributions in recent years, the European dimension is another subject awaiting further attention.[4]

It is administrative bodies that dominate implementation. Their sheer diversity has been noted; they range from ministers of state to social welfare officers, from prison warders to health and safety inspectors, including, on the way, a variety of tribunals, complaints bodies, and special commissions. A common factor is that all operate within a legal framework; they are empowered by legal rules and in exercising their powers they are guided by legal rules. The scope for different architectures is considerable, with some veering towards the judicial paradigm, others highly discretionary; some have well-defined and enforceable remedies, others depend on reaching agreement or persuasion; some are relatively autonomous and unaccountable, others tightly supervised. The idea of legal architecture was introduced in chapter 7 and is developed here as the first layer in understanding implementation. The architecture is the normative structure within which officials take action; it defines their tasks and how they are to perform them. It does more: it opens the way to interaction between the legal structure and its social context. Law is implemented in a social setting; but law is itself infused with social fragments, through interpretation, discretion, incompleteness, and even contradictions, with the result that it creates around itself a social environment, which in turn interacts with the fuller social environment. The significance of this structure in understanding implementation will become apparent in the course of this and the next chapter.

From these remarks, it is plain that implementation covers different

---

[4] Important recent contributions are: D. Robertson, *Judicial Discretion in the House of Lords*; J. Bell, *French Judicial Culture* (Londons, 2002); C. Guarnieri and P. Pederzoli, *The Power of Judges: A Comparative Study of Courts and Democracy* (Oxford, 2002); A. Stone Sweet, *The Judicial Construction of Europe* (Oxford, 2004).

approaches and processes, so that the task of proposing a general structure is daunting. Before even beginning, we need to deal with a lingering cloud on the horizon: it is the idea that 'anything goes', that once officials or organizations are given a mandate to take action, the process becomes a purely social one in which social factors determine what happens, with the law having at best a minor role. The image accompanying 'anything goes' is one of officials being free to pursue their objectives according to such plans and strategies as they think fit. The inaccuracy of this image, which haunts the discussion of implementation, should not drive us into the opposite and equally misguided camp where implementation is regarded as just a matter of applying legal rules and standards to situations coming within them, allowing some, but only limited, scope for judgment or discretion. One might reach that position by reading legal texts and judicial pronouncements, and mistaking their account of the law as a doctrinal system for one about implementation.

By whatever route one reaches either position, neither will do, it being no more satisfactory to abandon the law than to imagine that implementation consists in its unproblematic application. Both, however, contain a grain of truth to be cultivated; from the second comes the idea that implementation is a legal process, according to which officials are authorized by law, and their actions are directed, guided, and limited by combinations of primary and secondary laws. The clusters of laws regulating an activity are often complex, allowing variation in both the legal architecture and its environment. The law can be problematical, harbouring within itself unresolved matters, as we shall shortly see. Also, law has to be interpreted, standards have to be individualized, and discretion given content and structure. It is not just that law opens up gaps that have to be filled by looking to social factors; that is true, but it is only part of the process and not the most important part. While gaps in the law create direct links to social factors, the relationship between the two is more fundamental, the very process of applying law takes place in a social context in which it is interpreted, its limits set, and its weight assessed. Understanding its terms and ascertaining how it relates to other standards unavoidably invoke sets of social understandings and preferences, conventions and values that, even if not made explicit, are immanent in any rule-based setting.

Implementation depends on officials working in organizations, so introducing into the process another set of factors. Within organizations, ideas, meanings, and norms at large in the society are rendered more focused and particular for the purposes at hand. A culture of meanings and norms, of practices and conventions, of attitudes and approaches, of possibilities and boundaries, is created within organizations, which directs and guides officials, and necessarily interacts with the law and its environment. The process is also influenced and constrained by practical economic and political factors, so that plans and strategies have to be moulded and trimmed accordingly. The purpose of this chapter and the next is to navigate these currents of complexity and diversity, and show that, imperfect and unruly as implementation processes appear to be, they nevertheless have a structure that can be articulated and scrutinized.

Against this background, several issues are considered in this chapter and the next in understanding the process of implementation. The *first* is to examine more closely the legal architecture itself. A *second* follows: the law creates around it a legal environment, by which is meant that the officials responsible for implementation have to decide what the law requires and how to achieve it; different architectural styles promote different legal environments. The *third* step is to consider the fuller social context in which a legal regime occurs and implementation takes place; this includes the social spheres within which the officials work, the relationships between officials and those whose actions are regulated, practical economic factors, and a range of other matters.

15.3 ARCHITECTURE OF LAW

Architecture suggests design and here we are concerned with the design of legal regimes.[5] Just as buildings have common features and endless variation, legal regimes are similar. The framework of each legal edifice is normally created by a statute within which rules and standards are formulated, powers are allocated, and rights and duties are specified. It includes matters of procedure, mechanisms, participation of parties, and remedies. A statute has to be read subject to standards deriving from other sources, including the Constitution, the law of the European Union, the common law, and international covenants. Within this common framework, the details of legal design take different forms and involve such matters as: the normative structure, the mechanisms or instruments available to encourage or enforce compliance, and the remedies the implementing body may bring, or which may be brought against it. Legal architecture is the first step in understanding implementation.

[5] The discussion here builds on that in chapter 7. I first came across the architectural metaphor in Fiona Haine's excellent book *Corporate Regulation* (Oxford, 1997).

The simplest model of implementation is a rule imposing duties on X and giving authority to Y to take enforcement action in the event of non-performance. If X does not comply voluntarily, Y may take action to enforce compliance or to impose a sanction for non-compliance. X could be a private party, as in the case of an employer obligated to take action in the interests of the health and safety of its employees. X could itself be an administrative body with duties to do things, such as grant a licence upon stated conditions being met. In either case, Y has powers and duties to implement the law against X. This simple design is a good place to start for it opens a window onto more complex legal regimes marked by a range of variables.

Normative structure

One variable is the normative legal structure, by which is meant the nature of the legal rules and standards specifying what should be done and how. They can be in the form of basic dictates, such as 'all employees on building sites are to be issued with hard hats', which is fairly clear and easy to apply, although, even here, the apparent simplicity does not foreclose all room for interpretation. In the search for clarity and precision, and often to cope with complex matters, the clear and simple rule can be sacrificed in favour of clusters of rules of great detail and complexity. An attempt in Britain to formulate rules governing all aspects of entitlement to social welfare soon became so hopelessly complex, with rules piled on rules, that elements of discretion had to be restored. Too many rules create their own pathology, which has to be remedied, usually by officials assuming discretion to ignore some of the rules and create a simpler regime.

An alternative to high-density rules is a pattern of general standards (or standard-based rules). Standards do not try to provide for all matters in advance, but furnish general guidance to be made specific in practical cases. Instead of the hard-hat rule above, the law could state that: 'employees shall be provided with clothing suitable to protect them on building sites'. The logic here is different from that of a clear-line rule, since what amounts to suitable clothing is left open. Decisions have to be taken as what safety measures would be reasonable, which in turn requires consideration of context and the social conventions that prevail. There is room for judgement, evaluation, even policy, but it is not yet full-blown discretion. Over time, more precise understandings can be expected to evolve through the experience of those engaged, so that the scope for interpretation and discretion is narrowed. A body of law based on court decisions may emerge defining the measures that are suitable; alternatively, the implementing agency devises its own guidelines, which have different forms and significance, although they are prone, over time, to assume the character of rules.

Standard-based rules lead on to discretionary powers (or, in the language of rules, discretion-based rules), so that in place of clear-line rules or standards the authority is instructed by law 'to require such safety measures on building sites as it considers desirable'. The authority has discretion in the strong sense in that it has to decide what safety measures are needed, and it does so in the relative absence of guidance from the law. But it is not a matter of there being no legal constraints, since the law is likely to stipulate that certain matters should be taken into account in deciding what is desirable. Discretion is also subject to general standards, deriving from the sources earlier mentioned, standards of reasonableness and non-arbitrariness, relevance and proportionality, and due process.[6] Within those parameters, strong discretion means having scope to decide what safety measures are required, and so opening a direct path to the social context around it. The reference to social context, implicit in both clear-line and standard-based rules, becomes explicit in relation to discretion-based rules, for discretion is a legal concept inviting the holder to move directly into the social environment. Discretion also opens the way for different approaches and strategies of implementation. We now see how the normative structure is one major variable in the legal architecture, stretching from rules to standards, to discretion. Lines between the three are often not so clear in practice, and each to some degree merges into the other: rules merge into general standards; general standards are reduced to rules; and discretion appears in stronger or weaker forms. Nevertheless, whatever the design, no matter how simple or complex it is, social consequences follow: officials must work within the normative legal structure and give practical effect to it.[7]

Outcomes

The trajectory from rules to standards to discretion is the foundation of the legal architecture, around which other features are built. One is *outcomes* by which is meant the results expected from implementing the law; what has to be done for it to be complete and successful. Implementation

---

[6] See further, K. Yeung, *Securing Compliance: A Principled Approach* (Oxford, 2004).
[7] It is certainly true that 'the structure of legal rules . . . shapes the way in which consumer agencies operate': R. Cranston, *Consumers and the Law* (London, 1978), but they do much more as is brought out in the text.

is effected if X does what the rule requires: hard hats are supplied to all the workers, welfare payments are made, and licences issued. As we move away from clear-line rules to general standards and discretion, what is required becomes less clear, and the process for achieving it more diffuse. In such cases, the law leaves it to officials to decide what outcomes are acceptable, a practice not uncommon in regulatory arenas.[8] Suppose the law requires employers to create safe environments for their workers; this could be expressed in specific measures, such as hard hats, payments, or licences. Alternatively, the object could be to encourage the creation of safe systems over time without specifying the precise measures, allowing employers to take account of the features of their organizations, their resources, and so on. This purposive approach appears in diverse situations, including laws directed at eliminating discrimination in employment, laws inducing financial institutions to provide better protection for investors, or laws encouraging schools to improve the quality of education. A quite different kind of outcome is the reaching of agreement between officials and those subject to regulation, so that what the law requires is what the parties agree. A distinction is often drawn between laws dictating precise outcomes, and less precise standards conducive to agreed settlements between the parties. Among the forms this could take are informal contracts encouraging the regulatees to take a positive approach to compliance in return for restraint on the part of the regulator.[9] Some detect a tendency in regulatory arenas away from prescriptive laws to those encouraging 'a flexible, persuasive, individualized approach'.[10]

From these examples, it is seen that outcomes have their own trajectory from those that are clear and easily assessed, to others that are purposive, open-ended, un-stated, or evolving over time. Judgments as to what outcomes are mandated, and whether they have been achieved, may admit an additional element of discretion that is not always noticed. Such judgements need not be once-and-for-all but are revised as circumstances vary. The character of outcomes and the extent of their openness depend initially on the design of the legal regime: if it is open as to outcomes, whether by accident or design, the more closely the parties, implementer and implementee, are likely to be drawn together in learning what is required and how to achieve it. The legal context is the first step in ascertaining outcomes, but other factors soon enter the scene.

---

[8] See further: Z. Mikdashi, *Regulating the Financial Sector in the Era of Globalization* (London, 2003) p. *xxiii*.

[9] For discussion, see: J. Black, *Rules and Regulators* (Oxford, 1995), 133*ff*.

[10] K. Yeung, op. cit., p. 159*ff*.

Mechanisms

Another variation in the architecture centres on the mechanisms available to achieve compliance with law.[11] By mechanisms is meant legal instruments and techniques. Once again, the simple rule-application case comes first to mind: the rule specifies what X has to do, while in the event of failure Y takes action to enforce it. Among the mechanisms simple enforcement is probably the least used. Enforcement takes several forms, ranging from the very basic form the police officer exercises when he making an arrest, to a range of administrative processes, some quite informal, to formal court proceedings. Several intermediate steps often have to be taken before enforcement is invoked. A typical case is health and safety inspectors who have to issue notices to the enterprise before launching a prosecution.[12] The European Commission may ultimately take enforcement action in the European Court of Justice against a recalcitrant member-state, but only after it has followed an exhausting process of preliminary steps, both formal and informal, directed at inducing compliance. International organizations are notoriously hindered in their efforts to secure compliance by states with international law; lacking powers of enforcement, often the only mechanism open to them is persuasion.[13] A similar approach applies in other areas, national, regional, and international, where the mechanisms include investigations, inquiries, issuing notices, negotiations, reporting, and agreements – to name just some of them.

In some areas of regulation, formal enforcement is not available. Ombudsman institutions, which supervise a range of matters within government and administration, as well as private organizations such as financial services or insurance, normally lack enforcement powers, but depend on achieving compliance through persuasion, reporting, and publicity. A study of attempts by Japanese law to eliminate discrimination in the workplace against women and minority groups shows how legal standards lacked adequate enforcement mechanisms. Implementation had to be effected instead through mediation, the persuasion of employers, and the issuing by the administration of guidelines, with only limited

---

[11] For a fuller analysis of instruments and outcomes, see: D. J. Galligan, *Due Process and Fair Procedures* (Oxford, 1996).

[12] See: R. Baldwin, 'Health and Safety at Work' in Baldwin and McCrudden, and Public Law *Regulation* (London, 1987), p. 149.

[13] An important study is: D. Sandler, *State Compliance with International Law* (Doctoral thesis, Bodleian Library, Oxford 2000).

scope for recourse to the courts to seek enforcement.[14] These softer measures are more compatible with the Japanese tradition, but attract criticism for enabling the perpetuation of a powerful workplace culture, based overwhelmingly on male dominance and with which the government administration strongly identifies.

Implementation through enforcement is sometimes replaced by other mechanisms, including *exchange* and *persuasion*. They may be provided for expressly as part of the legal design, as in the Japanese case, at other times they are introduced informally. That may happen even in the face of clear-line rules and strict enforcement, perhaps motivated by the slightly cynical view that a rule is: 'a virtuous generalization around which a game can be played'.[15] For exchange to enter the process, the parties must have something to offer each other: one agrees to comply in return for concessions from the other. Plea-bargaining is a good example, where the suspect has something to offer the prosecutor, for whom a plea of guilty is well worth the effort of patience and compromise. Agreement is often reached only after what might aptly be described as *hard bargaining*.[16] Persuasion has a different character: it is achieved by appealing to shared norms and understandings or to common aims and purposes. Both exchange and persuasion, if successful, end in agreement, although agreements can be more or less voluntary. Those reached under the shadow of sanctions cannot be considered wholly voluntary, but are still normally preferable to the imposition of sanctions with the loss of respect and reputation that follows in its wake. In practice, the three mechanisms are not as distinct as they appear to be in principle, with elements of each present in the one situation.

In another familiar class of cases, the enforcement process is followed only to find that the penalties are not severe enough to induce compliance. To a large corporation, fines are merely annoying, being considered part of the costs of conducting business. A recurring problem in the new democracies of eastern Europe is the inadequacy of the measures available to enforce compliance against officials; administrative courts often lack the authority to order positive action to be taken by an official,

[14] F. K. Upham, *Law and Social Change in Japan* (Cambridge, Mass., 1987), R. L. Miller, 'Women's Job Hunting in the Ice Age: Frozen Opportunities in Japan', (1998), 13 *Wisconsin Women's Law Journal* 223.

[15] M. Edelman, quoted in: C. Touhy: 'Achieving Compliance with Collective Objectives: A Political Science perspective' in M. L. Friedland (ed), *Sanctions and Rewards in the Legal System: A Multidisciplinary Approach* (Toronto, 1989) p. 194.

[16] See further: H. Genn, *Hard Bargaining* (Oxford, 1986).

there being no equivalent of the common law writ of *mandamus*. Many examples could be given but the point is clear: the variety of legal mechanisms available in implementing laws is extensive, with each varying in its effectiveness. Just as in a building there can be several routes to a room, similarly in legal structures implementation can be brought about through different mechanisms. The softer measures of exchange and agreement have a natural attraction, and we shall see shortly that other factors support their having a prominent position in implementation. At the same time, behind the softer measures, enforcement through sanctions remains the dominant method in most contexts; and even where resort to softer measures is common, the harder side of implementation is never far away.

Remedies and procedures

Here the issue is what remedies are available to bring about compliance and what are the procedures for doing so. Sometimes they are clearly defined: the police officer uses force to effect an arrest; the regulatory agency imposes a fine on the employer who fails to issue hard hats; and the minister closes down a school that falls below the statutory standards of education. The remedy can be straightforward and easily executed, as in the case of the police officer, but often is more complicated. The inspector trying to enforce anti-pollution standards, rather than impose sanctions himself, may have to bring an action in the courts with the formality that entails; the minister endeavouring to uphold educational standards is constrained to follow complex and lengthy procedures before closing a school. British teachers complain that they have inadequate remedies for dealing with persistently ill-behaved pupils; lobster-fishing inspectors lament the inadequacy of remedies to deter poaching; administrative courts cannot force officials to act – the litany of inadequate remedies could go on. Courts are often hampered by restrictions on remedies, an issue that has made it difficult for U.S. courts involved in civil rights cases. The desegregation of schools requires the issuing of orders to local and state authorities of the kinds courts cannot easily issue; those authorized have to be tempered by realism, there being no point in ordering a full-scale reform of the school system if school boards lack the resources or the will to comply.[17]

Court proceedings usually mean a level of formality with greater concern for such matters as procedures, evidence, and standards of proof,

---

[17] See further; B. Flicker, *Justice and School Systems: The Role of Courts in Education Litigation*, pp. 7 *ff.*

than administrative bodies. The lobster-fishing inspectors found that the courts insisting on standards of evidence and proof that they could not meet, and that the courts' adherence to legal values such as fairness made enforcement impossible.[18] Consumer protection agencies, which had to go to court to have the law enforced, found the courts construed the law differently from them, and tended to favour business interests over those of consumers.[19] For reasons like these, it is not surprising that courts are regarded as the last resort, although the very threat of going to court may be enough to win compliance. The costs, uncertainties, and potential perils of court actions are an inducement to officials to be accommodating and to encourage negotiation and settlement. For similar reasons, officials use other approaches to secure compliance, some informal, roundabout, and often creative. The gaming inspectors relied on the threat of non-renewal of licences to conduct business as an alternative to going to court.[20] States are prompted to improve compliance with human rights standards when economic assistance is made conditional on them (a practice now common in international development). It is not uncommon for implementing bodies to complain that inadequate remedies hamper effective implementation, while the toothless tiger is not an unfamiliar figure in compliance circles.

It is possible here to convey only the barest sense of how important remedies are in the understanding of legal structures and, at the same time, how complex and problematical they can be. The involvement of third parties adds a further dimension. The role of third parties, usually meaning persons, associations, or organizations, which are in some way affected by failure to comply with the law, follows different patterns. Often the process can be started only by way of complaint or other expression of grievance, as in the case of an ombudsman inquiry or a court action. Even where the implementing body takes the initiative, success is likely to depend on the cooperation of one or more third parties; a prosecution for non-compliance fails unless witnesses are willing to give evidence. The recourse open to employees who feel discriminated against illustrates the point: a complaint may lie to a special commission which then has various courses available to it, including possibly initiating court proceedings; alternatively, action may be taken in the courts for damages or to restrain the employer from continuing the

---

[18] J.C. McMullin and D.C. Perrier, op. cit. p. 700.
[19] R. Cranston, *op. cit.*, p. 46.
[20] D. Miers, 'The Gaming Board for Great Britain: Enforcement and Judicial Restraint' in R. Baldwin and C. McCrudden, *Public Law and Regulation* (London, 1987) p. 48.

practices. The provision of legal remedies is a vital part of the architecture, of the legal structure within which implementation takes place. Around those legal provisions other informal or unofficial forms of recourse sometimes are created, which may affect and modify the formal ones in numerous ways.

Constraining standards

Apart from the limitations that inadequate remedies place on the implementation process, account also has to be taken of other legal standards deriving from sources such as the Constitution, the common law, or general codes.[21] A good example is due process, which imposes procedural rules on bodies such as courts, tribunals, ombudsman, and regulators. While the demands vary according to context, they often are exacting, with failure to comply invalidating the process.[22] Another set of constraints, touched on earlier, structures the exercise of discretion through notions such as reasonableness, relevance, and proportionality. Standards like these are developed by courts or stated in procedural codes, and often provide the basis for legal challenges to the validity of implementation processes. Other examples could be added, but again the general point is clear: without taking account of the limiting principles of these kinds, the legal architecture would be incomplete.

The architecture of law is a metaphor, but a useful one, in showing how rules and discretion, outcomes and remedies, the role of third parties, and general legal principles all combine in different ways in each legal setting. The metaphor helps to express the idea that legal regimes, like real buildings, have common features while allowing endless scope for variation, scope as to the patterns they form, how prominent each part is, and relationships among the parts. If we are to understand how law relates to other aspects of the process of implementation, the first step is to be clear about the law.

NOTES

On courts as implementing bodies

Within the extensive literature on courts, the most fruitful in understanding courts as implementing bodies are:

[21] Discussion of these constraints can be seen in: D. J. Galligan, *Discretionary Powers*, Chapter 3. In the context of regulation, Karen Yeung's recent study is indispensable: see K. Yeung, op. cit.
[22] For further discussion of this, see D. J. Galligan, *Due Process and Fair Procedures*.

M. Shapiro, *Courts: A Comparative and Political Analysis* (Chicago, 1981).

A. Stone-Sweet, *Governing With Judges: Constitutional Politics in Europe* (Oxford, 2000).

A-M. Slaughter, A. Stone-Sweet, and J. H. H. Weiler (eds), *The European Court and the National Courts – Doctrine and Jurisprudence: Legal Change in its Social Context* (Oxford, 1998).

On the use of law by parties to achieve social goals

M. McCann, 'How Does Law Matter for Social Movements?' in B. Garth and A. Sarat, op. cit.

For a recent review of the use of the legal process by Australian Aboriginies, see: R. Cranston, *How Law Works* (Oxford, 2006), Chapter 8.

A well-known account of the use of law in the political arena is: S. Sheingold, *The Politics of Rights: Lawyers, Public Policy, and Political Change* (New Haven Conn., 1974). A more recent account that assesses the value of legal recourse to victims of discrimination is: K. Bumiller, *The Civil Rights Society: The Social Construction of Victims* (Baltimore, 1988).

On individual persons or groups trying to get officials to implement the law against others

Apart from the study conducted by the Oxford Centre for Socio-Legal Studies referred to in the text, other useful studies are: J. S. Fan, 'From Office Ladies to Women Warriors?: The Effect of the EEOL on Japanese Women' (1999–2000) 103 *UCLA Women's Law Journal* 103; S. Olson, *Clients and Lawyers: Securing the Rights of Disabled Persons* (Westport, 1984).

Organizational culture

For an illuminating account of organizations and institutions, see: W. R. Scott, op. cit. The culture of corporations is considered at length in: F. Haines, op. cit.

Legal architecture

F. Haines shows how the common law covers issues and provides remedies within regulatory contexts; the intersection of common law and regulation is easily overlooked: op. cit., Chapter 8.

Administrative guidance as a remedy: the Japanese Equal Employment Opportunity Law restricted court actions and remedies to a minimum and inserted in their place administrative guidance in settling disputes.

Administrative guidance has been defined as: action 'of no coercive legal effect that encourages regulated parties to act in a specific way in order to realize some administrative aim'. M. Young, 'Judicial Review of Administrative Guidance: Government Encouraged consensual Dispute Resolution in Japan' (1984), 120 *UCLA Women's Law Journal* 923. In this case, administrative guidance was used to reflect the deeper social relations of the workplace, the business community, and government administration.

Mechanisms

For a good analysis of mechanisms in implementation, see: C. Touhy, 'Achieving Compliance with Collective Objectives: A Political Science Perspective' in M. L. Friedland, *Sanctions and Rewards in the Legal System: A Multidisciplinary Approach* (Toronto, 1989). Mechanisms are divided into *command, exchange,* and *persuasion,* with each context of implementation usually containing a mixture of the three, although one or other is likely to dominate.

Significance of the legal architecture

R. Cranston elaborates on the social effects of the legal architecture; he writes: '. . . law has a limited role and acts mainly to set the boundaries within which decisions are made. For consumer officers, law assumes a simpler form, for they could not cope with, nor do they need to, its full complexity, for their routine activity'. (*Consumers and the Law*, p. 7)

16

Implementation: the Legal and Social Environment

16.1 THE LEGAL ENVIRONMENT OF IMPLEMENTATION

The architecture of law is the first step in the implementation process, the social environment around that architecture the second. The social environment divides into two parts: one is the *legal environment*, by which is meant the issues and effects deriving directly from the legal design; the other is the wider social context that interacts with the law and its environment.[1] By introducing the officials responsible for implementing law, we move from the law to its environment. Officials have to ascertain what is required of them by the law and decide how to achieve it. In the same way that the design of a building influences and constrains the uses to which it can be put, the legal design directs the attitudes and practices of officials. The environment created by law is a vital part of the process of implementation; by placing law and its environment in the wider social context, the process is then complete.

The notion of a legal environment is best illustrated by considering the lines of the legal architecture etched above. Let us begin again with the simplest case of a legal regime based on clear and comprehensive rules. The officials' task is to apply the rules to cases that come within them. That means interpreting the rules and, in doing so, officials are led to that social world at their base and to the conditional contingencies it contains. The relations between legal rules and their social worlds need not be repeated here, except to note that officials interpret rules from the standpoint of that social world, which is also their social world, composed of their conventions and understandings.[2] Interpretation is just the first step. Officials must also devise procedures for reaching decisions about the application of rules; a choice may have to be made between an investi-

---

[1] A preliminary analysis of the legal environment is given in 7.8. [2] See Chapter 3.

gatory approach conducted by the officials themselves, or placing the onus on interested parties to present evidence. The demands of due process and other constitutional and legal values have to be taken into account. Provision has to be made for the role of the parties, as complainants, litigants, or witnesses. Consideration has to be given to mechanisms available for attaining compliance: is the process based on enforcement through sanctions, or is it more in the mode of negotiation and persuasion? Officials often find a sanction-based approach unsuitable in the circumstances, perhaps because the resources needed to mount prosecutions are lacking or infringements are difficult to prove. A threat of sanctions may simply be the wrong approach, being more likely to hinder compliance than help it. Officials feel the need to modify the legal approach, informally introducing softer mechanisms, while reserving punitive procedures for the worst cases.

The remedies available for non-compliance present another set of issues. Their potential unsuitability, inadequacy, or ineffectiveness has been noted. Officials find ways of coping, perhaps leading them to create other informal remedies to supplement or avoid the formal. The process is influenced by the extent to which and the ways in which officials may be called to account by other authorities, such as ministers, tribunals, or courts. A regime of strict accountability is likely to encourage attitudes quite different from those where accountability is weak or non-existent. The simple application of rules now appears more complex, with numerous aspects requiring decisions by officials, showing how the most straightforward legal design creates an intricate and contingent environment.

Moving from the implementation of clear-line rules to open discretion, we witness the emergence of a different legal environment. Here authority is conferred on officials with only general guidance on how to use it, leaving them to answer such questions as: what factors are relevant; should guidelines be drawn up or each case left to be considered with a relatively open mind? If there are to be guidelines, what force do they have? Should guidelines be left to evolve over time on the basis of experience and precedent? Procedures again have an important place in the process. The demands of due process, familiar in rule-based regimes, are likely to be absent or much reduced in discretionary contexts, perhaps replaced by quite different procedures directed at consultation and the making of representations by those whose case is at issue, and by a wider range of groups and interests. The formulation of suitable procedures is often left to the officials as part of their discretion, while other factors, such as remedies, legal constraints, and forms of accountability appear again but in different guises.

The differences between the rule-based and the discretionary are not as sharp in practice as in principle. Any legal environment consists in a changeable combination of direction from the law and discretion within the law. Some environments are plainly more discretionary than others, but even those that appear to be rule-intense rely for their practical application on the judgments, choices, and preferences of officials, with respect to remedies, mechanisms, procedures, constraints, and sanctions. The basis for the legal environment is the legal architecture; that is the first step, the laying of the foundations as it were; it then has to be turned into a social reality and given practical application by officials. That requires decisions about a range of matters on which the law itself probably furnishes incomplete guidance. And if to that is added the inevitable gaps, inconsistencies, and loopholes accompanying any regime of laws, and the inadequacies and foolishness that are never in short supply, it becomes clear just how important the legal environment is. It is equally clear that the legal environment does not come complete and ready-made; instead, around the law and within it, the legal environment has to be created, developed, and given practical effect.

16.2 CREATING LEGAL ENVIRONMENTS

In creating a legal environment, in considering what the law mandates and converting it into practical action, the underlying premise of a modern legal order is that officials accept the authority of the law.[3] By that is meant they regard it as binding on them and are obligated conscientiously to apply it. They are justified in taking actions directed at giving it effect and are justly criticized when they fail to do so. The role of the law is neatly captured in the idea of *benchmarks*: 'The law on the books is a benchmark for enforcers . . .', and, it should be added, for groups wishing to evaluate the actions of enforcers.[4] The general commitment to legal benchmarks is common to officials, although it varies in its strength from one group to another. Courts and court-like bodies are likely to be more legalistic, more concerned to apply the terms of the statute according to established canons of construction. Courts are expected to uphold the

---

[3] See Chapter 5.
[4] R. Kagan, N. Gunningham, and D. Thornton, 'Explaining Corporate Environmental Performance: How Does Regulation Work?' (2003) 37 *Law and Society Review* 51, p. 79.

law and have the final say regarding it; they also normally give public reasons justifying their decisions. A study of social security shows a marked difference between the appeal tribunals and the front-line officers, the former being strict with the law, the latter viewing it more flexibly.[5] Similar findings emerge from a study of consumer protection agencies where officials took a simplified view of the law compared with that of the courts, which placed emphasis on adopting a correct interpretation and on upholding due process.[6] Lobster-fishing inspectors were frustrated by the courts' insistence on high standards of proof, despite evidence being hard to obtain, and on strict observance of procedural fairness.[7]

The general commitment of officials to the law does not ensure that specific laws are given full effect, since in the process of application they have to compete with other social factors exerting other pressures, a matter to which we shall return shortly.[8] The idea of the legal environment follows from the acceptance of law as authoritative, since on the basis of that acceptance officials have to make sense of what it requires and devise ways of giving effect to it. Before examining the social factors that influence officials in implementation, several problems concerning the legal environment itself should be considered. The *first* is in knowing what exactly the law requires. Even the simplest rule sometimes catches cases it was not designed to, or misses those it was; similarly, strict application of the law may end in hardship or injustice and even fail to achieve its purposes. A study of a statutory freeze on wages, prices, and rents is a good illustration.[9] Here the question for regulatory officials was whether the strict and explicit letter of the law ought to be enforced, or whether it should be read subject to notions of effectiveness, fairness, and reasonableness. In practice, officials adopted the second approach, giving effect to what was described as a strong tradition of 'pragmatism and natural law'.[10] A basic legal question influencing the way officials construct the legal environment is whether the law should be applied strictly without regard to its effects, or whether there is a deeper duty to pursue the social objectives that led to the rule in the first place. If the obligation is one of strict implementation, the process takes on features analogous to the enforcement of criminal law, with prosecution and penalties the dominant mode. If, however, the rules are taken as signposts to underlying social

---

[5] J. Baldwin, N. Wikeley, and R. Young, *Judging Social Security* (Oxford, 1992), pp. 72, 98.
[6] R. Cranston, op. cit.   [7] J. C. McMullan and D. C. Perrier, op. cit.
[8] We shall see examples of those pressures in the next section.
[9] R. Kagan, *Regulatory Justice: Implementing a Wage-Price Freeze* (New York, 1978).
[10] *Ibid* p. 165.

aims and purposes, rather than ends in themselves, the approach has a different logic: implementation is centred not on the strict application of the rules but on achieving their point and purpose.[11] Once that is regarded as the goal, the strategies for achieving it are also affected; strict enforcement gives way to accommodation, negotiation, and persuasion as strategies for reaching acceptable compliance. As G. Richardson and others conclude in their classic study of enforcement officers in controlling pollution, once it was realized that enforcement was necessary in a particular case: 'Co-operation not confrontation was the aim'.[12]

The dichotomy between enforcement and accommodation is discussed in the literature on implementation, particularly in studies of regulation, where it is generally assumed that the regulatory body has a strategic choice between the two approaches.[13] To some degree that is true, but the issue is also legal and theoretical; it arises, at least in part, from the uncertainty as to what the law requires, an issue to which legal theory has no answer. Here we encounter the first problem for legal environments: at the heart of the implementation process is an unresolved problem about the nature of law, to which attention was drawn earlier, which creates a dilemma for officials in implementation. Different sets of officials will resolve it in different ways, according to how they view the law, a matter itself influenced by various factors, including their social spheres. If a generalization may be ventured (with ample allowance for exceptions) it would be that administrative officials generally take the 'signpost' approach, regarding the law as an instrument for achieving various ends and purposes, rather than as rules to be strictly applied. Having taken that view, officials are impelled towards encouraging compliance through negotiation and consensus, rather than threatening enforcement though sanctions. Courts are likely to lean the other way, although the position varies, with some judges assuming leeway in getting behind the letter of the law to ascertain its point and purpose. Once officials, whether administrators or judges, start to consider the point and purpose of a set of laws, they embark on an enquiry to which there is often no clear answer; at the same time, they open a door to the social context of legal rules through which other sets of social factors come flooding.

Similar theoretical uncertainty occurs in a *second*, slightly different way: here the issue is not what the law requires, but what counts as law.

---

[11] On rules as sign-posts, see Chapter 3.
[12] G. Richardson, op. cit, p. 123.
[13] A good summary is found in: K. Yeung, op. cit., pp. 158 *ff.*

Statutes and regulations enacted in accordance with the usual legislative procedures are normally clear, whereas guidelines, rules of interpretation, practices, informal directions, and the like, what was earlier designated *soft law*, are often of undefined status. And yet, in any context of official authority, clear-line rules of law are only part, and often a small part, of the fuller normative environment, where the questions often are: are the various kinds of soft law binding and to what extent are they binding? Standards of questionable authority qualify, moderate, or even oppose others whose legal credentials are more certain. We see here in practical form an illustration of the earlier discussion about the difficulty of identifying the precise scope of law, for even the clearest rules are subject to the contextual contingencies officials bring to bear in construing them. It is no solution to say that it is for the courts to decide what is law and what is not, for although that may be true, the great majority of issues never go to court but are left for officials to decide. The view they take of the scope of law, of what counts as law, and what legal weight it has, may well embrace a wider conception of law than that warranted by a strict rule-of-recognition approach. This is not just the result of inadequate judicial supervision, but a deep-seated, theoretical issue about the nature of law. If a set of officials consistently takes the view that a standard is legitimate and binding on them, where it is not just someone's subjective judgement but a standard acknowledged within the legal environment, it is hard, and possibly pointless, to insist to the contrary. The point for our present concerns is that the legal architecture, and the environment enveloping it, are likely to pose acute questions as to what sorts of rules and standards are included, and what weight they have. In most practical cases, that issue has to be settled by the officials themselves as part of their daily practice with little hope or fear that it will ever reach the courts.

The two previous matters reveal difficult, perhaps insoluble, questions about the nature of law, which infect legal environments. A *third* but equally problematic feature arises out of the use of rules. The fullest expression of law, and in a sense its ideal, is a set of rules that are clear and comprehensive, leaving as little scope as possible for interpretation, let alone discretion. By guiding behaviour and being the basis for evaluating it, rules create a very particular legal environment in which the task of officials is to ensure they are applied. That environment is not always free of difficulties. The well-intentioned and well-planned concern to achieve the ideal of law often leads to an excess of rules and details, which in turn create their own pathology. Where there are too many rules, interpretation is rife in piecing them together, in deciding an order of priorities, and in resolving inconsistencies and conflicts, the risk of which increases with the proliferation of rules. So, while high-density rule regimes reflect the desire to reduce the scope for interpretation and discretion, they are prone to encourage the opposite. The risks are aptly displayed in the study of attempts to regulate lobster poaching along the Canadian coast, in which the authors describe the laws, regulations, and policy guides as: 'a complex, bewildering, and ever-changing amalgam of legal rules, programmes, and procedures',[14] a description that would be at home in other legal contexts.

One consequence is the difficulty of taking all such laws seriously. Since they are unlikely to form a coherent and consistent whole, some may have to be discounted or ignored in favour of others. Officials dealt with the problem in the lobster-poaching case by concentrating on a few rules to the neglect of others. The need to select some and relegate others forced officials into a shadow-land of policy choices, which was not intended by the legislation, and which undermines the point of having high-density rules. Once implementation goes beyond the normal process of interpretation of rules and becomes a choice among them, the environment created by the law will have changed in significant ways. If other, external, factors are added, in particular the scarcity of resources, the need for selective enforcement is reinforced and the shadow-land becomes the reality. A variation on this theme occurs where the effects of one set of laws are reduced or dislodged by another. A law in Northern Ireland aimed at introducing standards of fairness into the workplace was limited in its effects by the use of common law doctrines, such as rules of statutory construction, the burden of proof, and judicial review of the implementing agency's powers.[15]

The claim here is that different areas of legal regulation are designed in different ways and that each creates a legal environment around it. Officials are at the centre of that environment, since it falls to them to make sense of the legal regime and put it into practice. The legal environment is of interest because it is structured and constrained by the design of the law, or, put differently, officials do not come with a free hand to make decisions about this or that, or to adopt one strategy rather than another; instead they come to a structured social situation, and work within it and around it; they have to make sense of it, even if finally they manoeuvre

---

[14] J. C. McMullan and D. C. Perrier, op. cit.
[15] S. Livingstone, 'Using Law to Change a Society: The Case of Northern Ireland' in S. Livingstone and J. Morison (eds), *Law, Society and Change* (Aldershot, 1990).

around it, avoid its requirements, or impose their own strategy on it. The argument is that each area of implementation is marked by a distinct legal design, that such design creates around it an environment, and that both are essential elements in understanding the implementation of law. And finally, the law and its environment are marked by features, some theoretical, others practical, that make them both problematical and unstable.

16.3 AUTHORIZED DISCRETION

Another way of bringing the legal environment into focus is through the notion of discretion. The word means the liberty of deciding as one thinks fit within some defined context. That matches nicely the legal sense of discretion, where it is taken to mean that, acting within a defined legal setting, one has a degree of liberty in deciding one way or another or of choosing among possible courses of action.[16] The legal settings of discretion vary. The interpretation of a clear-line rule involves discretion just in the sense that it leads to the social context and contingencies within it. Standard-based rules indicate more directly the need for discretion by using such terms as effectiveness, fairness, or reasonableness. Discretion, in its fullest sense, occurs when authority to act is granted with minimal guidance as to what to do or how to do it. Consider the example of a regulatory body with authority to specify 'such measures as it considers desirable in protecting the health and safety of workers'. The discretionary element in interpreting rules, whether clear-line, standard-based, or discretionary, is easy to see; the scope for discretion in other contexts is more subtle. Discretion implicit in fact-finding is an example: how much evidence and what sort is needed in a given case to prove the facts, and what amounts to adequate proof?

These and related questions require a discretionary assessment, which differs according to whether the context is a judicial process, an administrative one, or one that is deliberately discretionary. And whether or not the facts constitute a category or concept is another example of less obvious discretion. A study of mental health shows how doctors, families, lawyers, and judges have subtle forms of discretion in classifying a patient's symptoms as one or other category of mental illness.[17] Cases like

---

[16] For a fuller account, see: D. J. Galligan, *Discretionary Powers*, op. cit.
[17] P. S. Appelbaum, *Almost a Revolution: Mental Health Law and the Limits of Change* (New York, 1994), p. 215.

these reveal that, within the general framework of rules and standards, discretion can be disguised and appear in unexpected places. The more general point is that the subject matter of discretion is highly diverse, including not only substantive issues but also such matters as the choice of procedures or remedies. Once a procedure is chosen, discretion is likely to reappear at various points in its application; similarly, one remedy may be chosen as more suitable than another, but then as a matter of further discretion not granted. The idea often repeated that, wherever there is decision-making there is also discretion, is plainly true.

Powers conferred on officials sometimes come with discretion stamped on their backs, but officials are more likely to have to decide for themselves; they have discretion in deciding whether there is discretion. The interplay between different sets of officials introduces another variable into the legal environment, for what is rule-application to one may be discretion to another. Administrative officials are more likely to find discretion in places where courts would not; and since most actions of officials are unlikely to be tested in the courts, officials have a certain licence to see any law as offering some discretion, a licence to delve more freely into the social context than a stricter approach would permit.[18] The risk of later review by courts imposes some restraints, but they are usually weak; where there is no prospect of review, the natural inclination to assume some discretion in any context of decision-making will be harder to resist. Where courts do recognize discretion, legal consequences follow: they acknowledge the liberty of decision and are expected not to interfere with its merits. Discretion, in other words, is a legal concept with legal consequences; it is part of the architecture, and as part of the architecture it affects the environment. The legal concept of discretion, whose recognition depends on the courts, is much narrower than that which administrative officials use. Where the courts do find discretion, the liberty of decision on the merits is respected, but is subject to restraining standards of fairness, reasonableness, and procedural fairness. The practice of judicial review illustrates the point: courts do not review the content or merits of the decision, but ensure respect for standards such as procedural fairness and proportionality. The interplay between sets of officials and their different viewpoints in identifying discretion shows how complicated and diverse the legal environment can become;

---

[18] For a study of the interplay between officials and review bodies, see: R. Lempert, 'Discretion in a Behavioral Perspective' in K. Hawkins (ed), *The Uses of Discretion* (Oxford, 1993).

they also show a parallel interplay between the legal design and its environment. The interest and complexity of the two levels of interplay is increased when other factors are added, such as the tendency for discretion to become rule-bound, then raising issues as to the status of the rules and the different attitudes and approaches of sets of officials.

16.4 UNAUTHORIZED DISCRETION

The idea that the viewpoints of officials determine whether or not there is discretion leads onto the wider issue of *unauthorized* discretion. From the point of view of the courts, whether there is discretion is a matter of interpretation on which they have the final say; and if they find discretion, legal consequences follow. For other officials, the line between discretion and simple interpretation, between discretion and non-discretion, is less precise or significant. While their commitment to taking law seriously is generally sincere, administrative officials are likely to have views that are more directly linked to the social context in which they work. Their concern is with point and purpose rather than the strict letter of the law, while their understanding of what constitutes the point and purpose is linked to their social spheres and the underlying social relations. From that perspective, the law sometimes appears inadequate or unsuitable in advancing its own aims and purposes; it may also be contrary to the officials' view of how best to achieve them. At an indefinable point, the process of applying the law subtly becomes modifying, departing from, or marginalizing it. The concern to uphold the point and purpose of the law imperceptibly shifts to being a concern to advance other aims. A study of police behaviour makes the point well: the police regularly and systematically depart from the law in order to maintain a notion of public order as they understand it.[19] The law and the ideas behind it get in the way of a different conception of order based on organizational interests and managerial efficiency in detecting crime. Considering the tension between the two sets of factors, law on one side, order and efficiency on the other, the latter tends to prevail over the former.[20]

The tendency for officials to evaluate laws against their point and purpose is common to any legal system. Whether it is authorized or not is unclear, and again legal theory has no answer. *Unauthorized discretion* is a term meant to capture the ambiguity between applying rules according to their exact terms, or acting for other good reasons such as pursuing the

---

[19] J. Skolnick, *Justice Without Trial* (New York, 1966) pp. 68, 235.   [20] *Ibid* p. 238.

underlying purposes. Whether or not the term does so adequately, it draws attention to a common phenomenon that shows itself in many ways. One is the tendency of officials to modify the law in order to give effect to competing social considerations; in the police example this consisted in a conception of public order. In other cases, it is used to interpret laws in accordance with moral or other social notions, as in the case where laws freezing wages, prices, and rents were subject to notions of reasonableness and justice. It also frequently appears in regulatory contexts where enforcement is selective or made subject to ideas about how compliance is best achieved. Studies of enforcement of the criminal law show that police and prosecutors regularly assume discretion of selective enforcement, while studies of regulation in such matters as the environment show that officials often adopt a more accommodating approach.[21] This means adopting a disposition towards negotiation and persuasion rather than one of strict enforcement.[22] Originally environmental pollution was not regarded as classic criminal activity, so prompting an attitude of tolerance and understanding on the part of officials, and opening the way for consideration of non-legal factors; the duty to enforce legal standards was then filtered through those non-legal factors. The main issue in some studies of legal regulation is how those extra-legal factors influence and even determine the implementation process. Unauthorized discretion is a useful notion through which to view the way legal rules reach down into their social context. This, in turn, connects with the issue of what it means for officials to accept the authority of law, the suggestion being that general acceptance of the rule of recognition, and rules made under it, is part of a more complex process of acceptance, with the fuller account to be found in the institutional settings of officials. How law is regarded – what it means, how far it stretches, and how it relates to factors within the various social spheres – is resolved within that setting.

16.5 FROM LEGAL ENVIRONMENT TO SOCIAL CONTEXT

The final stage in understanding implementation positions the legal architecture and its environment in their social setting. One way of doing so is to return to a simple image of officials and implementation, and then

---

[21] See for instance: B. Hutter, *The Reasonable Arm of the Law* (Oxford, 1988) p. 179.
[22] Similar approaches are commonly found, see G. Richardson, *Policing Pollution* op. cit. pp. 123 *ff.*

to construct around it a social setting. According to this image, officials are grouped in organizations saturated with law: they are created by law, derive their mandates from law, and are restrained by law; they are accountable under the law, while the measure of success is effective implementation of the law according to its terms. To this should be added the general fact that officials within a modern legal order have a high level of commitment of respect for the law, even if among them the strength of commitment varies. In discharging their commitment, officials have both the authority of the legal order behind them and recourse to coercive measures to reinforce them. This image must now be placed in its social setting to see what adjustments have to be made. To a degree this has already been done, since points of intersection with the social setting are implicit in the notions of legal architecture and legal environment. The interpretation of law is infused with social meanings, while the grant of discretion is an open invitation to import social factors. We have seen how complexities, contradictions, and uncertainties in the law itself can be resolved only by resort to factors beyond the law. And if to that is added the inclination of officials to assume discretion where none is expressly authorized, the inter-relationship between law and its social context becomes even closer. From the analysis of law's structure and the questions it poses for officials, we have already learnt much about the social process of implementation.

In completing the picture, the starting point is to focus on the grouping together of officials to form a social world that, although heavily influenced by law, goes beyond it. Each group develops conventions and understandings about the point and purpose of the law, about how they should perform their tasks and relate to each other. The notion of a social sphere is intended to capture these elements and to convey the idea of groups of officials occupying a social world, which becomes distinct and tends towards detachment from other social worlds. Social spheres are formed from and react to influences, some flowing from the internal character of the organization and its legal foundations, others from external sources. The natural tendency of organizations towards autonomy, towards a social sphere of conventions and understandings, is further provoked by officials having to make decisions about how to perform their legal mandates. The very complexity of the legal architecture and its environment, and the issues and dilemmas they create for implementation, means that far from being a straight-forward matter of applying the rules, it requires decisions about approaches and strategies, about how best to achieve the stated objectives. Such decisions, in turn, need to be responsive to the social setting, to matters such as relations with those against whom the law is being implemented, the scarcity of resources, and the political context.

Social spheres, organizations, and institutions

Social spheres are of central importance to understanding the actions of officials in two main ways: first they absorb the influence of social factors and convert them into a manageable system of conventions and understandings; and secondly, the actions of officials then occur within and are guided by those conventions and understandings.[23] Social spheres are more or less dense depending on their normative structure and the understandings supporting them. Social spheres do not determine actions, not do they prevent individual officials from deciding differently; their use is in guiding decisions and in practice they are effective in doing so. One element in the formation of social spheres relating to implementation is the character of the organization, that is the grouping of officials as a department, a statutory agency, a regulatory body, or similar. Such organizations are created by law for the conduct of specific tasks – prosecuting offenders, granting licences, setting conditions and standards for the conduct of an activity, and so on. Another element is the normative structure that accompanies the organization. This consists of the legal architecture and its environment. These two elements are the bare bones provided by law around which a fuller social sphere is built.

Attitudes and understandings of officials

The attitudes and understandings of officials is another matter to add in developing a full sense of social spheres. The answers to questions such as the following will reveal much about attitudes and understandings: How do the officials see themselves? What do they consider their tasks and how do they approach them? What are the underlying values on which their actions are based? In answering these questions and others, several themes commonly occur. One theme is how seriously a set of officials takes the law; negative or equivocal views are bound to reduce their commitment to implementation to the point of modifying the law or even subverting it.[24] Another factor is whether a set of officials regards implementation as oriented to coercive enforcement or persuasion and

---

[23] Social spheres are considered more fully in Chapter 6.
[24] See further: R. L. Kidder, *Connecting Law and Society: An Introduction to Theory and Research* (Englewood Cliffs, 1983).

agreement. We noticed earlier how often the coercive approach is replaced by softer options; where the law stands in the way, officials can be expected to explore the opportunities for its creative interpretation, and in the process subtly assume unauthorized discretion. The self-image of consumer protection agencies was one of advisers rather than enforcers, although enforcement was part of their duties;[25] the same could be said of pollution inspectors,[26] anti-competition regulatory authorities,[27] and a host of other implementing bodies. Perhaps there is enough evidence to support the hypothesis that officials will normally strive to reach a satisfactory level of implementation through negotiation, compromise, and agreement before taking coercive action. The evidence on regulation shows a trend away from the command-and-control approach to one of persuasion, where the regulatee is encouraged to comply with the spirit of the law rather than its precise letter, 'spirit' meaning its aims and purposes.[28] The softer approaches are often prompted by the conviction that the interests of all parties are best served, or there may be practical reasons, such as inadequate penalties or the sheer expense of bringing prosecutions.[29] *Responsive regulation* is meant to capture the idea of its being responsive to the aims, processes, and structure of the activities being regulated.[30] On this approach, effective regulation subtly depends on the co-operative self-regulation of the parties affected.[31]

Another approach is to seek the optimum level of compliance with law by a combination of different techniques, beginning with persuasion and working up to enforcement through sanctions. This enforcement pyramid, as John Braithwaite, its creator, calls it, (although it has met some resistance) is realistic in acknowledging that persuasion does not always work and sanctions may be needed.[32] Some prefer the notion of regulatory pluralism to indicate the range of approaches and techniques available to secure compliance.[33] A full discussion of these ideas is beyond my present purposes, except to note that in implementing law officials are

---

[25] R. Cranston, op. cit.

[26] G. Richardson, op. cit., K. Hawkins, *Environment and Enforcement* (Oxford, 1984).

[27] K. Yeung, op. cit., p. 111.

[28] From an extensive literature, the following are especially instructive: J. Ayres and J. Braithwaite, *Responsive Regulation* and N. Gunningham and R. Johnstone, *Regulating Workplace Safety* (1999, Oxford), pp. 6 *ff.*

[29] These practical concerns are shown in: J. C. McMullan and D. C. Perrier, op. cit., pp. 703 *ff.*

[30] J. Ayres and J. Braithwaite, op. cit., p. 10.

[31] N. Gunningham and R. Johnstone, op. cit., p. 10; see also: N. Gunningham and P. Grabosky, *Smart Regulation: Designing Environmental Policy* (Oxford, 1998), p. 10.

[32] J. Ayres and J. Braithwaite, op. cit.   [33] K. Yeung, op. cit., p. 160.

likely to be influenced by them. The legal architecture places constraints on the extent to which these ideas may be followed in practice, although it is realistic to acknowledge that, as new ideas concerning regulation circulate, they are likely to influence the attitudes of officials, who will find ways of adjusting and orienting the implementation process to take them into account.

Confronting the normative structure of implementation

Another major variable is how officials view and deal with the legal architecture and its environment. We have seen how important these two notions are in the process of implementation; we have also seen how pervasive discretion is. In placing the normative legal structure in the wider social environment, we face the immediate issue of how discretion is viewed and used by officials. Where discretion is plainly conferred, officials have the opportunity to structure it through guidelines and policies, thus creating a direct and immediate link between the legal environment and their social world. The claim is often made that some discretion can always be found, enough to justify interpreting laws in a particular way, or to avoid unwanted directions or outcomes. In dealing with issues of interpretation and discretion, officials draw on various factors. One is their own understanding of the point and purpose of the law. The judge, the police officer, and the social welfare officer all have views about their work, what they are trying to achieve, and how best to do so. The law is their vehicle, but it has to be interpreted; discretion opens the way for direct reference to underlying aims, and when disparities appear the law can be creatively construed. Ways of regarding the law vary, the sight of rigid adherence to the rules being as familiar as departure from them. Where discretion is granted or assumed, the influences on the way it is exercised are many and varied, and are discussed at length in my earlier book *Discretionary Powers*. It is unnecessary to repeat the discussion here except to note that a range of other factors also have a place in piecing together the full social environment, matters as everyday as the capacity of the organization, the inevitably inadequate resources, and the political background. In addition to their responsibility to the law, officials often have relations with the government ministers or other political forces, whose influence is likely to be felt in the implementation process.

Social relations between implementers and implementees

Relations between officials and those to whom they are applying the law (implementees) is a major factor in the social context of implementation.

The views officials form of relations between the two shape their actions, while the different strategies of implementation discussed above owe much to them. Studies show that officials often develop lasting relationships, so that implementation becomes a continuing process rather than an isolated incident. Lasting relations encourage co-operation between the parties, which may lead on to accommodation and agreement in achieving compliance; if legal corners have to be cut to achieve co-operation, the results make it worthwhile. Ideas of punishment have no place in a cooperative relationship, the tendency being instead to bring out the best in the implementee. The implementee for its part must show it is trying to comply, is ethically sound, and is honest and open with officials. If officials conceive the relationship differently, as one in which coercion is appropriate, their response is also different. This is more likely to occur in situations that are one-off rather than continuing, although established relations with softer approaches can swing towards punishment where the implementee's actions warrant it, perhaps because of questionable behaviour.[34] The legal architecture itself limits the scope for cooperative relations; a regime of strict rules not only restricts the discretion of officials, but is a clear signal that the relationship is based on distrust rather than mutual trust.[35] The costs of one approach or another are likely to be a significant factor in settling the nature of the relationship. Punitive approaches encourage mutual hostility and incite the implementee to exploit legal loopholes, to resort to literal compliance rather than substantive.[36] A softer, more persuasive approach enables officials to 'coax and caress fidelity to the spirit of the law even where the law has gaps and loopholes'.[37]

Inside organizations

The internal character of an organization and relations among organizations are another set of factors in implementation. A full treatment would take us far into the nature of organizations, while our purposes are served by taking note of just a few main features. Of special note is the extent to which one set of officials depends on another set, or is subject to its scrutiny or review. The dependence of one set of officials on another is likely to influence the approach it takes to implementation, although

---

[34] G. Richardson admirably discusses these matters in *Policing Pollution*.

[35] See: J. Black, *Rules and Regulators*.

[36] See: J. Ayres and J. Braithwaite, op. cit., p. 27; on literal or creative compliance, see: D. McBarnet, *Crime, Compliance, and Control* (Aldershot, 2004).

[37] J. Ayres and J. Braithwaite, ibid., p. 27.

precisely how depends on the nature of the dependence. Officials who are free of such dependence are likely to act differently and to develop their own distinctive approach to implementation. Such freedom should be rare in modern legal orders, where extensive checks on the behaviour of officials is a basic feature, although the practical workings often fall short of the ideal. Where there is such freedom, it would not be surprising to find officials displaying a tendency to discover discretion where it is not obvious, and using it freely.[38] Lobster-fishing inspectors feel the effects of court supervision and bridle at not being able to apply the law themselves, having instead to prove the infringement in court.[39] The evidence, while convincing to the inspectors, is prone to fall below judicial standards; due process considerations also means more to the courts than to the inspectors. Apart from being frustrated by the experience, inspectors were driven to emphasize softer strategies of compliance through co-operation and persuasion. Consumer affairs officials have a similar experience; prosecutions have to be proved in court where the law is interpreted and applied more strictly than by the officials who tend to simplify it. The court system itself is far from uniform, with magistrates showing more understanding than higher courts of officials and their work.[40]

Relations within agencies between officers and managers are complex and significant; officers are expected to follow the policies of managers, who may overturn decisions on specific matters. Internal hierarchies and managerial strategies, which appear in complex and varied forms, add another layer to the social setting of organizations. Another set of relations occurs where the decisions of one set of officials are subject to appeal to another. Social welfare awards made by adjudication officers are subject to appeal to a tribunal, but only on narrow grounds; the claimant does not appear at the hearing, although the officer whose decision is in question does, a factor undoubtedly relevant to the way decisions are made in the first place.[41] The implementation process often involves different sets of officials working together, or perhaps against each other. A study of the regulation of gaming and betting shows the intricate relations between inspectors, their superiors, and the Gaming

---

[38] See for further discussion; R. Lempert, 'Discretion in a Behavioral Context' op. cit., p. 195.

[39] J. C. McMullan and D. C. Perrier, op. cit.

[40] R. Cranston, *Consumers and the Law*, pp. 46 *ff.*

[41] See: J. Baldwin, N. Wikeley, and R. Young, *Judging Social Security*, (Oxford, 1989) pp. 70 *ff.*

Board.[42] Despite a legal regime of strict standards, implementation is portrayed as a complex pattern composed of different kinds of decisions made by different officials at various stages.

Numerous other variables affect the workings of government organizations and much could be said about them; for our purposes the discussion must now end here, subject to brief concluding remarks. My purpose in these two chapters has been to provide an account of the implementation of the law by officials, the emphasis being on officials within administrative organizations applying the law to others with a view to securing their compliance. The emphasis could have been placed on other implementing bodies such as courts, or on how non-governmental organizations induce compliance in others. Much of what has been said about administrative bodies applies to other organizations, with suitable adjustments being made to take account of any special features. The account given here should be seen as a practical and down-to-earth application of the more general ideas about law in society developed in the earlier part of the book. Matters such as the character of legal rules, and the relationship between commitment to the legal order as a whole and dealing with specific laws, are very much in evidence here; the earlier account of social spheres, and their role in the reception of law, also has a major part in understanding implementation. And finally, in discussing the more practical issues of implementation, I have been guided by the framework of analysis developed earlier, which distinguishes between the legal design, the legal environment, and the fuller social environment. Implementation revolves around the recognition of these three aspects and the intricate relations among them.

NOTES

Legal environment

The two approaches to enforcement, strict application of legal rules on the one hand, a more accommodating approach on the other hand, is well-stated by in a study of implementation of environmental health law: see B. Hutter, *The Reasonable Arm of the Law* (Oxford, 1988). She writes: 'Such assumptions [that offenders are good and respectable] foster an accommodative approach to enforcement, since good respectable, fundamentally honest people are generally considered to be in need of advice and education.' (p.179)

[42] D. Miers, op. cit.

G. Richardson, in her study referred to in the text, writes: 'A series of enforcement devices which proceeded gradually from gentle persuasion to the more overt use of the formal law were commonly employed. Only in extremely rare cases was the ultimate legal sanction of criminal prosecution used (*Policing Pollution*, p. 124).

One of the most significant contributions to understanding law's environment is that of Lauren Edelman, who in a series of articles has shown its importance in particular relation to compliance by firms with due process laws. The difference between her account and mine is that I separate the legal environment into the law itself and then the environment the law creates for anyone who has to comply with or implement it. The reason for this approach is that the character of the law itself, its great internal variety and the problems and uncertainties it creates, is important and made more visible.

See: L. Edelman, 'Legal Environments and Organizational Governance: The Expansion of Due process in the American Workplace' (1990), 95 *American Journal of Sociology* 1401 and 'Legal Ambiguity and Symbolic Structures: Organizational Mediation of Civil Rights Law' (1992) 97 *American Journal of Sociology* 1531.

Social context of implementation

The literature on how organizations carry out their mandates is extensive and has influenced my approach. That literature has become interconnected with another stream, which is more specifically concerned with the institutional aspects of organizations, that is, their cognitive and normative character.

Among the sources that have been most useful here should be included the following:

J. March and H. Simon, *Organizations* (Oxford, 1993).

R. M. Cyert and J. G. March, *A Behavioral Theory of the Firm*, (Cambridge, Mass, 1992).

J. Meyer and W. R. Scott (eds), *Organizational Environments: Ritual and Rationality* (London, 1983).

On the more legal side, Philip Selznick's study of the Tennessee Valley Authority is of special note: P. Selznick, op. cit.

The research of Lauren Edelman, referred to above, is also most helpful in bringing the traditions of writing on organizations and institutions to bear on law.

More recently, Fiona Haines has drawn-on these bodies of literature in her illuminating study of compliance by corporations: F. Haines, op. cit.

Social context: attitudes and understandings

R. Cranston shows how the self-perception of consumer agencies as advisers rather than enforcers has an impact on the whole edifice of consumer protection: op. cit., p. 173.

A study of health and safety at work reinforces the emphasis officials put on consensus and cooperation: R. Baldwin, 'Health and Safety at Work' in R. Baldwin and C. Mc Crudden (eds), *Regulation and Public Law*.

The notion of an informal regulatory contract between regulator and regulatee, according to which the regulator does not interfere in the detailed operations, provided the regulatee complies with the spirit of the law; see: J. Black, op. cit., p. 136.

Normative structure of implementation

The suggestion is often made that implementing bodies have extensive discretion, and at the same time are given minimal direct guidance from the law as to how to use it; see: K. Yeung, op. cit., p. 26.

R. Lempert discusses the different attitudes different sets of officials have to the law and how that affects their interpretation of it: 'Discretion in a Behavioural Perspective' in K. Hawkins, op. cit.

Lempert also notes that perhaps the most significant feature of discretion is that it permits officials to formulate their own rules about how matters should be dealt with: 'Discretion in a Behavioral Perspective' p. 226.

The tendency for officials to modify and creatively interpret the law is a common feature of numerous studies. Cranston's study of consumer advice shows how officials were able to create discretion where none was directly given, the purpose being to enable them to restrict the use of prosecution to serious cases, while trying to reach co-operative results in lesser cases; see: R. Cranston, op. cit., p. 106.

This is not always the case: sets of officials, especially in courts or court-like bodies, are just as likely to take a stricter and more literal approach to the law. They may even underestimate the extent to which they have discretion. A study of social welfare found that the appeal tribunals adopted an approach of this kind, in contrast to adjudication officers who tended to simplify the law in order to achieve their aims : J. Baldwin, N. Wikeley, and R. Young, op. cit., pp. 72, 98 *ff.*

Social relations between officials and implementees

Although co-operative relations are desirable, it is not clear that they are more effective in securing compliance than a sanctions-based approach:

R. Cranston, *Consumers and the Law*. Other studies suggest that where the law makes clear the standards to be met, the threat of litigation can be effective. K. Yeung discusses at length the relative merits of the different strategies: *Securing Compliance*, pp 112 *ff*.

Change Through Law: the Contours
of Compliance

17.1 USING LAW TO CHANGE SOCIETY

It is a commonplace of modern societies that law is used to bring about social change. Social change occurs through changing the way people behave individually or in groups and organizations. The use of legislation and judicial decisions to change attitudes and practices concerning discrimination and segregation has probably attracted more attention than any other. In relation to issues of race in the United States, decisions such as *Board of Education v. Brown,* and laws such as the Civil Rights Act, have been much analyzed and discussed to determine what effects they have. Opinions vary. Few doubt that both had some effect on the behaviour of officials and citizens, on government and private bodies, although precisely how much influence they have remains unclear. This is not surprising, considering the difficulties of tracing the impact of a single judicial decision or a new law. But we need not travel abroad to find ample cases of laws aimed at changing behaviour; nor need we select attempts at fundamental social change, such as a system of racial segregation. More limited cases, some quite everyday, show how the process works, what difficulties it confronts, and how successful it is. Wherever we happen to be, examples are all around, with a few chosen randomly from the experience of the United Kingdom illustrating the point. One is a law passed for England and Wales in the early 1980s to regulate the way the police deal with suspects during an investigation.[1] The new standards require the police to act in ways quite at odds with their established practices. We have already considered another law, enacted shortly before, providing better protection for mental health patients who are compulsorily detained and treated.[2] The new standards ran counter to the attitudes and practices of psychiatrists responsible for making decisions about

---

[1] Police and Criminal Evidence Act, 1984.
[2] Mental Health Act, 1983.

patients. A final example is the Human Rights Act of 1998 whose objectives are to require administrative and judicial bodies to adopt practices and procedures that comply with the standards of the European Convention on Human Rights.

Cases like these are notable within a wider trend of enacting new laws to bring about changes in the way officials are required to do their jobs and citizens to arrange their affairs. The very idea of law, regulatory law in particular, is to change the way an activity is conducted; it could mean reducing the discharge of polluting materials, not driving a car without a licence, offering equal opportunities to employees, or a host of other matters, some of everyday interest, others of high significance. Law is at its most regulatory and directive when it sets standards that confront existing social practices and social relations, whether of government officials, professional groups, or private citizens. But it is not only in patently regulatory contexts that law tries to change and direct behaviour; private arrangements and transactions as common as entering contracts, transferring property, or launching a company must follow legal forms and standards. The criminal law is meant to ensure that certain standards of conduct are maintained, while increasingly international covenants stipulate the behaviour expected of nation states. Another familiar use of law is to create new legal regimes where none existed before, to distribute social welfare, for example, with officials being appointed to implement the law and in doing so to comply with its terms.

It is a sign of modern legal orders that law is used to achieve a range of social goals, although its legitimacy in doing so is a matter on which opinions differ. On a more cautious approach, law should reflect existing social relations and their social practices rather than try to change them. The early common law is cited as an example of that approach, which is also close to the outlook of legal pluralists. Enacted laws are often bolder, being instruments not only for reflecting social relations as they spontaneously occur, but also changing them in accordance with other interests and values. Regulatory law is the symbol of modern law and the sign of a bolder approach to its use in bringing about social change. By its nature, it lays down standards that tend to compete and conflict with existing practices, standards that are aimed at changing behaviour rather than reinforcing it. My object in this chapter is not to revisit the arguments for and against the role of law in modern legal systems; instead, accepting that role as one of their defining features, my intention is to consider what happens when a set of laws aimed at changing behaviour confronts established attitudes and practices, for therein lies the key to law's bringing about social change. The focus is the process of interaction between the two, rather than the impact in any particular case, the idea being that the process has a structure, which, once uncovered, can be used for enquiring into specific cases. The task of uncovering the structure is made easier by the availability of an array of empirical studies which are used liberally.

17.2 FRAMEWORK OF COMPLIANCE

The focus here shifts from officials, whose task it is to encourage or coerce others into complying, to those who are required to comply, including private citizens, whether individually or in associations and organizations, and other officials, who not only have to implement the law against others but have duties of compliance themselves. The framework for the reception of law and, therefore, compliance has already been laid, and has the following features. *First,* there is the issue of what the law requires: its architecture. *Secondly,* there is the legal environment experienced by those expected to comply, where the issue is: what action has to be taken in order to comply? *Thirdly,* how is law received within the fuller social environment? How does it fit within the social spheres of the people or entities required to comply? How are competition and conflicts with existing practices and understandings dealt with? What other factors enter into consideration?

Each of these issues is approached from within the social spheres of the person or entity faced with compliance, a notion whose features should by now be clear, but perhaps a reminder is in order. A social sphere is a web of understanding and conventions, within whose parameters much of human endeavour takes place. The way we view an issue and the way we deal with it, are influenced by the conventions and understandings of our social spheres. The foundation stone of social spheres is social relations, social relations between private parties, between private parties and officials, and among officials. Social relations refer to the manner in which one party interacts with another; they revolve around such social formations as the family, property, and employment; they include the way officials treat citizens and how officials work together within government organizations. Social relations generate conventions and understandings which, in turn, express the relations and guide behaviour in relation to them. Social spheres also respond to other influences, including moral and religious ideas, professional training, organizational structures, and political considerations. The list is not exhaustive, but is meant to convey the idea that, around the foundation of social relations, other factors influence them, some from within, others from outside. Social spheres are the vehicle for translating various features of the social world into a reasonably coherent set of conventions and understanding. When a set of laws tries to influence behaviour, it encounters social spheres, and is understood and acted upon from within social spheres. Social spheres influence the interpretation of the law; they guide the determination of what needs to be done and how it is to be done. Compliance is most easily accomplished when legal standards are compatible with the existing pattern of social relations, and so can be absorbed easily into existing social spheres. Conversely, the results are more uneven when social relations and social spheres have to be changed in order to absorb legal standards.

The encounter between legal standards and social spheres is illustrated in the following two cases. The first, concerning psychiatrists, is familiar: laws enacted to give better protection to patients compulsorily detained and treated have met resistance from the psychiatrists, who are responsible for deciding whether compulsion is necessary and when the patients are ready for release.[3] The measures are aimed at protecting the civil rights of patients 'against unjustified therapy or deprivation of their civil liberty'.[4] We noted earlier the tension psychiatrists experience between the legal provisions protecting patients and the clinical assessment that treatment is necessary. As a result, the social world of psychiatrists has difficulty absorbing the law and reformulating its relations with patients. The second example comes from a different culture: in recent years, the Japanese legislature passed an equal opportunity law aimed at eliminating discrimination in employment, the main victims of which are women and ethnic minorities. The law had to confront the social spheres of companies and other employers, where a strong male ethos prevailed with the support of entrenched attitudes, conventions, and practices.[5] Working on the assumption that a coercive, enforcement-based approach would have little impact on this social world, the legislature sought to bring about compliance by softer mechanisms. These include the voluntary resolution of complaints, mediation, and the co-operation of government and administration in issuing guidelines aimed at coaxing employers to change their ways. How successful the laws are is still debatable, for although supported by the constitutional entrenchment of equality, they

---

[3] Discussed in chapter 6.   [4] N. Eastman and J. Peay, op. cit., p. 4.
[5] Well-described in L. Parkinson, 'Japan's Equal Employment Opportunity Law: An Alternative Approach to Social Change' (1989), 89 *Columbia Law Review* 604.

encounter deep-seated opposition from the social spheres of employment which are, in turn, based on deeper social norms and attitudes. The diversity and flexibility that women and minorities would introduce, according to one commentator, would not only need fundamental changes to the workplace but would: 'threaten to destroy the social and psychological basis of Japan's political stability and economic success'.[6]

The encounter between law and social spheres is not always one of competition and incompatibility; acceptance can be smooth and uncontested, with several intermediate positions between the two. The purpose of this chapter is to examine this intersection of law and social spheres, while identifying other variables that gather around and influence the process. But first a few general points to note. One is to be reminded that social spheres, being based on social relations and the attitudes and conventions of the men and women who experience them, are always subject to change and modification. Social spheres tend towards autonomy and closure from outside influences and vary in their density; but they are open to influence from the wider environment. A second point follows: compliance with law is not generally a once-and-for-all or all-or-nothing matter; it is often more-or-less, stronger or weaker; it is approached through the use of different mechanisms, and where one fails another might succeed. Finally, the success of law in changing behaviour depends on several factors, each of which is liable to have an effect, the main ones being the character and strength of the legal environment, the density of social spheres, and their capacity to absorb outside standards and make adjustments in accordance with them. Against this background, we now turn to the main variables in the process of compliance.

17.3 LEGAL CONSCIOUSNESS

The image presented so far could encourage the idea that law is an external force whose aim is to change social relations and the social spheres expressing them. The image, so far as it goes, is accurate, as the cases of the psychiatrists and the Japanese employers show. In both cases, a set of legal standards is directed at changing the way the former treat patients, the latter women and minorities. That the image does not go far enough becomes clear when we consider the links between law and social relations, which are intertwined, as the discussion in chapter 4 shows. There we saw how law at its most elemental, rather than being handed

[6] F. K. Upham, op. cit., p. 214.

down from above, is the expression of social relations, and in that sense grows from the ground up. We also saw how spontaneous social relations persist in modern legal systems, despite the dominance of enacted law and its lack of social roots. Between social relations and enacted law, a complex and often tense situation occurs. Social relations generate their own social practices, practices that in a primitive sense constitute law. They exert influence on the making of enacted law and its application. The law in its many forms – enacted, common law, judicial rulings – expresses and reinforces social relations and practices in countless ways. At the same time, enacted law tries to change them. Both the complexity and the tension are displayed in the character of the Japanese workplace: it is constituted by social relations and practices, which are embedded socially and expressed and supported by sets of laws. At the same time, other sets of laws seek to change them.[7] The same should be said of psychiatry, and indeed of other sets of social relations, covering such disparate relations as property rights, employment contracts, and the way in which officials use their powers. All such relations are a combination of spontaneous social engagement and its expression and reinforcement by law. When new laws try to change the way people or entities behave, they encounter not only bare social relations and practices, but also the legal concepts and frameworks in which they are encased. Bringing about change in behaviour is hard enough; when the law itself legitimizes and fortifies the behaviour it is harder still.

The notion of *legal consciousness* is often invoked to convey the idea that law enters into social relations and practices through several openings. Enacted laws imposed from the outside are dominant in modern legal orders, but closer scrutiny shows how they are still only part of the fuller social reality in which law infiltrates social relations and practices in different ways by different means. We had an inkling of this idea before in the claim that law *structures society;*[8] we now see its point. It is not clear that *legal consciousness*, whose popularity outshines its utility, and whose emphasis on attitudes is misleading, needs be introduced to understand the ways in which law affects social relations, practices, and attitudes. Whether we use the notion or not, it alerts attention to a diffusion of law and legal ideas that merits further consideration. The *first* and most fundamental sense of legal consciousness is the elemental notion of law expressed in social relations, as it appears in traditional societies and the

[7] This is well shown by F. K. Upham in his excellent book *Law and Social Change in Postwar Japan.*
[8] Section *12.1*

early common law. According to that notion, the very expression of relations is an expression of law; and if, in a modern legal order, that attribution is out of place, the social reality and its importance remain intact. It is, moreover, not merely an historical curiosity, as is amply shown by considering how influential social relations, practices, and the attitudes supporting them are in the formation and application of enacted law.

A *second* sense of legal consciousness of near equal rank, but coming from above rather than below, refers to the way officials and citizens regard the legal order as binding. That both share a sense of commitment to the law, even though some variation among them is to be expected, is a defining element of modern legal orders and a recurrent theme in this book. Social spheres are the medium within which attitudes to law are formed. Different groups have different levels of commitment as earlier examples show. The sense of commitment to the legal order as a whole is a major influence on people's attitudes to specific laws, which may be considered a *third* meaning of legal consciousness. The attitudes people hold towards specific laws vary according to whether it is their behaviour that is subject to the law or someone else's. If they accept the authority of the legal system as a whole, they accept the authority of specific laws. Acceptance in principle then has to be put into practice, at which point other factors enter the arena. The issue then is how strong commitment to the law is in the face of competing factors. This sense of legal consciousness could be extended to those who are not directly affected by a particular law, but have views about it. Two cases of such laws are topical as I write, one to ban smoking in restaurants, the other allowing for the detention of terrorist suspects for long periods. Laws such as these cause strong reactions, not only in those who are directly affected, but also in observers. And the reason they do so is the threat they pose, or are perceived as posing, to settled social relations and practices, which are likely to be supported by a diversity of other laws. Studies show that how people experience and think about such matters as the criminal law, laws regarding offensive speech, restricting corporate behaviour, or guiding the social welfare system, are salient in revealing this sense of legal consciousness.

A *fourth* sense, consisting in an extension of the *third,* is advanced by the constitutional lawyer A. V. Dicey, when he wrote that the main importance of law is not its direct object but the effect it has 'on the sentiment or conviction of the public'.[9] He used the Reform Act of 1832 as an example.

[9] A. V. Dicey, *The Law of the Constitution* (E. C. S. Wade (ed), London, 1961), p. 79.

The direct legal change effected by the Act was the relatively minor matter of giving the vote to a limited class of people, but the effect on public opinion was of 'transcendent importance', for the enfranchising of one group was an irreversible step towards full enfranchisement. Minor changes to the voting laws effected a revolution of the English Constitution. In terms of legal consciousness, apart from their direct objectives, laws may change the way people think about wider issues, and create in them new expectations beyond the law itself. Support for Dicey's claim comes from such different contexts as anti-smoking laws in Japan[10] and judicial declarations against racial discrimination in the United States.[11]

A *fifth* sense of legal consciousness refers to the way people absorb ideas about law, either directly from their own experience or indirectly through the conventions and understandings of their social spheres. Views about what the law is or what it dictates, often mistaken views, are formed from a range of sources. Absorption can be either conscious and deliberate, or unconscious in the sense that one does not realize it is happening. A law student deliberately sets out to assimilate legal ideas, and a police officer has to master some law in order to do his job; on the other hand, the knowledge of law one gains from watching a film with a legal theme is more likely to be unintended and, in that sense, unconscious.

The way individuals and groups regard the law as an instrument for advancing their ends is the *sixth* and final sense of legal consciousness. This sense is sometimes linked to disadvantaged groups, such as an indigenous population in a post-colonial society, which has been excluded or alienated from law and legal remedies, but comes to view them as useful instruments in furthering their cause. Other marginal groups often share similar experiences. It is said in relation to them that their legal consciousness has been raised, meaning simply their realization that the law and its processes can be an effective weapon. Some say there is a growing tendency among such groups to use the law to advance their causes, sometimes after a history of rejecting that approach. The use of law to advance individual or group interests in this way is not new, with many groups and interests, from the weak to the powerful, taking advantage of it. The powerful and better-organized are likely to see this as normal, and in that sense have a more developed legal consciousness. A

---

[10] E. A. Feldman, 'The Landscape of Japanese Tobacco Policy: Law, Smoking and Social Change' (2001) 49 *American Journal of Comparative Law* 679.

[11] S. Sheingold, op. cit.

recent study shows how at this moment media groups are using the law to gain control of the internet.[12]

17.4 A SETTLED DISPOSITION TO COMPLY WITH THE LAW

Legal consciousness proves to be a fertile notion, but it is not the easiest to use to any clear purpose. Its several senses all help to illuminate the way law influences social relations, practices, and attitudes. The *second* and *third* senses are of special interest for our present purposes, a sense nicely captured in Hart's *settled disposition* to follow the law. The strength or weakness of that disposition is a significant variable in the process of compliance. Officials have that settled disposition in modern legal orders and share a commitment to uphold the law, although the strength of their commitment varies. Citizens, I have suggested, must also have a threshold of commitment in order to sustain modern legal orders. That the level of commitment may stretch to vanishing point is shown in a recent study of migrants from one part of China attempting to live and work in another.[13] The law for them meant nothing more than a set of factors to deal with, either as aids or as hindrances, in pursuing their ambition of being able to conduct business away from their native province. How well the disposition of respect for the law takes root is subject to wider social factors, and can be absent in some societies. Those emerging from a prolonged period of totalitarianism are likely to have low levels of commitment from both officials and citizens, as recent studies of attitudes to law in countries of the former Soviet Union show.[14] Negative attitudes towards law limit its effectiveness, whereas in a strong legal environment, respect for law is displayed in many aspects of social life.

From the fact that a social sphere displays general respect for law in its understandings and norms, it does not follow that specific laws are necessarily accepted. The discussion in chapter 7 shows how a general commitment to the system creates a presumption of compliance with specific laws; but being a presumption its priority over competing factors

---

[12] L. Lessig, *Free Culture: How Big media Uses Technology to Lock Down Culture and Control Creativity* (New York, 2004).

[13] Xin He, 'Why Do They Not Comply with the Law? Illegality and Semi-Illegality among the Rural-Urban Migrant Enterpreneurs in Beijing', (2005), 39 *Law and Society Review*.

[14] D. J. Galligan and M. Kurkchiyan, op. cit.

is not guaranteed. Individual persons and groups may regard the law as binding in a general way, and yet on occasions display a low level of compliance with particular laws. The explanation is simply that, despite the general commitment, compliance with particular laws encounters obstacles: these may be of a very practical kind, such as lack of resources to do what the law requires; or there may be incompatibility between the norms and practices of their social spheres and the law. The general commitment to obey the law 'because it is the law' is shown by Ayres and Braithwaite in their study of corporations; in the face of specific laws, considerations of profit compete with their sense of social responsibility.[15] They write: 'business executives have profit-maximizing selves and law-abiding selves; at different moments, in different contexts, the different selves prevail'.[16] The success of the law depends on how well the incompatibility with other factors is overcome, a matter which often takes time, and whose outcome is as likely to be an accommodation between the two as an outright victory for the law. The settled disposition to follow the law is a factor weighing in the balance, but how much weight it carries in the face of more compelling and immediate concerns is highly variable.

17.5 LEGAL ARCHITECTURE AGAIN

With the image in mind of law entering into social spheres at two levels, one in a general and indirect way influencing their cognitive and normative structure, the other seeking directly to bring about change to that environment, we now turn to consider other variables in the process of compliance. The law itself is the place to start and we need not repeat the reasons, except to remind ourselves of several points. One concerns the form the law takes. Despite all that has been said to the contrary, in unguarded moments we are still inclined to think of laws as clear and precise directions as to what should be done. Some take that form, but many others are expressed as standard-based or discretionary rules. The powers of the police in maintaining public order are a good example: if they decide a breach of the peace is occurring or threatened, a matter left to their judgement, the police are authorized to take a range of actions, the precise form of which is also left to their discretion, as are questions as to when they should adopt one rather than another. The law confers

---

[15] J. Ayres and J. Braithwaite, op. cit., p. 24. See also R. Cranston, op. cit., p. 170 where it is said that some businesses act out of social responsibility, others do not. It is suggested that in the absence of enforcement, a business acts rationally in not complying.

[16] *Ibid*, p. 31.

such wide powers that the real issue in practice is whether the police choose to use them and how.[17]

Even clear-line rules have to be interpreted, which means reaching into their social context, where the understandings and contingencies depend on who is engaged in interpretation, and their standpoint.[18] Judges of the House of Lords, the highest court in the United Kingdom, in deciding whether administrative bodies have exercised their powers according to legal principles, bring to the task a set of understandings and conventions from outside the law which shape their approach.[19] If superior court judges are swayed in this way, then how much more likely it is that other groups of officials and citizens will be guided in interpreting the law by the conventions and understandings of their social spheres. The interpretive process allows for the re-assertion of social relations that appear to be damaged or distorted by the law; it also allows for other factors to enter into consideration. Among many examples that could be cited to illustrate this point, an attempt by the Indonesian legislature to control aspects of family life, especially unilateral divorce, polygamy, and child marriages, is striking.[20] The law has had little success in prohibiting child marriages because the Muslim community interprets it according to Islamic doctrine, and in doing so leaves customary practices intact.[21] The community denies the legislature has any right to interfere in family matters, and interprets the law in a way intended to protect existing social relations. Interpreting a law out of existence is naturally more attractive than breaking it. Questions of compliance tend to merge into the prior one of what is required by the law, and control over interpretation makes it easier to ensure that what the law requires is compatible with, or needs only minimal changes to, existing practices.

Not only does the law itself often allow scope for creative interpretation, it may be uncertain, incomplete, and contradictory. A study of how suspects were treated in the criminal justice system found that many of the concerns about their treatment could be traced, not to police malpractice, as often alleged, but to the uncertainties and inadequacies of the law itself.[22] The due process rights of suspects were in jeopardy, mainly

---

[17] See D. J. Galligan, *The Right to Protest* (Inaugural Lecture, University of Southampton, 1986).

[18] The relationship between rules and their social context is examined in chapter 3.

[19] David Robertson, op. cit.

[20] M. Cammack, L. Young, and T. Heaton, 'Legislating Social Change in an Islamic Society – Indonesia's Marriage Law' (1996), 44 *American Journal of Comparative Law* 45.

[21] *Ibid*, p. 61.

[22] See D. McBarnet, *Conviction, the State, and the Construction of Justice* (London, 1983).

because the law did not properly provide for them: it was vague, incomplete, and uncertain, allowing the police and other agencies latitude as to how they behaved without breaking the law. As D. McBarnet's research shows, it was not only uncertainty and vagueness in the law, but also gaps that explain what happened. L. Edelman has come to similar conclusions concerning the way employers dealt with laws against discrimination.[23] The law gave little guidance as to what constitutes 'discrimination', so that employers were able legally to take a minimalist approach. They could then satisfy their legal obligations by adopting procedural adjustments and work-force reporting requirements, rather than make substantive changes in employment practices. The courts are responsible for clarifying laws that are unclear, but judicial rulings occur sporadically, and here the courts failed to take opportunities to make the law more certain. The outcome was that non-discrimination standards had only marginal impact on the social context of employment.

17.6 DEALING WITH THE LEGAL ENVIRONMENT

The legal environment in relation to compliance has two elements. One is the familiar one of an environment created by law in which those subject to it have to decide what is required in order to comply with it. The other adds as an extra dimension the strength of the legal environment, strength meaning here how compelling the law is in comparison with competing factors. The first of these elements is the reverse of the official who has to decide how to implement the law; here the issue is what the implementee has to do to meet its demands. The answer may be as simple as: pay the tax, get a driving licence, or deliver the goods under the contract. It soon becomes more complicated, as is clear by asking such questions as: how much tax is due or what does delivery mean? And as the law moves from clear-line rules to general standards, such as a safe environment or non-discrimination at work, the uncertainty is compounded; and if it depends on an official's discretion, what is required may be a matter of guesswork.

In unravelling this aspect of the legal environment, several points of guidance stand out. In the first place, complying parties are not passive recipients of the law, but construe it against a background of

---

[23] L. Edelman, 'Legal ambiguity and symbolic structures' (1992) *American Journal of Sociology* 531.

understandings and expectations about the law itself. Laws perceived as procedurally unfair, or as not being applied consistently and impartially, incite resistance.[24] The architectural metaphor teaches another lesson: laws, like buildings, need to be well-planned and well-constructed if they are to win approval and encourage compliance. Another important aspect is whether the party complying is a 'repeat player' (to borrow a useful expression) who knows from experience what is expected, rather than one whose encounter with officials is once only. What is expected in turn emerges from a pattern of relations with the implementing officials, for what constitutes compliance may simply be whatever satisfies them. Officials develop informal rules and understandings, some of which are open and public, while others become known only as the relationship develops. Around the legal standards, a world of informal norms and understandings is created. Officials sometimes dictate and others obey, although continuing relations between the two tend to be dynamic, with accommodation, bargaining, and compromise, common components in the way discussed in 16.3. The complying parties are naturally keen to protect their interests and to construe their duties accordingly. How zealous they are in doing so depends on various factors, including their sense of social responsibility, one measure of which is whether their incentive is the spirit of the law or its letter.

Attention to the letter of the law, generally known as *formalism*, is now sometimes replaced by the more evocative notion of *creative compliance* to depict the process by which the law is interpreted in the narrowest way possible, and the action taken the least tolerable. Creative compliance has a pejorative edge and is a hair's breadth away from manipulation, although the one does not necessarily mean or lead to the other.[25] The approach depicted in creative compliance has the consequence that complying parties do not properly assimilate into their social spheres the point and purpose of the law. It remains, instead, an external influence, intruding on a social world where it is unwelcome, encouraging what has been aptly called a 'paper response' rather than a substantive one.[26] At the same time, it cannot be said that minimizing law's impact through a formalist approach is never justified; laws can be foolish, ill-conceived, and unworkable, provoking parties to exploit whatever strategies of

---

[24] A point illustrated in N. Gunningham and R. Johnstone, *op. cit.*, p. 5.

[25] Doreen McBarnet has developed the notion of *creative compliance* in her research; see D. McBarnet, op. cit.

[26] N. Gunningham and R. Johnstone, op. cit., p. 74. The contrast between formal and substantive responses to law is well-discussed in: F. Haines, op. cit., pp. 166, 191*ff*

avoidance are available. Creative compliance is not the only way of doing so. One group of school administrators was so frustrated by the flush of court decisions, civil rights legislation, and federal and state regulations, all interfering with the effective and orderly running of schools as they saw it, that they devised ways of neutralizing the effects. Ignorance of the law was one, selective attention to the law another, and the 'force of institutional inertia' a third.[27]

Studies of regulation emphasize the advantages of moving on from the command-and-control approach and the opportunities it both provides and encourages for formalism. Clear-line rules, especially if backed by zealous officials, are prone to incite a formal, minimalist response from the complying parties, who may regard strict rules as a sign of distrust by officials.[28] The reverse is that strict rules are sometimes wholly justified, properly leave little room for discretion or negotiation, and should be rigorously enforced.[29] Some contexts are more suitably regulated by open standards and elements of discretion, encouraging a more spirit-of-the-law approach, which in turn directs attention to its point and purpose, puts it more closely in touch with the underlying social relations, and allows for a substantive response from the complying party. What is sacrificed by way of clear and crisp rules is gained by a longer-term prospect for co-operation and real change on the part of the complying party. The optimum outcome in the longer term is often put in terms of internalization, meaning here the assimilation of legal standards into its organizational and institutional setting, the acceptance at a systemic level of law's point and purpose. More open legal regimes also have distinct disadvantages and, instead of encouraging co-operation, may have the opposite effect. Divergent understandings of what the law demands, and what constitutes compliance, may lead to hostility and suspicion, to conflict rather than consensus, to the point of ending up in court. A different risk is that open standards and discretion allow the parties to seek solutions that are as much a departure from the purposes of the law as is acute formalism.

The effective realization of law's purposes is more probable when both parties, officials and those complying, are in agreement as to what is required and how best to achieve it. The potential for agreement between

---

[27] D.Tynack et al, *Law and the Shaping of Public Education* (Madison, 1991).

[28] J. Black, op. cit.

[29] When strict rules and strict enforcement are or should be the preferred strategies raises important issues of institutional design; for further discussion see: D. J. Galligan, *Discretionary Powers*.

the parties, or at least for constructive dialogue, is an attraction of open legal regimes. They open the way for relations to develop between the parties, often for the long term; they invite the softer measures of discussion and negotiation, accommodation and compromise. The natural appeal of soft measures is warranted by their effectiveness in reducing conflict, and in achieving harmony between the law's demands and the internal structure of complex organizations. Agreement, and the softer measures naturally accompanying it, also has its dark side. Whether agreement is a good thing depends on what is agreed; bad outcomes are not improved by agreement. Harmony easily slips into collusion, while close relations between powerful organizations and accommodating officials are at risk of inducing compromise and even capture. A final, and perhaps the most serious risk, is that the law itself is subverted: in the name of consensus, legal standards and the values supporting them are compromised beyond toleration. Subversion is sometimes justified, but normally the faithful application of the law is a social good of considerable worth; agreement between the parties is not then necessarily the most desirable goal, nor need it be the only one.

An alternative that is now gaining support could take the European Union's notion of a *directive* as its model. A directive is a law made according to the procedures of the EU, which is addressed to member states, stating the policies to be implemented, but leaving it to each member state to determine for itself how best to do so. The European Commission involves itself in the process, offering advice, encouragement, and the ultimate threat of enforcement. The adoption of a similar approach in areas of domestic regulation is often advocated, the general idea being that the law should specify the outcomes and then leave it to the other party to decide how to achieve them.[30] In practical terms, it means telling a firm not that it must obey a set of clear-line rules, but rather develop a system, culture, and structure that guarantees, for instance, the safety of its workers, or equal opportunities, or a reduction in the level of under-age drinking.[31] Regulation according to legal standards then becomes so close to self-regulation as to be indistinguishable, which in turn has both its virtues and its vices.

We see from this brief account how parties make sense of a legal regime with which they have to comply; we see the variable factors in their

---

[30] For discussion, see: Z. Mikdashi, *Regulating the Financial Sector in the Era of Globalization* (London, 2003) pp. *xxii ff.*

[31] See further: F. Haines, *Corporate Regulation*, pp. 164, 191 and N. Gunningham and R. Johnstone, op. cit., pp. 5, 141*ff.*

forming a view of what is required and how to achieve it. Enough has been said to show how these issues are sometimes straightforward but more often are not; different ways of approaching compliance soon appear, while the decision as to which to take, and how to handle such matters as relations with officials, themselves depend on other factors. Understanding the legal environment is not the final step in the process of compliance but, despite its unwieldiness, an essential step.

17.7 STRENGTH OF THE LEGAL ENVIRONMENT

Another aspect of the legal environment is its strength. Strength means several things. The case of zero-tolerance policing is an example of a strong legal environment; it means the police arrest or take other action against everyone who is suspected of breaking the law, so that anyone thinking of doing so has a strong incentive to refrain. By contrast, where it is known that the law is not enforced or is enforced only exceptionally, or that the sanctions are minor, the legal environment is weak. Between the extremes of zero-tolerance policing and non-enforcement, the strength of each legal environment can be assessed. The attitudes of officials and the likelihood of enforcement is a key variable, but not the only one; the chances of detection and the nature and severity of the remedies are also relevant. Where enforcement depends on officials having to prove the case in court, another set of factors is introduced into the calculation of strength, while a further factor is whether raising a complaint or bringing an action depends on a third party. Laws riddled with gaps and ambiguities are likely to contribute to weakness.

The plight of mental health patients compulsorily detained and treated is scarcely relieved by law because of the weakness of the legal environment meant to protect them. Social support for the well-being of patients was strong enough to find expression in the law, but the level of protection gained in practice is low, especially when pitted against the social spheres of psychiatrists. The weakness is explained on several grounds: remedies have to be sought by the patients themselves or on their behalf; the decision-making process, at both primary and appeal levels, is dominated by psychiatrists; while recourse to the courts is difficult to mount. It is not surprising, given the powerlessness of the patients and despite the efforts of interest groups, themselves hardly powerful, that the law has made only modest impact on the practices of mental health regimes. A weak legal environment may over time be strengthened, as seen in the case of environmental pollution, where early attempts at regulation created only a weak environment. Groups favouring regulation for reasons of conservation or environmental protection were in their formative stages, while the public was neither well-informed nor all that interested. The polluters were often powerful organizations with economic incentives to resist regulation. As more is learnt about pollution and its harmful consequences, the legal environment has strengthened; attitudes have hardened, the moral and social basis of pollution is better understood, and interest groups are better organized.[32] If extensive legal intervention in social relations is a defining feature of modern societies, then the strengthening of legal environments should be its companion in arms. Strength is a factor of such matters as the normative structure, the procedures for enforcement, and the remedies available; it also depends on the attitudes and approaches of the implementing officials.

The factors so far described are not the only ones determining the strength or weakness of the legal environment. That less tangible and more indirect factors that legal processes contribute is illustrated by a study of the effects of due process laws in the workplace.[33] The laws were enacted to ensure the fair treatment of workers, in whom they created, together with interest groups representing them and the public, expectations as to what constitutes fair treatment. The combination of factors created a strong environment around the laws, which put pressure on employers to respond by adopting the new measures, and incorporating them into employment practices. Their motivation was not so much the threat of legal action, but that the failure to meet public expectations about good practices and fair treatment could have a harmful effect on the enterprise. The harm itself could be diverse in its effects, including public opprobrium, conflict with interest groups, and dissatisfied workers.

17.8 DENSITY OF SOCIAL SPHERES AS A VARIABLE

The encounter between a set of laws and the social setting of the complying parties is the next step in compliance. The social setting is expressed in one or more social spheres, which are formed around social relations, with various other factors, both internal and external, influencing them. A set of laws is sometimes readily accepted by the members of a social

---

[32] See the discussion in: G. Richardson and others, op. cit.

[33] L. Edelman, 'Legal Environments and Organizational Governance' (1990) *95 American Journal of Sociology* 1401.

sphere and absorbed into its conventions and understandings, so becoming the normal way of doing things. That is most probable when the law is compatible with existing social relations, as they are expressed in the norms and understandings of an association or organization. The opposite happens when law tries to alter social relations; easy absorption is then replaced by competition and confrontation, with individuals, associations, and organizations having to change their practices accordingly. Their sense of social responsibility, their commitment to legal authority, may be strong enough to promote willing adjustments. But compliance is not always so easy or the parties so willing. Major changes to social relations pose real difficulties; existing social relations may be based on deep conviction, strengthened by history, and supported by economic and political structures. The level of compliance with law turns finally on how well social attitudes and practices are adjusted to meet law's demands.

The *density* of social spheres was proposed earlier as a way of expressing the idea that social spheres are more or less open to change, that their internal system of conventions and understandings is more or less open to absorbing outside influences, of which law is one. Attempts in Japan to introduce non-discrimination against women workers encountered social spheres of high density. Workers in Japanese firms, corporations, and public administration are traditionally men, with women kept at bay. This practice is embedded in the social relations of the workplace, and supported by conventions and understandings of high density. The workplace is designed for men; the attitudes of employers and managers are formed on the basis of the workers being men, with matching attitudes against their being women. But its springs run deeper: workplace culture is supported by and expressive of fundamental social relations between men and women in Japanese society, which are themselves confirmed and supported by many areas of law. Workplace practices have powerful support from the economic and political environment and the attitudes accompanying them. It is to be expected that changes proposed by law to the practices of the workplace are not easily absorbed, are resisted, and have only peripheral impact. Social relations are protected by the high-density workplace culture remaining intact.[34] Customary and traditional practices relating to the family and marriage, children and

---

[34] Studies of the Japanese law controlling discrimination against women (and minorities) include L. Parkinson, op. cit. J. S. Fan, op. cit. and T. Hanami, 'Equal Opportunity Revisited', (2000) 39 *Japan Labour Bulletin* 1,200.

property, are other examples of dense social spheres as studies from Indonesia and Israel show. Being the most fundamental social relations of all, they encase themselves in attitudes and practices resistant to outside regulation.

The main variables in setting the density of social spheres can be identified from the study of the workplace in Japan. The cognitive and normative environment, as the principal variable, is formed from several factors. The character of the activity is one factor. The closed environments of police stations, prisons, mental hospitals, and the like are resistant to outside supervision. When that is combined with a sense of high risk, even danger, in doing their jobs, the tendency towards close collaboration and solidarity is apparent; the wearing of uniforms, and possessing powers and privileges of an exceptional kind, strengthen density. The aims and purposes of the activity are another factor, so that groups like the police, which have a strong and shared sense of purpose, tend to develop impenetrable social spheres. Clarity of purpose and high consensus among the members are other factors in developing and strengthening density. The earlier example of teachers passively subverting laws they considered interference in the education of their pupils, is an example of a group whose organization is less dense than those of the police or the military, but whose commitment to its purpose can be effective in resisting threats to it. A similar lesson should be learnt from the psychiatrists whose sense of purpose, combined with professional expertise and buttressed by a clear vision of their relations with patients, produces high density. In the different context of business activities, the collective enterprise of profit-seeking provides a firm foundation for organizational solidarity. Since few things motivate more than the love of money, it is to be expected that businesses dedicated to that end should form dense social spheres. Legal changes attempting to introduce practices counter to the profit motive, such as equal opportunities, anti-discrimination, or greater social responsibility, naturally encounter stiff opposition, unless they can be interpreted as being in the long-term interest of economic prosperity.

The structure of the organization within which common purposes are pursued naturally influences the character of social spheres and their density. The university in which I work is a federation of colleges, departments, faculties, and research institutes. It is high in its commitment to learning, research, and teaching, but low on hierarchy and managerial direction, with a dons' parliament being the ultimate authority. It is committed to the free expression of ideas, celebrates heterodoxy, and allows its members to conduct research into whatever interests them, and to follow wherever it leads. Any attempt to interfere, to change the main aims and purposes, would unite the dons in opposition. But its fragmentation results in an institutional order of low density, which means weak capacity to resist outside intervention. By contrast, organizations which are hierarchical, managerial, and regimented, where one voice speaks for all, are likely to have high social density. Military organizations are striking cases, while business enterprises are more moderate cases. Administrative bodies, in the form of associations of civil servants, lack the profit motive, but have a surrogate of comparable force in the prospect of promotion, power, and the trappings of office. Their professionalism has to be tempered by the needs of government, and in the interests of conformity and obedience; free expression is curtailed, while performance according to settled criteria is paramount. Bureaucratic organizations are likely to generate internal rules and routines that become entrenched, and acquire their own momentum and rationality. They vary in character, but we should generally expect the result to be a dense social environment that is fairly impervious to change, as history and experience tend to show.[35] The main countervailing factor, the secret weapon against this social fortress, may be the strength of commitment of civil servants to the authority of law.

17.9 DEALING WITH THE LAW

One measure of how well an association or organization is able to absorb legal standards is whether the proposed changes are perceived as being in its interests or not. Those that are not are often deflected, neutralized, or complied with formally rather than substantively. Studies of attempts to raise standards protecting the health and safety of workers show the capacity of employers to make just enough changes to meet a threshold of compliance, without embracing a safety culture.[36] Within any association or organization, some matters are more clearly related to its core than others. Standards of an organizational or procedural nature can often be accepted because they do not impinge on vital matters. Procedural changes can normally be accommodated more easily, either because they make no real difference to core activities, or because they

---

[35] See further discussion in: D. J. Galligan, 'Authoritarianism in Government and Administration: The Promise of Administration Justice', 2000 *Current Legal Problems 79*.

[36] F. Haines, *Corporate Regulation*, p. 191ff.

can be neutralized by formal compliance.[37] Procedures directed at preventing discrimination and bringing about equal treatment might be satisfied by the appointment of an equal opportunities officer, whose powers are formal rather then real.[38] Institutions are adept at absorbing laws which are only superficially at odds with existing practices, while those perceived as striking at its core present real problems. Firms value their economic survival and competitiveness over other goals, even if they regard those other goals as commendable. Virtue carries little weight in the face of competitive advantage. However, things are rarely straightforward, with apparently incompatible standards creating new opportunities for improving core practices. L. Edelman has drawn attention to the way private businesses are able to link laws concerning the fair treatment of workers to considerations of efficiency; management came to realize that the workers' perception of being well-treated made the organization more efficient.[39] The employers may have been encouraged in their attitudes by the realization that the costs of change were modest.

First reactions are not always lasting reactions. When laws in England and Wales made fundamental changes to the way in which police forces conduct investigations and treat suspects, the police resisted on the grounds that they ran counter to entrenched attitudes and practices. Considering that police stations are closed institutions, the strength of police culture, and the weakness of judicial control over the police prior to the new law, it might reasonably have been expected that the changes would be problematical. However, the police's attitudes soon changed; they came to see that the procedures, exacting in the duties they imposed for reporting and recording their actions, and insisting on the division of responsibility among officers, protected them as well as suspects. Compliance with the procedures, although irksome, provided a shield against complaints of mistreatment of suspects. As the true consequences of the new law became plain, opposition from the police dissolved and acceptance was encouraged. Other factors, such as more vigorous scrutiny by the courts, may have played a part, but simple self-protection was incentive enough.

---

[37] Although it should not be assumed that procedural changes can always be assimilated into the social sphere; see: G. Richardson and D. Machin, 'Judicial Review and Tribunal Decision-Making: A Study of the Mental Health Review Tribunal' (2000) *Public Law 494*.

[38] See L. Edelman, 'Legal Ambiguity and Symbolic Structures: Organizational Mediation of Civil Rights' (1992), 97 *American Journal of Sociology* 153.

[39] *Ibid.*

Among the factors that influence parties in their attitudes to compliance with legal standards, the moral and social attitudes at large are important. It is often hard to know whether parties have changed their behaviour because the law requires it, or whether they are responding to deeper changes in moral and social attitudes. According to one school of thought, attitudes towards segregation on the basis of colour in the southern United States had already begun to change before the famous rulings of the Supreme Court or the enactment of civil rights legislation.[40] A few such rulings, even from such an influential source, are unlikely to overturn social relations and the attitudes, entrenched over centuries, supporting them. If the process of change has already begun, judicial pronouncements may accelerate it. A set of publicly pronounced standards challenging embedded attitudes and practices becomes a reference point, a benchmark, on the basis of which actions can be evaluated. What begins as conflict and competition between two sets of standards may give way to accommodation, and finally end in absorption of the new and adjustment to the old.

The conferring of rights by law does not bring automatic change, but provides individuals and groups with instruments for undermining existing practices. Public opinion is a powerful influence; being itself influenced by laws, it in turn influences the way individuals and groups deal with law. A study of attempts to control smoking in Japan shows how the legal environment was weak; law and litigation brought under it has had some effect on smoking, but much more important was the stimulus the law gave to informal norms against smoking.[41] Environmental protection laws are another example: laws appear to have influenced public opinion, which in turn reinforces the law and encourages compliance. What was acceptable practice even twenty years ago is no longer so; what was morally ambiguous is now condemned.[42] The same could probably be said for the well-being of workers, where considerable progress has been made since the first attempts at regulating the workplace, although standards of equal treatment and non-discrimination lag behind, partly because the attitudes of the public about these matters are still equivocal.

---

[40] A recent assessment of the debate surrounding these issues is contained in: D. A. Schultz (ed), *Leveraging the Law: Using the Courts to Achieve Social Change* (New York, 1998).

[41] E. A. Feldman, op. cit. p. 705.

[42] These changes in attitude are well-brought-out by G. Richardson op. cit.

17.10 CONCLUSION

At the very beginning of this book, I stated as my object how to take law seriously in law-and-society, to show how law is a distinct social formation, and how it interacts with other social formations and factors. What it means to take any social formation seriously has been expressed so well by David Garland, in his justly acclaimed study of punishment, that I could not improve on it; he writes: '. . . we need to think in terms of complexity, of multiple objectives, and of overdetermination. We need to think of it (punishment) as a distinctive form of life which is also dependent on other forms and other social relations. Somehow or other we must learn to view it both in its integrity, as an *institution*, and in its relatedness, as a *social* institution. Such a way of thinking may involve a degree of difficulty, and it certainly lacks the spare elegance of some of the more reductionist approaches'.[43] Although I discovered this quotation late in the day, without my knowing, it has, in effect, been my guide. The result is, I hope, both an approach to understanding law in society and a framework within which to do so. There are other approaches and other structures. But the one adopted and developed here has proved to be of considerable utility in guiding the social analysis of law and modern legal orders; it has also provided a useful focus on the interaction of law and other aspects of society, at both the theoretical level, as seen in earlier chapters, and at the practical level, as seen in the last three chapters.

Among minor milestones along the way, the relevance of analytical jurisprudence to the study of law in society merits mention, in the hope that others may come to the same realization and benefit from it. Another is the importance of developing methodological principles to guide research in law-and-society. Those proposed here may need refining and adding to, but they have served my purposes well and provided a way of marshalling into manageable order the enormous range of data about law. The importance of the third methodological principle warrants special mention. The notion of social spheres has been of considerable help in bridging the gap between individual actions and decisions, whether of officials or citizens, and the law. The idea that both view the law from diverse spheres, structured by conventions and understandings, is plainly important and of real utility. Mention should be made finally of the idea

---

[43] D. Garland, op. cit.

of narrowing the study to certain kinds of legal orders, those I have designated as modern. Legal orders with the features charted and discussed here are of interest and importance compared with other types of legal orders, not for reasons of western triumphalism, but because they have been effective in producing social goods that are valued in western societies and beyond. They are at the same time fragile and unstable, so that if they are to be sustained they must first be understood.

NOTES

Compliance by nation states

For a recent review of the issues concerning compliance with international law by nation states, see: D. J. Galligan and D. J. Sandler, 'Implementing International Law' in S. Halliday and P. Schmidt (eds), *Rights Brought Home* (Oxford, 2004).

Legal consciousness

Ewick and Silbey make the point in this way; after stating that: 'commonplace transactions and relationships come to assume (or not assume) a legal character', they go on to say: '. . . legality is an emergent feature of social relations rather than an external apparatus acting upon social life'. (P. E. Ewick and S. S. Silbey, *The Common Place of Law* (Chicago, 1998), p. 17). The authors marr an otherwise clear statement of the idea of law as the expression of social relations by going too far; it is also *an external apparatus*, the denial of which serves no point. The point is that law is both, and the tensions between the two are at the heart of modern legal systems. The authors modify this claim later in the book, on p. 22 for instance.

On the indirect effects of law on people's attitudes: changes in the law relating to rape and their effect on attitudes are examined in R. J. Berger, W. L. Neuman, and P. Searles, 'The Impact of Rape Law Reform: An Aggregate Analysis of Police Reports and Arrests' (1994), 19 *Criminal Justice Review* 1.

Settled disposition to comply with the law

On the inclination of people generally to accept the results of litigation, see L. M. Friedman, 'Disruptive Litigation' in H. W. Arthurs et al (eds), *General Theory of Law and Social Change* (York,1973), p. 30. The author suggests that the elites of American society accept the law generally and the results of litigation.

Legal architecture

A study of legislation passed by the Israeli parliament to regulate the age of marriage reached similar results to those of the Indonesian study, referred to in the text; certain Jewish groups who had a tradition of marrying early found ways of continuing their practices despite the legal restrictions; see: Y. Dror, 'Law and Social Change' in V. Aubert (ed), *Sociology of Law: Selected Readings* (Harmondsworth, 1969).

Relations between officials and complying parties

The Japanese experience with anti-discrimination laws in the work-place well illustrate the importance of relations between officials and employers. F. Upham describes it as 'a style of implementation and pol-icy-making that emphasizes bureaucratic leadership through informal processes' (F. K. Upham, op. cit. pp. 21 *ff*).

In relations between officials and corporations, the move from a puni-tive response on the part of officials to ones that 'seek to maximize good behaviour through . . . building trusting relationships with business' is discussed in: F. Haines, op. cit., p. 3. The idea is to emphasize 'corporate virtue'.

Legal environment

The difference between formal and superficial compliance, and absorbing the legal standards into the culture and structure of an organization, is discussed in: F. Haines, op. cit., pp. 127 *ff*.

On the tendency for an enforcement approach to provoke resist-ance in the complying parties see E. Bardach and R. Kagan, *Going by the Book: the Problem of Regulatory Unreasonableness* (New York, 2002). and Ayres and Braithwaite, op. cit., p. 25. See also F. Haines, ibid., pp. 3 *ff*.

Different procedural approaches ranging from rule-application to agreement are discussed in: D. J. Galligan, *Due Process and Fair Pro-cedures*, Chapter 8. Karen Yeung analyses the pros and cons of settlement in *Securing Compliance: A Principled Approach*.

On approaches to compliance

Ayres and Braithwaite suggest that governments are most likely to achieve their goals by communicating to industry that in any regulatory arena the preferred strategy is self-regulation. On this approach, the state negotiates the goals to be achieved, then leaves it to industry as to how best to achieve them (J. Ayres and J. Braithwaite, op. cit., p. 38; also N. Gunningham and R. Johnstone, op. cit., p. 10).

Gunningham and Johnstone give an illuminating account of the advantages of a systems-based approach over a command-and-enforce approach. A systems-based approach, which looks to the organization and its operations as a whole, is intended to encourage complying parties to go beyond compliance with the legal standards ibid., pp. 15, 23, 38.

Strength of the legal environment

Laws in Japan regulating both equal opportunities in employment and smoking are good examples of weak legal environments. In the case of equal opportunities, the law failed to provide 'effective enforcement mechanisms and makes only superficial procedural requirements of employers to comply with the standards': (J. S. Fan, op. cit, p. 136). Similar conclusions are reached in a study of the anti-smoking laws (E. A. Feldman, op. cit).

Density of social spheres

The conflict between legal standards and the social world of psychiatrists is brought out in an American study. See P. S. Appelbaum, *Almost a Revolution* (New York and Oxford, 1994). The author concludes: '. . . the mental health system so commands the allegiance of ordinary citizens and front-line decision-makers with regard to its core treatment functions that a legally precipitated apocalypse is unlikely. Even legal changes that on paper seem capable of causing significant disruption in the delivery of care are usually transmuted in practice into procedures that preserve the system's function. Not that other professions or the public at large will support flouting of patients' rights; they will not. Neither, however, will they facilitate legal initiatives that threaten to undermine care for those most in need'. (p. 215)

Dealing with the law

On the influence of judicial rulings, and their complex relations with deeper social and moral attitudes, a collection of studies of education is of considerable interest and importance; see: B. Flicker (ed) op. cit.

It is often said that the conferring of rights on disadvantaged groups, while having little immediate effect, can be used in the political arena to advance the cause; see for instance: S. Olson, *Clients and Lawyers: Securing the Rights of Disabled Persons* (Westport, 1984). As Olson states: law reform efforts 'were relatively successful, although their success came less from outright victories in court than from negotiation, political pressure, and advocacy whenever important decisions were made'. (p. 35) For an excellent review of this book and its arguments, see: N. G. Yuen, 'Alienation or Empowerment? Law and Strategies for Social Change' (1989), 14 *Law and Society Inquiry* 551.

Bibliography

Alexrod, R., *The Evolution of Cooperation* (New York: Basic Books, 1984).

Anon, 'Hart, Austin, and the Concept of the Legal System: The Primacy of Sanctions' *Yale Law Journal*, 84 (1974–5), 584.

Appelbaum, S., *Almost a Revolution* (New York, 1994).

Appelbaum, R., Felstiner, W. and Gessner, V. (eds.) *Rules and Networks: the Legal Culture of Global Business Transactions* (Hart, 2001).

Arlott, P., *The Health of Nations: Society and Law Beyond the State* (Cambridge: Cambridge U.P., 2002).

Arup, C., *The New World Trade Organization Agreements: Globalizing Law Through Services and Intellectual Property* (Cambridge: Cambridge U.P., 2000).

Ashworth, A., *Principles of Criminal Law* (Oxford: Oxford U.P., 1991).

Ashworth, A., *The Criminal Process: An Evaluative Study* (Oxford: Oxford U.P., 1994).

Atiyah, P., *Introduction to the Law of Contract* (Oxford: Oxford U.P., 2001).

Austin, J., *Province of Jurisprudence Determined* (1832, second edition 1954, Weidenfeld and Nicolson, London; Indianapolis: Hackett Publishing, 1998).

Ayres, J. and Braithwaite, J., *Responsive Regulation,* (Cambridge: Cambridge U.P., 1992).

Baert, P., *Philosophy of the Social Sciences* (Polity Press, 2005).

Baker, J.H., *An Introduction to English Legal History* (4th Edition, Butterworths, 2002).

Baldwin, R. and McCrudden, C. (Eds), *Regulation and Public Law,* (Weidenfeld & Nicholson, 1987).

Baldwin, J., Wikeley, N. and Young, R., *Judging Social Security* (Oxford: Clarendon, 1992).

Baldwin, R., 'Health and Safety at Work' in R. Baldwin and C. Mc Crudden (eds.), *Regulation and Public Law,* (Weidenfeld & Nicholson, 1987).

Banakar, R., *Merging Law and Sociology* (Galda and Wilch Verlag, 2003).

Bell, J., *French Legal Culture* (Butterworths, 2001).

Benton, L., 'Beyond Legal Pluralism: Towards a New Approach to Law in the Informal Sector' *Social and Legal Studies,* 3 (1994), 223.

Benton, L., *Law and Colonial Cultures: Legal Regimes in World History* (Cambridge: Cambridge U.P., 2002).

Berger, R.J., Nueman, W.L., and Searles, P., 'The Impact of Rape Law Reform: An Aggregate Analysis of Police Reports and Arrests' *Criminal Justice Review*, 19 (1994), 1.

Berman, H., *Law and Revolution: The Formation of the Western Legal Tradition* (Cambridge, Mass.: Harvard U.P., 1983).

Beveridge, F. and Nott, S., 'A Hard Look at Soft Law' in P. Craig and C. Harlow (eds) *Lawmaking in the European Union* (London: Kluwer, 1998).

Birks, P.B.H., *Unjust Enrichment* (Oxford: 2nd ed. Oxford U.P., 2004).

Black, J., 'Decentring Regulation: Understanding the Role of Regulation and Self-Regulation in a Post-Regulating World' *Current Legal Problems*, 54 (2001) 103.

Black, J., *Rules and Regulators* (Oxford: Clarendon, 1997).

Bohannan, P., *Justice and Judgment Among the Tiv* (London: Oxford U.P., 1957).

Bowen, J.R., 'Consensus and Suspicion: Judicial Reasoning and Social Change in an Indonesian Society 1960–1994' *Law and Society Review*, 34 (2000) 97.

Braudel, F., *A History of Civilizations* (New York: Penguin, 1995).

Briggs, A. and Markesinis, B., *Foreign Laws and Foreign Ideas in the English Courts*, (Amsterdam, 1998).

Bringham, J., *The Constitution of Interests: Beyond the Politics of Rights* (New York, New York U.P., 1996).

Bull, H., *The Anarchical Society* (London: Palgrave, 1977).

Bumiller, K., *The Civil Rights Society: The Social Construction of Victims* (Baltimore: John Hopkins U.P., 1988).

Burton, F., *Family Law* (Cavendish, 2000).

Cammack, M., Young, L., Heaton, T., 'Legislating Social Change in an Islamic Society—Indonesia's Marriage Law' *American Journal of Comparative Law*, 44 (1996), 45.

Campbell, D., 'Reflexity and Welfarism in Modern Law in Context' *Oxford Journal of Legal Studies*, 20 (2000), 473.

Cane, P., 'Administrative Law as Regulation' in C.Parker et al, *Regulating Law* (Oxford: Oxford U.P., 2004).

Chultz, D.A. (ed), *Leveraging the Law: Using the Courts to Achieve Social Change* (New York: Lang 1998).

Cini, M., 'The Soft Law Approach: Commission Rule-Making in the

EU's state aid regime' *Journal of European Public Policy*, 8 (2001), 192–207.

Coleman, Jules, 'Incorporationism, Conventionality, and the Practical Difference' in J. Coleman (ed) *Hart's Postscript* (Oxford: Clarendon, 2001).

Coleman, Jules, (ed) *Hart's Postscript* (Oxford: Clarendon, 2001).

Coleman, James, 'Social Capital in the Creation of Human Capital', *American Journal of Sociology*: Supplement 95, 94 (1988).

Coleman, James, *Foundations of Social Theory* (Cambridge, Mass: Harvard U.P., 1990).

Collins, H., 'Regulating the Employment Relation for Competitiveness' *Industrial Law Journal*, 30 (2001), 17.

Collins, H., *Employment Law* (Oxford: Oxford U.P., 2003).

Collins, H., *Regulating Contracts* (Oxford: Oxford U.P., 1999).

Collins, H., *The Law of Contract* (Butterworths, 2003).

Cooter, R., 'Law and Unified Social Theory' in D.J. Galligan (ed.), *Socio-Legal Studies in Context: The Oxford Centre Past and Future* (Oxford: Blackwell, 1995).

Cotterrell, R 'Law in Social Theory and Social Theory the Study of Law' in A. Sarat (ed), *The Blackwell Companion to Law and Society* (Oxford: Blackwell, 2004).

Cotterrell, R., *EmileDurkheim: Law in a Moral Domain* (Palo Alto: Stanford U.P., 1999).

Craig, P. and Harlow, G. (eds.) *Lawmaking in the European Union* (Springer, 1998).

Cranston, R., *How Law Works* (Oxford: Oxford U.P., 2006).

Cranston, R., *Legal Foundations of the Welfare State* (London: Weidenfeld and Nicholson, 1985).

Cranston, R., *Consumers and the Law* (London: Weidenfeld & Nicholson, 1978).

Cyert, R.M. and March, J.G., *A Behavioral Theory of the Firm*, (Blackwell, 1992).

Davies, A.C.L, *Perspectives on Labour Law* (Cambridge: Cambridge U.P., 2004).

Deakin, S. and Morris, G., *Labour Law* (London: Butterworths, 2001).

Diamant, W.J, Lubman, G and K.J O'Brien, *Engaging the Law in China*: *State, Society, and Possibilities for Justice* (Palo Alto: Stanford U.P., 2005).

Diamond, S., 'The rule of law versus the order of custom' *Social Research*, 38 (1971), 42.

Dicey, A.V., *The Law of the Constitution* (London: Macmillan, 1961).

Dickson, M., *The Revival of Pragmatism: New Essays on Social Thought, Law and Culture* (Durham and London: Duke U.P, 1988).

Douglas, H., 'Customary Law, Sentencing, and the Limits of the State' *Canadian Journal of Law and Society*, 20 (2005), 141.

Douglas, M., *Risk and Blame: Essays in Cultural Theory* (London: Routledge,1992).

Dror, Y., 'Law and Social Change" in V. Aubert (ed.), *Sociology of Law: Selected Readings* (Penguin, 1969).

Dupret, B. and Berger, M., *Legal Pluralism in the Arab World* (Kluwer, 1999).

Durkheim, E., *Rules of Sociological Method* (Free Press, NY, 1938).

Durkheim, E., *The Division of Labour in Society* (Free Press, NY, 1984).

Dworkin, R., *Hart's Posthumous Reply* (Unpublished paper).

Dworkin, R., *Taking Rights Seriously* (London: Duckworth, 1978).

Dworkin, R.M., *Laws Empire* (Cambridge, Mass: Harvard U.P, 1988).

Eastman, N. and Peay, J., *Law Without Enforcement* (Hart, 1999).

Edelman, L., 'Legal ambiguity and symbolic structures: Organizational Mediation of Civil Rights Law' *American Journal of Sociology*, 97 (1992), 1531.

Edelman, L., 'Legal Environments and Organizational Governance: The Expansion of Due process in the American Workplace' *American Journal of Sociology*, 95 (1990), 1401.

Eekelaar, J., 'What is Critical Family Law?' *Law Quarterly Review*, 105 (1989), 244.

Eekelaar, J. and Maclean, M., *A Reader on Family Law* (Oxford: Oxford U.P., 1994.

Ehrlich, E., *Fundamental Principles of the Sociology of Law* (Cambridge, Mass: Harvard U.P., 1936).

Elias, N., *The Civilizing Process* (Blackwell, 1994).

Ellickson, R., *Order Without Law* (Cambridge, Mass: Harvard U.P., 1991).

Engle Merry, S., 'Colonial and Post-Colonial Law' in *The Blackwell Companion to Law and Society* (Blackwell, 2004).

Engle Merry, S., 'Legal Pluralism' *Law and Society Review*, 22 (1988), 869.

Etzioni, A., "Social Norms: Internalization, Persuasion, and History" *Law and Society Review*, 34 (2000), 157.

Ewick, P.E. and Silbey, S.S., *The Common Place of Law* (Chicago: Chicago U.P., 1998).

Ewing, K., 'Democratic Socialism and Labour Law' *Industrial Law Journal*, 24 (1995), 103.

Falk Moore, S., *Law and* Anthropology: *A Reader* (Blackwell Publishing, 2004).

Falk Moore, S., *Law as Process: An Anthropological Approach* (London: Routledge, 1978).

Fan, J. S., 'From Office Ladies to Women Warriors ?: The Effect of the EEOL on Japanese Women' *UCLA Women's Law Journal*, 103 (1999–2000).

Feeley, E. and Rubin, M., *Judicial Policy Making and the Modern State* (Cambridge: Cambridge U.P., 1998).

Feldman, E.A., "The Landscape of Japanese Tobacco Policy: Law, Smoking and Social Change" *American Journal of Comparative Law*, 49 (2001) 679.

Ferguson, A., An *Essay on History of the Civil Society* (London: Cadell, 1782).

Finnis, J., *Natural Law and Natural Rights* (Oxford: Clarendon, 1980).

Fitzpatrick, P.F., *Modernism and the Grounds of Law* (Cambridge: Cambridge U.P., 2001).

Flicker, B.(ed.), *Justice and School Systems: The Role of Courts in Education Litigation* (Philadelphia: Temple U.P., 1990).

Fortescue, Sir J., *On the Laws and Governance of England* (Ed. S.Lockwood, Cambridge: Cambridge U.P, 1997) (Originally written around 1471).

Foucault, M., *Discipline and Punish: The Birth of the Prison* (London, Allen Lane, 1977).

Foucault, M., *The History of Sexuality: Volume I, An Introduction* (London: Penguin, 1981 and 1987).

Foucault, M., *Hommage a Jean Hyppolite* (Paris: Presses Univesitaires de France, 1971).

Friedman, L.M., 'Erewhon: The Coming Global Legal Order' *Stanford Journal of International Law*, 37 (2001), 347.

Friedman, L.M., 'Disruptive Litigation' in H. W. Arthurs et al (eds.), *General Theory of Law and Social Change* (York: York U.P,1973).

Fuller, L.L., *The Morality of Law* (New Haven: Yale U.P, 1969).

Galanter, M., 'Justice in Many Rooms: Courts, Private Ordering, and Indigenous Law' *Journal of Legal Pluralism*, 19 (1981), 17–18.

Galligan, D.J. (Ed), *Socio-Legal Studies in Context: The Oxford Centre Past and Future* (Blackwell, 1995).

Galligan, D.J. and Kurkchian, M. (Eds), *Law and Informal Practices: The Post Communist Experience* (Oxford: Oxford U.P., 2003).

Galligan, D.J. and Matczak, M., *Strategies of Judicial Review* (Warsaw, 2005).

Galligan, D.J. and Sampford, S. (Eds), *Law, Rights and the Welfare State* (Groom Helm, 1986).

Galligan, D.J. and Sandler, D.J., 'Implementing Human Rights' in S. Halliday and P. Schmidt (eds.), *Rights Brought Home* (Hart, 2004).

Galligan, D.J. and Smilov, D., *Administrative Law in Central and Eastern Europe* (Budapest: Central European U.P, 1999).

Galligan, D.J., *Administrative Procedures and the Supervision of Administration in Hungary, Poland, Bulgaria, Estonia and Albania* (Paris: OECD, Sigma Paper 17, 1996).

Galligan, D.J., *Discretionary Powers* (Oxford: Clarendon, 1986).

Galligan, D.J., *Due Process and Fair Procedures* (Oxford: Clarendon., 1996).

Galligan, D.J., *The Right to Protest* (Inaugural Lecture, University of Southampton, 1986).

Garland, D.J., *Punishment and Modern Society* (Oxford: Clarendon, 1990).

Garth, G., and Sarat, S., 'Studying How Law Matters: An Introduction' in G.Garth and S.Sarat (eds.), *How Does Law Matter?* (Evanston: Northwestern U.P., 1998).

Geertz, C., *Local Knowledge: Further Essays in Interpretive Anthropology* (New York: Basic Books, 1983).

Geertz, C., *The Interpretation of Cultures* (New York: Basic Books, 1973).

Genn, H., *Hard Bargaining* (Oxford: Clarendon, 1987).

Genn, H., and Genn, Y., *The Effectiveness of Representation before Tribunals* (Lord Chancellor's Department, London, 1989).

Gibbon, E., *The History of the Decline and Fall of the Roman Empire, Volume V* (First published 1776, Folio edition 1987).

Gluckman, M., *The Judicial Process Among the Barotse of Northern Rhodesia* (Manchester: Manchester U. P., 1955).

Goodin, R.E. and Klingemenn, H.D. (eds.), *A New Handbook of Political Science* (Oxford: Oxford U.P., 1996).

Green, L., 'The Concept of Law Revisited' *Michigan Law Review*, 94 (1996), 1687.

Griffith, A., 'Legal pluralism', R. Banakar and M. Travers (eds.), *An Introduction to Law and Social Theory* (Hart, 2002), 302.

Griffith, J., 'What is legal pluralism?' *Journal of Legal Pluralism*, 24 (1986),1.

Griffiths, J., 'Legal Pluralism and the Theory of Legislation: With Special Reference to the Regulation of Euthanasia' in H. Petersen and

H. Zahle (eds), *Legal Polycentricity: Consequences of Pluralism in Law*, (Dartmouth, 1998).

Gross, H., *A Theory of Criminal Justice* (New York: Oxford U.P., 1979).

Guarnieri, C. and Pederzoli, P., *The Power of Judges: A Comparative Study of Courts and Democracy* (Oxford: Oxford U.P., 2002).

Gunningham, N., and Johnstone, R., *Regulating Workplace Safety: Systems and Sanctions* (Oxford: Clarendon Press, 1999).

Gunningham, N. and Grabosky, P., *Smart Regulation: Designing Environmental Policy* (Oxford, Oxford U.P., 1998).

Habermas, J., *Between Facts and Norms*, (Cambridge, Mass: MIT Press, 1996).

Hacker, P. and Raz, J., (eds.), *Law, Morality, and Society: Essays in Honour of H. L. Hart* (Oxford: Clarendon, 1977)

Haines, F., *Corporate Regulation* (Oxford: Clarendon Press, 1997).

Halliday, S., 'The Influence of Judicial Review on Bureaucratic Decision Making' *Public Law*, 110 (2000).

Halliday, S., *Judicial Review and Compliance with Administrative Law*, (Hart, 2004).

Hanami, T., 'Equal Opportunity Revisited' *Japan Labour Bulletin*, 39 (2000).

Harding, A., *Medieval Law and the Foundations of the Modern State* (New York: Oxford U.P., 2002).

Harrè, R. and Secord, P., *The Explanation of Social Behaviour* (Blackwell, 1972.)

Harris, D. et al (eds.), *Compensation and Support for Illness and Injury* (Oxford: Oxford U.P., 1984).

Harris, J.W., *Legal Philosophies* (LexisNexis UK, 1997).

Hart, H.L.A, *The Concept of Law* (Oxford: Clarendon, 1st Ed. 1961, 2nd Ed, O.U.P.,1997)

Hart, H.L.A., 'Concept of Law in the Perspective of American Legal Realism' in Modern *Law Review*, *35* (1972), 607.

Hart, H.L.A., in 'Conversation with David Sugarman' *Journal of Law and Society*, *32* (2005) 267.

Hassard, J., and Parker, M. (eds.), *Postmodernism and Organizations* (Sage, 1993).

Hawkins, K (ed), *The Uses of Discretion* (Oxford: Clarendon, 1992).

Hawkins, K., *Environment and Enforcement* (Oxford: Clarendon, 1984).

Hayek, F.A., *Law, Legislation and Liberty* (Vol 1–3 in IV, Chicago: Chicago U.P., 1982).

Hayek, F.A., *The Road to Serfdom* (Chicago: Chicago U.P., 1944).

He, X., 'Why Do They Not Comply with the Law? Illegality and Semi-Illegality among the Rural-Urban Migrant Entrepreneurs in Beijing' *Law and Society Review*, 39 (2005).

Herring, J., *Family Law* (London: Longman, 2004).

Holmes, S., 'Lineages of the rule of law' in J.M. Maravell and A.Przeworski (eds.), *Democracy and the Rule* of Law (Cambridge: Cambridge U.P., 2003).

Holton, R.J., 'Classical Social Theory' in B. S. Turner, (ed.), *The Blackwell Companion to Social Theory* (Oxford: Blackwell, 1996).

Hooker, M.B., *Legal Pluralism: An Introduction to Colonial and Neo-colonial Laws* (Oxford: Clarendon, 1975).

Horwitz, M., *The Transformation of American Law, 1780–1860* (Cambridge, Mass: Harvard U.P., 1977).

Hume, D., *A Treatise of Human Nature* (Oxford: Oxford U.P., 1978 L.A.Selby-Biggs (ed.), 1st edition, 1888).

Hunt, A. and Wickham, G., *Foucault and Law: Towards a Sociology of Law as Governance* (Pluto Press, 1994).

Hunter-Taylor, E., 'H.L.A Hart's Concept of Law in the Perspective of American Legal Realism' *Modern Law Review*, 35 (1972), 606.

Hutter, B., *The Reasonable Arm of the Law* (Oxford: Clarendon Press, 1988).

Kagan, R., *Regulatory Justice: Implementing A Wage-Price Freeze* (Russell Sage, 1978).

Kagan, R., 'What Socio-Legal Scholars Should Do When There Is Too Much Law To Study' in D. J. Galligan (ed.), *Socio-Legal Studies in Context: The Oxford Centre Past and Future* (Blackwell, 1994).

Kagan, R., Gunningham, N. and Thornton, D., 'Explaining Corporate Environmental Performance: How Does Regulation Work?' *Law and Society Review*, 37 (2003), 51.

Kahn-Freund, O., Introduction to K.Renner, *The Institutions of Private Property and Their Social Functions* (Taylor and Francis, 1976).

Kelsen, H., *General Theory of Law and State* (Cambridge, Mass: Harvard U.P.,1945).

Kelsen, H., *The Pure Theory of Law* (University of California Press, 1967).

Kidder, R.L., *Connecting Law and Society: An Introducton to Theory and Research* (Englewood Cliffs, 1983).

King, M., 'Future Uncertainty as a Challenge to Law's Programme: The Dilemma of Parental Disputes *Modern Law Review*, 63 (2000), 523.

Kramer, M., *In Defence of Legal Positivism* (Oxford: Oxford U.P., 1999).

Kurckchiyan, M., in D.J. Galligan and M.Kurckchiyan, *Law and*

Informal Practices in Post-Communist Societies (Oxford: Oxford U.P., 2003).

Lacey, N. (ed.), *A Reader on Criminal Justice* (Oxford: Oxford U.P., 1994).

Lacey, N. and Wells, C., *Reconstructing Criminal Law* (Butterworths, 1998)

Lacey, N., 'Criminalization as Regulation' in C. Parker et al, *Regulating Law* (Oxford: Oxford U.P., 2004)

Lacey, N., *A Life of H.L.A.Hart: The Nightmare and the Noble Dream* (Oxford: Oxford U.P., 2004).

Larson, L.M., *The King's Household in England Before the Norman Conquest* (1904 quoted in C. B. Chrimes, *An Introduction to the Administrative History of Medieval England* (Oxford: Blackwell, 1959).

Lempert, R., 'Discretion in a Behavioural Perspective' in K.Hawkins, *The Uses of Discretion* (Oxford: Clarendon, 1992).

Lessig, L., 'The Regulation of Social Meaning' *University of Chicago Law Review*, 62 (1995), 943.

Lessig, L., *Free Culture: How Big media Uses Technology to Lock Down Culture and Control Creativity* (Penguin, 2004).

Livingstone, S. and Morrison, J. (eds.) *Law, Society and Change* (Aldershot, 1990).

Lloyd-Bostock, S., *Law in Practice* (British Psychological Society & Routledge, 1988).

Lockwood, S. (ed.) *On the Laws and Governance of England*, (Cambridge: Cambridge U.P., 1997).

Loveland, I., *Housing Homeless Persons* (Oxford: Clarendon, 1995).

Lubman, S., *Bird in a Cage: Legal Reform in China After Mao* (Palo Alto: Stanford U.P., 1999).

Lucas, J., 'The rule of recognition' in P.Hacker and J. Raz (eds.), *Law, Morality, and Society: Essays in Honour of H. L. A. Hart* (Oxford: Clarendon, 1977).

Luhmann, N., 'Operational Closure and Structural Coupling: The Differentiation of the Legal System' *Cardozo Law Review*, 13 (1992), 1419.

Luhmann, N., *Law as a Social System* (Oxford: Oxford U.P., 2004, translated by A.Ziegert).

Macaulay, S., 'Non-Contractual Relations in Business: A Preliminary Inquiry' *American Sociological Review*, 28 (1963), 55.

Machiavelli, N., *The Prince* (Oxford: Oxford World's Classics, 2005).

Macintyre, A., *After Virtue* (London: Duckworth, 1981).

Malinowski, B., *Crime and Custom in Savage Society* (London: Routledge, 1926).

March, J. and Simon, H., *Organizations* (Blackwell, 1993).

Marmor, A., *Positive Law and Objective Values* (Oxford: Oxford U.P., 2001).

McBarnet, D., *Conviction, Law, the State, and the Construction of Justice* (London: Macmillan, 1981).

McBarnet, D., *Crime, Compliance, and Control* (Ashgate, 2004).

McCann, M., 'How Does Law Matter for Social Movements?' in B. Garth and A. Sarat (eds.) *How Does Law Matter ?* (Evanston: Northwestern U.P., 1998).

McCann, M., 'Law and Social Movements' in A. Sarat (ed.), *The Blackwell Companion to Law and Society* (Blackwell, 2004).

McMullan, J.C., and Perrier, D.C., "Lobster Poaching and the Ironies of Law Enforcement" *Law and Society Review*, 36 (2002), 679.

Mercuro, N. and Medema, S.G., *Economics and the Law; From Posner to Post-Modernism* (Princeton: Princeton University Press, 1997).

Meyer, J. and Scott, W. R. (eds.), *Organizational Environments: Ritual and Rationality* (Beverly Hills: Sage, 1983).

Michaels, R., 'The Re-statement of Non-State Law: The State, Choice of Law and the Challenges from Global Legal Pluralism' *Duke Law School Social Studies Series*, Research Paper no.81, (2005).

Miers, D., 'The Gaming Board for Great Britain: Enforcement and Judicial Restraint' in R.Baldwin and C. McCrudden (eds.), *Regulation and Public Law* (London: Weidenfeld & Nicolson, 1987).

Mikdashi, Z., *Regulating the Financial Sector in the Era of Globalization* (Palgrave, MacMillan, 2003).

Miller, R.L., 'Women's Job Hunting in the Ice Age: Frozen Opportunities in Japan' *Wisconsin Women's Law Journal*, 13 (1998), 223.

Nader, L. and Todd, H.J. (eds.), *The Disputing Process: Law in Ten Societies* (New York: Columbia U.P., 1976).

Nagel, T., 'The Central Questions' *London Review of Books*, 3rd February 2005.

Nelken, D., (ed.), *Comparing Legal Cultures* (Dartmouth, 1997).

Nonet, P. and Selznick, P., *Law and Society in Transition: Toward Responsive Law* (Berkeley: Berkeley U.P., 1978).

North, D., *Institutions, Institutional Change, and Economic Performance* (Cambridge: Cambridge U.P., 1990).

Ogus, A.I., *Regulation: Legal Form and Economic Theory* (Oxford: Oxford U.P., 1994).

Olson, S., *Clients and Lawyers: Securing the Rights of Disabled Persons* (Greenwood Press, 1984).

Origo, I., *The Merchant of Prato* (Folio Society, London, 1954).

Ostrom, E., *Governing the Commons: The Evolution of Institutions for Collective Action* (Cambridge: Cambridge U.P., 1990).

Parker, C., Scott, C., Lacey, N. and Braithwaite, J. (eds.), *Regulating Law* (Oxford: Oxford U.P., 2004).

Parkinson, L., 'Japan's Equal Employment Opportunity Law: An Alternative Approach to Social Change' *Columbia Law Review*, 89 (1989), 604.

Payne, M., 'Hart's Concept of a Legal System' *William & Mary Law Review*, 18 (1976), 287.

Paz-Fuchs, A., Conditional Welfare: *Welfare to Work Programmes in Britain and the United States* (Doctoral thesis, University of Oxford, 2006).

Peerenboom, R., *China's Long March Toward Rule of Law* (Cambridge: Cambridge U.P., 2002).

Pettit, P., *Rules, Reasons, and Norms* (Oxford: Oxford U.P., 2002).

Piccioto, S., and Campbell, D., (eds.), *New Directions in Regulatory Theory* (Blackwell, 2002).

Pospisil, L., *Anthropology of Law: A Comparative Theory* (New York: Harper and Row, 1971).

Pospisil, L., *Kapauku Papuans and Their Law* (New Haven: Yale U.P., 1971).

Postema, G., *Bentham and the Common Law Tradition* (Oxford: Clarendon, 1986).

Priban, J. and Nelken, D. (eds.), *Law's New Boundaries: The Consequences of Legal Autopoeisis* (Ashgate, 2001).

Przeworski, A., 'Why Do Political Parties Obey Results of Elections?' in J.A. Maravell and A. Przeworski, *Democracy and the Rule of Law* (Cambridge University Press, 2003).

Putman, R., *Making Democracy Work* (Princeton: Princeton U.P., 1993).

Radcliffe-Brown, A.R., *Taboo* (Cambridge, Mass: Harvard U.P.,1939).

Rawls, J., *A Theory of Justice* (Oxford: Oxford U.P., 1971).

Raz, J., *Ethics in the Public Domain* (Oxford, Clarendon, 1994).

Raz, J., *Practical Reason and Norms* (Princeton: Princeton U.P.,1990).

Raz, J., *The Authority of Law* (Oxford: Clarendon, 1983).

Raz, J., 'The Functions of Law' in Simpson (ed.) *Essays in Jurisprudence*.

Renner, K., *The Institutions of Private Property and Their Social Functions* (Taylor and Francis, 1976).

Richardson, G. and Machin, D., 'Judicial Review and Tribunal Decision-Making: A Study of the Mental Health Review Tribunal' *Public Law*, (2000), 494.

Richardson, G. and Sunkin, S., 'Judicial Review: Questions of Impact' *Public Law*, (1996), 79.

Richardson, G., and Thorold, O., 'Law as a protector of rights' in N.Eastman and J.Peay (eds.), *Law Without Enforcement* (Hart Publishing, 1999).

Richardson, G., Ogus, A., and Burrows, P., *Policing Pollution* (Oxford: Oxford U.P., 1982).

Roberts, S. and Comaroff, J.L., *Rules and Processes: The Cultural Logic of Disputes in an African Context* (Chicago: Chicago U.P., 1981).

Roberts, S., 'After Government: On Representing Law Without the State' *Modern Law Review*, 68 (2005), 1.

Robertson, D., *Judicial Discretion in the House of Lords* (Oxford: Oxford U.P., 1998).

Robertson, G., *The Tyrannicide Brief* (London: Chatto and Windus, 2005).

Rorty, R., *Philosophy and the Mirror of Nature* (Oxford: Blackwell, 1980).

Rosen, L., *The Anthropology of Justice: Law as Culture in Islamic Society* (Cambridge: Cambridge U.P., 1989).

Rosenberg, G., *The Hollow Hope: Can Courts Bring About Social Change* (Chicago: Chicago U.P., 1991).

Rostain, T., 'Educating Homo Economicus' *Law and Society Review*, 34 (2000), 973.

Ruffini, J.L., 'Disputing Over Livestock in Sardinia' in L. Nader and H.F. Todd (eds.), *The Disputing Process: Law in Ten Societies* (New York: Columbia U.P.,1976).

Ryan, A., *The Philosophy of the Social Sciences* (London: Macmillan, 1970).

Sampford, C. and Galligan, D.J. (eds.), *Law, Rights, and the Welfare State* (Croom Helm, 1986).

Sandler, D., *State Compliance with International Law* (Doctoral thesis, Bodleian Library, Oxford, 2000).

Sarat, A. and Felstiner, W.L.F., *Divorce Lawyers and Their Clients* (New York: Oxford U.P., 1995).

Sarat, A. (ed.), *The Blackwell Companion to Law and Society* (Blackwell, 2004).

Scheingold, S., The Politics of Rights: Lawyers, Public Policy, and Political Change (Michigan: Michigan U.P., 2004).

Schultz, D.A. (ed.) *Leveraging the Law: Using the Courts to Archive Social Justice* (New York: Peter Lang, 1998).

Scott, W. R., *Institutions and Organizations* (London: Sage, 1996).

Selznick, P., *TVA and the Grass Roots: A Study in the Sociology of Formal* (Berkeley, Berkeley U.P., 1949).

Senden, L., *Soft Law in European Community Law* (Oxford: Hart, 2004).

Shakespeare, W., *The Tragedy of Coriolanus* (London: Guild Publishing, 1990).

Shapiro, M., *Courts: A Comparative and Political Analysis* (Chicago: Chicago U.P., 1981).

Shapiro, M., *The Supreme Court and Administrative Agencies* (New York: Free Press, 1968).

Shepsle, K.A. and Weingast, B.W. (eds.), *Positive Theories of Congressional Institutions* (Michigan: Michigan U.P., 1984).

Shepsle, K.A.and Weingast, B.R., 'The Institutional Foundations of Committee Power' *American Political Science Review*, 81 (1987), 85.

Sheridan, A., *Michel Foucault: The Will To Truth* (London: Tavistock, 1980).

Simpson, A.W.B., 'The Common Law and Legal Theory' in A. W. B. Simpson (ed) *Oxford Essays in Jurisprudence* (Oxford: Oxford U.P., 1973).

Simpson, A.W.B., *An Invitation to Law*, (Blackwell Press, 1988).

Skolnick, J., *Justice Without Trial* (New York: Wiley, 1968).

Slaughter, A.M., Stone-Sweet, A. and Weiler, J.H.H. (eds.)., *The European Court and the National Courts-Doctrine and Jurisprudence: Legal Change in its Social Context* (Hart, 1998).

Smith, S., *Contract Theory* (Oxford: Clarendon, 2004).

Sajò, A., *Limiting Government* (Budapest: European U.P., 2001).

Stapleton, J., 'Regulating Torts', in Christine Parker et al. (eds), *Regulating Law* (Oxford: Oxford U.P., 2004).

Stein, P., *Roman Law in European History* (Cambridge: Cambridge U.P., 1999).

Stone Sweet, A., *The Judicial Construction of Europe* (Oxford: Oxford U.P., 2004).

Stone-Sweet, A., *Governing With Judges: Constitutional Politics in Europe* (Oxford: Oxford U.P., 2000).

Sunstein, C., 'Social Norms and Social Roles' *Columbia Law Review*, 96(1996), 903.

Tamanaha, B., *A General Jurisprudence of Law and Society* (Oxford: Oxford U.P., 2001).

Tamanaha, B., *Realistic Socio-Legal Theory: Pragmatism and a Social Theory of Law* (Oxford: Oxford U.P., 1997).

Tamanaha, B., *On the Rule of Law* (Cambridge: Cambridge U.P.)

Teubner, G., 'Bukowina in World Society' in G. Teubner (ed.), *Global Law Without a State* (Dartmouth, 1997).

Teubner, G., 'Juridification: Concept, Aspect, Limits, Solutions' in G.Teubner (ed.) *Juridification of Social Spheres* (Berlin: Walter de Gruyter, 1995).

Teubner, G., *Law As An Autopoeitic System* (Oxford: Blackwell, 1993).

Thompson, E.P., *Whigs and Hunters* (London: Allen Lane, 1975).

Touhy, C., 'Achieving Compliance with Collective Objectives: A Political Science Perspective' in M. L. Friedland (ed.), *Sanctions and Rewards in the Legal System: A Multidisciplinary Approach* (Toronto: Toronto U.P., 1989).

Treitel, G., *The Law of Contract* (11th Ed, Sweet and Maxwell, 2003).

Twining, W., *Globalization and Legal Theory* (Butterworths, London, 2000).

Twining, W., 'General Jurisprudence' (World Congress on Philosophy of Law and Social Philosophy, Granada, May 2005) in M. Escamilla and M. Saavedra (eds.) *Law and Justice in Global Society* (2005, Seville) 609 (Spanish version, p.563).

Tynack, D. et al, *Law and the Shaping of Public Education* (Madison: Wisconsin U.P, 1991).

Ullmann, W., *A History of Political Thought: The Middle Ages* (Baltimore: Penguin, 1965).

Unger, R., *Law in Modern Society* (London: Macmillan, 1976).

Upham, F.K., *Law and Social Change in Postwar Japan* (Cambridge, Mass: Harvard U.P., 1989).

Van Caenegen, R.C., *European Law in the Past and the Future* (Cambridge, Mass: Cambridge U.P. 2002).

Vanderlinden, J., 'Return to Legal Pluralism: Twenty Years Later' *Journal of Legal Pluralism*, 24 (1989) 149.

Vico, G., *New Science* (First published 1744, Penguin edition, 1999).

Von Bender-Beckmann, F., 'Comment on Merry' *Law and Society Review* 22 (1988).

Warnock, G., *The Object of Morality* (London: Methuen, 1971).

Weber, M., in G.Roth and C Wittick (eds.) *Economy and Society (2 vols)* (Berkeley: California U.P., 1968).

Weber, M., *The Protestant Ethic and the Spirit of Capitalism* (London: Routledge Classics Edition, 2001).

Weir, T., *Tort Law* (Oxford: Clarendon, 2002).

Whitehead, L., 'Comparative Politics: Democratization Studies' in R. E.

Goodin and H-D. Klingemann (eds.) *A New Handbook of Political Science* (Oxford: Oxford U.P.,1996).

Winch, P., *The Idea of the Social Science and its Relation to Philosophy* (Routledge, 1958, 1st Ed. 1990, 2nd Ed.).

Winn, J.K., 'Relational Practices and the Marginalization of Law: Informal Financial Practices of Small Businesses in Taiwan', *Law and Society Review*, 28, (1994), 193.

Yeun, N.G,. 'Alienation or Empowerment? Law and Strategies for Social Change', *Law and Society Inquiry*, 14 (1989), 551.

Yeung, K., *Securing Compliance: A Principled Approach* (Hart, 2004).

Zuckerman, A.S., *The Principles of Criminal Evidence* (Oxford: Clarendon, 1989).

Index